D0392721

ALSO BY T. C. McLUHAN

Touch the Earth
Portraits from North American Indian Life
Dream Tracks

THE WAY OF

ENCOUNTERS WITH NATURE

IN ANCIENT AND

CONTEMPORARY THOUGHT

THE EARTH

T. C. McLUHAN

A TOUCHSTONE BOOK
PUBLISHED BY SIMON & SCHUSTER
New York   London   Toronto   Sydney   Tokyo   Singapore

TOUCHSTONE
Rockefeller Center
1230 Avenue of the Americas
New York, NY 10020

First Touchstone Edition 1995

TOUCHSTONE and colophon are
registered trademarks of Simon & Schuster Inc.

Manufactured in the United States of America

10 9 8 7 6 5 4 3 2 1

Library of Congress Cataloging-in-Publication Data
McLuhan, T. C.
    The way of the earth : encounters with nature in
ancient and contemporary thought / T. C. McLuhan.
        p.   cm.
    Includes bibliographical references and index.
    1. Philosophy of nature.   2. Nature—Religious
aspects—Comparative studies.   I. Title.
BD581.M379   1994
113'.09—dc20   93-49653   CIP
ISBN 0-671-75939-6
ISBN 0-684-80157-4 (Pbk)

Page 535 constitutes an extension of the copyright
page.

ACKNOWLEDGMENTS

Books like this one are especially dependent upon libraries. I have benefited greatly from the privileges of the Wertheim Study of the New York Public Library. Working at NYPL is a scholar's dream, and several staff members in particular are deserving of praise and thanks for their constant generosity and resourcefulness, their interest in the book and their delightful knowledge of arcane subjects: Philip Yockey and Jane Greenlaw in interlibrary loan services, and Wayne Furman in the Office of Special Collections.

I am grateful to geologian Thomas Berry for allowing me to browse at my leisure through his vast personal library; to Father Tom Bermingham, scholar and teacher of Greek studies at Fordham University, who set me on the path of discovery in the realm of Greek philosophy and art; to Emmanuel Skoulos for his excellent translations of materials of Greek origin, both literary and artistic; to author Beth Southcott for her interpretations of several of the Ojibway works of art; to Ann Spencer, Curator of Ethnology, the Newark Museum, for her whirlwind introduction to the African and Native American collections at the museum and for assistance in providing details about several pieces of African and Native American art; to Kate Flynn, Director of the Australian Art Advisory, who let me loose in her personal library of Aboriginal art and literature, which was once housed at the Australia Gallery; to Helen Ashton Fisher, Media/ Information Officer at the Australian Overseas Information Service for help in contacting museums and galleries; to Jan Weiss, Director of the Jan Weiss Gallery, for her unflagging enthusiasm for Aboriginal art and her generous efforts in alerting me to useful and important materials; to professors Faye Ginsburg and Fred Myers, Anthropology Department, New York University, for arranging screenings for me of Native American and Aboriginal films (Program in Culture and Media).

A special thanks to Dana Reynolds, who labored for a number

of months with me in the library, amassing the research that is necessary for a book of this scope.

I want to express my gratitude to computer wizard and teacher Estella Powell for her specific acts of mercy not only in setting up a computer program for the book, but also in displaying uncommon patience with a beginner's foibles.

I also thank my editor, Sheila Curry, for her attentions to the manuscript.

My agent, Loretta Barrett, was especially helpful and patient throughout the enormously intricate process of creating this book.

And a last appreciative word of thanks to production editors Ted Landry and Gypsy da Silva and copy editor Carol Catt for guiding me through an avalanche of detail with great good humor and devotion.

In loving memory of my father
Herbert Marshall McLuhan

CONTENTS

PROLOGUE

"All journeys have secret destinations of which the traveler is un-aware," wrote Martin Buber in *The Life of the Hasidim*. In my years of study for this book, I have sought to illuminate the unique possibil-ities of cultural patterns across the planet in reintegrating the frac-tured human spirit of the world in which we live. More than a hundred years ago, "culture" in the West (in one important sense) meant an ideal of spiritual and intellectual aspiration, "the study of perfection," in Matthew Arnold's words in *Culture and Anarchy* (1869). That definition of culture, as an idea and practice of transcen-dent achievement, is little more than a memory today. What I have encountered in my own pilgrimage are states of sacredness that are the birthright of every individual. The sacred is in the coming to-gether, an un-covering of what we've known before, a turning to the infinite treasures that rest within the human spirit. The early Christian mystics referred to the quest for wholeness as the way of "oneing." Oneing is active everywhere: in art, poetry, the human body and psyche, the eternal wisdom in a great many of the world's traditional cosmologies—a number of which are explored in this book—and above all in Nature. The task at hand is to re-ignite that spark of holiness that is associated with all of human life and which may contribute to the refinement of the heart. It behooves us to become more attentive to the potential of spiritual and cultural alchemy in the retrieval of what has always been ours—the living experience of the ultimate unity of the human spirit, the biosphere and the cosmos.

The Way of the Earth is an invitation to the discrete cultural traditions of the world to look to each other, to respect one another from the vantage point of a shared Earth—Earth as partner, not object; as Master Teacher, as the ideal One. The wisdom herein recognizes the mutual dependency of all that lives. In the words of eleventh-century visionary Abu Hamid Muhammad al-Ghazali, "the visible world was made to correspond to the world invisible and there is nothing in this world but is a symbol of something in that world."

T. C. McLuhan
New York City
December 31, 1993

Ultimately, the study of any Way is a labor of the heart.

SON'EN (1298–1356),
son of the emperor Fushimi
and one of the most influential
calligraphers in Japanese history[1]

The earth is at the same time mother, she is mother of all that is natural, mother of all that is human. She is the mother of all, for contained in her are the seeds of all. The earth of humankind contains all moistness, all verdancy, all germinating power. It is in so many ways fruitful. All creation comes from it. Yet it forms . . . the basic raw material for humankind. . . .

HILDEGARDE OF BINGEN (1098–1179),
poet, musician, Rhineland mystic[2]

[We have] the deep conviction that everything in the universe is connected, nothing stands alone. Any violation of sacred laws causes a deep disturbance in the cosmic balance, which results in huge upheavals on the earth.

AMADOU HAMPÂTÉ BÂ (1901–   ),
sage of Mali (West Africa)[3]

*. . . the completely profane world, the wholly desacral-
ized cosmos, is a recent discovery in the history of the
human spirit.*

MIRCEA ELIADE (1907–   ),
historian of religions[4]

*We clothe our souls with messages and doctrines and
lose the touch of the great life in the naked breast of
nature.*

RABINDRANATH TAGORE (1861–1941),
Bengali poet and essayist[5]

*Heaven is my father and earth is my mother, and even
such a small being as I finds an intimate place in their
midst. Therefore, that which fills the universe I regard
as my nature. All people are my brothers and sisters,
and all things are my companions.*

CHANG TSAI (1020–1077),
Confucian master[6]

INTRODUCTION

Man models himself on Earth,
Earth on Heaven,
Heaven on the Way,
and the Way on Nature.

LAO-TZU (ca. 6th c. B.C.)[7]

Something grievous happens to the spirit of civilizations when they engage in willful exploitation of their native earth. Cut off from the interactive and interdependent web of life on this planet, human communities wither. Just as plants are nourished by soil, so too is human character. Plumbing the deepest and most common intuitions of the race about the sacredness of life leads inevitably to a richer understanding of what it means to be a human being.

This is a book about Earth rather than Earth's decline and about the common threads that connect the ways the planet's inhabitants, from ancient times to the present, have understood it, related to it and celebrated it.[8] It sets out to discover patterns of culture across the planet rooted in the natural world. It constitutes a cross-cultural mapping of the human psyche. The texts are intended to reveal the deeper currents of energy that exist among cultures and how each has thought and felt about their home, the Earth—often amid struggles to defend its integrity and their own right to inhabit it.

The Way of the Earth offers some of the most vivid thinking about the race's relation to Earth: how traditional as well as contemporary peoples throughout history have perceived the nature of Earth, the nature of Nature and the nature of Human Nature, and the interaction of these three paradigms.

These insights may guide us toward "re-inhabiting" the Earth intelligently, humanely and effectively. And "re-membering" it as well: "re-collecting" how humans have imagined it, and "re-integrating" it as a vital, nurturing force.

The Way of the Earth is a book about timeless paths into the realm of the human spirit. It is a journey through Australia, Japan, Greece, Africa, South America and North America in search of essential truths that illuminate the nature of Earth and the attitudes—both ancient and modern—in these cultures about the sacrality of living on the planet. At each layover, we listen to the wisdom of poets, artists, philosophers, scholars and sages—known and unknown—

and how they imagine themselves as inhabitants of their earth worlds and spirit worlds. Each of the cultures in the book presents a challenging voice that we do not necessarily know we need until we've heard it. The book seeks to demonstrate the affinities that exist among the various cultural traditions while acknowledging their unique forms and discrete natures.

The voices are drawn from widely diverse sources in space and time: from Plato to Nikos Kazantzakis in Greece; from Canasatego to Henrietta Mann in Native North America; from Yagan to Galarrwuy Yunnupingu in Aboriginal Australia. We hear also from members of the Kogi tribe of Colombia, South America; from the Ainu indigenous people of Japan and the great visionary, poet and farmer Masanobu Fukuoka; and from such eloquent thinkers of the African continent as Ogotemmêli, Bessie Head and Kofi Awoonor. Each of the societies represented displays an unswerving commitment to the quest for meaning in life, all striving to make sense of the universe and their place in it. Individual expressions of the telluric spirit are a prominent feature of all the traditions. The effect is one of revelation: an unfolding of the manifold ways of seeing, inhabiting, listening to and understanding the earth.

The Way of the Earth is about the Way of sacredness, dignity, truth and laughter; it is also about the Way of Nature. The Way signifies not only the energy of the universe, but also the very essence of being. The Way is the reciprocal symphony of animals, plants, minerals, soil and humans.

The Way describes the pattern which, in meta-scientist Gregory Bateson's words, "connects the crab to the lobster and the orchid to the primrose and all four of them to me."[9] The pattern is the greater entity; greater than the parts that comprise it. It is an *open* environment where interrelationships prevail. Bateson's search for unifying principles led him to a pattern theory which shapes the thinking that frames this book. As he put it:

> THE PATTERN WHICH CONNECTS *is a metapattern.* It is a pattern of patterns. It is that metapattern which defines the vast generalisation that, indeed, *it is patterns which connect.*[10]

The connection of past and present *within* each culture has revealed a continuum of sacred beliefs that has sustained the traditions. Placing the cultures *side by side* exposes a commonality of themes that is illuminating. Juxtaposing knowledge and observations from diverse sources contributes to further knowing. The interaction of the information can lead to new ways of seeing and perceiving. Bateson emphasized the truism "two descriptions are better than one" and summarized the power of pattern to heighten human perception in this way:

> THE COMBINING OF INFORMATION of different sorts or from different sources results in something more than addition. The aggregate is greater than the sum of its parts because the combining of the parts is not a simple adding but is of the nature of a multiplication or a fractionation, or the creation of a logical product. A momentary gleam of enlightenment.[11]

Japanese philosopher and art historian Sōetsu Yanagi looks at pattern somewhat differently, yet complementarily. The value of pattern, Yanagi says, lies in its vitality, in its transformative powers and in its ability to metamorphose, symbolically, wisdom to its highest order. Pattern, he proposes, is the vital connector to an integrated universe and, ultimately, to all that is good and true. Pattern, he writes, is a "hymn to nature's mysterious power." It is charged with intuition, vision and true essence. In other words, "pattern contains the nature of nature."[12]

This is also a book about commonality. *The Oxford English Dictionary* defines the word *common* as "belonging to all mankind alike." Its root is thought to be *com*, "together," and *munis*, "obliging, ready to be of service." Human nature—across all lands and all time—displays a striking consonance. Our similarities as human beings are far more deeply rooted than our differences, especially when we consider the most profound themes that people of all eras and all localities have pondered: our relation to the planet we share; to the earth we walk upon and its fruits that sustain us; to the limitless cosmos that we observe in the great dome of sky above us; to the mysteries that confound us as a species; to the fears and exaltations that unite us.

A cross section of peoples and cultures from widely separated points on the globe dramatizes these intriguing similarities. In tracing the six-stop journey across a world map, I was pleased to discover that the track line—from Australia to North America—describes a graceful, careened letter *S,* spanning the world's great land masses.

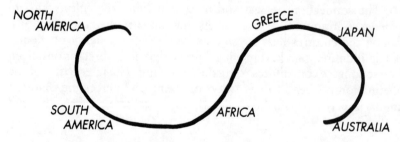

If we join the terminus points of the *S*, we create ∞ , the mathematical symbol for infinity, an instant, visual metaphor for the bottomless richness and variety of human imagination that infuses and informs these cultures.

There are a number of omnipresent themes in world cultures that mark their congruence:

THE PRIMACY OF EARTH

Earth, isn't this
   what you want:
      rising up
inside us invisibly *once more?*

RAINER MARIA RILKE (1875–1926)[13]

The thoughts of the earth are my thoughts . . .
The voice of the earth is my voice . . .

Song of the Earth Spirit,
Navajo origin legend[14]

The belief in Earth's essential nature as a living being wherein the changeless law of spirit prevails has endured since prehistory. This conviction is deeply cherished by the six cultures and many others the world over. The late-fifteenth-century German Benedictine monk and alchemist Basilius Valentinus expresses a universal view of Earth's creative powers and describes the planet's fundamental spiritual nature:

> THE EARTH IS NOT A DEAD BODY, but is inhabited by a spirit that is its life and soul. All created things, minerals included, draw their strength from the earth spirit. This spirit is life, it is nourished by the stars, and it gives nourishment to all the living things it shelters in its womb. Through the spirit received from on high, the earth hatches the minerals in her womb as the mother her unborn child.[15]

Similarly, the earth-nature of man may be perceived in an analogy that relates humankind to aspects of his cosmos. A seventeenth-century alchemical text states:

MAN IS TO BE ESTEEMED a little world, and in all respects he is to be compared to a world. The bones under his skin are likened to mountains, for by them is the body strengthened, even as the earth is by rocks, and the flesh is taken for earth, and the great blood vessels for great rivers, and the little ones for small streams that pour into the great rivers. The bladder is the sea, wherein the great as well as the small streams congregate. The hair is compared to sprouting herbs, the nails on the hands and feet, and whatever else may be discovered inside and outside a man, all according to its kind is compared to the world.[16]

For each of the cultures we examine, there is a trajectory of empathy for Earth that takes precedence over the impulse to exploit her (even, ironically, in Japan, a society which many perceive as one that has mercilessly despoiled its own living space). For each, the Earth is their historian, the sanctuary for their ancestors' bones. It is the fountainhead of their spirituality, knowledge, imagination, language and traditions. It provides them with guidance and nourishment, medicine, comfort and joy. It is the source of their liberation; it is their mother. She is adored; she is yearned for. Above all, she is held in great respect.

The notion that soil and soul are twin substances is raised by these cultures and proferred as an indispensable truth. "The spirit of the earth is the spirit of life," writes Japanese Zen Buddhist scholar Daisetz Suzuki. "Life that has no connection with the earth is not really alive . . . The earth and the self are one. The roots of the earth are the roots of one's own existence. The earth is oneself." Nikos Kazantzakis, Greek novelist and poet, suggests, "There is a mystical contact and understanding between this soil which fashioned us, and our souls . . . Your own feet sprout roots which descend into the earth and search, seeking to mingle with the great, immortal roots of the dead." Anthropologist E. E. Evans-Pritchard relates a story about the Nuer of the Sudan in East Africa that can hardly be more expressive or symbolic of a people's spiritual ties with the soil:

[M]EN WHO INTEND TO LEAVE the tribe of their birth to settle permanently in another tribe take with them some earth of their old country and drink it in a solution of water, slowly adding to each dose a greater amount of soil from their new country, thus gently breaking mystical ties with the old and building up mystical ties with the new.[17]

In novelist Ilias Venezis' story of the eviction of the Greeks from their homeland in Asia Minor in 1922, we encounter a complementary expression of that indivisible bond with one's natal soil and its life-giving forces:

> GRANDMOTHER WAS TIRED; she lay her head upon Grandfather's chest. But something, a small bundle, was there under his shirt. "It's nothing," said Grandfather shyly, taking it out and unrolling it. "It's nothing. Just a bit of soil." They would use it to plant some basil on their new land.[18]

Shortly after an earthquake devastated the valley town of Huaraz in the Peruvian Andes, one townsman who could have moved and begun a new life elsewhere confessed: "My heart and soul are happy here . . . Every morning I can see my Huascarán, my hills, my snowy peaks. The real reason I can't leave is that if I go away, Huaraz is going to suffer a little more. Huaraz needs people."[19] The identification of soil and soul as one involves a mutual recognition of the reciprocal needs of humans and earth and an acceptance of the wisdom of the dynamic forces, benevolent and treacherous, that animate and direct all that is.

The Vedas, those ancient scriptures and hymns of India and the repository of Hindu wisdom, are permeated with a reverence for life in which an all-encompassing sovereignty of the divine is at work. The Atharva-Veda contains the extraordinary "Hymn to the Earth" (Bhūmi-Sūkta), redolent of compassion for the Universal Mother and a touchstone of ecological wisdom:

> Earth, in which lie the sea, the river and other
> waters,
> in which food and cornfields have come to be,
> in which lives all that breathes and that moves,
> may she confer on us the finest of her yield.
> Earth, in which the waters, common to all,
> moving on all sides, flow unfailingly, day and
> night,
> may she pour on us milk in many streams, and
> endow us with lustre.
> May those born of thee, O Earth,
> be for our welfare, free from sickness and waste,
> wakeful through a long life, we shall become
> bearers of tribute to thee.
> Earth my mother, set me securely with bliss in full
> accord with heaven,

O wise one,
uphold me in grace and splendour.[20]

Earth as a source of solace and enlightenment is described by Aboriginal writer Sally Morgan as an old twisted peppermint tree that reached deep inside her and sowed the seeds of faith and courage. "Earth is . . . the lap, back, and maternal breast for mankind," writes Malian sage Amadou Hampâté Bâ in his description of the procreative powers of "the mother of beings." The farmer neither plants nor sows, Bâ says, without beseeching the earth to accept and protect the seed; and he begs the earth's pardon before ploughing it so that it will "accept this wound without anger."

The Kogi conviction that minerals in the earth play an important part in its life and their life is based on ancient knowledge tested over the centuries and found in their experience to be true. Gold, for example, is considered a precious gift, a sacred element that contributes to the ongoing fertility of the earth and therefore the planet. Digging out the earth's gold is tantamount to stealing the very thought and spirit of the Mother. "We don't take out the earth's gold. . . . We know where it is but we decide only to make offerings to it," they say. The Kogi believe that the removal of so much oil and so many minerals from the soil the world over weakens the earth and life itself. "[I]f there is a scientist like the *Mama* [Kogi master] who knows the earth . . . let him study the earth to see, is it declining or not? Does the world grow weak? Why is it weak? Because they take out much of its lifeblood, minerals, and the *Mama* is frightened. . . ."[21] When the earth is robbed of its minerals, life is robbed of its spirit and the Kogi are robbed of their soul. Native Americans and Aboriginal Australians share identical attitudes with the Kogi about the fecundity of the earth and its vital role in sustaining the life and spirit of the planet. Paiakan, the leader of the Kayapo tribe of the Amazon rain forest, expresses comparable ideas from a holistic viewpoint:

> THE FOREST IS ONE BIG THING; it has people, animals and plants. There is no point saving the animals if the forest is burned down; there is no point saving the forest if the people and animals who live in it are killed or driven away. The groups trying to save the animals cannot win if the people trying to save the forest lose; the people trying to save the Indians cannot win if either of the others loses . . .[22]

An inexpressible radiance dominates the worlds of those cultures that recognize the boundless spiritual significance of Earth. In being guided by the natural affinity that exists between the soil and its offspring, the cultures are animated by a common spirit. The cultivation and perfection of human beings is the goal of these societies and is nowhere better expressed than in the words of Masanobu Fukuoka: "If you understand the heart of one *daikon* [radish], you understand all. You see that religion and philosophy and science are all one." Put another way, and equally effectively, are the thoughts of Juan Pedro, a Totanac Indian from Mexico: "Those who never listen to earth and its elements while they are here regress to live again; and again and again until they take time to know the Source contained herein and follow it."[23]

LAND AND SELF

WE DON'T WANT MONEY, we want our land. Our spirits are in our land. Our old people are still in the land, our motherland, our dusty old land.

BANJO WOORUNMURRA,
Noonkanbah[24]

The idea of land as inextricably linked to culture, society, the human body and spirit is a pervasive expression of continuity for all indigenous peoples on the planet. Indigenous peoples are inhabitants of a landscape that inhabits them. The interests of the land are identical with the interests of its inhabitants. An attitude of regard for the land rather than one of exploitation motivates their human activities. In ancient religious traditions, land was not merely a beautiful vista but a true force that physically embodied the powers that ruled the world. In the ancient world, land could never be conceived of simply as a material thing. It was a home, a dwelling place, where humankind discovered its deep relation to the cosmic order. In China, for example, that interrelatedness is grounded not in any religious covenant, nor in any social contract, but in the very origin, structure and functioning of the universe. In the *Li Chi,* the *Book of Ritual,* we are given the definition of the human as the "heart and mind of heaven and earth." Here, the integration of the individual and the society requires an intimate knowledge of and communion with the seasons and the rhythms of the land. The ancient landscape of Greece was venerated and its spiritual forces were acknowledged, revered and continually propitiated. Shrines, temples and sacred enclosures of all kinds studded the countryside. Groves, meadows, springs and caves were inhabited by nymphs who stood for the gentle beneficence of nature. When an Australian Aboriginal speaks of land, it is within a framework of belongingness that is both physically and metaphysically binding: A Yirrkala native will say, "We belong to the ground; it is our power and we must stay close to it; or maybe we will get lost." In many African societies, land provides its peoples with the roots of existence; it serves the symbolic function of representing a living identity of the people who inhabit it, uniting them socially, historically and mystically. Kenyan novelist Ngugi wa Thiong'o gets to the heart of this relationship in *The Homecoming:* "Ngotho felt responsible for whatever happened to this land. He owed it to the dead, the living and the unborn of his line, to keep guard over this shamba [farm]." The Kiowa essayist and poet N. Scott Momaday addresses Native American attitudes about land from a position of reciprocal appropriation where, he explains, a person respectfully gives himself up to a landscape and at the same time "incorporates the landscape into his own most fundamental experience." Japanese Zen painter, calligrapher and teacher Kazuaki Tanahashi, on the other hand, views landscape as "what you see in yourself."

THE UMBILICAL CONNECTION

THE MOST HOLY ONE created the world like an embryo. As the embryo grows from the navel, so God began to create the world by the navel, and from there it spread in all directions.

Hebrew tradition[25]

Umbilical symbolism permeates many of the world's ancient traditions, providing a pattern of interaction among cultures today.

Umbilical imagery is an expression of continuity and completeness. It shapes the thought and form of many societies and cultures. It endows life with meaning, beauty and coherence. "In Homer, the whole world is a woof of organic umbilical cords," writes the modern Greek poet and scholar George Seferis. He is describing a unifying experience of life whose expression is found everywhere in the belief systems of the world's traditional societies. The notion of the umbilical provides a unitive template for human activity. It is a sacred and ancient belief widely held and acted upon in a broad range of cultures since time immemorial.

For instance, the burial ceremony of the placenta of a Kofon child in East Africa is of paramount importance to that child's sense of belonging and identity. "As the navel cord ties an unborn child to the womb," writes Prince Modupe, a Kofon, "so does the buried cord tie the child to the land, to the sacred earth of the tribe, to the Great Mother. If the child ever leaves the place, he will come home again because the tug of this cord will always pull him toward his own." In much the same spirit, the Bontoc of the Mountain Province of the Philippines believe that as "an unborn child is attached to his mother through an umbilical cord, so are we attached to the land."[26] The Diné (the Navajo people) of the American Southwest maintain they will always know who they are as long as the people remain on the land where their umbilical cords are buried. The carefully preserved cord anchors the child in the Earth, linking his or her spirit to the land. "Our rootedness to the Earth is like tying a string to yourself and the other end to your mother," explains Navajo elder Roberta Blackgoat. "The string thickens with each Offering, with each ceremony, each member of the family, each generation." Similarly, the Miskito, the native people of Nicaragua, say, "One wants to die where one's belly button is buried."[27]

In Polynesia, the Tikopia word *fenua* conveys an integrating experience of Creation—the inseparability of land, person and placenta. The word is used to express all three concepts. For the Aboriginal peoples of Australia, land is *life:* "Land is us; it is our mother," they say. The Aboriginal belief that land is a *parent* derives from a deeply held conviction that they are *of* the land and *belong* to the land because they were *conceived* of it. It is their spiritual source of existence, and they cannot imagine themselves as separate from it. A Worora elder, describes the ritual of the umbilical planting as a "marker" designed to put the mind and spirit in balance with the order of Creation. And South African writer Noni Jabavu tells us that her mother's people are referred to as "those of the umbilical cord."[28]

Even in exile, Senegalese writer Cheikh Hamidou Kane could never break the umbilical cord which held him to Nature and helped him endure the experience of "see[ing] less fully" and "no longer feel[ing] anything directly" during his years of expatriation: "I have not yet cut the umbilical cord which makes me one with her [Nature]. The supreme dignity to which, still today, I aspire is to be the most sensitive and most filial part of her." Sudanese Dogon elder Ogotemmêli underscores the symbolic nature of umbilical imagery: "When a girl is born the mother takes her spindle in her hand as a reminder that the granary which came down from heaven was attached to a spindle planted in the sky. The thread she winds is that which was unrolled in the descent."[29] At birth, in Dogon society, the child's body is touched to the ground so that the four limbs make contact with the earth. This ritual establishes a crucial umbilical link with the soil, which is called "the Thread of God."[30]

The Kogi of the Sierra Nevada de Santa Marta in Colombia consider that the universe developed in the form of a spiral, as do the Dogon. In addition, Kogi weaving starts with the spiraling of thread on a spindle to make their cloth; their pottery begins with a spiraled round of clay. In their circular ceremonial house, called the *nuhue*— whose floor represents the Earth, its structure a womb, and its conical roof the whole top half of the universe—the Kogi priests (the *Mamas*) sit at the center of the universe. The *nuhue* is the connector to all that is. It is the beginning, the way, the truth. It is the umbilical cord to the soul.

MOUNTAINS AND THE HUMAN SPIRIT

Come play on the mountains of myrrh.

The Song of Songs[31]

Sacred mountains, symbolizing the exaltation of divine providence, are to be found in all parts of the world. Moreover, the fusion of man and mountain into a living embodiment of truth and light as the way to knowledge of self and the universe is a fundamental belief of many extant traditions. Equally, mountains are metaphors for transcendent states of being; they are also living repositories of sacred energies and conduits of power and revelation.

Mountains occupy a prominent position in the spiritual life of innumerable cultures across the planet, including the six traditions which form the body of this book. For example, the thirteenth-century Japanese Zen master and teacher Dōgen tells us that "from time immemorial the mountains have been the dwelling place of the great sages; wise men and sages have all made the mountains their own chambers, their own body and mind." In much the same spirit, Masanobu Fukuoka believes that "those who make use of discriminating knowledge cannot grasp the truth of [Mount Fuji]. Without the whole, the parts are lost, and without the parts, there is no whole. Both lie within the same plane. . . . To know the real Fuji one must look at the self in relation to Fuji rather than at the mountain itself. . . . When one's eyes are opened by forgetting the self and becoming one with Fuji, then one will know the true form of the mountain."

The Kogi of Colombia make their home on a mountaintop and have instructions about the sacredness of the mountain world: "The Mother told us to look after all mountains. They are ceremonial houses. We know that all the mountains we see are alive. So we make offerings to them." The Kikuyu, with more than two million members the largest tribe in Kenya, revere Mount Kenya, Africa's second highest peak and the heavenly abode of their Supreme Being, *Ngai*. The Kikuyu refer to Mount Kenya as *Kere-Nyaga*, which means "mountain of brightness." In fact, the holy peak is considered to *be* their Supreme Being, "the possessor of light."

When Australian Aborigines speak of the billowing rock mound of *Uluru* (Ayers Rock) they describe it as a sacred record of their ancient origins, possessing the magical powers of a magician's rod to evoke the land's ancestral energies. A Pitjantjatjara elder and guardian of the living presence of this sacred site expresses his inalienable linkage to the place with these words: "I am Ayers Rock. . . . This is my great ceremony . . . this holy cave . . . this great camp with its holy tree."

Alphonso Ortiz, a Native American poet and writer, turns to a Tewa expression *Pin pe obi,* "look to the mountaintop," for a guiding vision of life. He believes that life is a journey in search of the transcendent meaning of these words. He conveys the potential of the summits when he recites a Tewa prayer, "Within and around the mountains, your authority returns to you." Marco Pallis, mountaineer, entomologist and music teacher, declares that genuine insight is "the true [Mount] Olympus." "The way to the Mountain," he says, "is nowhere and everywhere; it therefore cannot be specified in rational language, but it becomes immediately apparent to those who have earned that knowledge by paying the required price. That price is the renunciation of self or denial of self in its separative sense, in order to realize true Selfhood in the universal sense . . . [O]nly he who has attained the summit and made himself one with it knows the solution of the mystery . . . [A]t the summit all alternative routes become one."

No word for "Nature" (as an abstract concept separate from ourselves) exists in the Quechua language of the Peruvian Andes. Instead, the people say *nuestra naturaleza* ("our nature") and then begin to enumerate the mountains of the valley, identifying peaks, affectionately and respectfully, with a litany of names, images and stories that are intimately entwined with their lives. The mountainous landscape molds their psyche and gives shape and substance to their existence: "This landscape softens our character," explains a man from Huaraz. "We do not explode so easily when we live in this paradise. We endure like water dripping slowly into a gourd." [32]

Beyond those underlying common themes, there are others:

Modalities of the Sacred: Sacred sites are revered by all the cultures—waterfalls, mountain peaks, caves, hillocks, rocky outcrops, waterholes, groves and forests are but a few examples. Apart from these natural sites, there are man-made sacred places such as Stonehenge, Serpent Mound and the Great Pyramid. They all help to determine the quality of life, express the significance of attachment to place, encourage social and cultural cohesion and reveal spiritual laws.

The "Wildness" of Mind: The connection of Human Nature (mind) to Nature is revealed through patterns and pathways that disclose themselves in differing modes: N. Scott Momaday writes that the bond between humans and Nature is "so crucial as to be definitive of the way in which man formulates his own best idea of himself."[33] Cheikh Hamidou Kane emphasizes his essential unity with Nature: "Being Nature herself, I do not dare fight against her. I never open up the bosom of the earth, in search of my food, without demanding pardon, trembling, beforehand." Japanese philosopher Watsuji Tetsuro stresses Nature's boundless creativity and how it has stirred humankind's best potential: "Man sought consolation and assistance from nature. . . . Seeing his own reflection in nature, man felt that he was being shown the way to infinitely deep abstractions and the best artists tried through their experience to seek out and express this way." Sōetsu Yanagi places Nature at the heart of the beauty of craft: "[N]ature must be freely at work in the mind when anything is well made. Though painstaking efforts may have their contribution to make in carrying out a work, more astonishing is the effect that 'no-mindedness' has upon it. One gains greater insight into nature by open trust rather [than] by attempts at intellectual understanding."[34] Aboriginal storyteller Elkin Umbagai looks to Nature for guiding principles in life: "[The Aboriginal] is taught that the stars, birds and animals are his faithful friends and that he will always be guided by them. Throughout his lifetime, he keeps on studying about Mother Earth and Mother Nature."[35]

Childhood Encounters: Do early experiences of the natural world contribute to a mature understanding of the numinous in life? The recollections of Maurice Kenny, a Mohawk, suggest the answer is yes. "My childhood was spent wandering from [strawberry] patch to patch behind my mother and sisters," he writes. "I learned much in those northern fields under skies carved by birds and clouds and winds: thanks, respect, the importance of the family circle, the value of honest labor, the pleasures and the essential beauty of the natural, and the need to preserve and protect not only what is useful and beautiful, but all that the Creator placed on this earth to endure. . . . For me it is of the utmost importance to touch earth, the earth where the berries grow, bleed into the soil re-newing life. It is a re-newal, continuum; a symbol of my being and all beings, an image of my life and all life."[36] Similarly, Ilias Venezis recounts his childhood years in the farmlands of the Kimindenia on the Asian side of the Aegean. In the countryside, he began learning about "the secret life of trees" and the deep bond that exists between man and the sun, the soil, and water. It was the trees, however, that acquainted him with himself: "We lay down on the ground to try to hear the sound of the tree's blood in the young roots. . . . After a while, the miracle happened: we heard the tree's heart beating—or so at least we believed, for in fact we heard the beating of our own hearts." Mircea Eliade, historian of religions, relates two childhood incidents that marked his life and introduced him to otherwordly beauty. At about the age of two and a half, he saw in a forest "a huge resplendent blue lizard" that "dazzled" him; the image stayed with him for years. On another occasion, he crawled into a room that was totally green. He felt he "was inside a ripe green grape." But it was the exceptional atmosphere of the golden green light that impressed him and made him feel he was in paradise. The memory would haunt him for years.[37]

The Correlative Nature of Things: Ideas about the universe and one's place in its structure are frequently conveyed through the intricately constructed world of correlation that often takes shape in the natural world. Throughout this deeply humanizing landscape of the imagination a strange organic beauty blossoms everywhere capable of moving the most intransigent spirit. It taps into the intangible realms of memory and dream derived from the most profound human intuitions and arrests them for contemplation. The way of correlation is a manner of being in the six cultures.

Thinking by correlation means recognizing causal, complementary, parallel or reciprocal relationships between two or more entities. It also means perceiving a pattern that can manifest at different levels and in a variety of ways. Sōetsu Yanagi suggests "we touch on the mystery of beauty" in pattern. And "why should pattern be so beautiful?" he asks. Because "[i]t provides unlimited scope for the imagination," he replies. "[T]hat, for me is true beauty. . . . Pattern is nature seen in the best light."[38]

The use of correlation allows the grand patterns of Nature and being to be grasped. For instance, the Gagudju of Arnhem Land know that the maturing of the fiber on the pandanus tree is irrefutable proof of sharks in nearby waters giving birth to their young. Similarly, Nettie Jackson Kuneki, a Klickitat from the Yakima Indian nation, explains: "When the huckleberries are at full harvest, the fish are also at full harvest."[39] The Kogi, for their part, see the mutuality of all life: "You can't just cut banana trees. You can't cut them because banana trees are like your father, like your mother. You have to respect them as much as any person." And Cape Dorset artist Pitseo-lak (the Inuit word for the sea pigeon) derives a special sense of identity from observing her totemic namesake and spirit: "When I see pitseolaks over the sea, I say, 'There go those lovely birds—that's me, flying.' "[40]

The six cultures in many ways represent worlds dramatically different from each other, yet they are bound by universal home truths that are eternal in their continuing application to all ages and all of humankind. What can they teach us about ourselves? What can we learn from them? They show us how far we have strayed from our authentic roots. They can demonstrate how to achieve a measure of balance in a land of widespread psychic uncertainty. They can assist in bringing about a restoration of our true origins—the recovery of a state of grace.

Reaching for an understanding of the wisdom that lies in the richness of six ancient traditions—whose roots continue to nourish, inspire and challenge its peoples—is an opportunity for growth in each of us. The perennial nature of these truths is never so vividly revealed as in the battles that many of these peoples have fought to retain sovereignty over their lands and sacred sites and to right the imbalances of misguided progress. The shared touchstone of these world cultures is an expression of allegiance to the mystery of life. Each of the societies reveals a landscape of the human spirit that evinces an impeccable integrity which, in our finest moments, we behold in ourselves.

We are entering a new era. The old categories are dead and gone, for we have passed over into a different world—a world in which I suggest we sensitize ourselves to what Lévi-Strauss calls "entropol-ogy" (as opposed to anthropology)—the notion of a people recognizing and exploring its own disorientation, its own disintegration, its own running down, and then finally, perhaps, its own possibilities.

In the words of the sixth-century B.C. Persian prophet Zarathus-tra, "It is time for the human being to plant the seed of his highest hope."[41]

THE WAY OF THE LABYRINTH

IN ARCHAIC ART, the labyrinth—home of the child-consuming Minotaur—was represented in the figure of the spiral.

JOSEPH CAMPBELL (1904–1987)[42]

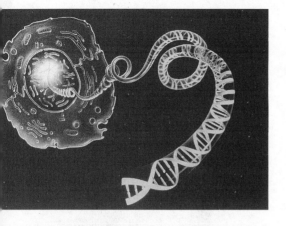

LEFT: The cell and its genetic components, the coiled structure of double-stranded DNA. BELOW LEFT: *Cucurbita*, pumpkin tendrils. BELOW: The cochlea of the human ear.

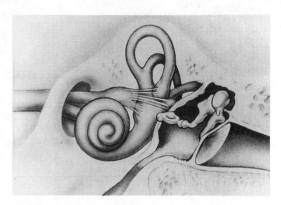

WORLD HISTORY has become everyone's task, and our own labyrinth is the labyrinth of all mankind.

OCTAVIO PAZ (1914–   ),
Mexican poet and essayist[43]

Art, nature, the human body and the human psyche are so intimately related that it is impossible to think of one without being reminded of the others. In my seven years of research, I found that their symbolic expression manifests itself in a fascinating set of patterns common to each of the six cultures—as many of the illustrations in this book demonstrate—and perhaps, by extrapolation, to every culture. Among their visual figurations are labyrinthine, umbilical and spiral images.

The natural and dynamic formations of the cosmos embody many forms but none, perhaps, is more universal than the spiral and its relative, the labyrinth. They embody a symbolic shape of human

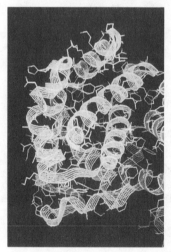

ABOVE LEFT: *An ammonite.* Coiled, corrugated fossil shell of an extinct mollusk showing surface pattern. ABOVE: *Silphium laciniatum,* Compass plant, rosinweed. Parts of dried leaf on the stem. LEFT: Helix of hemoglobin. Computer graphic molecular model of hemoglobin showing protein folding (helix).

LEFT: *Adiantum pedatum,* American maidenhair fern. Young rolled-up fronds. ABOVE: Fingerprint. ABOVE RIGHT: *Aspidium filix mas,* shield fern. Young rolled-up fronds.

experience. They set humankind's inner life in motion through a continual revisiting of basic principles that provides an ever-deepening and broadening perspective.

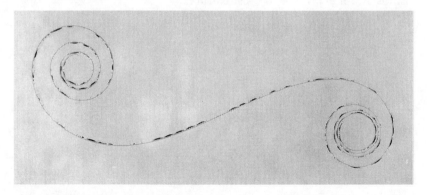

The logarithmic spiral, discovered in 1638 by the French mathematician René Descartes, is an archetypal shape mirrored in the fetus of humans and animals and is present in the growth patterns of many plants and flowers. The spiraling trunks of gigantic eucalyptus trees, the horns of goats, ram and reindeer, and mollusk shells, especially the *Nautilus pompilius,* assume the spiral form. A cross section from the trunk of a white pine reveals an exquisite spiraling configuration. Spirals can be found in the consecutive florets of the sunflower, the overlapping scales in the pinecone, the capsule of a shark's egg, a monkey's tail, a serpent's coil, an elephant's trunk, and in the spiral motion of the tips of a bird's wings; in an umbilical cord or in the cochlea of the inner ear, in the spiral muscles of the heart and stomach and, indeed, in galaxies millions of light-years distant, as well as in our own galaxy, the spiral-shaped Milky Way; and in the vortical laws that govern the movements of water, which composes nearly three quarters of our physical bodies. The spiral flow and winding motion of water are characteristics of its fundamental nature. This universal symbol, which is perpetually turning in on itself, embodies the principles of expansion and contraction.

The spiral impulse is the visual motif of this book.

The double spiral, one flowing into the other, is one of the most ancient symbols for eternity. It both comes from and returns to its source. The most celebrated example of this configuration is the double helix, the coiled structure of double-stranded DNA—the carrier of genetic information—which takes a double-spiral shape. Even the sun in its daytime path across the heavens describes a double spiral.

Charles Ross, *Solar Burn Spiral.* The equinoctial year, September 23, 1971, through September 22, 1972. Tracking the passage of the sun.

In the early 1970s, American artist Charles Ross tracked the movement of the sun over the course of a year by setting up a lens to focus the sun's rays across 366 wooden planks "so that cosmic elements," as Ross put it, "would reveal themselves." He photographed the resulting burn marks, and discerned in their pattern a double spiral —generated, he said, by "the sum of days."[44]

Artist and writer Robert Lawlor calls the spiral "our most profound image for the movement of Time," and thus central to our notion of evolution.[45] He explores the philosophic underpinnings of this geometric form:

> THERE IS A TELEOLOGICAL MESSAGE contained . . . in the spiral itself; for it moves in successively opposite directions towards the ultimate expression of both the infinitely expanded and infinitely contracted. The spiral is constantly approaching these two incomprehensible aspects of the ultimate reality, and therefore symbolizes a universe moving toward the perfect singularity from which it arose. Thus the spiral-like arms of our galaxy constitute an image of the continuity between fundamental polarities—infinite and finite, macrocosm and microcosm.[46]

The essential principle of rotation distinguishes the physical universe: planets orbit; atoms spin; the fetus grows in a spiral shape; time manifests as a cycle of existence. The circuitous windings of the labyrinth are also part of the creative furlings and unfurlings of the cosmic revolutions. Although intricate in form, a labyrinth is often an interrupted spiral. It represents a re-memberment, a return to the source. It is the path, the Way. It is a symbolic representation of the cosmos and it is present in most cultures.

I

ABORIGINAL AUSTRALIA

Hear us, White Australia, we are the spirit of the land. Our name is humanity. Our aims are self-determination and justice.
We will not be defeated.
We are our history, we are our culture, we are our land.
We are now.

> *Aboriginal Statement of Declaration,*
> *1982 Commonwealth Games,*
> *Brisbane, Queensland*[1]

The land, for Aboriginal people, is a vibrant spiritual land-scape. It is peopled in spirit form by ancestors who orig-inated in the dreaming, the creative period of time im-memorial. The ancestors travelled the country, engaging in adventures which created the people, the natural fea-tures of the land, and established the code of life, which is today called "the dreaming" or "the Law." The law has been passed on through countless generations of people through remembrance and celebration of sites which were the scenes of the ancestral exploits. Song, dance, body, rock and sand painting, special languages and the oral ex-planations of the myths encoded in these essentially reli-gious art forms have been the media of the Law to the present day.

Aboriginal ontology of The Dreaming[2]

Do not leave the home of your fathers, the home of your forefathers, the home of your ancestors ever from the be-ginning. Do not touch the sacred tjurunga [stone and wooden objects]. Leave them in their caves where they have rested through all the ages. Tend them, revere them, honour them. Do not rove continually through the territor-ies of other clans: honour the homes of your own ances-tors. Keep their ceremonial sites free from grass and bushes. Guard all sacred objects lest they should be stolen, lest they should decay.

Aranda teaching[3]

Darby Jampijinpa Ross, *Emu Dreaming*, 1987. The great themes of Aboriginal art derive from the events of *The Dreaming*. Darby Jampijinpa Ross's painting portrays an-cestors of the emu (an ostrich-like bird) represented by the arrow-like footprints. The spiraling lines indicate the animals' intestines. Spears and digging sticks—symbolic of men and women respectively—are suggested by the rows of bars.

INTRODUCTION

In Aboriginal Australia there is no geography without meaning or sacredness. Life is lived out in a constellation of relatedness anchored in the land. The whole of Aboriginal countryside is one living ageless family tree.

The physical landscape of Aboriginal Australia is of a primordial nature. Radiocarbon dating has indicated the existence of a society more than 40,000 years old. It is said Australia contains the oldest dry land in the world. The continent itself is the lowest and the flattest of all the continents, and three quarters of its land mass is desert or semiarid. The Australian continent was the last to be settled by Europeans, two hundred years ago. Estimates suggest that in 1788, at the time of the invasion of the Europeans, there was a population of between 250,000 and 500,000 Aborigines divided among more than 500 tribes. A 1987 official census reported 227,645 Aboriginal people in Australia. About 45,000 are full-blood Aborigines, the remainder being of mixed descent.

Australia has only one mountain that might be considered "tall." Named Kosciusko, it reaches a height of just 7,310 feet and is located in the Snowy Mountains of the southeast coast. There are mountain ranges, to be sure, that rim the continent and wind their way through the interior, but in the words of Asian studies scholar and mountaineer Edwin Bernbaum, "the long ages of erosion . . . have worn down these ranges into stubs of mountains . . . [while producing] some of the most spectacular geological formations in the world."[4] Bernbaum is referring to the enormous monoliths of ancient, glowing red sandstone that loom out of the deserts of central Australia and which are of paramount ritual and cultural importance to the Aborigines. One of these is the great sacred dome of Uluru (Ayers Rock), the world's largest isolated piece of rock and a site of incalculable meaning and sacredness to Australian Aborigines.

The worldwide surge in mineral exploration that began in earnest in the early 1960s has resulted in land rights and sacred sites issues, creating unprecedented pressures and anxieties in the lives of Aboriginal peoples. These life-threatening issues have prompted many Australian Aborigines to come forward and attest to the value and significance of their beloved land and their Law, each of which is validated through the Aborigines' adherence to *The Dreaming*. *The Dreaming* is an entirely Aboriginal construct of knowledge that shapes their perception of the universe.

The Dreaming is the otherworld. It is an everlasting and hallowed world that is peopled with great mythic spirit beings. "It is a big thing; you never let it go . . ." It is "like engine, like power, plenty of power; it does hard work; it *pushes*," explained one Aboriginal.[5] *The Dreaming* gives meaning to life, bestowing upon it depth and resonance through memory. *The Dreaming* is the ground of being.[6] It is also known as the Law: the generative principles of past, present and future; the body of ethics and the code of life. It has been called the "plan of life."[7] In other words, *The Dreaming* gave order to the world and laid down the Way (of the ancestors) for humans. Thus the spirit-essence of *The Dreaming* resides in all humankind.

The Dreaming is the period at the beginning of time when enduring shapes took form, enduring connections were established, and enduring events and exploits happened. Dreamings are the larger-than-life ancestral beings and heroes (human, animal and bird) who are eternally present. They are a ubiquitous presence in the landscape, and their power—their life force—is activated and maintained through right conduct, ceremony, song, dance, offerings, recounting of oral histories (Dreamtime stories), and the practice and preservation of Aboriginal traditions in general.

The Dreaming links people and place, ancestor and cosmos. "The ancestor became country," in the words of one Pitjantjatjara man.[8] The land then unites body and spirit, making country, spirit being, and Aboriginal inseparable. The place from which a person's spirit comes (where he or she was spiritually "conceived," as opposed to physically conceived and born) is his or her Dreaming Place, and the person is an incarnation of the ancestor who made that place. Anthropologist T. G. H. Strehlow writes: "Wherever they wandered, [the ancestors] left behind them a trail of what we might call potential life-cells which are only waiting for an opportunity to assume some visible, corporeal form. If a woman crosses any of these old tracks she is likely to conceive a child: the ancestor, or one of his sons, or one of the life-atoms that radiated from them on their wanderings, has entered into the body of the woman, craving for reincarnation."[9] In this sense, immortality is regarded as a natural Aboriginal birthright, an inherited and inherent state of beingness.

The Dreaming is the invisible framework that holds the world, substantiated by and reflected symbolically through the landscape itself. It is a metaphysical and binding reality; a transcendent form of human consensus that is not subject to negotiation. It is what is. A Pintupi's reflection, in this context, is both illuminating and instructive:

> IT'S NOT OUR IDEA, it's a big Law. We have to sit down alongside of that Law like all the dead people who went before us.[10]

When an Aboriginal speaks of "earth," he may use the word in a richly symbolic way to mean his "shoulder" or his "side," according to anthropologist W. E. H. Stanner, who tells us he has seen an Aboriginal lie down and embrace the earth he walked on.[11] In Aboriginal Australia, perhaps more than in any other society, land is a fountain of energy that invigorates their world. The real beauty of the landscape lies in one's belonging to it. Land is both giver and maker of life. Indeed, Aborigines say, *Walyaji Wankarunyayirni*— Land is life.[12] It is virtually impossible for an Aboriginal to deny his or her relationship with his or her "country." Consider the thoughts of an Aboriginal chairman of the Northern Land Council:

> I THINK OF LAND as the history of my nation. It tells of how we came into being and what system we must live [by]. My great ancestors who lived in the times of history planned everything that we practise now. The law of history says that we must not take land, fight over land, steal land, give land, and so on. My land is mine only because I came in spirit from that land, and so did my ancestors of the same land. . . .[13]

Landscape also is a humanized realm imbued with substance and consequence, as one Aboriginal explains:

> THAT COUNTRY KNOWS who is walking about in it. It can feel who is there. It knows if a stranger comes. And it can get angry—start a bush fire, or something. Not people, doing that—just the country itself.[14]

Aboriginal expressions of life are saturated with a rich oratory of belongingness which embodies their code of life. Narritjin Maymuru, a Yirrkala native, says,

> We belong to the ground
> It is our power and we must stay

Close to it or maybe
We will get lost.[15]

Charlie Jampijinpa Gallagher, a Nyirrpi native, speaks about his family's return to their ancestral home and the nature of this source:

> HERE WE ARE NOW, back in [our] own country, Nyirrpi. ... We've come back to our family's country, our grandfather's country, to live in this country, my own country, my father's country, father-in-law's, grandmother's and mother's country, so our children can grow up here. The children will mind this country. There are lots of children growing up here.[16]

Aboriginal writer and painter Goobalathaldin (Dick Roughsey) puts it another way when he says: "There is no such person as an unrelated stranger."[17] A traditional Aboriginal greeting to a stranger frames this aphorism nicely in the form of a question, "Of what family are you?"[18]

In the film *Desert Stories*, Nosepeg, a distinguished Pintupi elder from central Australia, guides a young anthropologist to an outcrop of gigantic boulders, pointing out to him that for the Pintupi people these boulders are much more than simply rocks. "They were," he said, "an old man and his many wives who had huddled together for warmth from the cold southerly wind."[19]

A towering compassion and exuberant affection for the land lies at the heart of all Aboriginal existence. It is hard to imagine, let alone understand, the depth and magnitude of this state of beingness, nor is it possible to calibrate its true significance. The following story touches upon the profound mystical attachment the Aboriginal holds with "country" and the life-sustaining power he derives from its intimate and eternal embrace.

Johnny Wararrngula Tjupurrula, an accomplished and renowned Papunya Tula artist, is returning home to Tjikarri, the inspiration for some of his most spectacular paintings and an important and sacred site in remote central Australia, 480 kilometers west of Alice Springs. His companion and driver tells the story:

> THE WHEELS SPIN over the ridge of the last dune and we are there. But it is not much—a rocky outcrop much like any other, perhaps even more ordinary than many that we have passed during the long day. The rockholes turn out to be dry and there's effectively nothing in the way of edible plant food; all the animal tracks are old so there will be no fresh meat tonight. And yet the old man is taken

away by it; he is crying, he is talking, singing to the rock, he is calling out its names, its stories, and he's clambering, almost crawling, over the rock face, this way and that way, stroking, rubbing, feeling his country. For the next twenty-four hours, late into the night and all the next day back to Papunya, it is as if he is in another world, ceaselessly telling the stories of the events and the creatures that passed through here and forged this landscape. But more than just telling them he seems to be living them, and actually seeing them still visible in the forms in front of him.[20]

Every atom of that rock represents the embodiment of some great ancestor, and its potential fertility is palpable.

"Law Written in Cave,
That Painting is Law."
—Bill Neidjie, Bunitj elder

Gagudju White Spirit Figure, rock painting, Cannon Hill area of Kakadu National Park, Northern Territory.

If our Dreaming and our laws and languages and our way of living die then that will be the end of Aboriginal people. . . .
Our bodies must keep doing the dances and living in the bush—we must teach in schools and get our people to perform dances for others.

These are the things we need to help us keep the head and body alive until we are given back our land, and the land can make us whole again.

LARRY LANLEY,
Aboriginal chairman,
Mornington Shire Council,
1978[21]

To wound the earth is to wound yourself, and if others wound the earth, they are wounding you. The land should be left untouched: as it was in the Dreamtime when the Ancestors sang the world into existence.

Aboriginal belief[22]

Singing up the country, boss,
Makes the country come up quicker.

Aboriginal saying[23]

THE DREAMING:
THE SONGS, MYTHS,
RITUALS AND STORIES

We live in a country . . . which possesses the original sources of mythology," writes Australian poet Roland Robinson. "Almost every feature of [the] beautiful and mountainous landscape has its mythical explanation." In a journey to "unlock the sacred voice of the country I called home," Robinson has "captured" and recorded some extraordinary Aboriginal narratives, songs and myths. He once said: "I was shown the mountain site of an ancestral being who still gives out songs to certain aborigines and caste-aborigines [of mixed descent] of this tribal area."[24] A rare and translucent accounting of the sources of inspiration for Aboriginal song-making and dancing was given to Robinson by Leodardi, a songmaker and dancer from Millingimbi in Arnhem Land in the Northern Territory.

I DON'T MAKE UP THESE SONGS and dances. The spirits give them to me. Sometimes when I am out hunting I come to a certain place. Something in that place tells me to keep quiet. By and by I see the spirits come out and start singing and dancing. They are painted up, and they are beating the songsticks together. I keep quiet. I catch that song. I catch that dance. I catch that painting. I come back to the camp and give this song, this dance, this painting to my people.[25]

Aboriginal music, song and dance re-collect the sacred forms of the inner world of mythic consciousness so that the singer, dancer and musician can engage in dialogue with "country." To enter a state "where all the earth has the power to converse with him" is the goal of the Aboriginal artist.

Song in Aboriginal Australia has a sacred life independent of those who sing it and those who listen to it. Song (and singing) is a sacred trust bequeathed by the Law and invested with singular power and grace. It is a life force. Songs are a retelling of the creative era, the activities of The Dreamtime, and through the singing of them the land comes alive and gives meaning to life. Songs are owned; they can also be inherited and transferred. Songs have their own living texture. Among the Pintupi people of central Australia, for example, the melody of a song is known as the scent *(mayu)*, or taste *(ngurru).*[26]

In *Wanamurraganya*, Aboriginal elder Jack McPhee, born Garimarra, tells his story to Aboriginal writer Sally Morgan, and with exquisite detail "sings" the praises of his Uncle Hector, "famous amongst the people as a songmaker" of *corroborees*—social and ceremonial gatherings.

WHENEVER HECTOR CAME UP with a new song everyone was always amazed. They were all so different, you see, so clever and so meaningful. There was a lot of respect for him because of this. When it came to song-making Hector was considered very special. How the whole thing worked out was like this. Hector would make all the different songs that were to be sung, then it was up to others to try and make a dance that would do credit to that song. This wasn't always easy because Hector's songs were so good people worried about having a dance that was up to standard. Hector had complete power to say yes or no to the dances that were invented. If he didn't like the dance or thought it wasn't good enough, it wasn't allowed to be performed. It was only when all this was settled that the corroboree went ahead. His songs became so famous that some even travelled up to the Kimberley area, as well as down to Meekatharra. . . .

The corroborees there [Corunna Downs Station] were wonderful too. We had them once a month. We would dance all night sometimes. There were some very good singers there amongst the women. Every corroboree we had was different and lasted a different length of time. Sometimes someone would make up a song and we'd all take a liking to it, we'd sing it over and over every night and still not get sick of it. We could make a good song last for weeks. Other times we'd get a song and teach it to others who didn't know it. Then they would go and teach it to another group and so on.

Some corroborees have what's called a Big dance in it. That's a special dance the women aren't allowed to see.

Some dances they are allowed to see, but not the Big one. That's just for men.

Corroboree time is a very busy time. There's meat to be gotten, arrangements to be made, headdresses to be constructed, dances to be worked out and songs to be learnt. It's very exciting. Depending on what dances are going to be on, you might have to make three or four different headdresses, and that takes time because some of them are quite complicated and they all have to be painted and decorated in the correct way. We used to make all our own paint and help decorate one another. It all takes time and it all has to be done properly, according to what the Law says. I used to join in all the dances and songs. I loved that time. You wouldn't recognise me now if I was dressed up like that.

I can't really explain to you how important those times were to me. To sing and dance, to hear the women's voices singing out high above the rest, it just made me feel good inside. I suppose to people listening, our songs all sound the same, but to us they are all different. Some were just for singing, some for dancing. They were all entirely different to us.

The people there were wonderful storytellers too. At night we'd sit around the campfire and the few old ones would tell us Dreamtime stories. Can you imagine how it was for me then? The fire, my friends, the moon and stars and us young blokes with our mouths hanging open believing every word they said. Some of those old people had a way of talking that sent shivers down your spine. . . .

[H]ere I am, old . . . and what keeps coming back to me? Dances, singing, stories the old people used to tell. Every night I lie in bed and sing myself to sleep with all my old corroboree songs. I go over and over them and I remember that part of my life. They're the things I love, they're the things I miss.[27]

Aboriginal country is a richly symbolic and deeply religious world that inspires great love. Singing is one expression of that profound affection. It keeps everything fertile, ensuring reciprocity between humankind and the natural and metaphysical worlds. Likewise, through the songs, as in this love song from the Oenpelli region of Arnhem Land in northern Australia, the spirits keep the people alive. Songs affirm the sacrality of life and the numinous nature of the Aboriginal universe.

> Come with me to the point and we'll
> look at the country,
> We'll look across at the rocks,
> Look, rain is coming!
> It falls on my sweetheart.[28]

"If we do not sing the songs, the animals will go away. Then we will all die."[29] This was the remark of an old Aboriginal tribesman to Australian writer and poet James Cowan. The singing of songs constitutes proof of aboriginality and guardianship of country. In the singing and the revelation of song a de facto assertion is made about self-identity and rights and responsibilites held in the land. A reciprocity of belongingness streams through this *Dreaming* song about country.

> Forked stick and rafters, floor posts
> with a roof like a sea eagle's nest
> lie by a billabong* where goose eggs
> give the water its huge expanse.
>
> My people build, thinking of rain—
> rain and wind from the west, clouds
> slowly spreading over the billabong—
> while we raise our grass huts.
>
> Our chests heave like clouds
> as we call out for the rain to fall.
> Rain! dampen us with your deluge
> as soon as we build our shelters.[30]

The dynamic traveling principle that is central to Aboriginal existence reflects a reenactment of the great journeys of their ancestral heroes who made their universe and continue to guide and protect all that lives and grows. Observance of the Law bequeathed by the creator-ancestors sanctifies all life and ensures an ongoing coherence

* A small lake or pool.

to Aboriginal life. The piquancy, humor and earthiness of the Tingari story-telling tradition of Pintupi country in central Australia is embodied in a poem by Billy Marshall-Stoneking called "The Promiscuous Old Man." The poem is based on a Tingari song cycle (part of a larger sacred cycle that tells of the mythological journeyings and adventures of the first ancestral spirit beings) and is told by Old Tutuma Tjapangati:

> "It went West!"
> The old man laughs as he tells me this.
> It's the end of a story
> about an old man who was worried
> all the time
> for tjiki-tjiki—
> "He liked women.
> All the time/all the time;
> one night wasn't good enough.
> One woman wasn't good enough."
> The storyteller grabs my hands
> and leans over close to whisper
> in my ear: "Law! Aboriginal law!"
> The story's about this old man
> who liked women;
> he loved a different kungka every night.
> "He couldn't think straight."
> One morning he woke up—
> "karlu wiya, ngaampu wiya"—
> his sexual parts were missing.
> "They'd gone walkabout by themselves.
> They couldn't wait for him anymore!"
> He tracked them for days and days,
> over sandhills and dry lakes.
> He tracked them at night,
> with a firestick in his hand,
> but "that penis wasn't going to stop;
> those balls weren't going to sit down."
> That penis has a long "dreaming track" now.
> It goes a long way—West!
> The storyteller sticks out his tongue
> and scrunches up his nose:
> "That old man—
> he never did catch up!"[31]

Most non-Aborigines think that the term "Dreamtime" refers to a long distant era of the past when Aborigines languorously drew patterns on the walls of caves and generally moved in a dream-like trance through life, without constraint of law and regulation, and generally slept in the sunshine. . . .

The Dreaming, the Dreamtime, not only refers to an historic heroic era in the long distant past but is a living continuation of spiritual life and instruction that continues today.

KEVIN GILBERT,
Aboriginal poet,
playwright and artist [32]

Aboriginal people will always live in their dreamtimes and their dreamtimes is the space that was once around them long before the coming of the white man. . . . [T]he Aboriginal dreamtime is true facts, and not just myth as the white man would put it or say it.

ROBERT BROPHO,
Fringedweller
and author [33]

The world-forming marvels of The Dreamtime—the heroic acts of the ancestors that sustain and validate Aboriginal traditions—continue to provide a philosophy for contemporary Aboriginal life. It is a system of knowledge that regards man and nature as one corporate whole, sacred and eternal. In Confucian terms, its goal is "to unite hearts and establish order." [34] The belief and ideal of The Dreamtime are at once the teaching of final things, which were also first things. [35]

Many Aborigines say that they "follow up the Dreaming," a metaphor for following a track. Traversing the Dreaming Tracks (literally the footprints of the ancestors) is a way to honor and vivify the great totemic ancestors and to quicken one's own spirit presence (and by extension that of the universe), while calling up the faith, courage and fortitude required to live in the fullness of Aboriginal life. From the Aboriginal perspective, the whole of Australia is perceived as a gigantic Dreaming Track, a communications system of the profoundest order, operating on a metaphysical, social and cultural level. One student of Aboriginal society has described these tracks as trails "of words and musical notes" along the line of the ancestors' footprints. He writes that these Songlines "could be read as a musical score," adding that "[t]here was hardly a rock or creek in the country that could not or had not been sung,"[36] and relates a conversation with an Australian cartographer of Aboriginal sacred sites to this effect.

> "A SONG," he said, "was both map and direction-finder. Providing you knew the song, you could always find your way across country."
> *"And would a man on 'Walkabout' always be travelling down one of the Songlines?"*
> "In the old days, yes," he agreed. "Nowadays, they go by train or car."
> *"Suppose the man strayed from his Songline?"*
> "He was trespassing. He might get speared for it."
> *"But as long as he stuck to the track, he'd always find people who shared his Dreaming? Who were, in fact, his brothers?"*
> "Yes."
> *"From whom he could expect hospitality?"*
> "And vice versa. . . . "
> *"So the land," I said, "must first exist as a concept in the mind? Then it must be sung? Only then can it exist?"*
> "True."[37]

This piece of prose poetry was recounted by Charlotte Williams, an old Aboriginal of mixed descent of the Gindavul tribe, whose country is the mountainous area around Woodenbong. Williams lived at the Aboriginal settlement at Woodenbong in New South Wales. The account that follows is an explanation and translation of one of her tribal songs. It is also a glimpse into an inner world, a whole world, where all worlds are one.

> THERE WAS A VINE which was the spirit of a man. These forest-vines, they were the spirit-people's vines. They were not made by men. And someone cut this vine, and there

this man is, struggling to be alive. Ngaranbul, this is my own grandfather's song. This vine is this man's spirit, it is his life, and there he is, struggling to be alive. "I am here," the song says. "I am this vine. My life is going away. It is going up into the sky. It is going up into the sky from this place, this ground, this dust. My ears are ringing. Gaungun, the spirit-woman, is making my ears no good. My ears are ringing. I'll never see this world no more."

And one man came along and saw this vine, struggling to be alive. He covered it with dust.

When I think of my old people, how they would sit down and sing their songs to me, I could cry. . . .[38]

Percy Mumbulla, son of "King" Jacky Mumbulla, a full-blood Aboriginal from the far south coast of the State of New South Wales, was a wonder of a storyteller, a poet who could neither read nor write. By a gum tree in a place called Tomerong, "a sound like a little bark coming out of the gum tree" triggered Mumbulla's explanation of the significance of the singing of the *Jarrangulli*, the tree-lizard:

HEAR THAT TREE-LIZARD *Jarrangulli*, singin' out. He's in a hole up in that tree. He's singin' out for rain. He wants the rain to fill that hole right up, to cover him with rain. That water will last him till the drought is gone.

It's comin' dry when he sings out, *Jarrangulli*. Soon as ever he sings out, he's sure to bring the rain. That feller, he's the real rain-lizard. He's just the same as them black cockatoos. They're the fellers for the rain.

He's deadly poison, that *Jarrangulli*. He'll bite you. You climb that tree and happen to put your hand over that hole, he'll bite you sure enough. He's a black lizard painted with white stripes. *Jarrangulli*, he's singin' out for rain.[39]

A myth is called a *butheram* in the tribal language of the Gullibul of the Clarence River in the northeast corner of New South Wales. It is also a sacred story "released" and handed over by an eternal being who lives in a mountain. These immortal spirits are also called *butheram*. Alexander Vesper, an elder of the Gullibul tribe, describes the essence of a *butheram*. His explanation is considered one of the best accounts of the nature of a myth.[40]

THE *BUTHERAM* WERE LIVING in the mountains in Australia before the three brothers, the first men ever to reach Australia, came here. When the tribes became clever, they found the *butheram* here and made them their gods. There was not one *butheram* that was ever told without the songs. When a *butheram* was told in the old days, it would take three or four nights to tell it. The story-teller would start the story just on dark. He would go on until it was late and everybody was sleepy. The next night he would pick up the story from where he left off, and go on again till everybody was sleepy. This kind of story had many songs in it. As the story-teller told the story, the people sitting round the fire would call out from time to time, at the sad parts, the exciting parts, or the beautiful parts, "*Ngain! Ngain!*" This would mean, "It is beautiful! It is good to hear this story!"[41]

I feel it with my body,
with my blood.
Feeling all these trees,
all this country . . .
When this wind blow you can feel it.
Same for country . . .
You feel it.
You can look,
but feeling . . .
that make you.

BIG BILL NEIDJIE,
Bunitj elder[42]

The Aboriginal universe is suffused with a vast sign system that directs life and gives it meaning. Dutiful use of and respect for the efficacious signs combined with the exchange and flow of signs constitute one aspect of Aboriginal reciprocal thinking.[43] The sign world is a complex, multilayered host of symbolisms where everything has meaning and a sense of mystery dominates. An inquiry about unexplained phenomena often results in the Aboriginal comment, "It must be something."[44] Similarly, most queries about myth, rite, song and things of a religious nature are met with a uniformity of response that these beliefs and rituals are observed to "follow up the Dreaming." All experience is encompassed within this foundational and fragile ontology of *The Dreaming*.

The presiding principle of Aboriginal society is life; that is, everything thrives, even in death. Songs are a means of reanimating and recovering the knowledge inherent in the land. Nothing is insignificant or meaningless, as Galarrwuy Yunupingu, son of Arnhem Land artist Munggurrawuy and former chairman of the Northern Land Council, demonstrates in this story about his father.

> WHEN I WAS SIXTEEN YEARS old my father taught me to sing some of the songs that talk about the land . . . One day, I went fishing with Dad. As I was walking along behind him I was dragging my spear on the beach, which was leaving a long line behind me. He told me to stop doing that. He continued telling me that if I made a mark, or dig, with no reason at all, I've been hurting the bones of the traditional people of that land. We must only dig and make marks on the ground when we perform or gather food.[45]

On a chilly September morning in 1979, at Tennant Creek in Blueberry Hill camp in the Northern Territory, Topsy Napurrula Nelson, a Warlpiri-Kaititj "teacher and philosopher," and elder with respect to her range of Dreaming knowledge, talked to her friend and "pupil" Diane Bell about the three most important things in her life —family, country and *yawalyu* (songs, rituals and knowledge). She spoke about the rights and responsibilities that come with being a woman "custodian" of sacred knowledge, objects, rituals and sites of her clanspeople's beloved land, Pawurrinji (southwest of Tennant Creek). On one occasion, reports Bell, when Nelson sought to convey the strength and power of song and body paint that emanate from their proper and sincere use in ceremonial ritual, she likened their potency and effect "to a blood transfusion: 'It's life, our life blood, but it comes from another.' "[46] Topsy Napurrula Nelson speaks of the ways in which women's *yawalyu* keep the sacred land alive.

> THAT COUNTRY . . . THAT PAWURRINJI—we're going back there. My father told me about it when I was child, and all

my aunties too [father's sisters]. They taught me the business [religious rituals], the songs and the painting-up for that country. We went into that country before with you, lots of times, but there was too much long grass, too much no road. We had to turn back all the time. We couldn't get right up close to that really place at Pawurrinji, where the *jintirrpiri* [Willie wagtail] and *kurlukuku* [diamond dove] dreamings come through.

But they told me about you [her pupil]—you got there. They told me here, where I'm sitting now. That country, it's all right now. They been burn it and make it clean. Now you can get right up to that Pawurrinji place. They were telling me and my father about when you got to that Pawurrinji, and he was happy. Rosie, his sister, was singing for that country. She was teaching me about that business, like before.[47]

Mick Namarari Tjapaltjarri, *Bandicoot Dreaming*, 1991. This painting is a highly figurative rendering of the significance of the bandicoot ancestors from *The Dreamtime*. It reveals the swirling and geometric scratch marks dug by Tjakalpa, the desert bandicoot (a rodentlike animal), as it digs a burrow at the Dreaming-site of Putja.

One area of widespread misunderstanding on the part of non-Aboriginal Australians is over the Aboriginal attitude towards sacred sites. One continually hears the complaint that whenever any development is proposed, the Aborigines suddenly find a new sacred site. In normal circumstances a sacred site would be secret and so would never be revealed. The Aboriginal people have now begun to disclose them only because they are under threat. If we do not ensure adequate protection for Aboriginal sacred sites in the future we will be making a mockery of religious freedom in this country.

HONOURABLE CLYDE HOLDING, M.P.,
Minister for Aboriginal Affairs [48]

We continue to follow the spirit of the people who have gone before us, who have handed down to us the laws for the land and the right way to establish human relationships for the maintenance of our religion and culture.

Despite what people from mining companies and others might like to think, our country still makes sense to us through sacred sites which criss-cross the continent.

We continue to love our land, the country that gives us life, our social, political and family institutions.

The question that we must ask is that do we, like our Kanaky brothers and sisters, have to go to Libya or some other country before the Australian Government comes to terms with our prior rights? . . .

We will not continue to sit at the foot of your table and watch you grow fat off our land.

We will not continue to accept the scraps which you choose to throw down to us, and threaten to take away.

We will not give up our struggle for recognition, independence and dignity.

Like our forebears, we will not die, we will not go away; our particular cultural genius has roots which reach back into time, beyond your recorded history, and continue to sustain us.

PAT DODSON,
Aboriginal spokesperson,
in an address to the National
Press Club, Canberra, 1985 [49]

SACRED SITES:
OASES OF KNOWLEDGE

Aboriginal perceptions of sacred sites, land tenure systems and the relationship that exists between a people, the land and its sacred sites constitute the heart of the Aboriginal Land Rights Legislation in Australia. The issues represent a complex web of rights and responsibilites *to* land and sites deemed sacred. Australian anthropologist Diane Bell has explicated the spiritual ties, kinship connections and conception rights that, from the Aboriginal's perspective, establish irrefutably Aboriginal "stewardship" of the land in general and "custodianship" of the sacred sites in particular. Sites became sacred through the activities of the "pioneering ancestors"—mythological figures of The Dreamtime—as they crisscrossed the country, giving it shape and meaning. Along the way they left behind clues about their presence: a rock marking where a dingo gave birth; a water hole as a gift to future life; a quartz formation as a manifestation of ancestral caterpillar eggs.[50]

Today the sacred sites continue to offer a lifeline to Aboriginal society. Through the re-acquisition of ancestral lands, the sites are gradually being returned to in greater numbers and their sleeping energies are being re-awakened through the renewed observance and practice of ritual, providing strength, guidance and solace to Aboriginal people. The sites are embraced as open-air cathedrals, ancient, holy and living repositories of the sacred images, eternal truths, physical, social and spiritual needs and profoundly human potential of Aboriginal culture. Jack McPhee, Aboriginal elder, describes the supernatural power stored in these sites and, by extension, invested in the land; and the unspeakable sadness experienced over the loss of any one site:

> A SACRED SITE could be a cave, a rock, a pool, anywhere where a big snake could be or where he comes now and then. I'm not talking about a real snake in the sense of something you can see, I'm talking about a very old spiritual thing. I suppose a white person's sacred site might be

his church, but you know when that church was built and you can feel it with your hands. Our sacred sites are more to do with the spirits, and they can't be dated because they've always been there.

There used to be a sacred site on the way back from the Comet mine, which is about six miles south-west of Marble Bar [in north Western Australia]. Just as you drive over the point of a big hill, there used to be a little bit of a creek that ran under a gum tree. It had been there for hundreds and hundreds and hundreds of years. When I was young you could always count on getting a drink of water there, even in drought time.

Unfortunately, white people didn't understand how special this place was. Someone went and dug a hole there, probably a prospector, hoping the water would build up, but of course it didn't, it just died away. You see, in doing that he killed Gadagadara, a snake with a strange head shaped like a horse's, who had placed his spirit there to live and keep the water for the people.

I remember the old ones being very upset when that site was destroyed. They had a meeting to try and work out who had killed Gadagadara, but no one knew. They were very sad for a long time after that.

There have been a number of places like that where I come from. In these special places there's been water, sometimes just a puddle, and then someone sends a grader in or someone tampers with it, and of course the water disappears because the spirit that kept it has been killed.[51]

All living things in Aboriginal culture share a common life principle derived from their creation in the Beginning, The Dreamtime. Specific land sites that are associated with The Dreamtime heroes are imbued with a life force that sustains Aboriginal life and the Law. Each person in Aboriginal society has a spirit connection with one of these sacred sites. As such, the site itself serves as the source of a person's being. For this reason, Guboo Ted Thomas considers the recognition and protection of Mumbulla Mountain, an Aboriginal sacred land base and initiation center, essential to the flourishing of Aboriginal culture. Furthermore, Thomas suggests that the spiritual resources of the mountain are an untapped frontier for the elucidation of white Australia's true heritage.

MY NAME IS Guboo Ted Thomas. I am a Tribal Elder of the Yuin Tribe on the South Coast of New South Wales. I am writing to you about Mumbulla Mountain, which is of vital importance to the culture and dignity of the 3,500 Aborigines living on the South Coast today. The Mountain is about 30 kilometres south-west of where many of us live at Wallaga Lake, not all that far from Bega.

For us Aborigines, it is a sacred mountain where initiations used to take place. These took place at sacred sites on the Mountain.

When they were old enough, the boys of our tribe were taken away to these special sacred sites. Here they were taught the special secrets of our Culture. So, you see, the Law comes from the Mountain.

They had to spend a long time on the Mountain away from their people, and they were put through special tests to prove that they were men. Then they were initiated and brought back to the tribe as young men who respected their Tribal Law and Culture. The Law has been handed down from one generation to the next, ever since the Dreamtime.

I was told about these things when I was young. I was told by my grandfather, my father and my uncle. Near Wallaga Lake where we live there is another important mountain called Goolaga—or, by white people, Mt. Dromedary. When I was a boy, I used to walk with my people from Wallaga Lake over Mumbulla Mountain to Bega. From Goolaga to Mumbulla is all part of the one walkabout.

When we were walking, the old people would sometimes point to places on Mumbulla Mountain and tell me there were special sites there. They told me that one day I would be taken there and have them shown to me. This would be when I would be initiated. They said that then I would have to help look after the Law and the Culture.

But the last initiations were about 1918, when I was still too young. These were done by our Tribal Elders. One of these was Jack Mumbulla, who has the same name as the Mountain. Some of the men initiated there were Percy Davis (my grandfather), Murrum Alf Carter (whose descendants still live at Wallaga Lake), Bukel Albert Thomas (my cousin) and Eric Roberts (who still lives at Wreck Bay).

We hope to bring back initiations on the Mountain in the near future. This will be very good. It will help make our Law and our Culture strong once again.

So I hope you can see now why Mumbulla Mountain is an important part of our Culture and why it should be protected. It is important to us Aborigines, but we think it should also be important to white Australians as well. It is something that should be important to our Australian heritage.[52]

Ayers Rock (known to the Aborigines as the great dome of Uluru) is a living, breathing temple, the locus of life for the desert people of central Australia. It is also immense. This astonishing piece of stone bursts from the earth to assume center stage in the middle of a desert plain, looming to a height of nearly 2,820 feet above sea level. It is $2\frac{1}{3}$ miles long and $1\frac{2}{3}$ miles wide, a mysterious reddish monolith of sandstone with, to paraphrase Emerson, the power of a magician's rod to awaken the sleeping energies of the land. For the Aboriginal people it is all Dreamtime, a vivid record of their ancient origins engraved and painted all over its cliffs, caves, waterholes and gullies. It is the embodiment of fertility—psychic, physical and universal. At the base of the rock is a small fecund stretch that is fed by the rain water runoff. This unexpected sanctuary makes it an important desert oasis for plant, animal and Aboriginal alike.

If sacred sites, like Ayers Rock, are not properly looked after, and if the desecration by tourists is allowed to continue (e.g., a sacred cave is unwittingly entered by a white person, as has frequently happened), there is no future. These holy sites *are* the Law, the lifeblood of the Aboriginal people. Paddy Uluru, Pitjantjatjara elder, whose own name (Uluru) is the same as that of the rock, was one of the traditional owners of the area. In Paddy's mind, this meant he *was* Ayers Rock; he was one with it. Today he is buried there. His five sons, together with other Pitjantjatjara and Yangkuntjatjara owners, carry on with the responsibilities of protection and generation. In November 1971, at a seminar in Ernabella, Paddy gathered with other Pitjantjatjara men to explain the significance of the site and to protest the ever-growing threats to its living presence. In their emotional testimony, all the elders pleaded for the recognition of the supersacred nature of the site and for the banning of all visitors in its immediate vicinity. Violations of this sort were considered a danger to everyone, they explained. The following words express Paddy's unconsolable anguish and concern over the repeated pollution of the site by insensitive and uninformed tourist traffic. They are also a testament to his inalienable linkage with this Dreaming Place.

AYERS ROCK IS MY CAMP. This is mine, this holy cave. Yes, this is a holy cave. I alone truly know about this place. I was put into this place. Yes, my fathers and grandfathers entrusted me with this cave. This holy cave. And girls have broken this thing of mine. And I have become very sad. This is my great ceremony, my holy ceremony, my great camp with its holy tree and Mutitjulu on this side is holy. Ayers Rock is holy. I am Ayers Rock and these things are mine. And now white people have broken that which is ours, our Law, ours, our great ceremony, the ceremony of the Mala wallaby [the plains wallaby] from which we are taught. And I am speaking truly to you. Mutitjulu is the main place at Ayers Rock and white people have gone through it. A white fellow, having frightened me, chased me away. Having gone from that place I wandered around, having left my things there I moved around. That was my camp, my home, mine, and I was going around from there. Finished! My fathers are finished. They are finished.

Having become one in that place I left it. This having happened I let everything go and later a white girl went through there. I do not know where she came from, from a long way away, but she went through this holy place. She broke this holy place. It is broken completely. . . .[53]

The whole of Aboriginal country is spiritually peopled. The land is alive. Not only does it give life, it is life. It is a life preserver that imbues Aboriginal culture with enduring value. Emotional and spiritual attachment to place is at the center of their ethos. As one Northern Aranda elder put it: "we all love the ancient soil around our soak, and it draws us to itself at all times, and there is not one amongst us who is ever heedless or forgetful of its call."[54] T. G. H. Strehlow, who was born and raised amongst the Northern Aranda and spoke their language, recorded in the 1930s that "the Northern Aranda clings to his native soil with every fibre of his being. He will always speak of his own 'birthplace' with love and reverence. Today, tears will come into his eyes when he mentions an ancestral home site which has been, sometimes unwittingly, desecrated by the white usurpers of his group territory."[55] Abandonment or desecration of one's ancestral home site can lead to one's spiritual death, and in many cases, to physical death as well. Gurra, an Ilbalintja of the Northern Aranda in central Australia, relates such a story of defilement.

THE ILBALINTJA SOAK [water hole] has been defiled by the hands of white men. Two white men came here to sink a well. They put down into the sacred soak plugs of gelignite, to blast an opening through the hard rock at the bottom. But the rock was too hard for them. They had to leave without having been able to shatter it; they took ill soon afterwards and died.

And now the soak has almost gone dry. No longer do men pluck up the grass and the weeds and sweep the ground clean around it; no longer do they care for the resting place of Karora [legendary Ilbalintja bandicoot chief]. Bushes have grown up on the very edge of the soak, and there is no one to uproot them. The bandicoots [rodentlike animals] have vanished from the tall grass in the mulga [small, spreading tree] thicket. Our young men no longer care for the traditions of their fathers; and their women bear no children. Soon the men of Ilbalintja will be no more; we shall all sleep in our graves as our forefathers do now.

There is little here for strangers to see; there is no mountain cave here, only a storehouse in a mulga tree. But though the soak has been foresaken by almost all our people, a few of us old men still care for it. It still holds me fast; and I shall tend it while I can: while I live, I shall love to gaze on this ancient soil.[56]

The importance of customary or traditional Law to the survival of indigenous peoples should not be underestimated. Customary law is a dynamic and holistic approach to life that evolves and adapts to new pressures and challenges. Possession of a traditional land base and the right of self-government are vital to the expression, meaning and flexibility of the Law and its spiritual nature. The Fringedwellers of Swan Valley are faced with the prospect of a pipeline boring into their Sacred Belief of Waughal, the Snake at Bennet Brook. Such an action would constitute a life-threatening violation of their Law, tantamount to a betrayal of *The Dreaming*. The Fringedwellers' original ancestors had touched Bennet Brook with their adventures, thus turning it into a sacred sanctuary where rites are performed and kept alive. The universality of the snake image as ancestor is associated with initiation, fertility and rain. The Australian Aborigines' snake ancestor is one that binds together as it throws asunder, re-members and ultimately transforms humankind. Thus an Aboriginal will say,

"I know Wonambi (the snake) because I have been inside his stomach."[57] In this way the mouth of the snake functions as a door and its body serves as a new habitat. This means that the initiate is disconnected from his childhood and then rejoined to a complex body of knowledge that provides a new focus in life. Initiation rituals act as rites of passage (as they do in most cultures). Their performance at the holy sites spells out a charter for social action whose goal is to unite body and soul and the spirit of the sacred place. The observance of ceremonies on Aboriginal sacred ground assures the continuity of life, the health of the land and the ongoing re-linking of the chain of the Law.

WE, THE ABORIGINAL FRINGEDWELLERS of the Swan Valley of the continent called Australia, who are a community of Aboriginal people who are the original owners and inhabitants on the Swan River on the west coast of the continent which was invaded by the white race, 150 years ago, we are writing to you for help and assistance where our Sacred Laws and Aboriginal Culture and Beliefs are concerned and which have to be protected. We, the fringedwellers of the Swan Valley, are the closest keepers of the Belief of Waughal, the Snake at Bennet Brook, on behalf of all Aboriginal people. We live in low living conditions in camps at Lockridge campsite on our Sacred Grounds beside the Belief which is Bennet Brook.

The Government of Western Australia through their State Energy Commission is making it really hard for us by deciding to bore a high pressure gas pipeline into the Sacred Ground of Bennet Brook which will desecrate our ancient dreamtime Belief. We agreed, 3 years ago, with the State Energy Commission for the pipeline to go across the land if it went *over* the Brook. . . .

The Federal Government of Australia is making it really hard for us by not assisting in the proper way, by using their powers to protect our Belief. This is why we have been forced to go to the Supreme Court of Western Australia to try to stop them. The Judge, Mr. Justice Rowland, gave us an injunction to stop them on 8th July, 1986, and advised all parties to get together to come to agreement. . . .

What is happening here at Bennet Brook in the Swan Valley is an attempt to move on and bore into sacred sites all over Western Australia. If this happens, if our sacred sites are destroyed, our Culture and what we live by, it is goodbye to Aboriginal people.

This here at Bennet Brook is only the one example. As soon as it is done here, boring into our Belief, that is a step against all Aboriginal people by the mining companies and this Western Australian government.

We the Swan Valley fringedwellers, who live in suffering and hardship on our Sacred Grounds, have been making a strong stand for many years. Your help is urgently needed now.[58]

The divine power invested in Aboriginal sacred sites is real and can be retributive in the case of wanton disrespect. Bob Turnbull, an Aboriginal of mixed descent of the Purfleet settlement in the northeast corner of New South Wales, recounts the story of an Aboriginal man, Frank Jock, who sold out on his Dreaming Place, his *jurraveel* (ancestral source of being), and hence his people.

YOU KNOW THAT WATER-HEN with the red beak? He sings out "Kerk," and "Kerk," and "Kerk," well, that bird is my totem. Every dark feller has a totem. It's his spirit. It looks after him and warns him of any danger. In my tribe, the Bunjalung tribe of the Richmond River, his name is *geeyarng.* And our native name for a totem is *barnyunbee.*

I want to tell you about a totem that belonged to a dark feller named Frank Jock. Frank Jock had a totem that was something like a little bantam rooster. Everyone would hear this bird singing out. They'd go to look for him, but they could never find him.

Away on the mountain in the lantana [notorious shrubby weed] he'd be, singing out. He was sort of minding that place, looking after it you'd say.

Well, the mayor of Coraki wanted to make a quarry in that mountain. There was the best kind of blue-metal there. He sent the men of the council to that place. They put three charges, one after the other, into the rock. But not one of those three charges would go off.

There was a dark feller in the gang by the name of Andrew Henry. He told the mayor of Coraki that he'd have to go and have a talk to Frank Jock. The mayor would have to ask Frank if he could do something so that they could blow up this mountain and make a quarry in it.

The mayor sent for Frank Jock, he said he wanted to see him. "Look," the mayor said to Frank, "can you let us blow this mountain up?"

"All right," Frank said, "but you'll have to pay me."

So the mayor gave Frank five gold sovereigns and two bottles of rum to let the council blow up the mountain.

The council men went back to the mountain and there they put in one big charge. When it went off, it blew the side right out of the mountain. That explosion shook Coraki. A big spout of black water rushed up out of the mountain-side. The council had to wait a long time until all the water cleared away before they could work that quarry.

The little bantam rooster, he disappeared. He didn't sing out any more. *Jurraveel,* that's what we call a place belonging to a totem. A dreaming, you say. That's right. That's another name for a *jurraveel.* . . .

Well, after the mountain was blown up, Frank Jock, the owner of that *jurraveel,* began to get sick. In three weeks he was dead. You see, like it says in the Bible, he'd sold his birth-right. It was the same as killing him. He'd sold his *jurraveel* to the mayor of the town.

That's why we call it in our language Gurrigai, meaning "blowing up the mountain." That's how Coraki got its name. . . .

These stories are dying out. They're lost to the young people. I'd like to think that one day the young people will read these stories and say, "These stories belong to us."[59]

The Aboriginal landscape consists of a network of traditional pathways—an intricate and sacred criss-crossing of mythical tracks (Dreaming Tracks)—marked by the passages of ancestral beings and punctuated by their legacy of a multitude of holy sites. The Aboriginal people today know these ancestral routes, and when they move across them they are both animating them and honoring their spiritual sources. Within the context of our own cash economy, "most sacred sites," writes Fred Myers in his study of Pintupi life, "are said, therefore, to be 'gold.' "[60] The active custodianship of these sites is essential to the fertility of the universe. For this reason, sacred sites like the extraordinary Ayers Rock—which has developed in recent years into a tourist attraction—have become a source of great anxiety to the senior clan elders and "owners" (male and female) who care for and protect these hallowed locations, the spirit source from which they came and to which they will return. The maintenance and nurturing of the sites through the vigilant performance of ceremonies and rituals is vital to the health of the tribe and the planet. Big Bill Neidjie, Bunitj elder from the East Alligator River of Arnhem Land, speaks about it this way:

> Our story is in the land . . .
> It is written in those sacred places.
> My children will look after those places,
> that's the law.
> Dreaming place . . .
> you can't change it.
> No matter who you are.
> No matter you rich man,
> no matter you king.
> You can't change it. . . .
> Rock stays
> Earth stays
> I die and put my bones in cave or earth
> Soon my bones become earth . . .
> All the same
> My spirit has gone back to my country . . .
> My mother.[61]

It all goes back to the land, that is why land rights are so important to us.

We need the land to be Aboriginal in our minds—that is why Governments must give back the land if we are to keep our culture.

Take away our land like the Queensland Government is trying to do and we're nobody, we will die out, finish. The land gives the true meaning to Aboriginal life.

At the heart of everything is land—it is the way we feel and think about the land that makes us Aboriginals. . . .

It is the only way to keep our culture, and without it we are scattered into a country that is not ours, where we feel hunted, like wild kangaroos and dingoes.

LARRY LANLEY,
Aboriginal chairman,
Mornington Shire Council,
1978[62]

How can Mr. Court say that his Government owns this country? It belongs to the Dreaming and not to him. Does Mr. Court also say that he owns the moon, and the sun and the sky?

FRED FORBES,
chairman, Ngaanyatjara Council,
Jamieson, WA, 26 August 1980[63]

WHOSE LAND
IS IT ANYWAY?

The Aboriginal fight for land rights began in earnest in the 1960s and continues in earnest today. "Land is a map," explains a Cape York Aboriginal;[64] in this sense, a Magna Carta, establishing the source of Aboriginal identity. Land is the basis of Aboriginal life. It is the Aborigines' raison d'être. Land *is* self.[65] It is also the umbilical cord to the soul. The inalienable nature of this relationship—land as origin of all life—is summarized eloquently by Aboriginal writer Kevin Gilbert. Land titles in the English tradition, he points out, were granted by the Crown and were then transferable. Aboriginal "land titles"—held by groups of people— were retained in perpetuity. Bartering and transferring land was never a factor because that would be trafficking in the very soul sustenance —*The Dreaming*—an act comparable to suicide for the tribe. Thus, while white squatters could, with permission of the tribe, use the land and share its fruits, they were never considered its real owners. Indeed, from the Aborigines' viewpoint, there were no owners, only custodians.[66]

In 1978, Billy Kayipipi, a Pitjantjatjara elder, addressed the Select Committee on Pitjantjatjara Land Rights. His moving and dignified statement is every Aboriginal's response to country.

> THE LAW CAME from our grandparents. It is a strong law and we want to keep it strong. We want to keep the land, hold the land, that is our strongest desire. It is our land, it cannot be changed. We have been holding it forever. We wish to do so. It comes down through the generations to be passed on from one generation to the other. We cannot change the law every year; it is one law and it is there forever. We hold the law and our beliefs in our head, not on pieces of paper. How will we stay there in the future? We want to live happily on the land. We do not want to

be sad. Our laws lie in the land, and the law is part of the land. We want to get and keep the land. I ask the Government for the rights to keep our land.[67]

Both women and men are caretakers of the sacred sites. Management of and responsibility for some sites can be an exclusively female trust; likewise, others are specifically the charge of the men; still others may be the province of both women and men ("that is the woman's side" or "that is the man's side" with reference to the sides of a site).[68] At the Willowra Land Claim Hearing in central Australia in 1980, the importance of women as the cherished, renewing and nourishing element in the ritual maintenance of country ("growing up" the land as they "grow up" children)[69] was underscored by a Warlpiri elder, Nangala, as she responded to a question about the woman's role in the guardianship of the land and its holy places.

When asked, "How do women look after the land?" Nangala replied with pride, cupping her hands before her and gesturing upwards:

"WOMEN lift up the country."[70]

Aboriginal women's spiritual heritage and their rights and responsibilities in land, conferred upon them as women by the all-encompassing Law of The Dreamtime, are well illustrated in this statement from a witness in a Land Claim Hearing in the Northern Territory in 1981. As "owners" of country, women are essential to the health of the whole of Aboriginal society. The power that is derived from this ownership is held in sacred trust and is used, on a cosmic level, to nourish, renew and restore happiness and harmony.

> MY FATHER WAS BOSS for that place. It was his to look after. He looked after two places and then I lost him; he passed away. Now it is up to me looking after my own country . . . so from when I was a young girl I kept on doing those ceremonies looking after that country . . . my sisters they are looking after that country too . . . we do that business for that place all the time . . . for the fruit . . . so that it will grow up well so that we can make it green so that we can hold the Law for ever. My father instructed me to always do it this way so I go on holding that business for that country.[71]

Kevin Gilbert wrote the following inquiry after watching a tribal Aboriginal berate Judge Furnell for his pretense of understanding Aboriginal affinity for tribal land. The incident took place on television, April 7, 1975.

Mister man
Have you stood on this rock
Have you come close to this ghost-gum tree
Have you stood on green fingers of grass
And felt deep their life surge like me?
Mister man
Have you entered the caves
And greeted your own totems there
Have they given directions to go
God-like through life's pathway like me?
Mister man
Have you stood on the shore
Of this land your own soul now rent bare
And discovered the hatred you wrought
The suffering the death you ploughed there.
Mister man
Have you looked at your face
Like mine that is mirrored in land
Yours reflects only on pools
My image goes deep in the sand
The soil and the rocks and the trees
The souls of my people are here
The birds and the clouds and the breeze
The sun and the moon and the stars
Talk to me are of me they dwell
Inside me they each are a part
Of me they live in my heart
All things all created by God
Are in me this whole universe
Are of me—we speak and we cry
We talk and we dance and we sing
And I bring them gifts of my soul
Of my love God has bidden me bring.
Mister man
If perchance you do find
The essence the life force in land
All giving expression to self

To soul-force then you'll understand
The God-soul in all things around
This essence of life then you live
Then indeed, Mister man, you do live.[72]

The Aboriginal people in Western Australia think this is
the promised land because we have promises and broken
promises. That's all we have.

> PEARL GORDON,
> executive member,
> Kimberley Land Council[73]

Comalco never asked for this land. This is our forefathers'
land . . . we cannot give away our land. It is not well for
the country to be destroyed and given away . . . we are
trying to save this land for our children to help them stand
firm and strong . . . No, we don't want the money, we
don't want the jobs, we don't want the companies to take
our land. All our children look very healthy here. They
don't just live on store tucker—we have our own food out
in the bush. If our country is destroyed, there will be no
hunting places left just like Weipa [on the western shore of
Cape York peninsula]. We don't want any mining. No, we
don't want any refinery. I speak on behalf of all my Peo-
ple's land.

> ALBERT CHEVATHEN,
> Arukun elder from Queensland,
> custodian of the land
> sought after for a mining port[74]

    Aboriginal society today is engaged in a common struggle waged
on behalf of all of humankind. Aborigines are battling for the preservation and growth of a cultural tradition that respects the Earth and

values humanity above material growth and exploitation. Loss of land or disconnectedness from it means loss of self. It has led to great poverty—spiritual, psychological, social and physical. Traditionally, inheriting land meant that it was passed along in perpetuity from one generation to the next, within the material and spiritual boundaries of the tribal area.[75]

The following statements by Gularrawuy Yunupingu and Silas Roberts, Aboriginal chairmen of the Northern Land Council (1976), describe the profound linkages that exist between Aboriginal spirit, country and culture.

> ABORIGINES HAVE A SPECIAL CONNECTION with everything that is natural. Aborigines see themselves as part of nature. We see all things natural as part of us. All things on earth we see as part human. This is told through the idea of *dreaming*. By dreaming we mean the belief that long ago, these creatures started human society; they made all natural things and put them in a special place. These dreaming creatures were connected to special places and special roads or tracks or paths. In many cases the great creatures changed themselves into sites where their spirits stayed.
>
> My people believe this and I believe this. Nothing anybody says to me will change my belief in this. This is my story as it is the story of every true Aborigine.
>
> These creatures, these great creatures, are just as much alive today as they were in the beginning. They are everlasting and will never die. They are always part of the land and nature as we are. We cannot change nor can they. Our connection to all things natural is spiritual. We worship spiritual sites today. We have songs and dances for those sites and we never approach [them] without preparing ourselves properly. When the great creatures moved across the land, they made small groups of people like me in each area. These people were given jobs to do but I cannot go any further than that here.
>
> It is true that people who belong to a particular area are really part of that area and if that area is destroyed they are also destroyed. In my travels throughout Australia, I have met many Aborigines from other parts who have lost their culture. They have always lost their land and by losing their land they have lost part of themselves.
>
> I think of land as the history of my nation. It tells of how we came into being and what system we must live.

My great ancestors who lived in the times of history planned everything that we practise now. The law of history says that we must not take land, fight over land, steal land, give land, and so on. My land is mine only because I came in spirit from that land and so did my ancestors of the same land. . . .

My land is my foundation. I stand, live and perform as long as I have something firm and hard to stand on. Without land . . . we will be the lowest people in the world, because you have broken down our backbone, took away my arts, history and foundation. You have left me with nothing.[76]

 When surveyors were first sent out into the Australian outback by the Surveyor-General to record the native names of geographic areas, including lakes, mountains, spectacular rock formations and rivers, surprising interpretations resulted. Lack of knowledge of native languages and reliance upon translators inevitably produced shaded meanings and misleading information about the localities in question.

The name of Lake Wendouree (as it is known today) is a poignant case in point. When asked the name of the lake, the wary aborigine replied: "Wendouree Wendouree," which means "Go away."[77]

Loraine Mafi Williams, Aboriginal writer and poet, gives a forceful overview of her people's history, origins and Law. The beloved gum tree emerges as a metaphor for the Aborigines' anguish, shame and despair over the despoliation of their "earth's back" by invading white settlers, and more recently, by corporate pastoral and mining interests and the cattle industry. It is Williams' invocation of Aboriginal sacred origins that holds out the promise of a full restoration of her people's culture and inheritance. These holy roots are collectively circumscribed by a complex system of beliefs, known as the Dreamtime, and to the canon of activities that surrounds it, known as the Law. This ancient body of knowledge lives in Aboriginal traditional lands.

FORTY THOUSAND YEARS AGO I came to this land from the Dreamtime. I came with knowledge that this land would care for me and I in return would acknowledge it as my Saviour.

I looked upon my surroundings and saw a land, like none other, with majestic mountains—so high their tops blended with the sky in blissful content. The gum trees whispered to me that they would shelter me from winds and rains and I understood and said "Yes, I will honour you and take only what you give, we will live here together. You will drink from the heavens and I will drink from the earth—the rivers and the streams."

The years passed and my people grew to be many tribes who share the land . . . As we grew, nature supplied us with food fit for our consumption and our bodies grew accustomed to the food nature provided, making us unique. Nature was good to us and looked after us well. We honoured our traditional land in song and ceremonies and kept sacred its secrets. We praised the creation that was ours in corroboree each day so our children could pass them on to their children. We lived thus for many years—until the white man came.

We saw the ships come bearing England's shame, a shame which they flaunted at us. We did not understand these murderers, beggars and thieves; nor did we understand the arrogant free settlers. We did not have anything in common with them. Their interests in us grew into greed as they saw how rich our land was. They spread across our country destroying and devouring fauna and wildlife until there was nothing left untouched above the earth. They found the treasures buried deep within its heart, a treasure so beautiful and priceless beyond the imagination —gold, silver, diamonds, and opals—given to us by the Creator. But now the earth's back is scraped by steel, harvest ploughs and tractor wheels. The old gum tree whose life spans hundreds of years, stripped of its bark and left to die in shame—when once its limbs reached the sky.

With its shame emerged our destruction. We were utterly confused, the white man hunted us down like dogs. Our death became their freedom. Our old ones, the keepers of the laws, slaughtered along with our Dreamtime, and sacred rules were left to wither and perish over the plains we roamed.

Soon our conquerors' blood mingled with our own, inflicting us with diseases. Added to our misery and despair we were detribalized and left confined in lands that were not our own; we became trespassers on sacred ground owned by other tribes. Our spirit could not condone; as the years passed our children lost their identity. Without our tradition we became aliens, soon we were victims of anthropologists' lust, archaeologists' insanity, and a museum's delight. . . . With our environment turned topsy-turvy our spirits rebelled. We began "to fight for peace"; with our backs to the sea we could not be pushed any further; we advanced, gathering together our mutilated race; we emerged on shaky legs to rectify the white man's disaster; we started the repairs.

Soon our individual organizations sprouted and started to bloom, kindling in our old ones a burning desire to delve into their memories for cultural strength to sustain us through the following years. Our slow reincarnation strengthened us to bury the colonialism that has plagued us over the last two centuries. In its place came patriotism moulding us into a political ball with new awareness. Departments grabbed us with iron claws, cementing us into categories, squeezing us into societies where we don't belong. The mighty force of oppression sapped our strength, we searched for spiritual guidance and left ourselves open to prey for other holy doctrines. With our spirits thirsting for holy guidance we devoured Christianity, a force so powerful and destructive to our cultural beliefs we were listless. Christianity showered over our own spiritual beliefs, turning us into believers of the white man's Christian doctrine, alienating us completely from the Dreamtime faith.

As a shattered race, we emerge in this new era and we are afraid. . . . We have stepped into a future that will ultimately be our destruction as our people become riddled with the concepts of the Western world, vice, and social mutilation.

For us to survive this new century we must have full control over our destiny, revive our culture and fulfil our inheritance, own our land; to restore us to the proud people that we are.[78]

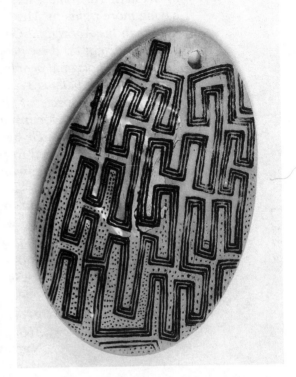

Engraved pearl-shell pendant. Collected in the 1930s, this specimen reflects a labyrinthine spiraling pattern and is an object of great value. Undecorated as well as engraved pearl shells are traded as currency, used in ceremonies and as personal decoration. They were in circulation before the arrival of Europeans, and continue in use today.

The dancing and artwork is your whole life—you have to know your traditional artwork that ties in with the land and ties in with the creation, where your boundary is, how far your ancestral creator has travelled. It's all written in the art. That is what the traditional art means: owner to the land.

BANDUK MARIKA,
Yirrkala artist[79]

We know every animal, every bird. First we learn their tracks, then where and how they live, and what they do. When we spear and cook them we find what they look like inside. That's why it is easy for us to paint the animals. We also look [at] and learn the footprints of people. We really look.

DICK NGULEINGULEI,
Aboriginal artist[80]

In Western Australia sheep and cattle were regarded as having more rights by Mr. Burke [government representative] than his Aboriginal Constituents. . . .

What right do these people [absentee landlords] have to alienate Aboriginal people from their land. Is it the right to a huge bank balance? . . .

There are aspects of the land claim process in the Northern Territory for instance which currently put Aboriginal people through agonisingly personal processes where they are required to publicly bare their souls in a way which most people would find offensive and indeed an invasion of privacy.

Our relationship with our land is so dear to us that we tolerate and try to live with this process that is forced upon us. We want to improve this process, build on it, broaden it, and find a way to develop a stronger, proper relationship between Aboriginal people and non-Aboriginal Australia.

PAT DODSON,
Aboriginal National Co-ordinator,
National Federation of Land Councils,
May 14, 1985[81]

Pat Dodson is an Aboriginal leader and writer. He was born Banaga near Broome in northwest Australia. On August 25, 1986, he addressed the Catholic Commission for Justice and Peace in Sydney, making an eloquent appeal for the restoration of Aboriginal land, dignity and life.

I WANT YOU TO TRY two exercises in imagination. The first is this. I want you to imagine you are black. An Aboriginal Australian. The time is the present. And I want you also to imagine that the white invasion is just about to occur.

How would you be living your life? About three days in every week would be devoted to gathering your food. Hunting, collecting. . . . The rest of your time would be spent socialising, or in religious observances of different kinds. As to your knowledge of the land, your country, you would know every tree, every rock, because in the Dreamtime the great ancestors came this way. And they are still here. They live. They must be revered, appeased, paid attention to. It is they who cause conception as a woman walks near. When the child is born he calls that part of the country "Father." You would husband the land. You would burn the grasses to promote new growth and to make sure that the delicate balance of nature that has been created has been preserved.

There is a rich and complicated legal system which is administered by elders and to which all are bound. The blind, the lame, the mentally defective are all to be looked after. Your spiritual and religious life is as rich as your material life is simple. The children are more deeply loved than perhaps any children on earth. Until puberty and initiation they can do no wrong. They are cuddled not chastised. They learn from love and from example. The children grow in security and confidence. They are tutored in the life of the spirit, in respect of the elders and kinship and the ways of the country.

Into this world comes the white invader. Their first act is to say that the land is terra nullius, that no-one owns the land, that it is not used. They knock down the trees, and blast the places sacred to you. They fence around the best water for their cattle. When you resist they shoot and poison your people. Thus begins the Australian Civil War. It can also be called the two hundred years war because it still continues. They still say that they know more than you about land and what your wants and needs are. They say it is important to fence it, to graze it, to mine it. You have difficulty in understanding how they could make such a preposterous claim to ownership. And only you call the land your father. If a whiteman stumbles into the hard country without water he will die. If the land is taken from you or if you are taken from the land your spirit will perish just as surely. . . .

In time the white people repent. For a very short time they have pangs of conscience. They pass one of their laws. You know about these white laws. How different they are from your own. The black man's law is straight: it never changes. How come the white man's law always changes?

But now, they say: "You come to us. You prove to us that you have always owned the land and we'll give it back to you." They want us to be grateful, but that is hard.

Land according to black laws cannot be given or taken away. You belong to the Land. Your birth has not severed the cord of life which comes from the Land.

But we come to them. No, they say, you can't have the land which we own. You can only have the land which no white man wants. The Land Council helps you. You go to the Land Commissioner. You tell of your love, duties and relationship with your land. You tell of your brutal eviction and sorrows for your country and your people. You bear the secrets of your soul to total strangers. You are given back the land which no-one wants. The land you cannot leave. The country you call father.

Then you hear about mining companies. They want to dig for gold, uranium, for other minerals. The pang of conscience of the white people has passed. They want to change their law, to make sure the miners cannot be stopped from coming on to your land. How come you gave that land to us and now you take it away? Give a thing, take a thing, a white feller's play thing. How come the white man's law always changes? . . .

The blacks of Western Australia have no right to their land because the mining companies don't want them to, and because there are no votes in it. By present indications there is no such thing as principle in politics. Politics is about votes and about power. The blacks are easy pickings. They have no princes or parliaments. Everyone has an equal say. The only constraint is the law that was handed down from the Dreamtime, a law that will never change. Up against the fast words and the money of the white politics the blacks don't stand a big chance. . . .

What would you do now if you were a black Australian in 1986? Not much you can do. You don't have control of votes. You haven't got the reserves of money that a mining company has. You can't use your investments to influence politicians and make their consciences change.

The position ought to be different for Christians. The moral ground ought to be theirs. The testaments are studded with exhortations to hold to principle. "What does it profit a man if he gain the whole world . . . ?" What is there to say to a government which says "To hell with principle. Our country needs money. We will amend the Land Rights Act. That will get us more money."

They may be right. We might get more money. Frankly I doubt it, but we might. If we do, we pay a price. We sacrifice our black people at the altar of expediency. We break faith with them yet again. We remove the opportunity for them to make their own contribution to the country in fidelity to our tradition and unique cultural genius.

One could be forgiven for thinking that the high moral ground should be taken by our leaders. We should expect them to say we will right the wrongs of the past. We will restore to black Australians the land which has always been rightfully theirs. We will not presume to interfere with how they run their affairs, any more than we would for any other Australian.

There is no special advantage in passing judgment on our politicians. That is a needless luxury. Let us do only two things. First, direct our legislators not to pass these cruel and heartless amendments to the NT Land Rights Act that do not respect our wishes. Secondly, restore to the ancient owners their dignity, their land, their life.[82]

Roland Robinson wanted to "hear" his country so he set out on a pilgrimage to its sources only to find "the voice . . . was inarticulate, locked up in its landscapes and the creatures of those landscapes."[83] That was until he met the natural storytellers, remarkable Aboriginal raconteurs, such as Alexander Vesper, who possessed an astonishing memory and revealed a superior knowledge of the sacred stories; magnificent Ethel Gordon with her mesmerizing oratorical gifts; and David Carpenter of Bundoola, the King of the Sea. These great people and others unlocked the voice for Robinson and released the ancient dormant energies of their land. All of their tales were for the strong of ear and, like all grand story telling, they exploit the basic elements of magic, humor, spirit beings, supernatural powers, thrills and frights of wizardry, intertribal fights, the wisdom of the old men, totemic spirits, love, greed, life and death. Some primarily instruct; others principally entertain; and many do both.

Robinson heard the following story at La Perouse Aboriginal settlement in Sydney from Thomas Kelly, a member of the Gumbangirr tribe and an Aboriginal teller of tales. Land is an inviolate trust, Kelly cautioned. There are consequences when that sacred charge is transgressed.

THERE WAS AN OLD DARK FELLER named Billy Joe. He had the possum for his property, or his totem, if you like. The possum was his messenger, his spirit. It was him himself. If we were to see a possum in a tree at night, we'd know that old Billy Joe would be there in a few hours. You couldn't frighten it away. It would climb down the tree and walk around the camp, smelling round and picking up things. The old people would tell us that the possum was Billy Joe himself. After a while the possum would go away and old Billy Joe would appear.

When we saw that possum the old people would say to us in the language, "*Ngudge wunarr. Ngarrun!*" That means, "Don't pelt anything! That's grandfather!" We call all old people "*Ngudge.*" That means "grandfather."

Well, there was a *jurraveel,* that's sacred ground, that belonged to the tribe. This *jurraveel* was in the mountains at Nymboida. There's a hydro-electric power-station there now. The old people had told Billy Joe never to lead the white man to this sacred tribal property. Well, he led the white man to that *jurraveel* and showed them where it was. There was gold, reef-gold, in that property.

The white men asked Billy Joe what he wanted for that property and he sold it to them for ten pounds.

The white men made the reef-gold mine, which was called The Black Mystery, in that place. The mine went on for years. It was only in the last few years that it petered out. The mine was finished. They still reckon there's gold in there, but she's flooded out.

Old Billy knew he'd broke the tribe's laws, so he shot across to the next river. He knew that they were after him. He also knew that he couldn't get away from them, that they'd get him sooner or later.

There's always two men who come for anyone who breaks the tribe's laws. These two men, *ngaloongirr,* we call them, travel at night. They never make fires to cook their food or anything. That would show them up, give them away. The feller they were after might walk on to their dead fire in daytime and then he would know that the men he was running from were right there.

These two men caught up with Billy Joe. It was five or six years after he sold that property, but they got him. They came right on to him while he was asleep. They cut a lock of his hair off. They took it away and sung it. Then they wrapped it up and buried it.

Old Billy could hear these two men singing him as he lay down at night. They gave him three days. Then old Billy got sick and in three days he was dead.

The night he was going to die, the property of these two men who had sung him came to his door and showed itself to him. That property was the black hawk. When old Billy saw that property at his door he knew he was finished.

• • •

The tribe had warned him. That *jurraveel* was sacred ground. There was no one allowed to touch it. He thought he'd get away with it, but they caught him after five or six years. That was the way with the old people. They had strict rules. Anything laid down by the old-fellers had to be carried out.[84]

We Yolnggus, we have been here in Australia since a long time. . . . We are not visitors like balandhas *[whites] who came from over there, from England, and then started to go after us vigorously. But they did not bother to see what we need. We want this very strongly, namely our land. No tree is going to be chopped down, and there is going to be no big road; no rock is going to be blasted off and our homeland is not going to be made miserable. This is in our eye and in our heart and in our life.*

> Ken Gunbuku,
> *a Yolnggu from northeastern*
> *Arnhem Land (Northern Territory),*
> *protesting a proposed road corridor through*
> *his people's land in 1983,*
> *at a special meeting held*
> *at their outstation in Gapuwiyak*[85]

Why do you white people come in ships to our country and shoot down poor blackfellows who do not understand you? . . . You listen to me!

The wild blackfellows do not understand your laws, every living animal that roams the country, and every edible root that grows in the ground are common property. A black man claims nothing as his own but his cloak, his weapons, and his name. . . . He does not understand that animals or plants can belong to one person more than to another.

YAGAN,
Nyoongarah leader, 1843[86]

Michael Anderson addresses white Australia on the humanity of his culture and the mothering nature of Aboriginal soil. Caressing the land was as important as caressing a child. Both acts were natural gestures, vital not only to the growth of the human spirit but also to the terrestial spirit, whose natures were intertwined.

WHITE MAN, your forefathers the early settlers, did not realize the special significance and the all-important bearings the land had in regard to our beliefs and way of life. For all [the] white man saw when he first came to this land, was a nomadic race of people, who may as well wander "over there" rather than "here."

There are no English words that could give sense in regard to the important link between my Aboriginal people and this country which is our homeland. This was not just "land," it was us, our way of life, our beliefs, it gives us security and richness in our spiritual world. When we walked on this land, we weren't just walking on it, we were embracing it, because it was the "Mother of things," in the white man's language "Mother Nature."

White man, when you started colonizing this country, you destroyed the most humane way of life ever seen anywhere on this huge planet called Earth.

Before the white man settled this continent, my people had a very clean and sustained nomadic society; we never had any form of poverty, or what you call a health or pollution hazard, because every living thing and dead thing played an important role in our society.[87]

In my forty-five years [I] have experienced and observed such a devastating loss to the environment that it shocks me to know that I have only a memory to pass on to my children. I cannot show or teach; material things have changed; the wild creatures are not there . . . Our flora suffers as a result, the fauna is forced into tiny pockets and corners. In such a short time, they are gone.

Aboriginal testimony on
the changes in the natural environment
of the East Kimberley, 1986[88]

The elements involved in the Aboriginal system are land, human beings and all other things that dwell with them. This system is in harmony and balance, and this is perfection.

The problem is that if any element of the system is destroyed, this circle of perfection is broken. 194 years ago this circle was broken, and in the Southern areas of the continent our society was all but destroyed.

The balance and harmony was lost but the strength of it lived within the survivors, and it gave rise to the identity that Aboriginals will carry with them into the 21st century and beyond. It is this identity which distinguishes them from anyone else who lives in their place. It is this identity that makes them what they are.

> We are Aboriginals, we are the desert winds, we are the sunlit plains, we are the bright waters, we are Australia. This land is our birthright. In this new world, in our new society, we have but a single principle. We are our brothers' keepers.
>
> Aboriginal Ideology and Philosophy of the Land,
> the National Aboriginal Conference, Canberra[89]

A woman's breast is like the Widaraga tree that grows on the sides of Karinya.

Kumalba song[90]

They [the Aborigines] believe that Aboriginal children are born of women but conceived of a spiritual source whose fonte is the land. And to them the land has two kinds of landscapes—one is physical, which all human beings can view. The other is spiritual, which only they can see. For aboriginal people there is only one way to own land and that is to be conceived of it. Land is a parent. This very important principle prevents any kind of land aggrandisement which has been the scourge of the rest of the world. The land, for Aboriginal people, is a vibrant spiritual landscape.

Aboriginal Ideology and Philosophy of the Land,
the National Aboriginal Conference, Canberra[91]

Bronwyn Bancroft, *Corroboree Created,* 1992. Bronwyn Bancroft describes her painting as "a celebration of the ancient traditional mythology and mysticism of Aboriginal ceremony of which the corroboree [social or ceremonial gathering] is an integral aspect. It is a statement about the strength of Aboriginal people and their struggle to survive and retain their culture through white invasion and two hundred and five years of oppression."

ABORIGINALITY

boriginal life is lived out in a framework of connectedness, beginning in the physical world with the umbilical cord. It is never really "severed" but rather re-connected and re-membered to its original primordial roots in Earth after birth. In other words, body and earth are made visible but indivisible. The umbilical cord is the initial living link of the child to the Earth and to the spirit world. Before its careful burial, the cord serves as an anchor, providing comfort and protection to the child. A Worora elder described the significance of the cord to the child's growth. The ritual of the umbilical planting is designed to put the mind and spirit —and all of life everywhere—in balance with the order of Creation. Upon the birth of the baby, said the elder, the umbilical cord is cut but not discarded. The mother wears the umbilicus, which has been carefully wrapped, around her neck. It is believed that the child derives comfort from the cord's proximity.

You build *Aboriginality, boy, or you got nothing. There's no other choice to it. It'll be easier, now, with bits of land handed back to us, here 'n' there. . . .*
Every person on earth can share in Aboriginality. It is a blessing you can give 'em to share in. The hungry, the homeless, the poor and the beaten, all those that are unhappy or in worse circumstances than yourselves are to be welcomed around your fires but they, too, must follow the rules. You've got the power; it's just a matter of giving all and everyone your nulli. That spirit, that great spirit will give you everything you need to live. That's what Aboriginality is! . . .

You don't have to try and "pass" as whites to be respectable; you don't have to hide in the borrowed respectability of some religion, either, unless you can get it to work for you and through you to help those around you. . . .

Each Aboriginal has to be another Aboriginal's keeper; each Aboriginal has to uphold the rules of right living because if we don't do those things then our Aboriginality will die out 'til there is nothing left . . . like the coals of a long-dead campfire.

KEVIN GILBERT,
Aboriginal writer and
playwright[92]

An enduring arrangement of sharing in Aboriginal life exists out of a mutual dependence on and respect for all that lives and grows. Greed is to be feared and, in fact, is intolerable. Ultimately, value rests in the land and, in the end, is not portable. The performance of fertility ceremonies to ensure an abundance of food—seeds, grasses, fruits, animals as well—is essential to the continuity of life. Jalna, an old woman of the Waddaman tribe, speaks out about the give-and-take of everyday life.

WHEN YOU DIG UP YAM, you must all time leave little bit end of that yam in ground . . . if dig it all out, then that food spirit will get real angry and won't let any more yam grow in that place.[93]

The Aboriginal poet Oodgeroo Noonucul (Kath Walker) expands on this principle:

TODAY, WHEN THE WHITE MAN'S FOOD is eaten so widely by Aborigines, the tribe no longer hunts the dugong [a dolphin-size marine animal]. They believe that to hunt dugong when their bellies are full would be to act against the natural law of "kill to eat." They believe that the Good Spirit would punish them severely if they killed dugong out of greed and that the Good Spirit might take one of the tribespeople to even the score.[94]

The Wuduu *touching will not stop. It is our strength.*

SAM WOOLGOODJA,
Worora elder, the Kimberleys[95]

... the Aboriginal people have kept the wunun, *the sharing of all things, till today. The* wunun *must follow the line from the north, right down to the west. It is a strict law. If a person didn't keep to the* wunun, *and didn't share, he or his family would suffer.*

Aboriginal elder

The teachings of *Wuduu* and *Wunun* embody the principles that are critical to the healthy development of an Aboriginal child and are generally conveyed through song and ritual. Sam Woolgoodja, a Worora elder from the Kimberleys in Western Australia, instructs his granddaughter, Dragon-Fly, in the way of *Wuduu*, through a language filled with poetic cadences.

> *Don't take*
> *Don't take from somebody else.*
> *Wuduu, Wuduu*
> *At the fire I touch you*
> *I hand you the strength of Wuduu*
> *Don't let yourself be turned.*
> *Here on your ankle,*
> *Here on your knee,*
> *Here on your thigh.*
>
> *Stay strong*
> *Don't let your forehead swell*
> *Wait, wait.*

Don't say the words of the men,
Don't go begging, granddaughter.

Namaaraalee * *showed us*
the Wuduu that we make for the little boys and
*   girls.*
The men who know still touch them
So each day they learn to grow.

Her two thighs, her two legs, her fingers.
The words are put there
That the Wandjinas gave us.
They said to keep on
And until today the words have lived.
The Wuduu touching will not stop.
It is our strength.[96]

The use of herbal preparations and plants in childbirth rituals
ensure the health and growth of the child and the renewed strength
of the mother. Aboriginal women possess extensive knowledge of the
plant world and its usage for the well-being of their society. It is true
that the Aboriginal childbirth experience has been almost entirely
usurped by white institutions, and traditional ceremonies around it
have been undermined by the presence of white "health authorities."
Magarruminya, a Mardarrpa (Yolngu) native urges a reevaluation of
traditional medicine.

> WE HAD OUR OWN MEDICINE. We had doctors of our own
> —doctors who used to give a man life again. Now young
> people are giving that away. The old people have still got
> this medicine, but they're frightened to show white people.
> Why? Because of the mission. I'm asking the old people to
> show the young people how, a long time ago, when we
> were hurt, [we knew] how to stop it—how to get up.[97]

Aboriginals believe that human beings are a synthesis of
mortal and spiritual parts. Unlike many of the world's

* A Wandjina spirit, an ancestral being who controls the elements and maintains fertility in humans and other natural species.

religions, they believe that personality is a product of this synthesis and not contained in any one part. At death the spirit persists and returns to the land.

The principle order is that of social organisation. When a child is born into the world he is related to every other human being that lives. He finds himself in a constellation of belonging. Aboriginals have one of the world's most extensive kinship organisations which interconnects, through religion, with all the world of living and inanimate things. Death cannot deprive a child of a mother or father or an uncle or an aunt or a brother or sister. Even today when Aboriginal people use the term brother or sister, it means far more than political brotherhood. . . .

Aboriginal ideology and philosophy of the land,
the National Aboriginal Conference, Canberra[98]

Sally Morgan is one of Australia's prominent writers and artists. She is also a great athlete of faith and courage by reason of her inhumanly difficult questing for her spiritual and racial roots. In *My Place,* her prose poem about three generations of Aborigines (her own family), "the blackfellas" of the Earth warily reclaim their dignity bit by bit as they guardedly retrieve their self-identity so deeply embedded in and entrusted to their dusty old beloved land. In the dedication to her family she writes, "How deprived we would have been if we had been willing to let things stay as they were. We would have survived, but not as a whole people. We would never have known our place." This passage is a lyrical reflection of that belief.

WE LOVED TO EAT the wild cranberries that grew in the bush, they were sweet and juicy. Year after year, we went to the same bushes, they were always laden. Trouble was, the goannas [monitor lizards] liked them, too. You could be eating from one side, and a goanna from the other, you never knew until you met in the middle. I don't know who got the biggest fright. . . .

Most of my happiest times were spent alone in the bush, watching the birds and animals. If you sat very quiet, they didn't notice you were there. There were rabbits, wallabies, goannas, lizards, even the tiny insects were interesting. I had such respect for their little lives that I'd feel terrible if I even trod on an ant. We'd come across all sorts of snakes, green ones, brown, black. We used to pick the green ones up and flick them. I wouldn't pick them up now. We never touched the black or brown ones, if we came across those, we just walked away. . . .

One day when I was on my own, I found some field mice under a rock near a honeysuckle vine. I often went to that vine, because the flowers were sweet to suck. It was almost as good as having a lolly. I thought the baby field mice were wonderful, they were pink and bald and very small. I decided it was a secret I'd keep to myself in case anyone harmed them. . . .

I had a crying tree in the bush. It was down near the creek, an old twisted peppermint tree. The limbs curved over to make a seat and its weeping leaves almost covered me completely. You didn't cry in front of anyone at the Home, it wasn't done. You had to find yourself a crying place. . . .

I'd sit for hours under that peppermint tree, watching the water gurgle over the rocks and listening to the birds. After a while, the peace of that place would reach inside of me and I wouldn't feel sad any more. Instead, I'd start counting the numerous rainbow-coloured dragon-flies that skimmed across the surface of the water. After that, I'd fall asleep. When I finally did walk back to the Home, I felt very content.[99]

Sally Morgan ponders her own delayed and ambivalent awakening to the significance of aboriginality. She was unaware that she was Aboriginal until she was fifteen. Much later on, as she was researching her autobiographical account of several family generations, she was stunned to discover in the drawings of a tribal relative in the Kimberleys of Western Australia the same technique and imagery she had used in her own art as a child. Morgan's autobiographical account of the process that led to the recognition of her own aboriginality is so poignant, so wise and so witty that an exaltation of wholeness of universal dimensions bursts through the pages.

THE KIDS AT SCHOOL had also begun asking us what country we came from. This puzzled me because, up until then, I'd thought we were the same as them. If we insisted that we came from Australia, they'd reply, "Yeah, but what about ya parents, bet they didn't come from Australia."

One day, I tackled Mum about it as she washed the dishes.

"What do you mean, 'Where do we come from?' "

"I mean, what country. The kids at school want to know what country we come from. They reckon we're not Aussies. Are we Aussies, Mum?"

Mum was silent. Nan grunted in a cross sort of way, then got up from the table and walked outside.

"Come on, Mum, what are we?"

"What do the kids at school say?"

"Anything. Italian, Greek, Indian."

"Tell them you're Indian."

I got really excited, then. "Are we really? Indian!" It sounded so exotic. "When did we come here?" I added.

"A long time ago," Mum replied. "Now, no more questions. You just tell them you're Indian."

It was good to finally have an answer and it satisfied our playmates. They could quite believe we were Indian, they just didn't want us pretending we were Aussies when we weren't. . . .

I feel embarrassed now, to think that, once, I wanted to be white. As a child, I even hoped a white family would adopt me, a rich one, of course. I've changed since those days.

I'm still a coward, when a stranger asks me what nationality I am, I sometimes say a Heinz variety. I feel bad when I do that. It's because there are still times when I'm scared inside, scared to say who I really am.

But, at least, I've made a start. And I hope my children will feel proud of the spiritual background from which they've sprung. If we all keep saying we're proud to be Aboriginal, then maybe other Australians will see that we are a people to be proud of. I suppose every mother wants her children to achieve greatness, or, at least, one of them. All I want my children to do is to pass their Aboriginal heritage on. . . .

I like to think that, no matter what we become, our spiritual tie with the land and the other unique qualities we possess will somehow weave their way through to future generations of Australians. I mean, this is our land, after all, surely we've got something to offer.[100]

The Gagudju of Arnhem Land know that the flowering of a plant is indisputable proof of the fatness of the stingray! The correlative nature of all things is a feature of aboriginality. It affects every aspect of Aboriginal thinking and is perhaps best summarized in this extraordinary statement about the ebb and flow of complex natural processes and forms that ground the Earth. The Gagudju display a profound understanding of the seasonal cycles that reveals an intimate knowledge and experience of the unity of all living energies.

> WE KNOW THAT DHARRATHARRAMIRRI [season] is coming to an end when balgurr starts to lose its leaves. At the same time the pandanus [tree] starts to fruit and Dhimurru [East-South-East] wind blows. The really cold mornings and mists are nearly gone. Sharks are giving birth to their young. They are called burrugu and so we call this season Burrugumirri. This is a very short season which only lasts for a few weeks. Stingrays are also called burrugu at this time. If munydjutj is flowering, then we are really sure that they are fat. . . .[101]

> *The important thing is that for Aboriginal people their home is where they come from. For white people their house is just something to be proud of. They may move on and lose the connection they have with that place. For Aborigines it's their home, the place they always want to go back to. I remember my grandmother, she came from Karua but lived here in Purfleet. When her time came she got sick, and we were looking after her. One morning she disappeared. We looked everywhere for her. Eventually we found her on the road back to Karua. She was returning to her home to die. That's the feeling Aborigines have for their homes.*
>
> WARNER SAUNDERS,
> *Secretary, Purfleet Housing Cooperative,*
> *Purfleet Aboriginal Community, NSW*[102]

The principles of interdependence have been central to notions of time in the Aboriginal universe. They determine all acts from sowing, gathering and hunting to harvesting, traveling, celebrating and dying. They also require highly discriminating perceptual abilities to direct the flow of life and assure survival. An Aboriginal tribal elder and leader describes a quality of attentiveness to and respect for the circulating and transforming energies of the natural world, whose function is to confer order and serve cosmic equilibrium and unity.

> *Aboriginal people live a communal life: a cycle of life which begins when they come out of the ground and is complete only when they go back to it, as they must. I would not sooner live permanently in Armidale than fly to the moon, because I came out of some ground over in Western Australia and I'll go back into it. That is where I'll go back to die.*[103]

As far as the rest of the world is concerned Aboriginals have the right to what they are, the right to independence, to self-determination, to their own destiny, the right to be. We are not mendicants. We seek only what is ours, and the land is ours. We live on the planet Earth and are citizens of that planet. We do not wish to make refugees of those descendants of the invaders or those who will come to live here. We will walk beside them in friendship and in goodwill, but we will not be subjugated nor will we allow this land to be subjugated to alien demands or greed. This is our world. We are prepared to share it, but not to give it away.

Aboriginal Ideology and Philosophy of the Land, the National Aboriginal Conference, Canberra [104]

VISIONS FOR LIVING

For more than two decades, Jack Davis, Aboriginal playwright, poet, activist, and recipient of the British Empire Medal for services to literature and the Aboriginal people of Western Australia, has fronted the Aboriginal fight for self-determination and better living conditions in the State of Western Australia. He suggests a plan for righting the Earth again.

[W]E'VE GOT WARDENS today to look after the forests. We've got wardens today to try and bring about weed control. But Aboriginal Australians for forty thousand years had their wardens, you know.

It's quite simple . . . give us a love of country whether we're white or black. Give every kid at school something to protect of our flora and fauna. O.K. you look after the kangaroos, you look after the beetles, you look after the ladybirds, you look after the quokka [small short-tailed kangaroo], you look after the emu [ostrichlike bird], look after all these things—that's your totem. Why should we kick an ant out of our path? Why should we deliberately tread on a beetle? They've got a purpose and they've been put there for a purpose. They're removing something that is [useful] to man's way of life. And Aboriginal people knew that, so everybody had something to look after as nature provided, some animal, some insect, some bird, fish, and Aboriginal men said, "No. I need him, because he's part of my survival."

You wouldn't need to "save the wild," all those types of things, coz kids, it's born within 'em. . . . And imagine us doing that for every Australian kid—giving him something in nature, flora and fauna to look after. And we'd be showing the whole world how to look after the world itself.[105]

The "spiritual flow" of Aboriginal life is an absolute in Aboriginal affairs. Unquantifiable, living and crucial to Aboriginal identity, it generates, through the life force of the land and its origins, the principles for all life. Kevin Gilbert, Aboriginal poet and writer, describes this state of awareness that is coexistent with the natural world and the cosmic galaxies. It is the Aboriginal way and it was devastated first by the colonists and later by government and corporate interests. Two hundred years later, Gilbert foresees the revival of "the spiritual essence" that underlies all Aboriginal thinking and being. The old men are beginning again to re-link the chain of Law through initiation ceremonies for the young and return to their rightful and sacred land base.

THE REAL HISTORY, or rather, the historic place of Aborigines in this land has not yet been written nor, unfortunately, even dimly perceived by the most learned anthropologists and archaeologists of the day. . . .

Aboriginal pre-history, archaeologically speaking, extends some 45,000 years and the actual period of any intensive archaeological study of Aborigines is a mere forty years or so. . . .

The Beginning, the Time before time began, when the world was a twilight zone. The Great Creative Essence of Life, the Creator, had filled the land with creative spirits and, in a transmorphosis, these spirits took on physical shapes and became the progenitors of the modern mammals, animals, earthforms we see today, imbuing them with spiritual being. Amidst this creative spiritual chaos humankind was created and spiritually generated. The "modern" type being came as a generative leap in physical and mental development. The Aboriginal Australian has been in this land from the Beginning. . . .

The people formed tribes. The tribes developed their civilisation. Land ownership rules regulated their daily lives, the Council of the Elders effectively maintained the government, created laws and gave judgement against the law breakers. They ascertained their land areas with neighbouring tribes and kept to their borders according to the Law.

As it was in the Beginning, the laws are such that every person, every sacred created thing has a precious valued status, for, since creation is sacred it follows that all things created are significantly sacred as well.

There were no barbaric wars, no slaves, no debasement of other humans, no prisoners. . . .

The Aboriginal religion, deemed animistic, is more akin to the Eastern religions in so far as the belief of spiritual return, telepathy, the silken cord, astral travelling, the third eye, tele-transportation, hypnosis and telekinesis are very much the basic part of Aboriginal religion. Most important is the spiritual knowledge, not only of creation and the Great Creative Spirit who maintains the soul, but also the fact that we are spiritually and physically co-existent and part of everything containing the life force; trees, soil, rocks, water, grass, clouds, celestial bodies, etc.

When tribes discovered Captain Cook, they discovered not only the man, but the injustice, the viruses and bacteria that had travelled with him from his barbaric, heathen world of England.

Then came Philip and the colonists. The world of magic and love, equal status, value for life and peaceful co-existence soon was shattered. The Council, the wisest of the wise men, sang and danced and cried but the remedies, the checks, the law against the law breakers and harbingers of evil did not work against the barbarians who were not only killing by sword and gun, but were burning, flogging, poisoning the people and killing with some invisible magic which they, the whites, called the flu, the pox, pneumonia, tuberculosis, syphilis, gonorrhea and leprosy. The old men, the old magic couldn't stop these less-than-men, these barbaric invaders, from slaughtering the hunter as he sought food, then raping and murdering the women and children. They couldn't understand a society that raped and murdered, for the sake of murder. They understood even less why their magic wouldn't work. Their spirit law-keepers and their God had recoiled in horror, leaving them to become hapless victims of these colonists and convicts, these dregs of English society who were amongst the most rapacious scum on earth.

Two hundred years has elapsed since our land was invaded by white Australians, 200 years of victimisation, debasement of our humanity, attempts at physical and cultural genocide and undeclared war.

The tribes, physically decimated and kept from their sacred areas and hunting/farming land, faced starvation and the terror of merciless unrelenting race murder. They hid in the remote areas, some finding protection and humanity with a few white settlers who, moved in human pity by the atrocities dealt the people, acted against the mainstream of opinion of their own white society. They nursed, fed, guarded and preserved the lives of the people.

After the land theft was accomplished by the whites, they placed the Aboriginal people into concentration camp areas, which they called "Aboriginal Reserves." When cries of outrage against the land theft and murders were raised in other nations, Australia defended its action by declaring to the world that the land was actually "waste land and unoccupied" and that the undeclared war was "peaceful settlement." Also, that Aborigines had no civilisation, no law, no artifact, no agriculture or economic use of the land, no status as human beings and latterly, that "Aborigines belong to the land, the land does not belong to the Aborigines."

But in 1981 the spiritual essence has returned. The old men are re-linking the chain of law through initiation. Revelation is amongst the people. The ceremony is having effect and the whiteman's God (his crops and cattle), reel under the drought dance.

Soon the land will be used as our ally to regain the land and our people, now numbering only 150,000 (less than a quarter of the number that populated this land when the white terror struck), are demanding a rightful share in the affluence of wealth ripped out of our country and forming the rich, high standard of health and living enjoyed by whites and rated as one of the highest in the world. A living standard gained by ill-gotten means; the murder, deprivation and denial of the original owners, the Aborigines, who have suffered an intense psychological battering over 200 years. Australians should remember that the last government-sponsored massacre occurred less than 60 years ago, within living memory, and the most recent attempt at individual massacre was the strychnine poisoning at Alice Springs in March 1981. Physical and health conditions approximate those of Bangladesh. Aborigines suffer amongst the highest infant mortality, leprosy, curable blindness (Trachoma), malnutrition and tuberculosis rates in the world, in a country where whites claim they have eliminated these eighteenth century diseases in *their* society.

To whom do we turn for justice? The heads of white society? Do we humbly beg the thief to act as judge? Do we ask the grazier, who fattens his cattle, his family, on land that was robbed from us in the most dastardly manner, for the return of our rightful property or at least a viable land base and reparation throughout Australia? No. It is not logical to expect the tyrant, the thief, to relinquish his unlawful gains.

We need the force of conscience and law to achieve justice. We need to let the other peoples of the world know the reality, the scumminess and lack of morality of white Australia. We need to gain allies. We need to teach young white Australians about the spiritual flow of our lives and, in accordance with Aboriginal Law, warn the offender, as I do, that if justice does not come soon from the offenders' quarter, come it will with terror and fire from another quarter; for from other corners of the world there are men and women who have a vested interest in justice and preserving the rights of humanity as conferred by the Great Creator.[106]

We want our ceremonies, we want our language, we want our stories told to our children, we want to sing, we want to dance. And why do we do it? We want to talk to our land and the land to talk to us.

GALARRWUY YUNUPINGU,
*Aboriginal leader and chairman
of the Northern Land Council*[107]

In 1983, the new school headmaster of the primary school at Yuendumu in the Northern Territory, commissioned senior Aboriginal Warlpiri men to paint the school doors (thirty in all) with traditional designs. The results were spectacular. The entire enterprise was a joint venture undertaken by many senior men of different kin relatedness. The men painted for the children, for the community, and that there may be a future for both. The old men and women (respectful term for senior men and women) reacted creatively to the presence of graffiti on the school walls and grounds and recognized an opportunity to use their own designs, the Dreamings (traditional mandates and ancient ancestral wisdom), to excite, guide and instruct their own. Paddy Japaljarri Stewart, one of the senior Warlpiri painters, voiced a shared concern in his statement about the motivating force behind the "painted" doors: "We painted these Dreamings on the school doors because the children should learn about our Law. The children do not know them and they might become like white people, which we don't want to happen."[108] That the children should know the Law, the Dreamings, became the powerful impulse behind the execution of the sacred charters and ancient truths of Warlpiri country. The senior men and women saw their expression of the Dreamings as a form of currency, a vital investment in the future of their own culture, land and, by extension, the whole planet.

Tess Napaljarri Ross gives an inside view of the Warlpiri people living at the Yuendumu settlement. Her willingness to come forward with such an abundance of detail about the closely held Dreamings attests to her determination to instill a dignity and self-identity that her community had not experienced before.

YUENDUMU IS NORTH-WEST of Alice Springs, in the middle of the Centre, a big place. There are many Warlpiri people living there. I am a Warlpiri living at Yuendumu.

The types of game that we hunt and kill are: emus [ostrichlike birds], kangaroos, wild cats, bush turkeys, blue-tongued lizards, skinks, goannas, birds, snakes, and perenties [large monitor lizards]. For vegetable foods, there are little seeds which fall from trees and onto the ground. These are ground with stone and prepared for seedcakes. Some of the seeds are from pig weed, grasses, mulgas, witchetty grub trees, and bean trees. From the flat country and sandy ground, we dig up bush potatoes, bush yams and bush onions. For sweet things, we chop down sugar bag from the tops of trees. We also get witchetty grubs [edible larvae of moths and beetles] from tree roots and white gum trees; from the ground, we dig up honey ants. Today, people are still hunting for game and other food. . . .

The country here is good, with sand hills, rocks, creeks, trees and flat country. There are water soakages lying some distance apart through the spinifex [prickly grass] country. There are rockholes in the hills. The names of some of the rockholes and soakages are Mirijarra, Wakurlpu, Yakurrukaji, Yurntumulyu, and so on. It is only after there has been a lot of rain that the rockholes get water. When there was no water, the people would walk around from place to place, from one water soakage to another, from one rockhole to another. This was the way the people brought up their children. Today, people are still walking around and are going back to the country of their ancestors where they grew up. They know that they want to live there forever now that the Europeans have given them back their land. . . .

The name of this place is "Yurntumulyu," which was the name of a Dreamtime Woman. Today, everyone calls it Yurntumu (Yuendumu). However, Yurntumu is over there, to the east, where we pass on the road to Alice Springs, beside the hills. Yakurrukaji is the name of the place where the houses stand, where the soakage is. This is the land where we live. Yuendumu people have been living here for a long time and, as the children grow up, this land will become theirs.

This is the land of Honey Ant Dreaming for Napanangka, Japanangka, Napangardi, Japangardi, Napaljarri, Japaljarri, Nungarrayi, and Jungarrayi.[109] It comes under and across from Papunya, then the Honey Ant emerges east, on this side of Mt. Allen. There are many other Dreamings—Water, Snake, Possum, Kangaroo, Budgerigar [small green-and-yellow parrot], Big and Small Yam, Goanna, and many others. These have belonged to our ancestors and they hold no lies.[110]

How did it begin?

First, from the children. Many people told the children about the Dreamtime by drawing on the ground and on paper; they told them a long time ago in the bush by drawing on their bodies, on the ground, and on rocks. This was the way men and women used to teach their children. Now, when children are at school, at a white place, they want to pass on to them their knowledge about this place. They want them to keep and remember it. They want them to learn both ways—European and Aboriginal. They want them to see the designs, the true Dreaming, so they can follow it on the land, hills and on the shields, boomerangs, nulla nullas, spear throwers, and on other things.

The old men and women said they wanted to show the children how to do it and said they wanted to draw their designs on the doors. The people were seeing graffiti on the school, and so instead they wanted to put their designs on the doors. . . .

We painted these Dreamings [adds Paddy Japaljarri Stewart] on the school doors because the children should learn about our Law. The children do not know them and they might become like white people, which we don't want to happen. We are relating these true stories of the Dreamtime. We show them to the children and explain them so that the children will know them. We want our children to learn about and know our Law, our Dreamings. That is why we painted these Dreamtime stories.[111]

I am a child of the dreamtime people,
Part of this land like the gnarled gum tree,
I am the river softly singing,
Chanting our Songs on the way to the sea,
My spirit is the dust devils,
Mirages that dance on the plains,
I'm the snow, the wind and the falling rain,
I'm part of the rocks and the red desert earth,
Red as the blood that flows in my veins,
I am eagle, crow and the snake that glides,
Through the rain forests that cling to the mountainside.
I awakened here when the earth was new . . .
There was emu, wombat, kangaroo.
No other man of a different hue!
I am this land and this land is me.
I am Australia.

HYLLUS MARIS,
Aboriginal poet and author[112]

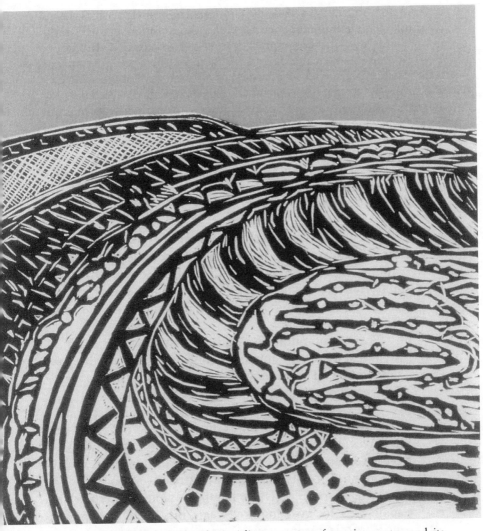

Ellen José. *Sea Scape*, 1987. The swirling currents of moving water and its teeming life of vegetation and mammals are reflected in this dynamic linocut. "No matter how dull or uninteresting the landscape may appear to some of us," says José, "there is life, color and space of boundless beauty [within it]. Lines, circle and oval shapes, tell us of the world and its shape and that we are part of it."

We hear the history of the Gurabulu through the informed and vivid family stories of Peter Yu, a social activist who was appointed by the Australian government to the Aboriginal Development Commission in the 1980s to oversee a budget of $130 million. He has been closely associated with the Kimberley Land Council and is a Community Aboriginal Consultant. Yu is a passionate and tireless advocate of Aboriginal self-determination. The principal obstacles to reassuming their humanity, he says, are the absence of their traditional lands and the consequent impotence to exercise traditional Law. Both are inextricably linked and without them self-government is impossible. Yu spends a great deal of his time developing strategies and programs to reassert Aboriginal dignity, to regain sacred country and to educate white Australians ("they do not have any culture because they are descendants of convicts")[113] about their *real* history.

Yu suggests that when a system of respectful reciprocity is operative within Aboriginal life, Aborigines are rarely denied the essentials for living. He is after recovering a depth in Aboriginal society that has no bottom, a landscape where life springs forth joyously and eternally, as it always has.

My people live on the coast in West Kimberley. We are what we call the Gurabulu—the seaside culture. Our stories, legends and dreamings relate to the sea; it is important to us not only for food but because it provides an identification of who we are and where we come from. . . .

My grandmother was a Bunuba woman, and a hundred years ago we numbered about two and a half thousand people. Today we only number about two hundred. The rest were all shot and murdered in ninety years. . . .

This is the sort of history that Australia has today. People know this, the whites don't want to believe it, but it is true. They have to come to terms with it. We have every reason to feel angry but we use our anger in a positive manner because that is our nature—we Aborigines are not violent people. There has been violence perpetrated against us for two hundred years but it has changed to more subtle means now. Australia is a very frustrating place to live in because it is very racist—in a very subtle way.

Australians are basically culturally insecure and ignorant about the issues of indigenous people. . . . [W]hite Australians do not have any understanding and appreciation of our culture; they do not have any culture because they are the descendants of convicts. . . .

According to our culture, we put our hand out in friendship and generosity believing that it is a reciprocal process—according to our rules it is. You can go anywhere and take something as long as you give back. That is our policy and that is why there has been no fighting. . . .

The problems really started when the white man landed in Australia. But they came to a head in the 1960's. Before then most people lived close to their traditional lands on cattle stations or cattle properties. They lived in bondage and worked as slave labour where they were only paid in tobacco, some flour and maybe some clothes. But in 1964 wage work came in and the white ranchers had to pay proper wages to Aboriginal people. It was no longer profitable for them so they kicked the Aboriginal people off the stations and they moved into towns—to the fringes of towns which became quite depressed areas with a lot of social problems because they were living away from their traditional countries. They came into contact with alcohol and it is the same story that happens all over the world with indigenous people. They came in contact with the missionaries—the social discipline structure was breaking down. There were different groups living on other peoples' traditional country. There were all kinds of internal conflicts. All these problems carry on today and are still evident—the problems still exist and the main reason is because people do not have their land.

The elders in my community were very concerned about this and decided that the only way to solve this question was to get back their traditional land, reassert their authority and try to get more discipline from the young people and to educate them in our way—in our tradition—to enable them to have strength, to be able to deal with outside influences and technology. . . .

But the problem in Australia has been that policies have been developed by the bureaucracy with little or no understanding of Aboriginal peoples' lifestyle. We have been trying to influence the policy-makers, to try to change their way of thinking, to get them to acknowledge that we are the master of our own destiny and we know what is best for us—not some white bureaucrat who sits in an office in the city some 2,000 miles away. So that has been basically the direction of our endeavours—to establish Aboriginal systems of administration structures and programmes so that we are in charge, not to receive money and be dictated to by government policies and programmes. . . .

In the history of Australia there have been three different phases, beginning about 100 years ago with the idea that Aboriginal people were dying out. The government, at that time, had a policy called the "smooth dying pillow" and that basically meant doing nothing and just allowing the people to die. The second phase was when they realised that we were not dying and they tried to assimilate us by making indigenous people white in their brain, denying us our language, culture, and kinship structure.

In 1967 there was a referendum which gave the Commonwealth government the authority to make laws for the benefit of Aboriginal people and recognize Aboriginal people as citizens. We were not Australian citizens until 1967 and if you wanted to become a citizen you had to apply and fill in a form. You were then given what we call a "dog ticket" and you had to be sponsored by a white person. That gave you the right to drink alcohol. My father was Chinese and was arrested in 1950 for living with my mother, for co-habiting with a native, and was fined 30 pounds. This is the only time he has been in jail. And there was a curfew. Aboriginal people had to be out of town after 6 p.m. in the 1950's. We were not considered human beings until 1967. So when we talk of Aboriginal development we are only talking about 21 years, a relatively short time. . . .

If we are to survive, and if we are to maintain the status quo, we have to develop new modern strategies and be able to manipulate new technology to our own advantage. . . . [W]e have just established our own Aboriginal publishing house and we have so far published four books. Aboriginal people have their oral history, oral tradition, so what we do is to get people to take tape-recorders and go and sit down, listen and get stories which we prepare and publish. . . . We are aiming for other Aboriginal people to read them so that they can be proud. We have to educate our own people, not only the white people, so it serves a dual purpose. . . .

The next book that's coming out is about the cattle industry from the Aboriginal point of view. The Aboriginal people were running the cattle industry in Australia, they were doing everything, but this was never recognised. They were the bosses, the white man just sat in his house and did nothing. The Aboriginal people know more about the cattle business than white people. So we have these old people, traditional people, who worked on the cattle stations and they talk and we write down what they tell. It will be very strong, very powerful politically, so people will have to come to terms with it. They cannot deny that the Aboriginal people were responsible for the development of that industry and that they contributed to the development of the country. This is going towards providing the facts of history because Australian history is very deliberate in its ignorance of Aboriginal peoples' role and that continues to be an excuse for white people to suppress us further; so we have to break down that myth by providing the factual evidence. That is what we are doing.[114]

ABORIGINAL PRESENTER [INTERVIEWING MINISTER]: *I've always been fascinated by white people. The evidence of their culture is all around us. What do you think about white people?*

ABORIGINAL MINISTER FOR WHITE AFFAIRS: *They're a developing people. They're starting to take an interest in the world around them. This is a good sign.*

Babakiueria *(film)*[115]

We say this: the Whiteman of Australia has more compassion and kindness for the Koala bear than for us Koorie people, but even our bones will not stop talking.

RIKKIE SHIELDS,
Aboriginal poet[116]

II

JAPAN

The ocean speaks and mountains have tongues—that is the everyday speech of Buddha. . . . If you can speak and hear such words you will be one who truly comprehends the entire universe.

DŌGEN KIGEN *(13th century),*
Zen master and thinker [1]

Stencil design for fabric

Make the universe your companion, always bearing in mind the true nature of all creation—mountains and rivers, trees and grasses, and humanity.

MATSUO BASHŌ (1644–1694)
haiku *poet and pilgrim* [2]

Trees and plants bring the magnificence of heaven to the human spirit.

TACHIBANANO TOSHITSUNA (11th century),
*author of the bible of Japanese gardening,
Sakuteiki* [3]

. . . the Japanese mind is so attached to the earth that it would not forget, however mean they may be, the grasses growing under the feet.

DAISETZ SUZUKI,
Zen Buddhist scholar [4]

Kano Hogai (1828–1888), Kannon, *The Bodhisattva Ava-lokitesvara,* "The Compassionate Mother," 1888. Created in the last year of his life, upon the birth of his grandson Shinji, the painting exhibits a distinct Western religious influence. It is considered by some the greatest painting of the Meiji era (1868–1911). The androgynous Kannon pours from her vase the water of life from which is produced an infant symbolizing humankind. In her left hand Kannon holds a willow branch denoting mercy and compassion. The whorl of creation is very much present in this magnificent painting. It is thought the "globe" represents the womb and the baby descends within this capsule toward the dark ragged mountains below while casting a glance back toward the Creator with a pained look, suggesting the suffering to be faced in life.

INTRODUCTION

Japan is a land of volcano, earthquake, tidal wave and typhoon. Born on the Pacific Rim's Ring of Fire, it is an island nation of approximately 150 million people. An archipelago of four main islands and thousands of smaller ones, Japan has a total land mass roughly the size of California.

Japan is crowned with mountains. According to one source, it has 354 major sacred mountains, not to mention countless minor ones.[5] They are the lifeblood of Japan's spiritual and physical landscape. For eleven centuries people have come to pray to the spirit of the Kamo River that flows into Japan's ancient onetime capital, Kyoto. Shincho Tanaka,* a priest and keeper of the Shimyo Buddhist mountain temple, speaks of the shrine as "a refuge" for the many Japanese who visit. "Places like this," he says, "are important for the sense of balance in their lives." The shaping influence of the natural environment and its elements upon Japan's living heritage is of particular importance to Tanaka:

> THIS TEMPLE WAS BUILT at the source of the Kamo River. The water of the Kamo River was the water of life. That caused people to believe that if they do not worship the Kamo River they cannot live peacefully. For a long time it was an important role for this temple to protect the nature around the source of the Kamo River.
>
> On this small island that is Japan, forests and mountains are very important and the rivers bring water to the oceans on each side of Japan in a very short time. Rivers and mountains maintain our water supply, the water is created in the mountains, then goes to the rivers. That is the important natural cycle. For a long time, Japanese cul-

---

* For Japanese names I have used the American name order.

118

ture and history had been nurtured in such a great environment.

People nowadays have to look very deep into the woods and really search to find anything real or natural in this area.[6]

Yamato, the ancient name for Japan, shares a rich association with Japan's mountain world, say philologists. *Yama* means "mountain." The name *Yamato* has been explained as "mountain door," "mountain tracks" and "mountain stop."[7] An aerial view of Japan reveals an intricate and highly variegated pattern of mountain landscapes. The Japanese philosopher Sōetsu Yanagi states that "nature depends on pattern." Moreover, "[t]o divine the significance of pattern," writes Yanagi, "is . . . to understand beauty itself."[8] Yanagi suggests that pattern is a lode of intuition, vision and true essence. Referring to the commonplace five-leaf bamboo grass crest that is used as a motif on Japanese clothes, Yanagi asks, "How is it that one sees the bamboo in the pattern?" He responds: "Because the essence of bamboo is there." A good pattern, he continues, is "but an enhancing of what is true." Pattern, he writes, "is the transmitter of beauty. Through pattern we learn how to look at nature. Without pattern, man's view of nature would be far more vague and equivocal than it is. Pattern contains the nature of nature."[9]

In Yanagi's eyes, pattern is a transcendent experience of nature:

> PATTERN IS A SUMMING-UP of a view of nature. Via pattern we see nature at its most wondrous. In a sense, an age without good patterns is an age that does not look at nature carefully. . . . Pattern may be compared to a spring of water that can be drawn on eternally. To provide a source of imagination that never dries up—that, for me, is true beauty. Through pattern, the world and our own hearts are made beautiful. . . . Pattern . . . obeys [natural] laws. . . . It is . . . a hymn to nature's mysterious power. In pattern man gets a view of a mighty world transcending man.[10]

One aspect of that "mighty world transcending man" is the belief in the sacredness of mountains. "Mountains are in fact . . . the spiritual homes of the Japanese," writes one scholar of Japanese religion. "They are where the souls go after death, and, as the permanent gathering-place of the souls of the ancestors and the family gods, are the source of prosperity and happiness."[11] Japan has one of the world's oldest traditions of mountain climbing. Ascents of and pilgrimages to the major peaks, divine abodes of the *kami* (the sacred deities believed to animate all features of the natural world) were recorded as early as the ninth century A.D.

Peerless among the mountains is Fuji—"Wondrous Sovereign of the Great One," "the axis and embodiment of all things, truly breathed"[12]—by far the grandest and highest, but also incomparably the loveliest. "Countless are the mountains in Yamato," wrote a seventh-century emperor in a verse known to every educated Japanese, but sublime Fuji reigns supreme in divine preeminence: "Lo! There towers the lofty peak of Fuji. . . . / It baffles the tongue, it cannot be named, / It is a god mysterious."[13]

Another feature of that "mighty world" flourishes in the original root of Japanese culture, "the way of agriculture," in the words of Japanese farmer, poet and microbiologist Masanobu Fukuoka. Fukuoka believes that we cannot isolate one aspect of life from another and uses the growth of a tree as an analogy for the infinite knowledge to be derived from the illumined composition of the natural world:

> [I]F WE TAKE AS OUR STARTING POINT the view that a tree grows of its own accord, the uptake of nutrients by the tree's roots is no longer a cause but, in the eyes of nature, just a small effect. One could say that the tree grew as a result of the absorption of nutrients by the roots, but one could also claim that the absorption of nutrients was caused by something else, which had the effect of making the tree grow. The buds on a tree are made for budding and so this is what they do; the roots, with their powers of elongation, spread and extend throughout the earth. A tree has a shape perfectly adapted to the natural environment. With this, it guards the providence of nature and obeys nature's laws, growing neither too fast nor too slow, but in total harmony with the great cycles of nature. . . .
>
> The more scientists learn, the more they realize just how awesome is the complexity and mystery of nature. They find this to be a world filled with boundless, inscrutable riddles. The amount of research material that lies hidden in a single gram of soil, a single particle, is mindboggling.[14]

The natural world was thought by the Japanese to have intrinsic value. For all time, the Japanese ethos has been marked by an emotional conjunction with nature. Thus emotion became the underpinning for their sensitivity to the animal, vegetable and mineral kingdoms.

Japanese philosophy is suffused with intimations of ecological awareness—for example (as one Western scholar points out), the expressions *wa* (harmony), *shugyō* (cultivation), *jinen* (naturalness), *mitsu* (intimacy) and *ma* (interval) reflect a reciprocal dependency of humankind and nature,[15] and this reciprocity is demonstrated in a third characteristic of the mysterious and almighty world that transcends man in the way of *cha-no-yu,* the art of tea.

"The Philosophy of Tea . . . expresses our whole point of view about man and nature," writes art historian Kakuzo Okakura (1862–1913). The Way of Tea, he says, instills naturalness, harmony and "the mystery of mutual charity."[16] "The art of tea . . . its ideal, [is] to come closer to Nature," writes Zen Buddhist scholar Daisetz Suzuki.[17] The tea ceremony has three elements: the setting, the pottery and the tea itself. The tea environment—the tea hut, its interior and the garden—correspond to three essential aspects of Buddhist doctrine: the impermanence of all things, "the selflessness of all elements" and Nirvana. The way of *cha-no-yu* helps perfect consciousness. The goal of the great tea practitioners was that which was simplest and most essential in human life.[18]

Even in painting, poetry, the dramatic arts, flower arrangement, calligraphy and the martial arts, the precepts of tea are the highest ideal. "Naturalness"—the essential essence—is at the heart of creativity.

Zen master Takuan (1573–1645) explains the principles of the Japanese tea ceremony as a means to establishing universal harmony:

> THE WAY OF *cha-no-yu* . . . is to appreciate the spirit of a naturally harmonious blending of Heaven and Earth, to see the pervading presence of the five elements *(wu-hsing)* by one's fireside, where the mountains, rivers, rocks, and trees are found as they are in Nature, to draw the refreshing water from the well of Nature, to taste with one's own mouth the flavor supplied by Nature. How grand this enjoyment of the harmonious blending of Heaven and Earth![19]

One of Japan's best-known art and literary critics, Shuichi Kato, offers a unique view on the significance of the *raku* teabowl (the archetypal teabowl adopted by the early masters of tea, and dating back to the sixteenth century). According to Kato, the whole universe is contained inside the teabowl. The cosmos, he suggests, rests in the palm of the hand:

THIS TEABOWL embraces all the characteristics of the psychological passage of human nature. We can feel with our senses that it's a summary of all the emotional ups and downs we experience with the passing of time. I'm growing old too and approaching the twilight of my life. So for me too this is very meaningful. As I look back on my life I somehow feel that everything, all the things I have experienced over the long years, is represented in this teabowl. To me this is a visible symbol of my own universe and this is by no means a simplified version of beauty. The teabowl stands for all the complex developments in life, yet everything is concentrated within a very small vessel. This unique form was created by the Japanese at a certain period in history, and you won't see it anywhere else.[20]

Life and nature are projected into the teabowl and, in fact, become the teabowl. One sign of this is the name given to each individual *raku* teabowl. Just as each of us is given a name at birth, so too with the teabowl. Each teabowl, in effect, has its own personality, and names such as Firefly, Sunset, Twilight, and Memories are bestowed upon these vessels.[21]

Nature as a universal force creating unity of feeling and existence is the way of *cha-no-yu*. "Who would then deny that when I am sipping tea in my tearoom I am swallowing the whole universe with it," muses Daisetz Suzuki, "and that this very moment of my lifting the bowl to my lips is eternity itself transcending time and space?" "The art of tea," he continues, "really teaches us far more than the harmony of things, or keeping them free from contamination, or just sinking down into a state of contemplative tranquillity."[22]

Claude Champi, A French potter who has been profoundly inspired by Japanese ceramics, states that "the teabowl reflects the individual's relationship with nature. . . . The Japanese have succeeded in making the very earth and stone speak"; adding, "that's why the teabowl is time, [and is] timeless."[23]

In the process of his own development as a potter, and in continuing the *raku* way of pottery, Kichizaemon Raku XV, a gifted contemporary craftsman, experienced a recognition of truth of profound proportion, which he stated in an interview with Shuichi Kato: "I came to the conclusion," he said, "that the whole of nature is contained within each of us."[24]

Painting by Icho, *Water*, with Buddhist image of the Flaming Jewel.

All you under the heaven! Regard heaven as your father, earth as your mother, and all things as your brothers and sisters.

SHINTO
oracle of Atsuta [25]

A virtuous man, when alone, loves the quiet of the mountains. A wise man in nature enjoys the purity of the water. One must not be suspicious of the fool who takes pleasure in mountains and streams, but rather measure how well he sharpens his spirit by them.

MUSO SOSEKI (1275–1351),
Buddhist monk,
National Teacher and painter [26]

THE AINU
OF JAPAN

Japan is generally, but mistakenly, regarded as a homogeneous nation. It does, in fact, have several minority groups and two indigenous minorities, one being the Ainu. The Ainu are considered to be the oldest inhabitants of the Japanese archipelago.[27]

The Ainu are the ethnic group that makes up the indigenous population of the island of Hokkaido, Japan's northernmost island (they once occupied the Sakhalin and Kurile Islands and northern Honshu as well). The word *ainu* (human being) distinguishes this people from their nonhuman counterpart, their *kami,* or deities. In this sense, interspecies communication was and is a natural part of life. The Ainu call their homeland *yaun moshir,* or "the country on land," "the mainland," and they, the inhabitants, are *yaunkur,* "people of the land," according to scholar of Ainu culture Donald Philippi.[28]

"The first written account of the Ainu refers to their presence in the prefecture of Akita in northern Honshu in 642," reports anthropologist Douglas Sanders. Surviving accounts of warfare between the Ainu and the Japanese describe hostilities in northern Honshu in 658, 789 and 811, relates Sanders.[29] Treated for centuries as aliens as well as an inferior minority group by the Japanese, and reduced in numbers by disease and a low birthrate since the turn of the century, the Ainu now number, officially, around 24,000 (local estimates, however, place the figure at closer to 80,000). Hunting and fishing and the gathering of wild fruits and leafy plants were the traditional sources of livelihood for the Ainu. These have been replaced by rice and dry-crop cultivation, commercial fishing, and the collection of kelp and shellfish.

Ainu culture and physiognomy have always been markedly different from that of the Japanese. They are known for their extreme hairiness, in contrast to the relatively hairless Japanese, and in earlier times, Ainu men used to grow very long beards. Today the Ainu language has almost entirely disappeared from everyday use. Fortunately, songs, dances, sculpture, textiles and a small body of oral literature have been preserved and retrieved in this century and are in the process of being learned and relearned through an organized and flourishing native interest in Ainu ways. No art of painting appears to have emerged from this ancient people, but the art of being is very much present in so many of their expressions of daily living.

Takeichi Moritake, a sixty-three-year-old Ainu *ekashi* (respected elder) and poet, greets the universe with his poems entitled *Genshirin (Primeval Forest)* fervently declaring "All humanity are brothers," while explaining "that means I am dead set against discrimination."[30] In this poem he recalls the fullness of another time.

> *Fire, water, plants, animals, . . .*
> *Everything was divine*
> *In the primeval life*
> *Of our* utari [village]:
> *Prayers of thanksgiving!*
> *Life of devout faith!*
> *Memories dear to me*
> *Of our ancestral life*
> *Primitive but full*
> *Of awe and reverence*
> *Toward every being.*[31]

Ainu oral literature is saturated with aesthetic qualities and is of great antiquity. The oral folkloric tradition is rich in song, prayer, speeches and mythic epics. "Before massive acculturation," writes scholar of Ainu oral literature Donald Philippi, "eloquence *(pawetok)* was regarded by the Ainu as one of the chief manly virtues."[32] Travelers commented on the astonishing body of lore, its richness of detail and dramatic recitations, remarks Philippi.[33] The oldest lyric genre of Ainu song is the *yukar,* long epic poems, traditionally sung, about ancestral heroes and totemic gods of the race. There are songs for all occasions—work (especially for brewing sake and pounding flour for the bear ceremony), festivals, ceremonies, pleasure and lullabies. Many songs imitate the sounds of the natural world, including birds and animals.[34]

Utomriuk, the Ainu chieftain of the village of Shumunkot in the Saru region, provides the following hunter's prayer, addressed to newly slain deer and according them great respect, while praising the deities who appeared to the hunter in the disguise of animals or birds.

Let your spirits
return
atop the summit
of our native country.
May you
abide there
as newborn gods.
Take these inau [*ritualized*
and precious whittled sticks],
these lovely inau,
and may you
enhance with them
your glory
as deities![35]

The elements and the growing and living things of the earth are prayed to, adorned with respect and thanked for the giving of their substance. An Ainu elder from Rankoshi recalls the essential ideals of his village life.

MY PARENTS TAUGHT US to revere and express gratitude to the *kamui* [deities] of fire, water, and mountains, in which are found the essentials for our living. Older persons in our *kotan* [village] often told us children to appreciate our natural resources, especially our trees and rivers. We were to be careful not to damage or destroy young trees when we played in the woods or to set fire to the trees. Trees, our old people said, hold water which comes forth from the earth when it is needed. Trees on mountains, too, are the homes of our bear and deer. We were taught to respect our rivers and not to pollute them. They were the home of our fish.

As children we were taught that mutual help of any kind was a great virtue. Every *kotan* must help a needy one, especially if the need is due to failures in the hunt. The best deed of all was to save the life of another. A child who saved a life or helped anyone to do so was showered with praise by parents and the people of the *kotan*. . . .

My parents said that every piece of food is sacred and that leftovers were not to be treated carelessly. We were not to help ourselves to more food than we could eat, for there should be no leftovers. We were never to step on food of any kind.

The Ainu child was taught to care for both parents and old persons. We have an Ainu word which means "to take good care of your parents" and another that means "to take good care of an old person."[36]

Millet, a staple of Ainu life, is considered the divine seed with male and female counterparts, which taken together are called "the divine husband and wife cereal." Gestures of homage and words of prayer and thanksgiving, such as the following, are offered in earnest to the millet deity by the Ainu elders, before the millet is pounded and made into cakes.

> O THOU CEREAL DEITY we worship thee. Thou hast grown very well this year, and thy flavour will be sweet. Thou art good. The goddess of fire will be glad, and we also shall rejoice greatly. O thou god, O thou divine cereal, do thou nourish the people. I now partake of thee. I worship thee and give thee thanks.[37]

Sasaki, an Ainu elder, discusses the way of the Ainu:

> FAITH IN THE AINU WAY! Faith, the kind we Ainu used to have. Ainu people were pious prayerful people. We communed with our *Kamui* [deities] about everything and everywhere—when we went to the mountains, we communed with *kamui* of the mountains; when we went to the river, we communed with *kamui* of the river. We saw *kamui* in all things of nature; through nature we prayed and worshipped. As soon as a child was old enough to walk, its parents took it into the woods and fields and taught it about the *kamui* in nature. Soon that child had faith. As he grew older and developed his ability to comprehend, his faith was enhanced. Today our young people have no faith, a regrettable thing. In those days we prayed for our children on many occasions. Maybe we have neglected to do so and should again pray for them.[38]

Nature's simplicity hides a greater complexity than man's.

SŌETSU YANAGI (1889–1961),
*philosopher, writer
and founder of Japan's
folkcraft movement* [39]

THE HEART OF NATURE
IN
JAPANESE THOUGHT

aigyō (1118–1190) is regarded by the Japanese as one of
Japan's foremost medieval Buddhist nature poets. Poetically,
the latter part of the twelfth century was an exceptionally
brilliant age, and Saigyō was one of its most gifted and important presences. Buddhist priest and monk of the Shingon sect,
Saigyō was greatly admired for his poetic talents by contemporary
court poets as well as succeeding generations. His classical *Waka*
compositions (thirty-one syllable verse), the conventional form of his
time, had a profound influence upon Bashō, another of Japan's leading poets. Saigyō has been described as "preeminently a poet of *Sabi*
(lonely, austere beauty)."[40] The elements of the natural world, Saigyō
discovered, were the elements of his higher self. Nature stirred his
soul to such a degree that he felt unworthy of his commitment to
surrender all worldly attachments. In his poetry, the love and emotion
that were kindled in his soul by nature are expressed and questioned.
Nonetheless, he felt compelled to surrender to the beauty and truth
of nature, yielding to what he perceived as a "sensation of being /
Made pure to the base of the heart";[41] in other words, the very
essence of his true self. When his heart and mind were "taken" by
the blossoms of spring, only then did he feel ultimately in contact
with what was real and true.[42] Even when voicing his doubts about
this lingering attachment, he seems unable to restrain his tender affection for this eternal friend. It is this confession of personal suffering
and inadequacy for which his poetry was especially esteemed. Lament
upon such misfortune is almost cherished by Saigyō in the following
transcendent expression of his communion with the natural world.

> *Methought, I had no desire of living longer;*
> *Yet, why should I not long to see another year,*
> *Again this pure moonlight of restful autumn?*

> *My gaze is caught by the butterflies*
> *Playing among flowers that bloom on the hedge;*

Do I envy them?—yes, perhaps—Am I envying
These little creatures, friends of the flowers?

Charmed by the flowers, I seem to feel a love for them.
How can this passion still possess my soul,
When, methought, I had utterly renounced the world![43]

[A]ll who have achieved real excellence in any art possess
one thing in common, that is, a mind to obey nature, to be
one with nature, throughout the four seasons of the year.

MATSUO BASHŌ (1644–1694),
poet and pilgrim[44]

Matsuo Bashō (1644–1694) was "a great wandering poet, a most passionate lover of Nature—a kind of Nature troubadour," in the words of Zen Buddhist scholar Daisetz Suzuki.[45] In fact, Bashō is a pen name the poet took for himself, after the bashō tree, a certain species of banana tree to which Bashō developed a special attachment. Bashō devoted his life to seeing into the living heart of Nature. He spent all his time traveling from one end of Japan to another. In one of the prefaces to his travel diaries called *Oku no Hosomichi (The Narrow Road of Oku)* he describes his irresistible hunger for journeying: "I do not remember when, but I have conceived the strong desire for a wandering life, giving myself up to the destiny of a solitary cloud as it is wafted in the wind. After spending some time along the seashore, I settled last autumn for a while in a tumbledown hut that stands by the river . . . But as the year approached its end, my wandering spirit violently asserted itself once more. It was as if I were pursued by a supernatural being whose temptation was more than I could resist . . . Finally, giving up my hut to a friend, I started on the northern trip, my heart filled with the moonlight that would soon greet me at Matsushima."[46] Bashō was "a poet of Eternal Aloneness," states Suzuki, and was best known for his *haiku* and *renku* verse. According to Bashō, the spirit of Eternal Aloneness is the spirit of *fūga*, the chaste enjoyment of life and Nature, and "he who cherishes it accepts Nature and becomes a friend of the four seasons. Whatever objects he sees are referred to the flowers; whatever thoughts he conceives are related to the moon. When objects are not referred to the flowers, one is savage; when thoughts are not related to the moon, one resembles the lower animals. Therefore, I declare: Go beyond savagery, be separated from the lower animals, and accept Nature, return to Nature."[47]

Bashō's love for the ancient pine and cedar trees of his beloved country occupies a prominent place in his poems and travel diaries. On a visit to the outer shrine of Ise one evening just before dark, he wrote: "As I stood there, lending my ears to the roar of pine trees upon distant mountains, I felt moved deep in the bottom of my heart."[48] His pursuit of and insistence upon truth and unity—the hidden vital forces that shape all things—in the infinite variety of existence was the primary impulse in his life. He explains this himself in the following way:

> GO TO THE PINE if you want to learn about the pine, or the bamboo, if you want to learn about the bamboo. And in doing so, you must leave your subjective preoccupation with yourself. Otherwise you impose yourself on the object and do not learn. Your poetry issues of its own accord when you and the object have become one—when you have plunged deep enough into the object to see something like a hidden glimmering there. However well phrased your poetry may be, if your feeling is not natural—if the object and yourself are separate—then your poetry is not true poetry but merely your subjective counterfeit.[49]

Humans are born through the beneficence of nature; they receive its heart and make it their own. They live amidst nature and partake of its nourishment. Thus they receive an infinitely great favor, but most people do not realize it. This is what is meant by "Peasants use it every day and are unaware of it."[50]

To rest under a willow tree, bathed in the cool evening breeze, and watch the moon rising above the trees, is sufficient to drive away selfish desires, and uplift every thought.[51]

KAIBARA EKKEN (1630–1714),
teacher, writer and philosopher

Kaibara Ekken (1630–1714) was a great teacher. He has been called "the Aristotle of Japan"[52] as well as "the grandfather or fore-father of macrobiotics."[53] Nearly three centuries after his death, Kaibara Ekken, regarded by his contemporaries and later generations as "a major figure in Japanese intellectual history," in the words of religious scholar Mary Evelyn Tucker, feels like a familiar presence.[54]

Ekken was a popular educator concerned with transmitting the eternal verities of the Sages to the widest audience possible. His ap-peal was to the peasant farmers (the vast majority of the population of the Tokugawa period, 1600–1868), the samurai, artisans and mer-chants alike. Ekken eschewed pretense of any kind and advised sincer-ity in all matters of learning and living. He once wrote that "the aim of learning is not merely to widen knowledge, but to form character. Its object is to make us true men, rather than learned men. The chief reason why the teachings of the Sages are not more appreciated by the people is because scholars endeavour to show off their learning, rather than to make it their endeavour to live up to the teachings of the Sages."[55] Tutor, lecturer, researcher, agronomist, botanist, pro-lific writer (more than 110 works), and extensive traveler, Ekken developed the neo-Confucian position of the human forming one body with all things: "Thus we must, of course, love humanity," he taught, "but we should also love all things."[56] He expressed symboli-cally the profound connection that exists between human, heaven and earth: "As children of heaven and earth, human beings must take heaven and earth as the model for their conduct; heaven and earth have nothing else at heart than to be sympathetic to all things. They have no other purpose or function than to bring forth and nourish all things. Humans also receive this heart and should always aspire to have a heart which is sympathetic and kind to others."[57]

Ekken perceived man and nature as interdependent, in perpetual renewal of one another and of all life. He affirmed the sacredness of all living things and revealed the natural birthright of the universe to be one of harmony and joyful contentment in the human heart. He believed, as did many other neo-Confucians of the Tokugawa period, that "the ceaseless activity of nature was . . . a field of knowledge that human minds must engage in to contribute to the social good."[58] In the following passage from his essay the *Way of Contentment*, Ekken describes, with gratitude, the great beneficence of nature pres-ent in the vitality and harmony of the natural world, of which, he insists, we are an integral part.

> THIS SPIRIT OF HARMONY exists not only in human beings but also in birds and animals and in plants and trees. Ani-mals play, birds sing, fish leap, and plants and trees flour-ish, bloom, and ripen. All have this spirit of harmony. . . .

The expansiveness of heaven and earth which is always replete before us is a source of great joy—the light of the sun and moon; the continual return of the four seasons; the beauty of various landscapes; the changes from dawn to dusk in clouds and mists; the appearance of the mountains; the flow of the streams; the rustling of the wind; the moisture of the rain and dew; the purity of the snow; the array of flowers; the growth of fresh grass; the flourishing of trees; the diverse life of birds, animals, fish and insects. If we constantly appreciate this varied beauty of creation, our spirit of harmony will be ceaseless by expanding our mind-and-heart, purifying our emotions, cultivating a moral sense, enkindling joy, and washing away all regrets from our heart. This is called being in touch with the mysteries of heaven. This means by contact with external things our inner goodness is aroused.[59]

Ryōkan (1758–1831), of the province of Echigo, has been called "a grand Nature-mystic."[60] A Zen Buddhist monk, poet and calligrapher who "had a most sensitive heart for all things human and natural," he was, in the words of another Zen Buddhist monk, "love incarnate."[61] All creatures and vegetation of Nature were dear to him. Ryōkan had an intense love for trees. Japan is the country of pine trees and cedars, and Ryōkan never tired of singing their praises. Here is his declaration of solidarity, respect and fascination for a solitary old pine at Kugami:

> At Kugami,
> In front of the Otono [grand hall],
> There stands a solitary pine tree,
> Surely of many a generation;
> How divinely dignified
> It stands there!
> In the morning
> I pass by it;
> In the evening
> I stand underneath it,
> And standing I gaze,
> Never tired
> Of this solitary pine![62]

Ryōkan's empathy for a rain-drenched pine tree at Iwamuro is saturated with a spirit of oneness. He offers consoling words to an arboreal friend:

A lone pine stands
In the fields of Iwamuro
And how miserably soaked
It was in the rain,
When I looked at it today.
Oh, Solitary Pine,
How gladly would I have
Protected you with my paper-umbrella
Or with my straw-coat
Were you only flesh and blood.
What a pity—to see you drenched so![63]

... the characteristics of nature should be understood as related to the spiritual make-up of those who live with that nature.

... while the Greeks sensed through sight, the Japanese saw through sense, a difference that it would be wrong to disregard. Japan shares this characteristic with China and India.

TETSURO WATSUJI,
philosopher, poet and essayist[64]

In a philosophical study of climate, Tetsuro Watsuji expressed wonder at the idealized natural beauty and refinement he found inherent in the detailed construction of the Japanese garden. "Here is a unity," he writes, "gained not by geometrical proportion but by a balancing of forces which appeals to the emotions, a unity of a meeting of spirit. Just as spirits meet between man and man, so do they also meet between moss and stone or even between stone and stone. Every effort is made to avoid the orderly in order to achieve this 'meeting of spirit.' In such a style of composition, the more intricate the materials that make up the garden, the more prominent becomes this 'meeting of spirit.' "[65]

The same application of spirit, he felt, could be applied to the artist's landscape. He has said that "this characteristic [of spirit] can be discovered also in the No [theatre], in the tea-ceremony and in Kabuki, all of them arts born of a 'meeting of feeling.' "[66] He once wrote that in a gathering of Japanese poets, the poets will "combine their feelings and reveal their individual experience in a symphonic concord of each other's hearts," while at the same time preserving their own individuality. He calls this coordination of imaginative power "a meeting of the heart," where "the order of a whole" is achieved through a total composition of "linked verse."[67]

But, always, Watsuji returns to a contemplation of what he calls his country's "gentle nature," a nature he once referred to as a "sweet intoxication . . . one of the most remarkable characteristics of Japanese culture, running through all the stages of its development."[68] Commenting upon this unique Japanese feature, Watsuji has written that "the peculiar beauty of Mother Earth in Japan has bequeathed the same beauty to the children born to her," adding with distinctive fervor that "all inquiries into the culture of Japan must in their final reduction go back to the study of her nature [in all its manifestations]."[69] In his classic work A Climate: A Philosophical Study, Watsuji describes the meaning of such a return.

> IN THE EAST . . . nature was treated not as something that is to be mastered but as the repository of infinite depth. Man sought consolation and assistance from nature; the [Japanese] poet Bashō, who was typically oriental, came into aesthetic, moral and even religious association with nature; but he showed not the slightest trace of an intellectual interest. His concern was to live, to live with nature; so his view of nature was directed to religious salvation. This could only come with the protean fecundity of nature in the East. Seeing his own reflection in nature, man felt that he was being shown the way to infinitely deep abstractions and the best artists tried through their experience to seek out and express this way. Even in a landscape the artist made not the slightest attempt to capture in his experience the method or the immutability of the structure of the landscape; rather, just as the Zen sage expresses his mental tranquillity in deliverance in a simple nature sketch poem, so the artist tries to express illimitable depth using the landscape as a mere symbol. I am not saying, of course,

that every artist in the Orient was and is capable of this. I am merely trying to point out that in the "meeting of feeling" of the artist who was capable of comprehending what was most significant in the savage disorder and the teeming abundance of nature there is a powerful expression of such a purpose. . . .

Today, now that the world seems to have become one, the stimuli of differing cultures appear to be toppling the distinctiveness of nature. Yet natural distinctiveness is not something to disappear without a trace. As ever, man will be restrained unconsciously by its curbings, as ever he sinks his roots in it.[70]

"I wonder what sort of men create great monuments—such as the sculptures and buildings of the Asuka (593–710) and Nara (710–794) Eras of Japan. What are they really like?" It was these questions, Tetsuro Watsuji tells us, that first aroused his interest in the antiquities of Japan. He did not know it then, but in 1917, at the age of twenty-eight, a lifelong interest in "ethics as the science of man" (in Watsuji's words) had taken root. Tetsuro Watsuji was to become the *new progenitor* of a dynamic system of learning—of being and perceiving—based on the Japanese word for ethics, *rinri,* the essence or principle that enables humankind to live in friendly communion and community.[71] In 1920, *Ancient Japanese Culture,* an imaginative and interpretative study of Japan's ancient culture, was published, revealing Watsuji's intense admiration for the ancients. But the things of old were placed in a new and refreshing perspective. In his preface to *Guzo Saiko* (a collection of critical essays published in 1918), Watsuji explains, with great poetic insight, his intentions behind the transcendent significance he attributes to the past masters and masterpieces: ". . . a mere 'revival of the old' is not my object. Even the old, when revived, shines with a new life, casting off its old crust. Here is no longer any restraint of time; it is eternally young and eternally new. What I wish to do is nothing more or nothing less than to advance such life as lives in the everlasting New."[72]

In the following passage from Tetsuro Watsuji's book *Koji Junrei* (*Pilgrimages to Old Temples*), published in 1919, the poet-philosopher, philologist and essayist writes about a visit he made to the Toshodaiji temple at Nara. The journey amounts to an awakening— "a meeting of feeling"—where the synergy of Nature and native architectural forms awakens Watsuji to an enhanced vision of Creation.

I FOUND MYSELF in front of the Temple and spent a few

minutes of happy contemplation. A clump of tall pine trees surrounding the Temple gave me an ineffable feeling of intimacy. Between the pine-grove and this monument of ancient architecture there certainly is an affinity both intimate and ineffable. I do not think a piece of Western architecture, of whatever kind or style, would match so well with the sentiment aroused at the sight of the pine-grove. To encircle the Parthenon with a clump of pine trees would be unthinkable. Nor can we, by even the furthest stretch of imagination, conceive that a Gothic cathedral would in any way match with the gently sloping curves of these graceful pine branches. Such buildings should only be contemplated in conjunction with the towns and cities, forests and fields of their respective lands. Just so do our Buddhist temples have something intimately connected with and inseparable from the characteristic features of our native shores. If there are to be found some traces of the Northern forest in Gothic architecture, can we not say with equally good reason that there are in our Buddhist temples some traces of Japanese pine and cypress forests? Do we not feel in those curving roofs something of the influence of the branches of our gentle pine or cypress? Is there nothing to be perceived in the look of the temple as a whole with its reminiscences of a stately old pine or cypress adorned with thick evergreen foliage?[73]

Is there a greater wisdom than nature's, which outstrips anything that man can conceive? Knowledge of the deepest order is to be described as that which is in accordance with nature.

SŌETSU YANAGI[7]

In *from the desert of japan,* poet and novelist Shimpei Kusano offers a dynamic graph of the human heart in his scenario for a radically "new" human world that mirrors the ideals and ageless wisdom of the natural world and where "all cultures will move towards becoming classics."

> like a hedgehog shedding light.
> soon the great sun of morning will rise.
> light will shine all around and.
> the scent of the green element will also come full.
> science will wander off into mountains and
> fields and towards precipices.
> literature will go on probing probing to see human
> beings in full depth.
> parks between air and air will be born and.
> in the sea neon will bloom.
> school a preparation.
> society will be school.
> politics will be the melting-pot of wisdom and
> devotion.
> everyone will start to make a living.
> inventions will produce inventions.
> great philosophies will be born.
> music will stir the aged.
> medical science will be common sense.
> cosmic rays will be more abundant and developed
> anew.
> atomic energy will be made into fuel.
> all cultures will move towards becoming classics.
> duels will occur everywhere over beauty.
> the unnecessary will be realized as unnecessary.
> only beauty will vie with heaven and its eternity.
>
> but these possibilities also.
> if they just remain so.
> will be retrograde.[75]

*Mountains and rivers
and the great earth:
Everything reveals
the Body of Buddha.*

Sayings of the Masters[76]

THE LAW
OF ONENESS

Muso Soseki (Muso Kokushi—1275–1351) explains the Law of Oneness that permeates all of Creation. Its truth is visible in all things of the earth, both animate and inanimate. The entire universe bears its mark joining all worlds—natural, human, spirit, vegetable and mineral—in the perpetuation and illumination of existence.

The following discourse was given by Muso Soseki in the year 1345 upon the opening of the Tenryu-ji monastery, a Zen temple garden at Kyoto, of which he became founding abbot.

THE APPEARANCE IN THIS WORLD of all Buddhas [fully enlightened beings], past, present and future, is solely for the purpose of preaching the Law and helping all creatures to cross over to the shore of Liberation. . . .

What is that which we call the "Law"? It is the truth inherent in all its perfection in every living creature. The sage possesses it in no greater measure than does the ordinary man. Enlarge it and it will fill the universe; restrict it and it can be contained in a fraction of an inch. Yesterday or today, it undergoes no change or variation. All that the Buddhas have taught, whether as the Mahāyāna, the Hīnayāna [the earliest branch of Buddhism], the pseudo or the authentic, the partial or the complete—all are embraced in it. This is the meaning of the "Law."

Everything the world contains—grass and trees, bricks and tile, all creatures, all actions and activities—are nothing but manifestations of this Law. Therefore is it said that all phenomena in the universe bear the mark of this Law. If the significance of this were only grasped, then even without the appearance in this world of a Tathāgata (Buddha), the enlightenment of man would be complete, and even without the construction of this Hall the propagation of the Law would have achieved realization.

As for myself, appearing before you today on this platform, I have nothing special to offer as my own interpretation of the Law. I merely join myself with all others —from the founder Shākya Tathāgata, the other Buddhas, bodhisattvas, saints and arhants, to all those here present, including patrons and officials, the very eaves and columns of this hall, lanterns and posts, as well as all the men, animals, plants and seeds in the boundless ocean of existence—to keep the Wheel of the Law in motion.[77]

Only when human beings purposively subdue the random "chatter" that afflicts their minds in every moment of the awakened state do they achieve the tranquillity that makes them most creative and induces an experience of unity with all nature, advises Zen Buddhist scholar and teacher Daisetz Suzuki.

MAN IS A THINKING REED but his great works are done when he is not calculating and thinking. "Childlikeness" has to be restored with long years of training in the art of self-forgetfulness. When this is attained, man thinks yet he does not think. He thinks like the showers coming down from the sky; he thinks like the waves rolling on the ocean; he thinks like the stars illuminating the nightly heavens; he thinks like the green foliage shooting forth in the relaxing spring breeze. Indeed, he is the showers, the ocean, the stars, the foliage.[78]

Masanobu Fukuoka provides a theory and practice of working with nature that is based on a transcendent perspective of the entire natural world order. Its source, he says, lies in the universal principle that "all is fundamentally one."[79] His explanation of nature as transcendent light comes closest to describing the real meaning of his natural way of being at large and at one in the universe.

NO WAY EXISTS to describe nature as it truly is. The best I could do would be to say that if one casts off everything, absolutely everything, from human thought, what emerges thereafter in one's soul—that indefinable something that one apprehends after having transcended even the light of which the *haiku* poet Bashō wrote in his poem: "Oh, how splendid! The sunlight on the young, green leaves"—that could be called nature. I believe that no better explanation is possible.[80]

Shōji Hamada, master potter and Living National Treasure of Japan, was fond of quoting a phrase of a Buddhist monk of the Tokugawa period (1600–1868) who said, "Not yet born means never die." "It's the same with Hamada, he's always being born," declared Hamada, on one occasion, in an illumined moment of playfulness and true clarity![81] Bernard Leach relates a conversation with Hamada in which the potter confesses that he did not begin to feel mature or authentic until well into his seventies.[82] In the following passage, Hamada discusses the vital forces at play in the creation of a pot. A symphony of unity with the universe itself emerges in this radiant expression of self-discovery.

> IT WAS NOT FROM MY MIND that it came but from my whole body; it emerged out of my middle, my lower abdomen. I have such a good feeling about having done this pot. . . . This work does not come out of my thought; rather I simply permit the movement that my hands have learned over many years. In fact, in the work forged by my body during sixty years, there is an unconscious revelation. I sense the work has become more comfortable. . . . I now hope that, rather than made things, born things will increase in my work.[83]

For forty years, Satomi Myōdō, a monk and pilgrim, wandered in search of the Way. In her spiritual autobiography, *Passionate Journey,* she describes an event that revealed to her "the real essence of Buddhism." In that moment of realization, she "found the door leading inside" to a state of oneness. In the following passage, Myōdō has returned home, pregnant, to her impoverished family farm in a mountain village in Hokkaido.

> ONE DAY I WENT AS USUAL to the fields, working and getting covered with dirt. From a distance, my father urgently called my name. I went to see what he wanted and

found Father squatting at the edge of the field, gazing intently at something. A moment passed. I felt a little strange squatting quietly by my father's side. Absently, my eye caught his line of vision. There was nothing but a single weed growing there. Softly, Father began to speak.

"I've been watching this for some time . . . it's quite interesting. . . . Look! A winged ant is crawling up the weed. It climbs up, little by little . . . it seems to want to reach the top. Oh, it fell! There—it's climbing again! For some time now it's been doing this over and over again." Just as he said, a winged ant was climbing up the weed and falling, falling and climbing up again.

"Here! Climbing again! Look, it must be tired now. When it's tired, it stretches its legs and beats its little wings up and down like that. That's how it restores its energy. Then, when it's rested, it starts climbing again."

Father continued to speak without taking his eyes off the brave little insect. I too inadvertently became intrigued. I stared at it intently for quite a while. Suddenly, it hit me—I understood what my father was getting at! It was unbearable! I quickly got up and left his side. I ran to the shady side of the field where no one could see me and fell down wailing. I cried and cried in anguish.

"Oh, Father, I understand; I really understand! Do you love me so much? I'm so unfilial! Do you still cherish such hope for me, when I am so disgusted with myself? How unworthy I am! But how grateful! I'm sorry! Oh, Father, from now on I promise to be a filial daughter! I promise to make you happy!" I determined to repay my father's love, no matter what. Just then, an iron shackle was broken and at once a broad expanse of light burst upon the world.

I have never known such a wonderful world as the one I experienced in that moment. I saw the grass and trees, the hills, river, fields, and stones, the hoe and sickle, the birds and dogs, the roofs and windows—all shining brightly under the same sun. For me it was a wonderful breath of fresh air. Both the animate and the inanimate were vividly alive, familiarly addressing me and waving their hands. Struck by the unearthly exquisiteness of this world, I broke into tears and lifted my face, weeping, in ecstasy. . . .[84]

Those who know the earth only through the fruits or blessings it imparts to them really do not know the earth. To
be familiar with the earth is to taste its sufferings. It does
not reveal its secrets merely by the raising and lowering of
the hoe. It does not make any criticism, yet it will take to
itself those who work upon it, if they are sincere and become one with it leaving their self-centeredness behind.
The earth hates deception. The farmer's simplicity and
honesty derive from his receiving the spirit of the earth.
Those absorbed in the explanations of old books know of
the earth's blessings and the taste of rice only conceptually.
The experience of Absolute Love through spiritual insight
cannot spring from such conceptual foundations. . . .

That the earth has political and economic significance goes
without saying. That by virtue of this the earth is man's
very body should also be comprehensible.

DAISETZ SUZUKI,
Zen Buddhist scholar and teacher[85]

THE SPIRIT OF EARTH/
THE SPIRIT OF LIFE

Daisetz T. Suzuki wrote *Japanese Spirituality* between trips to the air-raid shelter during some of the heaviest bombing of World War II. The book was published in 1944 and was directed to the Japanese at a time of growing doubt and despair, when humankind was experiencing uncertainty in the strivings of the soul. Suzuki, a Zen Buddhist scholar, wished to show his country its true unmilitary might, namely spirituality, as it existed in the history of Japanese religious thought. He uses the terms "religious consciousness" and "awakening" in addition to "spirituality" as he explores the spiritual foundations of Japanese culture. He writes that a "vital awareness" took root in Japan during the Kamakura period (1185–1333) when "the true significance of religious thought and faith and mood—in a word, spirituality—grew in all directions." "Its essence," he tells us, "exists in the earth."

Like another great Japanese teacher, Kaibara Ekken, Suzuki perceives the earth as a sustaining and affectionate mother—"this mother of all things"—and as a profound source of joy, which comes from contact with the natural world. The following passage from *Japanese Spirituality* soars with immense compassion for the good earth, as boundless love, a source of wisdom, and an enduring wellspring of life.

THE EARTH is where one experiences the blending of man and nature. He adds his power to that of the earth, and with industry harvests its products. It assists him in his work in proportion to his exertion. He is able to measure his own sincerity according to the degree he is helped by the earth. It does not falsify or cheat or delude, nor will it be deceived; it reflects man's heart as honestly as a mirror reflects his face. It does not hurry, knowing that summer can come only after spring. If the sown seed's season does not come, the sprout does not appear. Without the appearance of the leaf, the branch does not lengthen, the flower does not blossom, and therefore the fruit does not come forth and ripen. It does not disrupt this order in any way. Man learns from this the order of things, and is taught the need for patience. The earth is man's great educator and his great disciplinarian. How much of his own excellence he has attained because of it. . . .

The spirit of the earth is the spirit of life. This life always unfolds itself within the individual, who is a continuation of the earth—he has his roots there, there is where he appears, and there is where he returns. The spirit of the earth breathes at the inmost recesses of the individual, so that reality is ever present in him, sharing a pole in opposition to the world of ideas.[86]

Kunio Yanagita (1875–1962), poet and pioneer of ethnographic studies in Japan, documented the customs, beliefs, traditional tales and festivals of those he called the "unchanging people," the villagers of rural Japan; the social elite he left to others. He perceived the worlds of the "unchanging people" as the constants of his culture and he dedicated his life to observing, learning, and interpreting just how they held the country together. Yanagita believed that he just might begin to understand the *bases* of Japanese self-identity through the ways of the common people of his country. As he navigated this vast and unexplored field of the common folk of the provinces and the isolated mountain and island communities, he systematically explored the lifeways of not only the farmers and fishermen but also the outcast minorities or "itinerants" as he referred to them. At the time of Yanagita's extraordinary endeavor to enlighten Japanese culture to the fundamental nature of its own spirit through a sensitive examination of the treasures of the "unchanging people," the common people were scarcely thought of in Japanese society. This is what makes Yanagita's undertaking unique.

"The question that runs through all his work," writes cultural historian Shuichi Kato, is "what is it that basically underpins Japanese society when it is in flux."[87] The following passage from *About Our Ancestors,* written in the months of April and May 1945, during the tragic firebombing raids carried out over Tokyo, suggests some answers—one being that land, family and ancestors are indivisibly linked. The rice fields in particular were of an inherently spiritual nature, owing their existence to the divine beneficence of nature and the deity of agriculture on the one hand, and the watchful omnipresent ancestral spirits on the other. The rice-field deity *Ta-no-kami* (sometimes referred to as the agricultural deity *No-gami*) presided over the continuity of life, ensuring good yields when the prerequisite rites were carefully and faithfully observed.

ARABLE LAND was in principle safest property. There were many places which could conceive of no other foundation for a plan of living. Among them the farmer-developer, the man who turned the wilderness into gardens with his own strength, could continue to live well under good conditions without working too much, and even a tenant farmer who paid the usual land tax could feel easy about food and clothing if he were willing enough to work, and he could bring up his children in security. That is why from old times there was a common feeling among the upper and lower classes that land should be left to the family, and it is rooted deeply even today. . . .

There was a time when the sole basis for establishing a family was land holding. Rice fields were the necessary property for the continuance of the family, and without exception they formerly counted the generations of the family from the first reclamation or the inheritance of the land and not always from the origin of the lineage, and even now land and family are inseparable. We might say that all the efforts of ancestors for their descendants were identified with the effort they put into land. What we must take into consideration is that among the many crops on farms, the rice plant had special significance; that is to say, it had a spiritual character as something offered to the lord or emperor or deity on the one hand, and on the other, its production depended upon more than man's effort, its greater dependence in cultivation being upon sunlight and water. It was natural that many people believed that the souls of the ancestors who had provided the rice fields for the existence of the family were more concerned than anyone else in the success of the fields year after year and they would try to lend them their strong support. This is one of the bases for my supposition that the *Ta-no-kami* [rice field deity], sometimes called *No-gami* or *Saku-gami* [deity of agriculture], who has been excluded from Shinto studies and is always ignored regardless of its native origin, was identified as well as the *Toshi-no-kami* of New Year with the ancestral spirit worshipped in each family. . . .

[T]here is one matter about which we have given careful thought for a long time—the tradition that in the spring the *Yama-no-kami* [mountain deity] descends to the farming settlements and becomes the *Ta-no-kami* and ascends again into the mountains at the end of autumn to become *Yama-no-kami* once more—which may not seem to amount to much, but it is found throughout the land from the farthest north to the farthest south, places in which the belief is not transmitted being scarce, and that it is so wide-spread makes it a fact of great importance, although there are many people who have not yet taken notice of it. . . .

If there was an idea that instead of crossing into the Buddhist Paradise, the souls of our ancestors remain in a quiet, calm place in our land to return at a fixed time each year, then instead of in early autumn when the rice stalks are starting to flower, would not that time be when men are preparing to plant rice seed beds and their hearts are sensitive as they hopefully await the return of the *Kami*. . . .

I hesitate to mention the names of . . . mountains to which men and women in fields at rice planting look up together, singing songs in praise of them as places in which the *Ta-no-kami* lodges, the deity who is deeply concerned about the fertility of the fields. The protector of the farmer who descends and ascends is their mutual ancestor of long ago, and formerly the faith was more clearly held than now that it would continue forever to protect the original holdings of the family. . . .

Japan is a land of *Kami*. . . . [T]here is certainly a faith among our people, unchanged from long ago, that spirits remain in our land and are trying slowly to attain the position of our national deities. The time has come when we must understand that fact more clearly instead of regarding it as groundless legend.[88]

When he parts from the land, man is no longer able to maintain the stability of the heart.[89]

The ultimate goal of farming is not the growing of crops, but the cultivation and perfection of human beings.[90]

[A]n agriculture joining animals, crops, and human beings into one body existed as the mainstream of Japanese farming up to modern times.[91]

MASANOBU FUKUOKA,
visionary, farmer and poet

One of Japan's most visionary and, indeed, revolutionary figures is Masanobu Fukuoka—farmer, author, philosopher and microbiologist. Acclaimed as a "modern-day Lao-tzu" by fellow Japanese for his paradoxical wisdom, Fukuoka reaches back to the source of agrarian traditions for guidance, inspiration and truth. He has written that the inevitable "revival of nature means more than just returning to the beginning; it means nature creating a new nature." At the same time he maintains that "the ultimate aim of my natural farming that returns to nature is the freeing of the human spirit."[92]

Born in a small farming village on the island of Shikoku in southern Japan in 1913, Masanobu Fukuoka was trained in microbiology as a plant pathologist and then worked for several years as an agricultural customs inspector, running tests on incoming and outgoing plants at the port of Yokohama. Then rather suddenly, at age twenty-five, he experienced a *metanoia*. He began to question everything and doubt all he had ever learned about the "wonders" of modern agricultural science. This awakening led to the gradual development of a "new way" of farming as a spiritual path.

Fukuoka suggests that people do not have a clear idea of what is natural and what is not and insists that "the road of true man is an inner road. It cannot be followed by advancing outward."[93] To follow the path of natural farming, he says, "one must tear the robes of human action from nature and remove the innermost garments of subjectivity."[94] This rare, gentle and beguiling man once said "natural farming is the only future for man."[95] He attributes this knowledge and faith to an earnest lifelong search for the wellsprings of agriculture and therefore of the human spirit. His extraordinary crops —rice, barley, and mandarin oranges—are testimony to the efficacy of his beliefs. Fukuoka does not plough his fields, nor use chemical fertilizers, herbicides or compost; nonetheless, his results have confounded and astounded both scientist and farmer alike. His impossibly high yields have brought visitors from all over the world to his eight acres of mandarin grove and one-and-a-half-acre paddy field overlooking the Inland Sea.

In a rare moment of reflection about his life, Fukuoka has written:

> I AM FORTUNATE TO HAVE GROWN RICE AND BARLEY. Only to him who stands where the barley stands, and listens well, will it speak and tell, for his sake, what man is.
>
> As I look out now at the ripening head of barley standing golden before me under the sunny May sky, I recall the words of a young visitor from a southern island. After seeing this barley, he left, saying, "I have felt the awesome energy of the earth. What more can I say?"
>
> On the same day, a university professor told me, "It's best to keep philosophy and religion out of the world of science." If the barley had heard, it probably would have answered, "Don't bring science into the world of barley."[96]

The Japanese people have long been fond of calling their country the Land of Ripening Grain, states Masanobu Fukuoka. "Rice cultivation," he says, "held a deeper meaning for farmers than simply the growing of a staple food crop. The farmer did not grow the rice, nature did; and the people born to this land partook of its blessings. The words 'Bountiful Land of Ripening Grain' expressed the joy of the Yamato people [of ancient Japan], who were able to receive the rich blessings of heaven and earth with a grateful heart."[97]

Today, after nearly fifty years of "wander[ing] about in search of nature"[98] and living only in farming, Fukuoka believes his path to natural farming is a first step toward the restoration of nature and a regeneration of the human spirit. "Man's true joy and delight was natural ecstasy," remarks Fukuoka, and "[t]his exists only in nature."[99]

> LEANING AGAINST THE LONG HANDLE OF MY SCYTHE, I pause in my work in the orchard and gaze out at the mountains and the village below. I wonder how it is that people's philosophies have come to spin faster than the changing seasons.
>
> The path I have followed, this natural way of farming, which strikes most people as strange, was first interpreted as a reaction against the advance and reckless development

of science. But all I have been doing, farming out here in the country, is trying to show that humanity knows nothing. Because the world is moving with such furious energy in the opposite direction it may appear that I have fallen behind the times, but I firmly believe that the path I have been following is the most sensible one. . . .

To grow crops in an unplowed field may seem at first a regression to primitive agriculture, but over the years this method has been shown in university laboratories and agricultural testing centers across the country to be the most simple, efficient, and up-to-date method of all. Although this way of farming disavows modern agricultural development, it now has come to stand in the forefront of modern agricultural development. . . .

Now suddenly it is a completely different story. You might say that natural farming has become the rage. Journalists, professors, and technical researchers are flocking to visit my fields and the huts up on the mountain. . . . Few are able to grasp correctly that natural farming arises from the unmoving and unchanging center of agricultural development.

To the extent that people separate themselves from nature, they spin out further and further from the center. At the same time, a centripetal effect asserts itself and the desire to return to nature arises. But if people merely become caught up in reacting, moving to the left or to the right, depending on conditions, the result is only more activity. The non-moving point of origin, which lies outside the realm of relativity, is passed over, unnoticed. I believe that even "returning-to-nature" and anti-pollution activities, no matter how commendable, are not moving toward a genuine solution if they are carried out solely in reaction to the overdevelopment of the present age.

Nature does not change, although the way of viewing nature invariably changes from age to age. No matter the age, natural farming exists forever as the wellspring of agriculture.

My fields may be the only ones in Japan which have not been plowed for over twenty years [now forty], and the quality of the soil improves with each season. . . . By spreading straw, growing clover, and returning to the soil all organic residues, the earth comes to possess all the nutrients needed to grow rice and winter grain in the same field year after year. By natural farming, fields that have already been damaged by cultivation or the use of agricultural chemicals can be effectively rehabilitated. . . .

In olden times there were warriors, farmers, craftsmen, and merchants. Agriculture was said to be closer to the source of things than trade or manufacturing, and the farmer was said to be "the cupbearer of the gods."[100]

Takashi Nagatsuka's novel *Earth* is an evocation of rural Japan in the early 1900s. It appeared around the time when urban Japanese intellectuals were awakening to the extreme disparities between rich and poor. While the novel describes the living conditions of poor peasants—not sparing us the details of their superstitions, cunning, vulgarity and greed—it also contains exceptional observations about the natural world that are engrossing in their beauty.

SPRING GRADUALLY BEGINS TO QUICKEN, both in the heavens and the earth. The westerly gale that has been stirring up dust almost every day somehow suddenly drops. Cotton-like clouds stay hanging where the heavens and the earth meet, having risen, as it were, from the earth in order to bask in the warm sun. The wet soil near the water absorbs the warm sun to the full. The soil conveys the subtle stimulus of its animated life to the roots of alders at the edge of rice fields. Their somber-colored flowers in bud grow imperceptively longer, ready to flutter in the wind. Stimulated by the warmth of the soil, frogs, still hiding in the earth, begin to croak here and there. The sunshine showering from the sky gradually gets warmer and the earth never tires of absorbing its warmth. The earth stimulates every plant slowly, and at the edge of a channel, ditch reeds and *todashiba* and other grasses stick up straight towards the heavens, their green in harmony with the blue of the sky. The flowers of alders flutter incessantly and spread their soot-like pollen, thus making the soft balmy air even hazier. Frogs, woken from hibernation, sit up on the soft grass and cast their stupefied looks up toward the sky. They release their croaking sounds in a flurry to tell the heavens that they have woken from their long sleep.

Heard in the distance their noisy croaking vibrates in the heavens and seems to indicate their pleasure.

The frogs endeavor to inform every creature of the arrival of spring. They never cease croaking until the grasses and trees, aware of its arrival, quicken with new growth. The alders have already dropped their flowers and have put out fresh green leaves. Under the blue sky their yellowish young leaves, bathed in the invigorating and cheerful morning sun and shining with a pleasant lustre, look towards the still hesitant groves about them. The trees of the groves that surround the rice fields extending like a headland assert their individuality by putting out whitish, reddish or yellowish leaves according to their nature, and then when spring advances they remember hurriedly to merge into one deep green. Barley and wheat in the coppice clearings here and there thrust their heads up straight. The flowers of broad beans show their pretty black eyes and peep around from behind the leaves shyly. In the coppices cogongrasses also thrust their hard leaves upright into the sky. Skylarks, sheltered in wheat and barley fields and at the foot of cogongrasses, sometimes monopolize the heavens and tell the world of the advancing spring. Then frogs, thinking the voices of their tribe should fill the air, croak even louder, jumping upon one another, to overpower the sounds of larks. The larks, outnumbered, descend and take shelter at the foot of barley plants and cogongrasses. And only during the day when the croaking ceases, do the larks, as if to avoid being dazzled, disappear in the glaring light far above, and sing till their throats almost burst. The frogs croak triumphantly and are never content until their voices seem to shake the old leaves off trees such as big evergreen oaks all at once.

At this time of year the trees and weeds that lay flat on the earth during the winter, stretch on tiptoe towards the sky, yearning for warm light. The earth has a firm hold on them and never lets go, so that the plants form a right angle to the ground. . . .

Trees and plants grow during the night, cradled by the lullaby of croaking frogs which try to make their voices reach everywhere. *Kunugi* and Japanese oaks and other trees in the coppices never cease to grow thicker and leafier as long as the frogs continue croaking. In coppices hairy caterpillars and other noxious insects sometimes devastate the fresh leaves. Yet the new leaves are as deeply green as if the rain drizzling upon the treetops had transferred the blue of the sky to them, overshadowing the ground and shedding a cool and refreshing shade.[101]

Over the course of eight years, Dr. Junichi Saga, a general practitioner, recorded the stories of sixty old men and women from his hometown of Tsuchiura, which lies forty miles northeast of Tokyo. Every day after finishing work in his clinic, with his portable tape recorder in his medical bag, he would go on foot to visit the elderly. He talked to people from all walks of life: tradesmen, fishermen, yakuza (gangsters), geisha, day laborers and farmers. Dr. Saga discovered that the people of his village, through their attitudes and experiences, "provided the sole surviving links with the feudal period which ended with the overthrow of the last shogun in 1868."[102] The reminiscences of these old people reveal something about modern Japan that not even the Japanese themselves understand, says Dr. Saga. "The Japan which now prides itself on being an advanced high-technology nation," he writes, "had, until only recently, a very different type of society; and that indeed it was this very society, backward though it may have been, which created the basis for what Japan has become today."[103]

Mr. Takamasa Sakurai (1903–   ), a fisherman and one of Dr. Saga's interviewees, gives us a sense of what it must have felt like to be growing up on the shores of Lake Kasumigaura—the second largest freshwater lake in Japan and bordering the town of Tsuchiura—nearly a hundred years ago. Knowing the lake was indispensable to the survival of any fisherman.

> IT WAS IMPORTANT TO GET A FEEL FOR THE LAKE while you were still young. If you wanted to survive, you had to be able to recognize the telltale signs of danger and know what to do in a difficult situation. My parents drummed these sorts of lessons into me day after day until I could feel their advice oozing out of my ears. The old fishermen knew the lake like the backs of their hands and they'd happily go on fishing even in the strongest winds—it was almost unheard of for a fisherman to drown. The only people who ever died in the lake were the ones who didn't realize how deadly it could be. . . .

To take just one example: at the beginning of winter, rather peculiar clouds—dark and fast-moving—used to pass over Mt. Tsukuba, and if you looked carefully at the way they moved, you could roughly judge the speed of the wind on the lake and predict how the weather would change. I mean, there'd be days when the sky overhead was clear and blue, and the fishermen would look at the clouds over the mountain and reckon it was wiser to head for home. . . .

The fishermen had so much confidence in their own forecasting they even ignored typhoon warnings on the radio and went out fishing. "With a cloud formation like that, we won't get a typhoon," they'd say. And they were never wrong, either.

We also reckoned you could tell the weather by listening to the sound of the sea in the distance. If you could hear the waves off Kashima to the north, you knew a storm was on its way. . . . And then all of a sudden we'd hear the distant roaring of the sea from the far shore of the lake. If the sound came from the northeast we knew the weather would turn bad, but if it was from the southeast, even though there might be a few spots of rain, we could be sure it'd clear up after a while.

My grandfather told me I should think of the lake as a pot of boiling water: if I ever fell in I wouldn't have a chance. This, particularly in winter, meant that fishermen always kept a sharp eye on the weather before deciding to take the boats out. And as far as I can remember there were only two fatal accidents on the lake.[104]

RAPE-FLOWERS EVERYWHERE
RAPE-FLOWERS EVERYWHERE
RAPE-FLOWERS EVERYWHERE
RAPE-FLOWERS EVERYWHERE
RAPE-FLOWERS EVERYWHERE
RAPE-FLOWERS EVERYWHERE
RAPE-FLOWERS EVERYWHERE
FAINT FLUTING WITH A WHEAT-BLADE
RAPE-FLOWERS EVERYWHERE.

RAPE-FLOWERS EVERYWHERE
RAPE-FLOWERS EVERYWHERE
RAPE-FLOWERS EVERYWHERE
RAPE-FLOWERS EVERYWHERE
RAPE-FLOWERS EVERYWHERE
RAPE-FLOWERS EVERYWHERE
RAPE-FLOWERS EVERYWHERE
AND THE BABBLE OF SKYLARKS
RAPE-FLOWERS EVERYWHERE.

RAPE-FLOWERS EVERYWHERE
RAPE-FLOWERS EVERYWHERE
RAPE-FLOWERS EVERYWHERE
RAPE-FLOWERS EVERYWHERE
RAPE-FLOWERS EVERYWHERE
RAPE-FLOWERS EVERYWHERE
RAPE-FLOWERS EVERYWHERE
AND THE DAY-MOON AILING
RAPE-FLOWERS EVERYWHERE.

BOCHŌ YAMAMURA
(1884–1924),
poet,
"Landscape"[105]

The beautiful landscape
   as we know
      belongs to those who are like it.

MUSO SOSEKI (1275–1351),
Zen monk and poet[106]

Landscape: what you see in yourself.
Self-portrait: how you want others to see you.
Figure: better to talk to than to draw.
Still life: something that moves too fast to capture.

KAZUAKI TANAHASHI,
Zen painter, calligrapher
and teacher[107]

We are a landscape of all we have seen.

ISAMU NOGUCHI,
sculptor and designer
of gardens[108]

Tawaraya Sotatsu (1614–ca. 1639), *Waves at Matsushima*, Japan. Edo Period. A section from a pair of sixfold screens portraying a famous scenic spot in Miyagi Prefecture in northeastern Japan.

I like the gardens designed long ago by the great Zen teacher Muso [Muso Soseki (1275–1351)]. Take his name, Muso. "Mu" means "dream" in English and "so" means "window." Muso's name is very evocative to me. Dreams are interior, inward looking, while windows open outward. They are two different kinds of energy. The gardens Muso designed have a good deal of this tension about them. Of course, no matter what genius may have designed a garden, it's a living thing and time re-makes it. The garden at Saiho-ji for instance. There was originally no moss in the garden. Now there's so much we call it the Moss Temple. Muso seems to have allowed for the changes that time would bring.

Toru Takemitsu,
composer[109]

Within its limits, the Japanese garden swims. It works, it navigates, it floats within the imagination of the people who experience it . . . Can we really re-create nature or do we go on and do something other?

Isamu Noguchi[110]

GARDENS OF
THE HUMAN SPIRIT

J apanese gardens exemplify a view of being. They are visions of existence intended to transcend time. Not merely decorative landscapes or objects of human use, gardens are conceived of paths into the realm of the human spirit. In the words of Japanese poet Makoto Ooka, "gardens are designed to create a mood; some to bring one into a state of poetic creativity."[111] The temple, the teahouse and the garden (the fundamental components of many gardens) are treated as one. In fact, the 17th century Shugaku-In imperial garden at Kyoto is called the Teahouse. Thus boundaries between nature (in the case of a garden an idealized configuration of nature), religious observance and architecture are indeterminate as are the boundaries between sculpture, painting, architecture, spiritual practice and the natural world.

Muso Soseki (1275–1351), poet, painter, calligrapher, designer of famous gardens (some of which are still in existence, including the gardens at Saiho-ji in Kyoto, Zuisen-ji and Kencho-ji at Kamakura, Rinsen-ji near Kyoto, and Tenryu-ji at Kyoto), Zen monk and revered National Teacher, lays out some of his teachings on the Way and Gardens in *Dialogues in the Dream*. The three-volume collection of his writings was assembled by his students, who numbered some 13,145, according to a recorded figure of his time. Counted among them were monks, nuns, laity and seven emperors. Muso describes the different impulses by which individuals are led in their approach to gardens. He perceives the realm of gardens as an entry point into "the spirit of the Way."

> FROM ANCIENT TIMES until now there have been many who have delighted in raising up mounds of earth, making arrangements of stones, planting trees, and hollowing out watercourses. We call what they make "mountains and streams." Though all seem to share a common liking for

this art of gardening, they are often guided by very different impulses.

There are those who practice the art of gardening out of vanity and a passion for display, with no interest whatever in their own true natures. They are concerned only with having their gardens attract the admiration of others.

And some, indulging their passion for acquiring things, add these "mountains and streams" to the accumulation of rare and expensive things that they possess, and end up by cherishing a passion for them. They select particularly remarkable stones and uncommon trees to have for their own. Such persons are insensible to the beauty of mountains and streams. They are merely people of the world of dust.

Po Lo-t'ien dug a little pool beside which he planted a few bamboos, which he cared for with love. He wrote a poem about them:

> *The bamboo—its heart is empty.*
> *It has become my friend.*
> *The water—its heart is pure.*
> *It has become my teacher.*

Those everywhere who love mountains and rivers have the same heart as Lo-t'ien and know the way out of the dust of the world. Some whose nature is simple are not attracted by worldly things and they raise their spirits by reciting poems in the presence of fountains and rocks. The expression "a chronic liking for mist, incurably stricken by fountains and rocks" tells something about them. One might say that these are secular people of refined taste. Though they are in the world and without the spirit of the Way, this love of the art of gardens is nevertheless a root of transformation.

In others there is a spirit that comes awake in the presence of these mountains and rivers and is drawn out of the dullness of daily existence. And so these mountains and rivers help them in the practice of the Way. Theirs is not the usual love of mountains and rivers. These people are worthy of respect. But they cannot yet claim to be followers of the true Way because they still make a distinction between mountains and rivers and the practice of the Way.

Still others see the mountain, the river, the earth, the grass, the tree, the tile, the pebble, as their own essential nature. They love, for the length of a morning, the mountain and the river. What appears in them to be no different from a worldly passion is at once the spirit of the Way. Their minds are one with the atmosphere of the fountain, the stone, the grass, and the tree, changing through the four seasons. This is the true manner in which those who are followers of the Way love mountains and rivers.

So one cannot say categorically that a liking for mountains and rivers is a bad thing or a good thing. There is neither gain nor loss in the mountain and the river. Gain and loss exist only in the human mind.[112]

Toru Takemitsu, a Japanese composer, creates the kind of music that embodies all the crucial elements of a Japanese garden. Tension *and* harmony are one facet of his unique orchestration of the echoes and shapes of Nature and the syncopation of her vast spatial, auditory and timeless realm.

MORE THAN BEING AN INFLUENCE on my work, gardens give me energy. They provide a kind of self-affirmation. What I like most about gardens is that they don't exclude people, just as music mustn't exclude people . . .

I'm a composer and music is often called the art of time. On the other hand, gardens are constructions of space. But when I am in a garden what impresses me most are the layers of time. Various kinds and qualities of time form layers. They accumulate. Rocks hardly change at all. They're a stable presence. The plants change with the seasons. They come and go. They die away. I try and work these elements into an orchestra—parts that change quickly, others that don't change at all, like the rocks. Enveloping it all is the earth and the sky; and sometimes it rains. So really what I do, I design gardens with music.[113]

Sobin Yamada, abbot of the Shinju-an temple at Daitoku-ji in

Kyoto, describes the synchronous nature of the Japanese garden where, ideally, mind, spirit, universe and nature coalesce into a unified experience of creation.

ONE SHOULD JUST SIT QUIETLY and look at a garden. What you see depends on what you bring to it. When we meditate we can't separate ourselves from Nature. It's very important. The entire universe is concentrated in a garden. The garden allows us to contemplate, to become one part of Nature. For our approach is based on these things.

In Zen we don't look outside for God or Buddha. They are within us. Where we live is the Buddha's realm, the world of the gods. That's why it must be clean and beautiful; why we work to keep it from getting soiled. We think of *this* world as the Buddha's realm. Paradise is where we live so we clean it and keep it beautiful. This is the most important principle. That's why we tend our gardens so carefully and treat them with such artistry.[114]

Riverbanks lined with
    green willows, fragrant
    grasses:
A place not sacred?
Where?

Sayings of the Masters[115]

Katusushika Hokusai (1760–1849), *The Great Wave off Kanagawa*, with Mount Fuji in the background. Edo period.

A burst of laughter
in that wild movement of
the rising waves *and*
wind. . . .

"Ballad from Aikawa,"
Japanese folk song[116]

On the great sea of truth unsullied,
How brightly the moon of pure insight shines!

BODHISATTVA FUGEN[117]

THE LANDSCAPE
OF THE SEA

In *Kugai Jodo,* Michiko Ishimure has written a riveting account of the landscape of the sea, with its vast and magnificent array of living forms and fluctuating oceanic energies. She approaches the heart of the marine world, metaphorically, through an unforgettable description of the symptoms of a grossly disfiguring disease that shocked the world when it first became known to the public in the the 1960s.

With compassion, Ishimure tracks the inner and outer worlds of a fictional character named Sakagami Yuki, a fine fisherman who is struck down in midlife by Minamata disease, caused by the irresponsible disposal of industrial refuse. The disease is named after the city in Japan where it was first documented. It is the direct result of eating fish that has been severely contaminated by methyl mercury compounds from factory wastes.

Ishimure, herself a native of Minamata, moves as a cartographer would. With keen observance she maps the psyche of Yuki, who begins to recognize the inevitable physical separation she must face from the life-giving forces of the sea. Nonetheless, when Yuki speaks she does so as an indivisible part of the sea world and its wonderful creatures. What we come to understand is that the creative and sustaining force of nature itself is imprinted upon the body, mind and heart of Yuki in all her agony, in all her courage, in a myriad of halting words.

> "IT WAS GOOD, WORKING OUT ON THE SEA. My husband would pull on the main oar, and me on the side one. We would row out to pull up our cuttlefish baskets and octopus pots. Grey mullets—those fish, and octopuses— they're lovely. From April to October it was always very calm off Lion Island. . . ."
>
> Yuki knew by instinct where there were lots of fish to be found. She would navigate the boat to such a place,

stop rowing, and look down into the deep forests of sea-weed. Then she would address the fish: "Ahoy there! Here we are again!" Fishermen often talk to the fish like this; but as she was from Amakusa, Yuki knew how to call to them in a specially cheerful and kindly way. The sea and Yuki would seem to be lulling the boat, so that Mohei [Yuki's husband] would feel as if he were a child being rocked asleep. . . .

"The sea is like my own garden. The good-luck god Ebisu is kindly disposed to a boat rowed by a woman. . . .

"It was really lovely, working out at sea. Those damned cuttlefish though are mean devils, and when we catch them, they spurt their ink; but the octopuses are very loveable. We would pull up a pot and find an octopus that didn't want to come out, his feelers gripping the bottom of the pot and rolling his eyes at me. 'Hey, you,' I would shout, 'you've got to come out now you've been pulled into the boat. Get a move on. Come on out!' That's the way I used to talk to them, but sometimes he still wouldn't come out. . . . We feel a deep love for the things of the sea—even for the fish we are going to eat. Oh, it was lovely in those days.

"—We've had to sell the boat, now.

"When I was in the University Hospital, I kept think-ing only of the boat whenever it was windy or raining. My husband hoisted a flag on her and launched the boat when we were married. It's like our own child. You know how much care I took of that boat? I would mop the whole body of the boat clean. Between the fishing seasons, I would pull up all the octopus pots. I would scrape all the oyster shells and barnacles and weeds off the outsides of the pots and pile them in a hole in the rocks so they would be out of the rain. The pots are their houses. I wanted to make their houses clean for them. . . . [W]hat I think about most often are the things of the sea. It was so wonderful to be out working on the sea.

"In the sea, all kinds of flowers bloom in spring and summer. Our sea was very beautiful once. There are some famous places in the sea, just as on land—'Teacup Point,' 'Naked Rapids,' 'Dark Rapids,' 'Lion Island' and so on. When we go round these places, the scent of the sea in early summer is something overwhelming even for us. The smell is different from the factory the poisoned water comes from. The sea water is like flowing streams. Where the water flows slowly, there are acorn shells, sea anemones, sea pines all swaying like flowers in the sea. The fish especially are beautiful. The sea anemones are like full-blown chrysanthemums. The sea pines grow on the shoulder of a hill under the water and their beautiful branches are like stairways. The spindle-shaped bladder leaves look like weeping willows. The seaweeds stir like bamboo forests. The landscapes in the sea change from season to season just as they do on land. I believe in the legend of the Dragon's Palace at the bottom of the sea. The world under the water is beautiful as a dream. I have never tired of being on the sea. Even the smallest islet has somewhere a fissure in the rock under the water which often gives a spring of pure fresh water. Where the pure water flowing from such a spring and strong sea-water meet, you find good sea-lettuce just before springtime. Among the various scents of the sea, I miss most of all that of dark *aosa*— sea-lettuce—warmed by the sun when the water has ebbed. . . .

"I want to have two strong legs firmly supporting my body. I want to have two strong hands on my body. With those two hands I want to row my own boat and go to collect fresh sea-lettuce.

"I feel like crying. I want so much to go back to sea again."[118]

A deep emotional affinity with nature in Japanese thinking serves as a ground for being and a basis for interspecies awareness. This intuitive attitude that predominates in much of Japanese philosophy is frequently summarized by Japanese scholars in the famous dictum *mono no aware*, "sensitivity to things."[119]

Yoshiro Kunimoto describes an intense sense of intimacy which the Japanese experience with the creatures of their sea world. It is wedded to seasonal changes and is emotionally and spiritually sustained through Japanese art and literature.

FISH, FOR THE JAPANESE, is not simply food. It has delicate ties with the traditional spiritual life of the Japanese race. The seasons in Japan are not clear-cut. They go through one continuous chain of diverse changes. Fishing, as in the case of farming, is closely linked to the seasons and has helped foster a sense of the seasonal changes unique to Japan. This sense of seasonal change forms the basis of the aesthetics that are evident in the traditional life, the arts and the literature of the Japanese people. Each type of fish that can be caught in the seas surrounding Japan has its own season or time of the year when it tastes the best. This period is known as the *shun* of that type of fish. Because of the increasing dissemination of frozen fish on the Japanese market, the traditional feeling of the Japanese people of treasuring these *shun* periods of various fish is gradually being lost. However, the vestiges of this feeling still have deep and strong roots. The vast schools of herring that at one time churned through the waters of the northern seas from the end of February until early April used to be called *harutsuge uo,* the spring heralding fish. The bonito that can be caught in the season of fresh new verdure is greeted with joy as the harbinger of early summer with all its pleasant greenery. The mackerel-pike caught around the end of September is called the "autumn fish that is shaped like a sword," while the Chinese character for *tara* (the codfish) that can be caught in winter is composed of the characters for "snow" and "fish." In addition, lobsters and shrimps, sea bream, carp and dried squid are regarded as auspicious and are used on festive occasions.

In this way, fish play a special role in the daily life of the Japanese people in a manner unparalleled in any other country.[120]

On the island of Ishigaki, near the southernmost tip of the Okinawan island chain, the fate of a village and its coral reef have become intertwined. The people of the village of Shiraho and their way of life are inextricably tied to the living systems of the coral reef, both physically and spiritually. The spiritual connection to the coral reef is reflected in the names they give to it, ranging from *Sakana Waku Umi* ("Fountain of Fish") and *Umi No Hatake* ("Sea Fields") to *Inochi Tokeau Umi* ("Life Uniting Sea"). The largest stands in the world of rare blue coral grow here. A new airport site has threatened the delicate health and diversity of the coral. This sacred treasure of the sea supports a variety of life, including the villagers. Seaweed, algae, fish and shellfish from the reef provide many of life's necessities. Handwoven cloths are colored with dyes derived from the coral. Setsuko Yamazato, a silk weaver from Shiraho, cannot imagine a meaningful life without these sacred reefs.

> ON THIS ISLAND, the eastern sea is seen as fulfilling our dreams for the future. The goodness of the sea blesses us with many different good things, such as fish, sea weeds, and many other living things. And the coral reef is extremely valuable as a place where fish and other life are born and raised. And then, the coral reef protects the island from rough seas, typhoons, and tidal waves. If these coral reefs die out, the heart of our lives will be damaged.[121]

I will sing the praises
Of this exalted peak
As long as I have breath.

AKAHITO YAMABÉ,
8th-century poet,
expressing reverence
for Mount Fuji[122]

I went to China with the thought of receiving instructions
from masters, yet I found no masters but the mountains
and waters of China.

SESSHU (1420–1506),
Zen seer and artist[123]

You climb
Mount Hiei
on ladders of cloud

MUSO SOSEKI (1275–1351),
Zen monk and poet[124]

According to the world view of the Japanese mountain
religions, the mountains were where the gods (kami) were
in attendance; a beautiful mountain was called a kan'nabi
(god's mountain). Usually a stone sacred area was con-
structed on it and called iwasaki *(divine throne); the ap-*
propriate gods attended the rites.

YASUO YUASA,
writer and scholar[125]

MOUNTAINS:
OF ENLIGHTENMENT,
OF INDIFFERENCE,
OF COMPASSION

For the Japanese, the mountain *is* sacred; and Mount Fuji is magnificent in its sacredness. In the words of one of Japan's great portrayers of Fuji *(One Hundred Views of Mt. Fuji)*, Hokusai (1760–1849), the mountain is "peerless."[126] Hokusai perceived Mount Fuji as the realm of the Immortals and actively sought admission into its life-giving heart. He came to understand that the incomparable Fuji preceded itself! Fuji scholar Royall Tyler reports that once while traversing a Japanese mountain trail he encountered a sign that read: "I am in the mountains, the mountains are in me. Am I the mountains? Are the mountains myself?"[127] There are human counterparts to the mountain form; according to Roy Andrew Miller: "A mountain has a *chūfuku*, a "midbelly," and it has *suso*, "skirts."[128] Of paramount importance, moreover, is the mountain's capacity to radiate boundless love, and it does this through *zenjō*, or *samādhi*, which is perfect meditation, explains Miller.[129] In other words, the exalted peak is the state of perfection.

The exquisite, fragile beauty, rare dignity and perfection of form of splendid Fuji, "a god mysterious,"[130] has been acknowledged through the ages. At 12,385 feet, Fuji is by far the highest mountain in Japan (about 20 percent higher than its nearest rivals). It is a volcano of celestial proportion. It is also an aspired and transcendent state of being. Poetry and art have celebrated Mount Fuji for hundreds of years. These lines by poet and monk Akahito Yamabé, from Japan's first collection of poetry, the eighth-century *Manyōshū* of the Nara period (710–794), written when the volcano was still active, express what countless people have felt about the divine and inspired nature of this "pillar of the cosmos."[131]

> *Ever since heaven and earth were parted,*
> *It has towered lofty, noble, divine,*
> *Mount Fuji in Suruga!*

When we look up to the plains of heaven,
The light of the sky-traversing sun is shaded,
The gleam of the shining moon is not seen,
White clouds dare not cross it,
And for ever it snows.

We shall tell of it from mouth to mouth
O the lofty mountain of Fuji!
When going forth I look far from the shore of Tago,
How white and glittering is
The lofty Peak of Fuji,
Crowned with Snows![132]

Born to a noble family in Kyoto, Zen master and teacher Kigen Dōgen (1200–1253) was a revered figure of formidable intelligence. As the esteemed founder of the Sōtō Zen school in Japan, Dōgen's treatment and teaching of the nature of knowledge featured a technique that he himself described as "presenting sideways and using upside down" to break up and shake up the resisting "nest of cliché"; in other words, any stereotyped, traditional view.[133] In 1225, while advancing his learning and meditation in China with his last teacher, Zen master Nyojo, Dōgen experienced a *metanoia,* an awakening of great magnitude, when early one morning he overheard his master scolding a dozing monk with the words "Zen study requires the shedding of body and mind."[134] Within two years, Dōgen would return to Japan to begin his own transmission of Zen wisdom.

In his lifelong pursuit of perennial truths and their fundamental unity, Dōgen turned again and again to the mountains for re-collection, re-memberment and retrieval of what he called the "original face."[135] He confides that his profound love of mountains increased with age. He sought out their transforming powers and surrendered to their impossible compelling force and beauty. In his essay "The Scripture of Mountains and Waters" (from *Shōbōgenzō*), mountains as symbolic manifestations of the Path point up the Way to a fully realized life.

MOUNTAINS HAVE BEEN THE DWELLING PLACE of great sages since beyond the past and beyond the present. Wise people and holy people both have made mountains their inner sanctum, have made mountains their body and mind; due to the wise and holy people, mountains have become manifest. Though it seems that so many great saints and great sages have gone into the mountains and gathered there, after having entered the mountains, there is not a single person who has met a single person—it is only a manifestation of the livelihood of the mountains. There are no further traces even of having entered. . . .

Though mountains belong to the territory of the nation, they are entrusted to people who love the mountains. When mountains definitely love the "owners," saints, sages, and those of exalted virtue are in the mountains. When saints and sages live in the mountains, because the mountains belong to them, *the trees and rocks are abundant, the birds and beasts are holy.* This is because the saints and sages affect them with their virtue. You should know that the fact exists that mountains like sages and saints. . . .

Shakyamuni Buddha left the palace of his father the raja and went into the mountains, but his father didn't resent the mountains, nor did he suspect the people in the mountains who taught his son. Most of the Buddha's twelve years of training were in the mountains. The beginning of his teaching was also in the mountains. Truly even a supreme ruler doesn't coerce the mountains. Know that the *mountains* are not the realm of human society, not the realm of heavens. One cannot know or see the *mountains* by the measurements of human thought. If they did not take the flowing of the human world as the standard of comparison, who would doubt the *flowing of the mountains* or the *nonflowing of mountains?*[136]

Mountaintops as centers of learning and culture are woven into the fabric of Japanese society. The story of the monk Saichō (767–822) provides a context for the genesis of this treasured tradition. One day in the seventh moon of 788, in the words of one scholar, Saichō made his way up the side of Mount Hiei with the intention of establishing a very small "temple." By the year 1571, Saichō's humble desire had mushroomed into a 3,000-temple complex, which at that time was completely demolished by a mercurial military leader. Nonetheless, for nearly 800 years, Saichō's little temple had flourished as the heart of culture for an entire nation.

This was the song of prayer Saichō composed as he climbed to the mountaintop.

O Buddhas
Of unexcelled complete enlightenment
Bestow your invisible aid
Upon this hut I open
On the mountain top.[137]

According to Professor Hitoshi Takeuchi at Tokyo University, the present Mount Fuji is not that old. It was formed, he says, "as a result of a third volcanic eruption [and] is approximately 10,000 years old. It covers an older Mount Fuji, called Ko-fuji in Japanese. This second Mount Fuji was active about 50,000 to 60,000 years ago. Under this second Mount Fuji we have the original mountain, which was known as Mount Komitake. This first volcanic mountain was active 500,000 to 600,000 years ago."[138] It has been recorded that since the Heian period in Japanese history (794–1185) Mount Fuji has erupted as many as fourteen times. The last volcanic quake occurred in 1707, creating a hump on Fuji's right side, and producing a parasitic volcano that has come to be known as Mount Hoei. People believe that when a *kasagumo* (hat-shaped cloud) forms above Mount Fuji, there will be rain. At the very top of the sacred peak is a *Sengen-jinja*, a shrine, that is considered to be the hallowed abode of medieval samurai spirits.[139]

It is said that the Japanese so respected Mount Fuji, reports novelist C. W. Nicol, that they used the honorific for humans, calling the mountain "Fuji-san" (Mr. Fuji).[140] The fusion of mountain and man into a living embodiment of truth and light is central to notions of Japanese spirituality. Fuji, states Masanobu Fukuoka, is a metaphor for the desired state of completeness.

THE MOST COMMON VIEW is that one can best know the true nature of Fuji by both listening to the ecologist speak of his research on its fauna and flora and looking at the abstracted form of Fuji in Hokusai's paintings. But this is just like the hunter who chases two rabbits and catches none. Such a person neither climbs the mountain nor paints. Those who say Fuji is the same whether we look at it lying down or standing up, those who make use of discriminating knowledge, cannot grasp the truth of this mountain. . . .

To know the real Fuji, one must look at the self in relation to Fuji rather than at the mountain itself. One must look at oneself and Fuji prior to the self-other dichotomy. When one's eyes are opened by forgetting the self and becoming one with Fuji, then one will know the true form of the mountain.[141]

Why climb a mountain?

Look! a mountain there.

I don't climb mountain.
Mountain climbs me.

Mountain is myself.
I climb on myself.

There is no mountain
 nor myself.
 Something
 moves up and down
 in the air.

NANAO SAKAKI,
poet, wandering scholar and
itinerant artist[142]

Mount Fuji, as moral exemplar and living repository of truth, and as a national symbol of pure munificence, did not escape the attention of Zen Buddhist scholar Daisetz Suzuki. He suggests that a palpable intimacy exists between the Japanese heart and the heart of the good earth, its ideal embodied in Fuji.

THE JAPANESE LOVE OF NATURE, I often think, owes much to the presence of Mount Fuji in the middle part of the main island of Japan. Whenever I pass by the foot of the mountain as a passenger on the Tokaido railway line, I never fail to have a good view of it, weather permitting, and to admire its beautiful formation, always covered with spotless snow and "rising skywards like a white upturned folding fan," as it was once described by a poet of the

Tokugawa period [Ishikawa Jozan, 1583–1672]. . . .

Fuji is now thoroughly identified with Japan. Wherever Japan is talked or written about, Fuji is inevitably mentioned. Justifiably so, because even the Land of the Rising Sun would surely lose much of her beauty if the sacred mountain were erased from the map. The mountain must be seen in order to impress. . . .

[N]ature to us has never been uncharitable, it is not a kind of enemy to be brought under man's power. We of the Orient have never conceived Nature in the form of an opposing power. On the contrary, Nature has been our constant friend and companion, who is to be absolutely trusted in spite of the frequent earthquakes assailing this land of ours. The idea of conquest is abhorrent. If we succeed in climbing a high mountain, why not say, "We have made a good friend of it?" To look around for objects to conquer is not the Oriental attitude toward Nature.

Yes, we climb Fuji, too, but the purpose is not to "conquer" it, but to be impressed with its beauty, grandeur, and aloofness; it is also to worship a sublime morning sun rising gorgeously from behind the multicolored clouds. This is not necessarily an act of sun worship, though there is nothing spiritually degrading in that. The sun is the great benefactor of all life on earth, and it is only proper for us human beings to approach a benefactor of any kind, animate or inanimate, with a deep feeling of gratitude and appreciation. For this feeling is granted to us only; lower animals seem to be wanting in this delicate sentiment.[143]

Minako Ohba (b. 1930) is one of Japan's most important women writers of fiction. A central motif of her storytelling is the Japanese legend of the *yamanda,* or the old woman of the mountain, depicted as a mystical embodiment of light, hope and inspiration on the one hand, and an awesome and terrible force on the other. In 1969, Minako Ohba was awarded the prestigious Akutagawa Prize for her story "Three Crabs," which marked her literary debut. The following passage is from "Candle Fish," a short story dealing with memory—the fusion of present and past—an unmapped region in which Ohba creates and explores new experiences.

"Candle Fish" is a search for universal truths embedded in the natural world, as those insights emerge from a reverie about mountains.

A DOG BARKED while I was crossing the desolate land; it sounded like a wolf. As I walked, the wet ground sank under my feet, soaking my socks. Walking on the moss-covered ground in summer was always like that. In winter, the frozen ground would resist the shoes walking over it and make a small, hard sound. I saw the Three Sisters looming up beyond the roof of Olga's house. The mountain was bare, with a few patches of snow here and there. How many years have I lived here looking at this view, I wondered as I walked.

I was in my twenties, but I felt like the old cedar tree that had been standing at the foot of the Three Sisters for thousands of years. Dry moss hung from some of the branches of the cedar, looking like long white shrouds of hair; higher up on the tree I sometimes saw a bald eagle perched in perfect composure. The eagles were near extinction in most places but some still survived in the northern regions where we lived.

I was born and raised in Japan, an ancient country with a long history, but when I lived there I had never felt like an old cedar. Yet when I separated from my country a strange part of me, which seemed to have been covered by moss before, revealed itself. I became aware of a power inside me, informing me of things I had no way of knowing. . . .

I am awake now as I was in those days, and I am thinking of the Three Sisters in that remote land. Someday I shall go back there to see the mountain, and I will murmur those famous lines to myself: "There's nothing I want to say to the mountain; so precious is this mountain of my native place."

The time I spent in the shadow of the Three Sisters was the most precious period in my life, a time when I searched for meaning beyond words.[144]

Yasushi Inoue (1907–   ) is considered to have had one of the most enduring and distinguished careers in modern letters in Japan.

Novelist, poet and short-story writer, Inoue was awarded the prestigious Akutagawa Prize for literature for one of his exquisite short stories, "Tōgyu" ("Bullfight"). Another outstanding Inoue story is "Kobandai" ("Under the Shadow of Mount Bandai," 1961), a personal account of the earth gone wild and the subsequent rubble of devastation wreaked upon body, mind, spirit and cosmos.

In the course of Inoue's re-creation of the calamitous event of the eruption of Mount Bandai, the awesome and massive peaks of Daibandai, Kobandai and Akahani assume an almost existential character of vulnerability, ephemerality and indifference. In his description of the cascading nightmare, Inoue confronts us with a palimpsest of creation, destruction and, somehow, excitement as the mountain blows its top. The seismic upheavals are imprinted upon the land, and once again the earth is in formation. Yet it is the shouts of defiance of several village children, as they challenge the exploding mountain to "give it all you've got," that awakens Inoue to the true significance of that unimaginable explosion "so terrifying as to be not of this world."

I NOTICED THAT THE GROUND WAS LITTERED with small stones and the morning sunlight touched these stones, glinting off the blades of grass that grew between them. Even though it was still early, the sunlight sent up shimmering heat waves which promised a hot day ahead. To be watching something as insubstantial as this haze of heat and at the same moment to feel the ground begin to tremble filled me with uneasiness, as though even the earth itself were not to be relied upon. But the tremor passed in an instant, like the shadow of a bird sweeping over the ground, and though an ominous feeling flickered through my mind, as soon as the trembling stopped I forgot all about it.

After leaving the flat land along the river we found ourselves confronted by the three massive peaks of Daibandai, Kobandai, and Akahani. Gazing at these lofty summits, we were deeply impressed by their grandeur. . . . From the lower slopes of the great mountain down to the river plain stretched large natural forests of cypress, oak, zelkova, and maple, which gave a dark, almost gloomy aspect to the landscape. The slopes of Bandai itself were covered with stands of red pine, white birch, and other sorts of trees. From where we stood on the riverbank the whole view was one vast wooded panorama. It was hard to believe that the three villages we planned to visit were somewhere out there beneath that sea of living trees. Indeed, it was a bit frightening to think that people spent their whole lives beneath the canopy of that seemingly endless forest. . . .

At exactly 7:40 the earth gave a great heave and shudder. This was different from the tremors we had felt before, much more violent, and I was knocked to the ground. I could not tell if it came from the mountain or the ground beneath me, but I heard the most terrifying sound issuing from the bowels of the earth . . . I scrambled to my feet only to be thrown down again by a second violent jolt. This time I used my right arm to brace my body against the bucking earth. I glanced up at the outcrop to see if the children had also been thrown down, but there was no sign of them. All I could see was a swirl of dust slowly rising in the air.

By this time I knew better than to try and leap up again, but after the second quake subsided, I carefully rose to my feet. . . .

At the same moment, I saw two or three small heads poke up above the edge of the outcrop. Soon all the heads appeared in a row and I heard one of the children cry out in a loud voice, cadenced almost as though he were singing, "Blow, mountain, blow! Give it all you've got!" Soon several of the others joined in, shouting with all their tiny might, "Blow, mountain, blow! Give it all you've got!"

Their chant—or scream of defiance, whatever it was —was scarcely finished when in thunderous answer a roar came rolling back over the earth. It was a blast so powerful that I was lifted off my feet and hurled to the ground several yards to my right. On and on went the roar while the earth heaved in convulsive spasms. Later, when I tried to recall the exact sequence of events, I was never sure just when it was that I happened to catch sight of Mt. Bandai, but I know I saw a huge column of fire and smoke rising straight up into the clear tranquil sky; like one of the pillars of Hell it rose to twice the height of the mountain itself. The whole mountain had literally exploded and the shape of Kobandai was blotted out forever. It was only much later, of course, that I realized what had occurred.

I cannot say with any certainty how I survived the

explosion. The entire north face of Mt. Bandai came avalanching down in a sea of sand, rocks, and boulders. I remember it now as a nightmare vision, as something so terrifying as to be not of this world. The avalanche obliterated the forests that covered the lower slopes of the mountain. The wall of debris swept down with terrible speed and force. I saw the purple kimono swirl up in the air like a scrap of colored paper, and in a flash it was swept away in that tide of mud. I do not know exactly where or when it was that the kimono disappeared from sight. The air was so thick with clouds of ash and pebbles I could not tell whether it was day or night. I staggered along the bank of the Ono River and sought refuge on the high ground north of Akimoto. That alone saved my life. . . .

Within an hour of the time Mt. Bandai exploded, the villages of Hosono, Ōsawa, and Akimoto were all swept away, and whatever remained was buried under yards and yards of stone. . . .

What remains indelibly burned upon my memory and ringing in my ears is the defiant challenge—"Blow, mountain, blow! Give it all you've got!"—uttered by those brave children, who could do nothing else in the face of the mountain's awesome power.[145]

> *I push my way through,*
> *push my way through,*
> *green mountains.*
>
> TANEDA SANTOKA
> *(1882–1940),*
> *Zen priest and poet*[146]

> *In thoughts today*
> *my sleeves are wet*
> *for the memory of dew*
> *Travels into the mountains*
> *of olden days.*
>
> KAZUAKI TANAHASHI,
> *Zen painter, calligrapher and poet*[147]

The notion of the local mountain as compassionate guardian, eternal abode of the ancestors, and hence spiritual and palpable link with the world of the living is described by Japan's pioneering ethnographic writer, Kunio Yanagita (1875–1962).

IN THE COUNTRIES that surround Japan the idea that once you die you go to an infinitely distant place is prevalent in more or less sophisticated forms. Only in these islands is it thought that even if you die you do not leave the area but watch over the lives of your children and grandchildren from the heights of the local mountain, looking fondly on their prosperity and diligence. This is something that has come down from who knows what age and is infinitely affecting.[148]

I have locked the gate on a thousand peaks
To live here with clouds and birds.
All day I watch the hills
As clear winds fill the bamboo door.
A supper of pine flowers,
Monk's robes of chestnut dye—
What dream does the world hold
To lure me from these dark slopes?

ZEKKAI (1336–1405),
"Mountain temple"[149]

Looking up, the heavens are seen extending;
Looking down, the earth is seen stretched,
Both to the farthest ends of the horizon!
Beyond, there shines a white pearl,
The only one, and no second!

"Homage to Mount Fuji,"
anonymous,
8th-century Manyōshū [150]

Art is what reveals to us the state of perfection.

KUKAI (KOBO DAISHI, 774–835),
founder of Esoteric Buddhism,
gifted artist and calligrapher[151]

Enku, *Koma-Inu*, ca. 1675–1695. Lion dogs guarding a Shinto shrine orna-mented with the auspicious cloud pattern that takes the shape of huge, com-malike spirals. The seventeenth-century monk Enku completed 100,000 pieces of sculpture in his lifetime. Revered by the common folk of his time, he is said to have carved many of his images with a hatchet. Enku is now recognized as one of the most important sculptors in the history of Japanese art.

The rotting driftwood
picked up
—now,
the guardian gods
of children.

ENKU (1632–1695),
itinerant Buddhist monk
and sculptor[152]

In my hands I hold a bowl of tea.
I see all of nature represented in its green
color.
Closing my eyes I find green mountains
and pure water within my own heart.
Silently drinking I feel these become a part
of me.

> Description of the practice
> of the Way of Tea[153]

The taste of tea is like the mists of Spring,
the cuckoo hidden in the fresh green leaves of
summer,
the loneliness of the evening sky of autumn,
the daybreak in the snow of winter.

> ENSHIŪ KOBORI (1579–1647),
> Japanese tea master, poet
> and garden designer[154]

ARTS AND CEREMONY: REFLECTIONS OF THE NATURAL WORLD

The *Book of Tea* is an exquisite evocation of the living appreciation of beauty in ordinary things. As such, it is a timeless description of tea gathering—its history, practice and humanity. The book is also a reminder of the beneficence of nature experienced through the prism of flowers and their regenerative power.

Written in 1906 by Kakuzo Okakura, *The Book of Tea* was intended to convey the spirit and atmosphere of *Chanoyu,* widely known as the "tea ceremony," or *Chado*—literally "the way of tea" —to readers in the West. The author suggests how *Chanoyu* "represents the true spirit of Eastern democracy by making all its votaries aristocrats in taste!"[155] Okakura perceives *Chanoyu* "as a form of spiritual culture, a discipline that transforms itself into an 'Art of Life,'" according to tea master Soshitsu Sen XV.[156] Okakura states that "[t]he Philosophy of Tea is not mere aestheticism in the ordinary acceptance of the term, for it expresses conjointly with ethics and religion our whole point of view about man and nature."[157] Elsewhere, he describes "teaism" as "moral geometry, inasmuch as it defines our sense of proportion to the universe."[158]

In the following passage, Okakura pays homage to the religious veneration held by the tea and flower masters for flowers—"gentle flowers, teardrops of the stars, standing in the garden nodding your heads to the bees as they sing of the dews and the sunbeams . . ."[159]

IN THE TREMBLING GREY of a spring dawn, when the birds were whispering in mysterious cadence among the trees, have you not felt that they were talking to their mates about the flowers? Surely with mankind the appreciation of flowers must have been coeval with the poetry of love. Where better than in a flower, sweet in its unconsciousness, fragrant because of its silence, can we image the unfolding of a virgin soul? . . .

In joy or sadness, flowers are our constant friends. We eat, drink, sing, dance, and flirt with them. We wed and christen with flowers. We dare not die without them. We have worshipped with the lily, we have meditated with the lotus, we have charged in battle array with the rose and the chrysanthemum. We have even attempted to speak in the language of flowers. How could we live without them? It frightens one to conceive of a world bereft of their presence. What solace do they not bring to the bedside of the sick, what a light of bliss to the darkness of weary spirits? Their serene tenderness restores to us our waning confidence in the universe even as the intent gaze of a beautiful child recalls our lost hopes. When we are laid low in the dust it is they who linger in sorrow over our graves. . . .

When a tea-master has arranged a flower to his satisfaction he will place it on the Tokonoma, the place of honour in a Japanese room. Nothing else will be placed near it which might interfere with its effect, not even a painting, unless there be some special aesthetic reason for the combination. It rests there like an enthroned prince, and the guests or disciples on entering the room will salute it with a profound bow before making their addresses to the host. . . .

When the flower fades, the master tenderly consigns it to the river or carefully buries it in the ground. Monuments even are sometimes erected in their memory.[160]

The following *haiku* (a form of traditional Japanese poetry that has seventeen syllables, divided into three sections of five-seven-five) composed by the poetess Chiyo of Kaga (1703–1775) celebrates her encounter with the spirit of beauty. One late summer morning, upon her arrival at a nearby well, Chiyo discovered a blooming morning glory entwined around the well bucket; so taken by its loveliness, she experienced a moment of holiness. Leaving the flower undisturbed, Chiyo went in search of water elsewhere.

> *Ah! Morning-glory!*
> *The bucket taken captive!*
> *I begged for water.*[161]

Japanese poetry has the human heart as seed and myriads of words as leaves. It comes into being when men use the seen and the heard to give voice to feeling aroused by the innumerable events in their lives. . . . It is song that moves heaven and earth without effort, stirs emotions in the invisible spirits and gods, brings harmony to the relations between men and women, and calms the hearts of fierce warriors.

KI NO TSURAYUKI (ca. 872–945),
poet and writer[162]

Shōji Hamada is Japan's most renowned potter. He was designated a Living National Treasure in 1955 by the Japanese government and thirteen years later was awarded the Order of Culture. Hamada was a major figure in the Japanese Folk Crafts (*Mingei*) movement and established a permanent collection of folk-craft products in Mashiko (Tochigi Prefecture), the place of his pottery beginnings and his workshop, and an old ceramic center since the latter part of the Edo period (1600–1868).[163]

Hamada's pursuit and perpetuation of fundamental universal values through his work is reflected in his approach to art and living. "The right way," he has said, "lies in plainness and naturalness." Hamada referred to the goal of his "true craft" (a state of "always being born") as "the way of pottery"—ageless wisdom he found mirrored in the four seasons. In fact, the sugar-cane fields outside his workshop became his greatest inspiration and an emblem of his trademark. In a series of conversations with Bernard Leach, a close friend and equally renowned European potter, the master potter contemplates some aspects of the potter's way as he recalls a trip he made to America in 1952. Hamada wore Japanese country clothes and chose not to speak English when he gave wheel demonstrations. Many thought he was just a peasant.

WHEN I WENT TO AMERICA they thought I was a very simple person because I talked of ash glazes and they had long complicated formulas of calculated glazes. They did not realize that nature's glazes are infinitely more complicated than any man can conceive. . . .

What is best for a particular pot must come out of the

Jōmon Earthenware Jar, ca. 3000–2500 B.C. Jōmon ("cord-marked") pottery vessels were used primarily for storage and cooking. The tall body is decorated with bands of swirling clay spirals terminating at the rim of the vessel in three applied bands of clay that wind their way into a high-relief sophisticated ornament that suggests a stylized serpent.

potter himself. . . . The appropriate technique for any pot has to emerge from the potter or the result is forced. . . .

The point is not to be purposeful but to be natural. . . . It is not necessary to be concerned with achieving regularity or irregularity; the effort of the potter to achieve a specific effect will weaken the piece. If you are not worried about the pigment being even or uneven, the effect will certainly be good. . . .

Once you have done something with your body, with the whole being, the whole body, then I feel that you are getting somewhere in understanding that you are in it. . . .

Most potters think that unless they put specific patterns or drawings on the pot they are not making a pattern. They should realize that the pattern was being created from the very beginning of the pot-making process; the material itself creates the pattern. The potter must learn to see and to recognize this. . . . I began to realize that there are two kinds of patterns to consider: the natural ones that come from the material itself and the kind that is intellectually conceived. . . .

I remember the delightful experience of living in Okinawa with my wife and son for more than a year. The sugar-cane fields stretching endlessly in front of my workshop inspired me to create a pattern, which has continued to capture my interest, to my surprise, for these many years, without my becoming tired of it.

I drew the cane leaves, stem, and tops as they appear after being stricken by the violence of a typhoon. My style of drawing this pattern has changed naturally with the years, and my good friends tell me that they can detect changes in this sugar-cane pattern about every ten years. Now this pattern has become my trademark. . . .

I have said for many years that I would try my hand at raku [a common, simple, low-fired ware of a soft body and dark tones, introduced around 1577–80 by the son of a Korean immigrant] when I reached the age of seventy, but I have not done much yet. Because the low temperature firing keeps the form intact, with no firing distortion, I have been afraid that it would be essential for me to throw every pot with greater freedom and sensitivity. . . .

The simplicity of raku [asymmetry and irregularity] causes it to be the most difficult of all to make. The reason is that *the usage* of raku ware by the Japanese is very subtle. It is so simple that you go through the full cycle of your development. I see it in terms of the four seasons. The best bowls are made by children who are unselfconscious. But just as you are reaching the peak of skill—summer— this is when the danger sets in. You become aware of your skill, and then you must get beyond that awareness before you can reach autumn and then winter. Then you must come into the next spring. This is the period Japanese handcraftsmen know to be the time to develop their true craft. It is the second apple we are talking about, that is why it must be born, not made. Very often the craftsman does not live long enough, and not only that, when he is so old he may become brittle, rather than have a second childhood. If he becomes brittle, he must be very cautious. The second childhood must be a supple one, not a brittle one. To be able to make good red or black raku in Japan is the height of good potting because of the difficulty.

No craft is easy to master. Pottery is among the most difficult to encompass. The reason may be that the glazing technique (which should be more properly called *yugi*, play or pastime) and the firing technique are over-stressed. We should put aside this over-emphasis. The right way lies in plainness and naturalness. If we reflect on our motive for making pottery we can make a start without mistakes. I think we can approach the way of pottery much more easily then.[164]

Temple ornament. Asuka, early Nara period, seventh century. Gilt bronze. The canopies of the *kondō* ("golden hall") of the Hōryū-ji Buddhist temple at Nara, the ancient capital of Japan, were decorated with openwork ornaments such as this one. The exuberant whorls and curls reflect a bold flame pattern evoking the head of a dragon.

In Buddhism, one day a year is set aside for "releasing [and giving] life" by preventing the destruction of living creatures. Human beings are largely dependent on other living things such as fish, animals and vegetables for their existence. To remember how much we are indebted to them and to express our grateful feeling, fish and birds . . . are freed to return to nature accompanied by the chanting of sūtras.

DAISETZ SUZUKI,
philosopher and teacher[165]

Yes, the young sparrows
If you treat them tenderly
Thank you with droppings.

ISSA KOBAYASHI
(1763–1828),
haiku poet[166]

Whatever one sees is a reflection of oneself. Without you there is not the objective world or the subjective—the object never exists without the subject. This is not taught in schools; this is what the cuckoo taught me on the cliffs in Cornwall.

SHŌJI HAMADA (1894–1978),
master potter[167]

The voice of the cuckoo has been heard; it seems to come when the voices of other warblers have become feeble. In China the note of the cuckoo is disliked, while with us it has been appreciated from the earliest times. Thousands of odes have been sung in its praise. In some parts of the country we hear them all night, yet never feel annoyed with their notes. In others they are so rare, that we prize each occasion on which we hear them, and when the bird has flown away we regret, and yet regret not, for it has only sped to another village to delight those who love it as much as we do.

KAIBARA EKKEN (1630–1714),
philosopher and essayist[168]

RECIPROCITY
WITH THE ANIMAL
AND VEGETABLE KINGDOMS

T he Lady Who Loved Insects is a tender story that chronicles the affection of a court lady for "disagreeable" insects like caterpillars rather than cherry blossoms. It's a delightful twelfth-century anonymous account of female rebelliousness that defies some of the most precious social conventions of a court society in the Heian period (794–1185). Attentive to all things natural, the insect lady proves inimitable in her observations about the natural world and her disdain for the artifice of every sort that was the modus operandi of her time.

NEXT DOOR TO THE LADY who loved butterflies was the house of a certain provincial inspector. He had an only daughter, to whose upbringing he and his wife devoted endless care. She was a strange girl, and used to say: "Why do people make so much fuss about butterflies and never give a thought to the creatures out of which butterflies grow? It is the natural form of things that is always the most important." She collected all kinds of reptiles and insects such as most people are frightened to touch, and watched them day by day to see what they would turn into, keeping them in various sorts of little boxes and cages. Among all these creatures her favorite was the common caterpillar. Hour after hour, her hair pushed back from her eyes, she would sit gazing at the furry black form that nestled in the palm of her hand. She found that other girls were frightened of these pets, and her only companions were a number of rather rough little boys, who were not in the least afraid. She got them to carry about the insect-boxes, find out the names of the insects or, if this could not be done, help her to give them new names. She hated anything that was not natural. Consequently she would not pluck a single hair from her eyebrows nor would she blacken her teeth, saying it was a dirty and disagreeable custom [an aristocratic convention of the court]. So morning, noon and night she tended her insects, bending over them with a strange, white gleaming smile. People on the whole were frightened of her and kept away; the few who ventured to approach her came back with the strangest reports. If anyone showed the slightest distaste for her pets, she would ask him indignantly how he could give way to so silly and vulgar a prejudice, and as she said this she would stare at the visitor under her black, bushy eyebrows in a way that made him feel extremely uncomfortable.

Her parents thought all this very peculiar and would much rather she had been more like other children; but they saw it was no use arguing with her. She for her part took immense trouble in explaining her ideas, but this only resulted in making them feel that she was much cleverer than they. "No doubt," they would say, "all you tell us is quite true, and so far as we are concerned you may do as you please. But people as a rule only make pets of charming and pretty things. If it gets about that you keep hairy caterpillars you will be thought a disgusting girl and no one will want to know you." "I do not mind what they think," she answered. "I want to inquire into everything that exists and find out how it began. Nothing else interests me. And it is very silly of them to dislike caterpillars, all of which will soon turn into lovely butterflies." Then she again explained to them carefully how the cocoon, which is like the thick winter clothes that human beings wear, wraps up the caterpillar till its wings have grown and it is ready to be a butterfly. Then it suddenly waves its white sleeves and flits away. . . .

This was no doubt quite accurate, and they could think of nothing to say in reply; but all the same her views on such matters made them feel uncomfortable. She would never sit in the same room with her elders, quoting in self-defence the proverb, "Ghosts and girls are best unseen"; and the above attempt to bring her parents to reason was made through a chink in the half-raised blinds of the living room. Hearing of such conversations as this, the young people of the district were amazed at the profundity of her researches. "But what things for a girl to play with!" they said. "She must be an oddity indeed. Let us go and call upon the girl who loves butterflies."

Hearing some of the unflattering comparisons that were being made between herself and the butterfly lady, she rejoined: "I do not see anything very admirable in making a fuss over butterflies. Even those young men must know by now that the prettiest butterflies are but the shed-dings of creatures like my hairy caterpillars, who discard them as a snake drops its skin. And caterpillars are much friendlier playthings. For if you catch hold of a butterfly it frees itself as soon as it can, leaving its golden powder on your hand, and this powder is very dangerous, often caus-ing fevers and agues. Fancy trying to make pets of butter-flies! It is horrible to think of."

To the little boys who formed her retinue she would give pretty things such as she knew they wanted, and in return they would give her all kinds of terrifying insects. She said the caterpillars would be unhappy if there were no creatures with them to admire their glossy coats, and she therefore collected a number of snails, and also of grass-crickets whose ferocious and incessant cries seemed to suggest that they were at war with one another, thus recalling to her mind the line, "For the ground between a snail's horns what use to fight?" She said she was tired of ordinary boys' names and called her servitors by insect-names, such as Kerao (mole-cricket boy), Inagomaro (lo-cust-man), Amabiko (centipede), and the like. . . .[169]

 Stand like a shakuyaku *(herbaceous peony), sit like a peony; as you walk, imagine you are a lily.*

Advice to young Japanese women who wish to be charming[170]

Go to the cicada, consider her ways and be wise; they stay long in the ground, but when they come out into the world, they sing at the top of their voice.

SANKI ICHIKAWA,
*counseling young graduate students
in a hurry to make their mark
in the literary world*[171]

In his short prose-poetry piece "Mating," Motojirō Kajii (1901–1932) describes a spontaneity in the natural world that he comes to realize is the source of his own being. The instinctiveness of nature—the nature of nature—is observed in all its wonder through the single event of the mating of a frog. The experience releases Kajii's own true nature and enables him to recognize the common ground shared by the natural world and himself.

Kajii has provided us with an inspired approach to understanding our existence in the natural environment. His revelatory story is characterized almost entirely by feeling—for a oneness with all things.

I ONCE WENT TO OBSERVE some singing frogs. To see them, one first has to venture resolutely to the edge of the shallows where they sing. Since they will hide no matter how cautiously one approaches, it is just as well to move quickly. One then hides by the shallows and remains perfectly still. Imagine you are a rock. Nothing moves but your eyes. If you are not careful it is difficult to distinguish the frogs from the stones in the shallows and you won't see anything. After a while, from the water and the shadows of the rocks, the frogs slowly show their heads. As I look on they seemed to emerge from almost everywhere. All at once, as if by previous arrangement, they timidly appeared.

I remained still as a rock. Letting their fear pass, they all climbed out to where they were before. In front of me they took up their interrupted courtship song again.

I was overcome at intervals by an odd feeling, watching from this proximity. Akutagawa Ryūnosuke wrote a novel about men going to the land of the mythical *kappa*,[172] but in fact the land of the frogs is much more accessible. Through observing just one frog I suddenly entered their world. This frog sat by the small current that ran between the rocks in the stream and, with something uncanny in its look, stared at the rushing water. Its appearance was exactly like the human figures in classical literati paintings: something between a fisherman and a *kappa*. As I thought about this, the small current suddenly widened and became an inlet. And, in that instant, I had a sense of being a lone traveler in the universe. . . .

Scientists say that the first living things with a "voice" were amphibious creatures that appeared during the Carboniferous Period. Thinking of their voices now as the first living sound to chorus forth on the face of the earth gave me a sense of the sublime. It was the kind of music that touches the listener's heart, makes it throb, and finally moves him to tears.

In front of me was a male frog. Obviously drifting with the waves of the chorus, his throat trembled intermittently. I looked around, thinking that his mate must be nearby. A foot or two away in the stream, in the shadow of a rock, another frog was sitting with quiet reserve in the background. I thought it must be the mate. Whenever the male croaked, I noticed that the female answered "geh! geh!" in a contented voice. As this went on, the male's voice grew clearer. My heart responded to his earnest cries. Then he suddenly broke from the rhythm of the chorus. The intervals between his cries grew shorter and shorter. The female continued to reply. And yet, perhaps because her voice did not carry, she sounded a bit nonchalant in comparison to that other passionate call.

But now something had to happen. Impatiently, I waited for the moment. As I expected, the male frog abruptly stopped his ardent croaking, smoothly slipped off the rock, and began to cross the water. Nothing has ever moved me so much as the tenderness of that moment. Swimming across the water toward the female, he was like a child who has found its mother, crying appealingly as it runs to her. As he swam he cried out, "geeyo! geeyo! geeyo! geeyo!" Could any other courtship be so tender and devoted? I watched, feeling an awkward envy.

He arrived happily at the feet of his mate, and there they copulated in the fresh limpid stream. Yet the sight of their desperate mating came nowhere near the tenderness of his crossing the water. Feeling I had seen something in the world that was beautiful, for a while I submerged myself in the cadence of the frogs' voices vibrating in the shallows.[173]

Turnips and Zen monks,
Are [both] best when they sit well.

> SENGAI (1750–1837),
> *Zen monk, master,*
> *teacher and artist*[174]

Turnips are best-tasting when they are plump and some-what flat at the seat. Zen monks are best qualified for further training when they are able to sit well in the cross-legged posture of deep meditation.

> DAISETZ SUZUKI (1870–1966),
> *Zen Buddhist scholar,*
> *commenting on Sengai*[175]

There isn't a child, or for that matter an adult, in Japan who does not know some of Shimpei Kusano's frog poems. With engaging humor, insight and hope, they are a universal force orchestrating humanity. In the words of Kusano's translator, Cid Corman, his laughing and singing frogs "are the voices of nature—in its largest sense—and of absolute innocence. They sing in the face of every moment's doom. They live beyond any idea of PROGRESS. They are the gaiety and spontaneity and love and rootedness of fear in man. They mock our pretensions, but share them too—gently. They are a society whose limits are prehistoric and posthistoric. They live beyond abuse within the nature of man's spirit."[176]

Born in 1903, Shimpei Kusano is a translator, lecturer, novelist and critic. He is a well-known personality in Japan who has, on occasion, written poems for Japan's royal family. He has run numerous poetry magazines as well as bars and eating stands. Kusano is best described by his own frogs: "our hearts big (we've got plenty of nerve). / on this side and the other of the earth. / we're smiling . . ."[177] Kusano's soliloquy to a perfect world includes these lines: "from Jurassic times on. / the frog world has had no god. / sexual relation is the commonwealth. / songs are the form of government. / and all frog-kind are common kin."[178] Kusano presents a common habitat of his singing creations in an uncommon scenario, entitled "the day snow first fell on earth":

> *in a jungle of monster ferns parasol fungi and*
> > *banana trees.*
> *beam on purple beam of sunlight smouldering.*
> *a muddy muddy swamp dims mistfully.*
>
> > *frogs two or three hundred.*
> > *in the muddy muddy swamp.*
> > *dwelling.*
>
> > *of night and day do we sing*
> > *songs for living   songs of joy*
> > *by night and day we offer*
> > *songs for living   deep sweet songs*
>
> *and with all singing together.*
> *erect on the tip of a spectral flower.*
> *Kuku with his baton led the singing to its*
> > *climax. . . .*
>
> *a strange chill came wavering down.*
> *had never happened before. in fact.*
> *like shrivelled satin.*[179]

> *There is craft in this smallest insect,*
> *With strands of web spinning out his thoughts;*
> *In his tiny body finding rest,*
> *And with the wind lightly turning.*
> *Before the eaves he stakes out his broad earth;*
> *For a moment on the fence top lives through his life.*

When you know that all beings are even thus,
You will know what creation is made of.

> SUGAWARE NO MICHIZANE (845–903),
> "The Spider"[180]

> There was a cicada.
> He spent the whole summer singing.
> The winter came.
> What a fix, what a fix!
>   (Moral)
> It was worth it.

> DAIGAKU HORIGUCHI
> (b. 1892),
> poet, "The Cicada"[181]

III

GREECE

And when Greece *is silent,* Humanism *disappears. And when the* Greek *imitates the* Barbarians, *he commits suicide and there is no longer a* Greek *on earth. There is no longer* Nature. *And there is no longer a* Spirit. *And there is no longer* Beauty.

PERICLES YANNOPOULOS *(1869–1910),*
poet and essayist [1]

Painting on a libation jug from Phaistos.

. . . the name of Earth is dear, I ween, and is precious to every Greek, and it is a custom handed down to us by our fathers to revere her like any other deity.

PLUTARCH *(46–120),*
Greek biographer[2]

Greece is . . . the world's geographical and spiritual cross-roads.

NIKOS KAZANTZAKIS *(1883–1957),*
novelist and poet[3]

Sirenes, emerging from flowers; silver, fifth century B.C. Part of the handle of an urn. Sirens were fabulous creatures of the sea that drove men to destruction by the magic of their songs. They are often represented as birds with the heads and torsos of women.

INTRODUCTION

The Greek tradition, in its expression of human values, is of great importance to humanity. One might say that the Greek Way is common to the entire human community. The quintessential Greek ideal is unity: humankind in a single human; literature and life at-one-ment; the perfect reflection of the inner in the outer; the coalescing of the real with the unreal through the harmonization of things seen and not seen. A state of harmony is the key to the arching essence of Greek civilization and it is demonstrated in its purest form in Greek art. In this inspired realm, an exalted expression of the human spirit reigns supreme, reflecting, in the words of one scholar, "an absence of struggle, a reconciling power, something of calm and serenity the world has yet to see again."[4]

"Democracy and the other accomplishments of Greek civilization, however real or imaginary, remain so precious to us that virtually every modern civilization has wanted to claim them for itself," writes humanities scholar Mary Lefkowitz.[5] George Seferis, Greek poet and essayist, and recipient of the Nobel Prize for Literature in 1963, comments on this universally valued legacy through a geography of the imagination, land and spirit:

> ... I HAVE A VERY ORGANIC FEELING that identifies humaneness with the Greek landscape. . . . I should never use such adjectives as "grand" or "stately" for any of the Greek landscapes I have in mind. It is a whole world: lines that come and go; bodies and features, the tragic silence of a "face" . . . it is my belief that in the Greek light there is a kind of process of humanization. . . ."[6]

Nearly twenty-five hundred years ago, with the creative efflorescence that was so much a part of the fifth and fourth centuries B.C.— an astonishing time that brought us Socrates, Plato and Aristotle—

the ancient Greeks broke through the mythopoeic-magico realm into the air of reason. It began as early as the first quarter of the sixth century before Christ, when Thales of Miletus, an inventor and engineer, asked a new kind of question, "What is the world made of?" and replied "Water." It was the inquiry, not the answer, that led to the collapse of the prevailing belief, based on unquestioning faith, in a mythological universe. Succeeding it was the study of logic grounded in systematic inquiry. The Greek mind blossomed. The development of "philosophy" (*philos:* love; *sophia:* knowledge) in all its branches took shape—from metaphysics to economics; from the natural sciences to mathematics, history, drama and poetry.

It is misleading, of course, to think that the ancient Greeks spent the majority of their time in high-minded discussion. They were flamboyant, passionate and opportunistic. They engaged in the savagery of warfare, owned slaves and inflicted brutal and tyrannical leaderships. During one period of bloody turmoil (the Peloponnesian War, ca. 431–404 B.C.), the strengths and frailties of human character and the ultimate struggles of human life were being exposed in the dramas of Euripides and Sophocles and parodied in the comedies of Aristophanes. Clearly everything of value, especially the theater—a prime temple of Greek culture—was worth fighting for.[7]

Out of a small group of Greek city-states, a handful of truly outstanding philosophers and poets emerged to shape forever our understanding of the world and to challenge our perception of the significance of human life. Their instinct was to take the widest view, to fix a universal frame, to see things as an organic whole. Plotinus (ca. A.D. 205–270), Roman writer and Neoplatonist, called the Greek ideal "beauty, absolute, simple, and everlasting . . . the irradiation of the particular by the general."[8] In *The Colossus of Maroussi*, Henry Miller describes a coherent Greek universe, calling it a miracle of the human spirit:

THE GREEK COSMOS is the most eloquent illustration of the unity of thought and deed. It persists even today, though its elements have long since been dispersed. The image of Greece, faded though it be, endures as an archetype of the miracle wrought by the human spirit. A whole people, as the relics of their achievements testify, lifted themselves to a point never before and never since attained. It was miraculous. It still is. The task of genius, and man is nothing if not genius, is to keep the miracle alive, to live always in the miracle, to make the miracle more and more miraculous, to swear allegiance to nothing, but to live only miraculously, think only miraculously, die miraculously. It matters little how much is destroyed, if only the germ of the miraculous be preserved and nurtured.[9]

Who exactly were the Greeks? It is said that the question of their racial origins was of no particular importance to them, not even to Herodotus, who, ironically, was called "the Father of History" by Cicero. They did believe, however, that their ancestors were sprung from the land, the very earth that they themselves and their descendants were born into. The Athenians considered themselves to be *autochthonous* in every sense, that is, of the soil, of the ground (*chthōn*) itself. The language they spoke they deemed to be solely their own. A distinguishing Greek feature was a friendly, but serious, patriotic boastfulness. Pericles (ca. 495–429 B.C.), the preeminent Athenian statesman during Greece's period of intellectual and economic ascendancy ("the Olympian," as Aristophanes called him), in his widely admired Funeral Speech exhorts the people to be "*erastai* of Athens"—freely translated by historian H. D. F. Kitto to mean, "Let Athens be to you something that thrills you to the very marrow!"[10]

The Greeks regarded language other than Greek as nonsense (*barbar*), writes Mary Lefkowitz. She says "they did not seem to know or to care that the word 'barbarian' is itself a loan word, from the Babylonian-Sumerian *barbaru*, 'foreigner.'"[11] The Greeks called all foreign peoples barbarians (*barbaroi*). In the opening sentence of Herodotus' *Histories* (written between 430 and 425 B.C.), the writer adopts the prevailing Greek view that divided humankind into Hellenes and barbarians ("Greeks on the one hand, barbarians on the other").[12]

The ancient Greeks were fascinated by genealogy. In the Platonic dialogue, *Hippias Major,* Socrates asks the famous sophist Hippias what most interested his students. Hippias answered:

> THEY TAKE MOST PLEASURE, Socrates, in hearing about the genealogies of heroes and men, and about foundations— how cities were founded long ago—and in general about all *archaiologia.* . . ."[13]

In legend-wrapped Greece, the quality of one's *original* lineage determined the radiance of the reflected light of ancestral glory in which every member bathed. "Hence how far back will the Greek go genealogically to found his family or dynasty?" asks historian Van Groningen, in *In the Grip of the Past.* "A pedigree," he muses, "is in perfect order, as soon as it goes back to the mythical world of gods and heroes."[14]

The profound, shaping presence of the past is embedded deep within Greek consciousness. A continuity of inheritance from the ancient Greek world is most evident in the Greek experience of history and the present. Its manifestation, however, has less to do with "genealogy" than it does with a commonality of thought and feeling, belief and practice. For the poets, writers, artists and visionaries who have trod the same path over the centuries—"we who set out upon this pilgrimage," in the words of George Seferis[15]—it has inspired an invigorating freshness, clarity *and* timelessness about the age-old truths that refuse to die, but rather light up the universe of those who have chosen to be directed by them.

O earth! what a sound, how august and profound! it fills me with wonder and awe.

ARISTOPHANES (ca. 450–ca. 388 B.C.), playwright of comedies[16]

The Earth yields fruits, therefore glorify Mother Earth.

Verse chanted by Doves, Greek priestesses, at the oracular shrine of Dodona[17]

A pot of basil may symbolize the soul of a people better than a drama of Aeschylus.

ION DRAGOUMIS (1878–1920), writer and poet[18]

NATURE OF EARTH/
NATURE OF NATURE
IN GREEK THOUGHT

The holiness of the earth was a matter of primary importance in antiquity. Its sacred status is reflected in this beautiful *Homeric Hymn* about the beatitudes of benevolent Earth, attributed to Homer, Greece's first epic poet, and thought to have been composed and sung by him sometime during the "Homeric" period (a range of several hundred years, and, depending on the source, reaching as far back as the Trojan War of 1220 B.C.; some modern historians, however, favor the eighth or seventh century B.C.).[19]

To Earth, Mother of All
Homeric Hymn XXX

I shall sing of well-formed Earth, mother of all
and oldest of all, who nourishes all things living on
land.
Her beauty nurtures all creatures that walk upon
the land,
and all that move in the deep or fly in the air.
O mighty one, you are the source of fair children
and goodly fruit,
and on you it depends to give life to, or take it
away from,
mortal men. Blessed is the man you favor
with willing heart, for he will have everything in
abundance.
His life-giving land teems with crops, and on his
fields
his flocks thrive while his house is filled with
goods.
Such men with just laws rule a city

of beautiful women, while much prosperity and
wealth attend them.
Their sons glory in youthful glee
and their daughters with cheerful hearts in flower-
dances
play and frisk over soft flowers of the field.
These are the ones you honor, O revered goddess
of plenty!
Hail, mother of the gods and wife of starry
Ouranos [sky]!
For my song do grant me livelihood that gladdens
the heart,
and I shall remember you and another song, too.[20]

The pre-Hellenic myths emphasize the consanguinity of humankind with animals and the natural world. They honor the ineffable. "Pre-Hellenic mythology is matriarchal," says classicist Charlene Spretnak, "and classical Olympian mythology is largely patriarchal."[21] The pre-Hellenic goddesses are potent and lovingly empathetic. They represent "a more integrated view of life on Earth," declares Spretnak.[22] They are, she says, our earliest archetypal images. She has assembled fragments of this 3500-year-old oral tradition and reconstituted the myths of the goddesses from archaeological finds and classical writings. Throughout her unique study of the lost goddesses of early Greece, she has followed Jung's advice about trying to divine archetypes and myths. He said: "The most we can do is to dream the myth onwards and give it a modern dress."[23]

The Earth Mother who birthed the world is called Gaia. She is lauded in the preceding passage as "the oldest of divinities."[24] She was *the* Deity before she was the mother of deities. At Delphi, writes Spretnak, the priestess addressed the gods with the salutation: "First in my prayer before all other gods, I call on Earth, primeval prophetess."[25]

FREE OF BIRTH OR DESTRUCTION, of time or space, of form or condition, is the Void. From the eternal Void, Gaia danced forth and rolled Herself into a spinning ball. She molded mountains along Her spine, valleys in the hollows of Her flesh. A rhythm of hills and stretching plains followed Her contours. From Her warm moisture She bore a flow of gentle rain that fed Her surface and brought life.

Wriggling creatures spawned in tidal pools, while tiny green shoots pushed upward through Her pores. She filled oceans and ponds and set rivers flowing through deep furrows. Gaia watched Her plants and animals grow. In time She brought forth from Her womb six women and six men.

The mortals thrived but they were continually concerned with the future. At first Gaia felt this was an amusing eccentricity on their part. However, when She saw that their worry about the future nearly consumed some of Her children, She installed among them an oracle. In the hills at the place they called Delphi, Gaia sent up steaming vapors from Her netherworld. They wafted up from a cleft in the rocks, surrounding a priestess. Gaia instructed Her priestess in the ways of entering a trance and in the interpretation of messages that arose from the darkness of Her earth-womb. The mortals travelled long distances to consult the oracle: Will my child's birth be auspicious? Will our harvest be bountiful? Will the hunt yield enough game? Will my mother survive her illness? Gaia was so moved by their stream of anxieties that She sent forth other portents of the future at Athens and Aegae.

Unceasingly the Earth-Mother manifested gifts on Her surface and accepted the dead into Her body. In return She was revered by all mortals. Offerings to Gaia of honey and barley cake were left in a small hole in the earth before plants were gathered. Many of Her temples were built near deep chasms where yearly the mortals offered sweet cakes into Her womb. From within the darkness of Her secrets, Gaia received their gifts.[26]

This is what I believe, then, said Socrates. In the first place, if the earth is spherical and in the middle of the heavens, it needs neither air nor any other such force to keep it from falling; the uniformity of the heavens and the equilibrium of the earth itself are sufficient to support it. . . .

Although we live in a hollow of the earth, we assume that we are living on the surface, and we call the air heaven, as though it were the heaven through which the stars move. . . . If someone could reach to the summit, or

*put on wings and fly aloft, when he put up his head he
would see the world above, just as fishes see our world
when they put up their heads out of the sea; and if his
nature were able to bear the sight, he would recognize that
that is the true heaven and the true light and the true earth.*

PLATO (ca. 427–ca. 347 B.C.),
Phaedo [27]

Twenty-five hundred years ago, Plato delivered a stunning view
of Earth as a self-sustaining system in space. Long before an American
astronaut called it "the big blue marble," Plato—without benefit of
rocketry—achieved a vision of our planet from afar and described a
perfect orb upon which humans and animals lived a superior life. In
the words of Socrates' last speech (from the *Phaedo*), Plato limns a
world of kaleidoscopic color, of precious stones and god-inhabited
sanctuaries—which can be perceived only by the "blessed." Pondering that vision, Socrates declared, "Such is the nature of the earth."

THERE ARE MANY HOLLOW PLACES all round the earth,
places of every shape and size, into which the water and
mist and air have collected. But the earth itself is as pure
as the starry heaven in which it lies, and which is called
Ether by most of our authorities. The water, mist, and air
are the dregs of this Ether, and they are continually draining into the hollow places in the earth. We do not realize
that we are living in its hollows, but assume that we are
living on the earth's surface. . . .
[T]he real earth, viewed from above, is supposed to
look like one of these balls made of twelve pieces of skin,
variegated and marked out in different colors, of which
the colors which we know are only limited samples, like
the paints which artists use; but there the whole earth is
made up of such colors and others far brighter and purer
still. One section is a marvelously beautiful purple, and
another is golden; all that is white of it is whiter than chalk
or snow; and the rest is similarly made up of the other
colors, still more and lovelier than those which we have
seen. Even these very hollows in the earth, full of water

and air, assume a kind of color as they gleam amid the different hues around them, so that there appears to be one continuous surface of varied colors. The trees and flowers and fruits which grow upon this earth are proportionately beautiful. The mountains too and the stones have a proportionate smoothness and transparency, and their colors are lovelier. The pebbles which are so highly prized in our world—the jaspers and rubies and emeralds and the rest—are fragments of these stones; but there everything is as beautiful as they are, or better still. This is because the stones there are in their natural state, not damaged by decay and corroded by salt water as ours are by the sediment which has collected here, and which causes disfigurement and disease to stones and earth, and animals and plants as well. The earth itself is adorned not only with all these stones but also with gold and silver and the other metals, for many rich veins of them occur in plain view in all parts of the earth, so that to see them is a sight for the eyes of the blessed.

There are many kinds of animals upon it, and also human beings, some of whom live inland, others round the air, as we live round the sea, and others in islands surrounded by air but close to the mainland. In a word, as water and the sea are to us for our purposes, so is air to them, and as air is to us, so the ether is to them. Their climate is so temperate that they are free from disease and live much longer than people do here; and in sight and hearing and understanding and all other faculties they are as far superior to us as air is to water or ether to air in clarity.

They also have sanctuaries and temples which are truly inhabited by gods; and oracles and prophecies and visions and all other kinds of communion with the gods occur there face to face. They see the sun and moon and stars as they really are; and the rest of their happiness is after the same manner.

Such is the nature of the earth as a whole and of the things that are upon it.[28]

Human impact upon the earth was also a subject that Plato

addressed. He was a keen observer of the frailty of the planet. He provides us with one of the best descriptions in ancient times of the havoc created by the careless infringements of humankind on the natural order. In the *Critias,* Plato compares Attica to "the bones of a wasted body . . . a mere remnant of what it once was." Plato was an astute observer of the ravages of deforestation caused by the wanton felling of trees (which resulted in extensive erosion of the entire Greek countryside) and the overgrazing by goats and sheep. What was once a lushly wooded Mediterranean world had been reduced, largely by human activity (as well as nature's fury: earthquakes and mud slides), to a generally stark and treeless landscape. Plato reflects upon the loss of the verdant slopes and grassy terrain in this disturbing passage from the *Critias* and struggles to retrieve any remaining potentialities that may rest within the desolate Greek soil.

> [W]HAT NOW REMAINS compared with what then existed is like the skeleton of a sick man, all the fat and soft earth having wasted away, and only the bare framework of the land being left. But at that epoch the country was unimpaired, and for its mountains it had high arable hills, and in place of the "moorlands," as they are now called, it contained plains full of rich soil; and it had much forestland in its mountains, of which there are visible signs even to this day; for there are some mountains which now have nothing but food for bees, but they had trees not very long ago, and the rafters from those felled there to roof the largest buildings are still sound. And besides, there were many lofty trees of cultivated species; and it produced boundless pasturage for flocks. Moreover, it was enriched by the yearly rains from Zeus, which were not lost to it, as now, by flowing from the bare land into the sea; but the soil it had was deep, and therein it received the water, storing it up in the retentive loamy soil; and by drawing off into the hollows from the heights the water that was there absorbed, it provided all the various districts with abundant supplies of springwaters and streams, whereof the shrines which still remain even now, at the spots where the fountains formerly existed, are signs which testify that our present description of the land is true.[29]

Greatly favored by poets and mystics, the *Phaedrus* describes madness, in one of its manifestations, as ascribed to him who is enthralled by the "love [of] or the inspiration of beauty and knowledge."[30] Socrates, who left no writings of his own, discourses (as relayed by his pupil Plato) with Phaedrus on the true nature of things earthly and celestial. They are sitting under a plane tree, by the banks of the Ilissus River. As recorded in this famous dialogue, they debated the topics of philosophy and poetics, including "the nature of the body and the rhetoric of the soul."[31] Socrates declares that it is through the experience of the higher beauties of earth and reflection upon the sight of such brightness that the awareness of true beauty is reawakened and regained.

THUS FAR I have been speaking of the fourth and last kind of madness, which is imputed to him who, when he sees the beauty of earth, is transported with the recollection of the true beauty; he would like to fly away, but he cannot; he is like a bird fluttering and looking upward and careless of the world below; and he is therefore thought to be mad. And I have shown this of all inspirations to be the noblest and highest and the offspring of the highest to him who has or shares in it, and that he who loves the beautiful is called a lover because he partakes of it. For, as has been already said, every soul of man has in the way of nature beheld true being; this was the condition of her passing into the form of man. But all souls do not easily recall the things of the other world; they may have been unfortunate in their earthly lot, and, having had their hearts turned to unrighteousness through some corrupting influence, they may have lost the memory of the holy things which once they saw. Few only retain an adequate remembrance of them; and they, when they behold here any image of that other world, are rapt in amazement . . .[32]

We bless you, cicada,
high in the branches.
You sip a dew drop
and whistle like a king.
What you see is yours:
all the soft meadows
and furry mountains.
Yet you do no harm
in the farmer's field,
and men exalt you
as the voice of summer.
You are loved by Muses
and Apollo himself
who gave you clear song.
Wise child of the earth,
old age doesn't waste you.
Unfeeling and bloodless
you are like a god.

ANAKREON *(ca. 560 B.C.),*
lyric poet of Teos[33]

All men have need of gods.

HOMER,
Odyssey[34]

From the gods come all possibilities of mortal achieve-
ment; by them men become wise and strong of arm and
mighty in speech.

PINDAR
(ca. 518 B.C.–ca. 438 B.C.),
lyric poet[35]

Dear Pan, and all ye other gods that dwell in this place, grant that I may become fair within, and that such outward things as I have may not war against the spirit within me. May I count him rich who is wise, and as for gold, may I possess so much of it as only a temperate man might bear and carry with him.

Prayer of Socrates,
Plato's Phaedrus [36]

How did the ancient Greeks perceive Nature? They organized it into a system of gods and goddesses who had jurisdiction over all aspects of human activities. An intricate network of deities emerged. Devotional songs, poems or hymns were sung in honor of a god or goddess, usually at religious festivals, weddings, contests or game events; informal and private occasions may also have been included. According to one Greek scholar, the ancients called these poems or hymns, *prooimia* (preludes or preambles), because it is thought that in many cases "the poets used them as warm-up pieces for the singing or recitation of longer portions of the Homeric epics."[37]

In his translation of *The Homeric Hymns,* poet Charles Boer suggests that "the gods as Homer presents them are divine perspectives on the human condition." The Greek gods and goddesses were many and varied; they "were different styles of experience," proposes Boer, "different ways of feeling, of seeing, of desiring. *All* were blessed."[38] The *Hymns* appealed to and honored a grand panoply of deities—living entities who were perceived as the *real* dynamic forces that pervaded, guided and inspired the whole of ancient Greek life.

The *Homeric Hymns* are regarded by some scholars not only as poetry and historical literature but also as living myths. Boer refers to the *Hymns* as some of "the most important primary documents we have of Greek mythology," in that they offer us "a firsthand view of the Greek mythographic experience at an early date. It is an enthralling view."[39] The Greek deities, as they appear in Boer's translations, have been described as dynamic presences, "moving and radiant irruptions of the sacred."[40]

In his fluid rendering of three of the *Homeric Hymns,* the vital grace of the deities is revealed, invoked and honored, as it was indispensable to human existence.

THE HYMN TO THE MUSES

I begin
with the Muses[41]
and with Apollo
and Zeus
because
it's through
the Muses
and the archer
Apollo
that there are men
on earth
singers and
lyre players
and because
it's through Zeus
there are kings
you're a lucky man
if the Muses
like you
sweet
is the sound
that flows
from your mouth
hail
children
of Zeus
favor
my song

I
will remember
you
in another[42]

THE HYMN TO THE MOTHER OF THE GODS

Chant your hymn for me
   this time,
     Muse,
clearly,
   daughter of great Zeus,

to the mother of all the gods
the mother of all men
She loves the sound
of castanets
the sound of kettle-drums
and on top of this noise
she loves the shouts
of flutes
and the clamor of wolves
and the cries of bright-eyed lions
and hill echoes
and wood hollows
she loves them
And that's
how I greet you, goddess,
and all the other goddesses
with this song[43]

THE SECOND HYMN TO APOLLO

Apollo,
it is for you
that the swan sings
so loudly

self-accompanied
on its own wings
beating

beating its way
to the shore of the river,
the Peneus
stirring

It is for you
that a poet shapes
language,
holding in his hand
a lyre that is loud too.

First and last and always
it is for you.
Here is my prayer.
Here, god, is my song.[44]

The union of Heaven and Earth whereby the earth is fertilized—through the sacred pairing of a god and goddess—was a central and unchallenged feature of Greek mythological life. The primary function of this ancient and important belief was to provide a paradigm for human life. The universe was a metaphor for human life: the feminine principle, earth; the masculine, sky and the fertilizing seed, the rain. Aeschylus (born ca. 525 B.C.), the revered dramatist and tragedian, describes the procreative energy of this conception in a classical expression of the divine archetype in a fragment from his play *The Danaids*. The speaker is Aphrodite—goddess of love and beauty and maker of morning dew—who sprang from the foam of the sea.

> THE PURE SKY longs passionately to pierce the Earth, and passion seizes the Earth to win her marriage. Rain falling from the bridegroom sky makes pregnant the Earth. Then brings she forth for mortals pasture of flocks and corn, Demeter's gift, and the fruitfulness of trees is brought to completion by the dew of their marriage. Of these things am I part-cause.[45]

Athena, originally a Cretan goddess, was protectress of hearth and town. Serpent and tree symbolism link her to fertility and renewal. She is the revered goddess of wisdom, arts, and sciences and she watches over potters, weavers, spinners, sculptors and architects. She is the originator of the spiral pattern which she formed from the clay of the Earth.

> IN THE MINOAN DAYS OF CRETE an unprecedented flowering of learning and the arts was cultivated by Athena. Dynamic architecture rose to four stories, pillared and finely detailed, yet always infused with the serenity of the Goddess. Patiently Her mortals charted the heavens, devised a calendar, kept written archives. In the palaces they painted striking frescoes of Her priestesses and sculpted Her owl and ever-renewing serpent in the shrine rooms. Goddess figures and their rituals were deftly engraved on seals and amulets. Graceful scenes were cast in relief for gold vessels and jewelry. Athena nurtured all the arts, but Her favorites were weaving and pottery.
>
> Long before there were palaces, the Goddess had ap-

peared to a group of women gathering plants in a field. She broke open the stems of blue-flowered flax and showed them how the threadlike fibers could be spun and then woven. The woof and warp danced in Her fingers until a length of cloth was born before them. She told them which plants and roots would color the cloth, and then She led the mortals from the field to a pit of clay. There they watched Athena form a long serpent and coil it, much like the serpents coiled around Her arms. She formed a vessel and smoothed the sides, then deftly applied a paste made from another clay and water. When it was baked in a hollow in the earth, a spiral pattern emerged clearly. The image of circles that repeat and repeat yet move forward was kept by the women for centuries.

As the mortals moved forward, Athena guided the impulse of the arts. She knew they would never flourish in an air of strife, so She protected households from divisive forces and guarded towns against aggression. So invincible was the aura of Her protection that the Minoans lived in unfortified coastal towns. Their shipping trade prospered, and they enjoyed a peace that spanned a thousand years. To Athena each family held the olive bough sacred, each worshipped Her in their home. Then quite suddenly the flowering of the Minoans was slashed. Northern barbarians, more fierce than the Aegean Goddess had ever known, invaded the island and carried Athena away to Attica. There they made Her a soldier.[46]

I am Hermes. I stand in the crossroads by a windy
belt of trees near the gray shore of the sea
where the weary traveler may rest: here a fountain
bubbles forth a cold and stainless water.

ANYTE (fl. ca. 290 B.C.),
woman poet of Arkadia
in Peloponnesos[47]

Aphrodite is a fertility goddess. Love and eternal beauty are her hallmarks. She was born from the foam of the sea. Sometimes called *Antheia* (flower goddess) in recognition of her connection with herbalism, she is linked to the rose, apple myrtle, poppy and water-mint.[48] Aphrodite came to Greece via Cyprus.

> LIFE WAS YOUNG AND FRAIL when Aphrodite arose with the breath of renewal. Born by gentle winds on the eastern sea, She alighted on the island of Cyprus. So graceful and alluring was the Goddess that the Seasons rushed to meet Her, imploring Her always to stay. Aphrodite smiled. Her stay would be never ending, Her work never complete. She crossed the pebbled beach and wandered over the hills and plains, seeking out all living creatures. Magically She touched them with desire and sent them off in joyous pairs. She blessed the females' wombs, guarded them as they grew, and warded off love's pains at birth. Everywhere Aphrodite drew forth the hidden promise of life. Every day She kissed the earth with morning dew.
>
> The wanderings of the Goddess carried Her far, yet each spring She returned with her doves to Cyprus for Her sacred bath at Paphos. There She was attended by Her Graces: Flowering, Growth, Beauty, Joy, and Radiance. They crowned Her with myrtle and lay a path of rose petals at Her feet. Aphrodite walked into the sea, into the pulsing moon rhythms of the tide. When She emerged with Her spirit renewed, spring blossomed fully and all beings felt Her joy. Through seasons, years, eras, Aphrodite's mysteries remain inviolable, for She alone understands the love that begets life.[49]

"Which God?" Kosmas asked, surprised.

"The ancient God, of course. Do you think I'm the only one who's seen him? The villagers know that the ancient Gods roam our land on clear nights . . . Everyone knows the statues are haunted . . . Don't you believe that here on our island these Gods never died; they just became spirits. . . ."

Kosmas lived without feeling the loneliness that used to torment him, in this faraway corner of Ikaria, in an old world, warmed by the breath of people that passed over this island thousands of years before. A world that left its tracks behind it, warmed by old tales of gods that hadn't entirely died. Pan lived on, as a satyr, and his companions changed their names and became kallikantzaroi.[50] They lived in the deep caves by the cape or under the ruined temple. And on moonlit nights in January, many were the villagers who saw them roaming the deserted land.

LILIKA NAKOS, *novelist,*
Ikarian Dreamers *(1963)*[51]

For all things come from earth, and all things end by becoming earth.

XENOPHANES OF COLOPHON
(b. ca. 580 B.C.),
moral philosopher[52]

And I felt the earth was crystal beneath my feet,
       the soil transparent,
for the strong and peaceful bodies of tall plane trees
       rose up around me.

ANGELOS SIKELIANOS *(1884–1951)*[53]

Late Minoan Period Vase, ca. 1500–1400 B.C. The design of this three-handled vase displays a vitality and beautifully controlled precision in its depiction of the complex interlocking spiral pattern that was a valued feature of Minoan pottery. Believed to have been inspired by the natural world and its forms, the "scroll decoration" is referred to as the Palace style. The vase is thought to be from Knossos, Crete.

> *SEE! how the plane-tree round those lovers weaves*
> *its untranslucent canopy of leaves,*
> *and how the vine, the summer's dark delight,*
> *adds purple to the branches' greener night.*
> *SO! flourish plane! and may you ever prove*
> *green refuge for the lover and his love.*

> THALLUS OF MILETUS,
> *first century* A.D.[54]

In Homer's *Odyssey,* the gardens of King Alkinoos are an enchanted landscape of paradisiacal abundance. It was there that Odysseus was washed ashore and rescued by Nausicaa, the King's daughter. Some scholars believe that Alkinoos's kingdom—called Phaeacia by Homer—may have been modeled on northern Corfu.

> OUTSIDE THE COURTYARD but stretching close up to the gates, and with a hedge running down either side, lies a large orchard of four acres, where trees hang their greenery on high, the pear and the pomegranate, the apple with its glossy burden, the sweet fig and the luxuriant olive. Their fruit never fails nor runs short, winter and summer alike. It comes at all seasons of the year, and there is never a time when the West Wind's breath is not assisting, here the bud and here the ripening fruit; so that pear after pear, apple after apple, cluster on cluster of grapes, and fig upon fig are always coming to perfection. In the same enclosure there is a fruitful vineyard, in one part of which is a warm patch of level ground, where some of the grapes are drying in the sun, while others are gathered or being trodden, and on the foremost rows hang unripe bunches that have just cast their blossom or show the first faint tinge of purple. Vegetable beds of various kinds are neatly laid out beyond the furthest row and make a smiling patch of never-failing green. The garden is served by two springs, one led in rills to all parts of the enclosure, while its fellow opposite, after providing a watering place for the townsfolk, runs under the courtyard gate towards the great house itself. Such were the beauties with which the gods had adorned Alkinoos' home.[55]

Nature of another sort was explored by comedy playwright Aristophanes (ca. 445–ca. 380 B.C.) in *Birds,* which, as fantasy, has no rival in surviving Greek literature for hundreds of years thereafter.[56] Produced in 414 B.C., the play has two general themes: the rebellion of humankind against the gods and the mutiny of animals against the tyranny of man.

The birds proclaim themselves necessary ingredients in the lives of humans.

AND MORTALS GET all their greatest blessings from us birds. In the first place we make known the seasons of spring, of winter, of autumn: the time to sow, when the crane departs noisily for Africa; at that time it also signals to the shipowner to hang up his steering-paddle and go to sleep, and to Orestes as well to weave himself a warm cloak, so he won't feel cold when he's out stripping other people. After that, again, the kite appears to herald another season, when it's time to shear the spring wool from the sheep; and then the swallow, when you ought to be already selling your winter cloak and buying a thin one. And we are your Ammon, your Delphi, your Dodona, your Phoebus Apollo; for you embark on all your activities only after going to consult the birds—on a trading voyage, on the acquisition of assets, on man's wedlock. And everything that has decisive significance in relation to divination you classify as a "bird." Is it not plain that we are your prophetic Apollo? So, if you recognize us as gods, you will have musical prophets to consult at all seasons, in the winter, in the summer, in the moderate heat. And we won't flit away and sit snobbishly up there among the clouds, like Zeus; no, we will be with you and will give to you, to your children, to your children's children, health-and-wealth, happiness, life, peace, youth, laughter, dances, festivities—and birds' milk. In fact you'll find it possible to tire yourselves out with good things, so wealthy will you all be.

CHORUS: Muse of the thickets—
tiotiotiotiotinx!
Muse of intricate song, with whom I,
among the mountain glens and peaks—
tiotiotiotiotinx!—
perched on a leaf-clad ash tree—
tiotiotiotiotinx!—
bring forth from my vibrant throat
sacred melodies of song for Pan
and holy choral strains for the
Mountain Mother—
totototototototototinx!—
from whence, like a bee,
Phrynichus was ever sucking the

nectar of deathless
music
to produce his honeyed songs—
tiotiotiotiotinx![57]

All the Greek dramatists used nature imagery, but perhaps Sophocles (b. 496 B.C.) leaves us with one of the most striking examples of natural "scene painting" in his magnificent *Oedipus at Colonus.* The prevailing note of Sophoclean drama is reconciliation, harmony and peace. Sophocles was known in antiquity as the "Attic bee" because of his power to extract sweetness from all he touched.[58] An epitaph written by a contemporary poet and recited in a comedy produced just after Sophocles' death describes the benevolence of his character: "Happy was Sophocles. He died after a long life, blest by the gods and skilful in his art having composed many beautiful tragedies. He suffered no evil, and his end was peace."[59] One historian reports that "the charm of his character was such that all men everywhere loved him, and he was dear to the Gods beyond all other men."[60] In *Oedipus at Colonus,* written at the age of ninety, Sophocles pays a farewell tribute to his own cherished birthplace, "white Colonus," an esteemed spot in Athenian lore.

> Here in our white Colonus, stranger guest,
> Of all earth's lovely lands the loveliest,
> Fine horses breed, and leaf-enfolded vales
> Are thronged with sweetly-singing nightingales,
> Screened in deep arbours, ivy, dark as wine,
> And tangled bowers of berry-clustered vine;
> To whose dark avenues and windless courts
> The Grape-god with his nursing-nymphs resorts.
>
> Here, chosen crown of goddesses, the fair
> Narcissus blooms, bathing his lustrous hair
> In dews of morning; golden crocus gleams
> Along Cephisus' slow meandering streams,
> Whose fountains never fail; day after day
> His limpid waters wander on their way
> To fill with ripeness of abundant birth
> The swelling bosom of our buxom earth.[61]

Theocritus (b. ca. 300 B.C.) is celebrated as the inventor of bucolic poetry. His *Idylls* are a cornucopia of Nature's bounty. They show the strong attachment of the poet to his home ground, which included Alexandria and the island of Cos in the eastern Mediterranean. Idyll 7 records a personal experience of a harvest festival that took place on the island of Cos at the height of summer. It is Nature as pure auditory and sensorial experience.

> *Above our heads a grove of elms and poplars*
> *Stirred gently. We could hear the noise of water,*
> *A lively stream running from the cave of the*
>   *Nymphs.*
> *Sunburnt cicadas, perched in the shadowy thickets,*
> *Kept up their rasping chatter; a distant tree-frog*
> *Muttered harshly as it picked its way among*
>   *thorns;*
> *Larks and linnets were singing, a dove made moan,*
> *And brown bees loitered, flitting about the springs.*
> *The tall air smelt of summer, it smelt of ripeness.*
> *We lay stretched out in plenty, pears at our feet.*
> *Apples at our sides and plumtrees reaching down,*
> *Branches pulled earthward by the weight of fruit.*[62]

> *The sun fell in love and married the moon,*
> *and he invited his in-laws the stars to the feast,*
> *fluffed out the clouds for them to sit,*
> *served them a feast of nectar and flowers,*
> *seas and rivers of wine to drink.*
> *All the stars were there but the star of morning;*
> *and at dawn the morning star appeared,*
> *bearing a gift of lively sleep for the bride and groom*
> *and lanterns to light the in-laws on their way,*
> *to leave and return to their homes; the newlyweds are*
>   *sleepy.*

> Greek wedding song,
> Byzantine period (A.D. 300–
> 1453), and still sung[63]

In 1094, the Byzantine Emperor Alexios Comnenos exempted the monasteries of Mount Athos from taxes in the hope that "the most royal and divine Mountain should stand above other mountains of the universe, as Constantinople stands above other cities." Through the wealth and patronage of a succession of Byzantine emperors, Mount Athos became the repository of priceless works of Byzantine art and literature, much like the Monastery of Saint Catherine on Mount Sinai. Formerly the sacred abode of the revered ancient Greek gods Zeus and Apollo, Mount Athos has been the special preserve of the Virgin Mary since the Greeks converted to Christianity more than fifteen hundred years ago. Athos—its Greek name, *Aghion Oros,* means the Holy Mountain—rises to a height of 6,670 feet, isolated on the nearly inaccessible little peninsula that bears its name. It is narrowly joined to the mainland of northern Greece in Macedonia by a slim isthmus. Since the ninth century, the holy mountain has been a sanctuary to several hundred monasteries and hermitages; twenty still survive, inhabited by about three thousand monks and hermits who are committed to a life of spiritual contemplation and physical labor, the preeminent vocation being the working of the soil, the art of tillage and rejoicing in the earth.

Konstantinos Dapontes, in *The Garden of Graces,* describes a monk's life on Mount Athos in 1880. The routine there has changed very little.

> AND A SMALL AXE I HAD and I cut and cleared away pine-trees, holm-oaks, and in their place olives I planted, and pear-trees, and here apples, and here, for my delight, almonds, and then cabbages and leeks and garlic. And I rejoiced in the earth as you rejoice in money. I stood in a garden of graces, in a true paradise of love. And often I went down and gathered limpets, shells, crabs and sometimes prawns; and I was more happy with these things than with all my lordships and all my lordly banquets and all my ladyships. . . .
>
> Towards God I was all gratitude, my heart beat with unspeakable happiness, the place full of scents, the trees of fragrance, birds flying round, you chanting to them, they responding to you, earth offering flowers and lilies to the eyes' delight—I burn at the recollection, am torn with regret: birds charming the ears, you happy, and again and again falling to praise God: hearing, sight, touch, smell gratified, giving thanks and praise to God. You are bored in your cell? Go out and walk, stroll through the blessed

solitude: go to the spring, go down to the lovely sea-shore, go into the caves, cells of the old ascetics, divine palaces; only do not forget the "Kyrie Eleison," lest the springs of mercy close.[64]

Called "the first Greek woman prose writer,"[65] Elisavet Moutzan-Martinengou (1801–1832) describes life on the small Mediterranean island of Zakynthos (also known as Zante) at the end of nearly three hundred years of Venetian rule. *My Story* is a rare autobiographical account of an aristocratic girl's upbringing in the 1800s on the southernmost island of the Ionian chain, in the Ionian Sea, an arm of the Mediterranena Sea between southern Italy and western Greece. Zakynthos was at the crossroads of trade and commerce and was therefore a natural port of call for a diverse range of nationalities, including the Turks, the French, the English and the Russians. The island culture itself was a mix of Greek and Italian influences, the language mostly Greek, the expression and intonation of it mostly Venetian! Bilingualism was commonplace.

Elisavet Moutzan-Martinengou, like all aristocratic girls on Zakynthos, led a secluded life engaged in the prerequisite activities of embroidering and crocheting. The old custom of confining women to the home was very much enforced during Moutzan-Martinengou's brief life. This oppressive atmosphere had a profound effect upon the young Elisavet, driving her to devour books, learn new languages and dream about being a writer, all of which was discouraged (after a point) by her family. Lack of information about the lives of women of this period and region was due in large part to the harsh constraints of isolation imposed by the culture, leading one well-known male writer of the time to comment: "One could hardly guess what sort of lives they led; one never meets them anywhere."[66] Marriage did little to alter these restrictive circumstances. Convents, on the other hand, were considered a refuge, a hope that Moutzan-Martinengou's parents denied her. They "resembled finishing schools," writes her translator, "in that girls spent much of their time there entertaining guests, singing, dancing, and reciting."[67]

Despite the opposition of a hostile environment to an education of any significance for women, Moutzan-Martinengou was determined to pursue her passion for knowledge and her ambition to become a writer. It is this single-mindedness along with an active awareness of the barbaric and prevailing inequities of her society that sets Moutzan-Martinengou apart and makes *My Story* not only unique but, in fundamental and universal ways, a forerunner of feminist literature and a champion of the oppressed everywhere.

Sitting at home day after day, Moutzan-Martinengou lived *out* of the world but *in* a universe of her own making where her only teachers were the literary characters in the books she consumed, monks who visited her parents, the immediate natural environs outside her window and the ideals of Nature, which, we are led to believe, inspired her to write. From a severely repressed social position in Zakynthos society, Moutzan-Martinengou shows others it's possible to find liberating and spiritual exemplars in the smallest and most ordinary experiences. She discovered this insight in the natural and commonplace world around her. This short passage reveals the indomitable spirit of an eager and thirsting sixteen-year-old who wishes to leave her mark on the world:

> A WIDE SKY crowned by hilltops, a valley of grape vines, trees scattered here and there, zephyrs blowing mildly, a village violin sounding in the distance, a walk on the soft grass, a stroll with simple village girls, how much happiness, how much delight, they must have justly given to my heart! . . . At this time, without having studied any art or science yet and having been taught only by nature, I composed several maxims in Italian and two myths in Romaic [spoken Greek language]. I showed these compositions to my teacher [a visiting monk], and he was overjoyed because he realized that I had a creative mind. . . .
>
> At this point I thought of composing Aesopian fables in Greek, and I composed a few . . . to show what nature can do when it does not have the help of art.[68]

This earthen womb knows unerringly the worth of each of her children.

NIKOS KAZANTZAKIS (1883–1957),
Report to Greco[69]

Nikos Kazantzakis had a prophetic fury about him and about everything he did. He is described by an old friend and biographer as a "wild and tender soul" possessed of an exotic face that resembled "something like an African mask." Above all he was passionate.

Kazantzakis—novelist, newspaper columnist, travel writer, translator, poet, author of the much-acclaimed and popular novels *Zorba the Greek* and *The Last Temptation of Christ,* among others— is the most widely translated Greek man of letters. His cosmological principles—a wide-angle view of the universe—are embodied in *The Saviors of God.* They are of an evolutionary, involutionary and cosmic nature: all life, all the cosmos—the universe—is perpetually evolving toward self-consciousness.

Kazantzakis' work is deeply rooted in the Greek natural world, especially in its rock and earth, informed by its ancestors, haunted by past glories and defeats, and given relevance through memory and imagination. But it was the shepherds and the fishermen of his birthplace, Crete, who were to become his moral exemplars. Kazantzakis observed their reciprocity with nature and was inspired by it. They taught him about simplicity and humility. Nowhere else on earth did he feel such solidity of being as he did in the Cretan countryside. The earth of Crete became a talisman of great persuasion for Kazantzakis. It filled him, supplied him with strength and exerted a mystical and embracing influence upon him that extended to all humankind.

> COMPASSIONATELY, TRANQUILLY, I squeeze a clod of Cretan soil in my palm. I have kept this soil with me always, during all my wanderings pressing it in my palm at times of great anguish and receiving strength, great strength, as though from pressing the hand of a dearly loved friend . . . I hold this Cretan soil and squeeze it with ineffable joy, tenderness, and gratitude. . . . This soil I was everlastingly; this soil I shall be everlastingly. O fierce clay of Crete, the moment when you were twirled and fashioned into a man of struggle has slipped by as though in a single flash.[70]

The magnitude of the earth's appeal, the identification of soil and soul as one, and the union between man and nature—all formed a large part of Nikos Kazantzakis' life's quest for self-discovery. It was from the earth that he found his dignity and moral autonomy. He expressed these ideas with passionate clarity in the following passage about his maternal lineage and the ancestral mandates that dominated his life in his autobiographical *Report to Greco:*

> ALL MY FOREBEARS on my mother's side were peasants— bent over the soil, glued to the soil, their hands, feet, and

minds filled with soil. They loved the land and placed all their hopes in it; over the generations they and it had become one. In time of drought they grew sickly black with thirst along with it. When the first autumn rains began to rage, their bones creaked and swelled like reeds. And when they ploughed deep furrows into its womb with the share, in their breasts and thighs they re-experienced the first night they slept with their wives. . . .

There is a mystical contact and understanding between this soil which fashioned us, and our souls. Just as roots send the tree the secret order to blossom and bear fruit so that they themselves may receive their justification and reach the goal of their journey, so in the same way the ancestral soil imposes difficult commandments upon the souls it has begotten. Soil and soul seem to be of the same substance, undertaking the same assault; the soul is simply maximal victory. . . .

Man can feel no religious awe more genuine and profound, I believe, than the awe he feels when treading the ground where his ancestors—his roots—repose. Your own feet sprout roots which descend into the earth and search, seeking to mingle with the great immortal roots of the dead. The tart fragrance of the soil and camomile fills your vitals with tranquility and also with a desire for free submission to the eternal laws. . . .

The emotion I felt in walking over the ancient grounds of Knossos was so superabundantly rich, so embroiled with life and death, that I find myself unable to analyze it clearly. Instead of sorrow and death, instead of tranquility, stern commandments rose from the decomposed mouths. I felt the dead hanging in long chaplets from my feet—not to lower me into their cool darkness, but rather to take hold of something and rise into the light with me in order to recommence the battle. Unquenchable joy and thirst, together with the living bulls bellowing in the pastures of the world above, the sea salt and the perfume of grass, had penetrated the earth's crust for thousands of years and prevented the dead from dying.[71]

The natural world of Crete is woven into the fabric of Nikos Kazantzakis' existence. He sought refuge in it. Sun and sea are everywhere. His reverence for both is palpable. They bring him to life. The lemon and orange trees perfumed his air, and "from the vastness of the sea," he wrote in *Zorba the Greek,* "[there] emanated an inexhaustible poetry."[72]

IN THE MORNING the world was resplendent and steaming. A violent squall had broken out during the night; the parched soil had received the celestial waters and been refreshed. When I went to my window, I found the earth and sea sweetly fragrant, the sky freshly washed and sparkling, brilliantly white from the sun's radiance. My breast, like a parcel of land, had been refreshed as well; like parched soil it had received the entire night-time squall. The joy I felt was so great that I found it impossible to bend over my paper on this day and turn the world into octameters. Opening the door, I went outside.[73]

The Aegean is not only light and sea: it enters the body of men and becomes heartbeat, blood, and memory. It calls to them forever.

ILIAS VENEZIS (1904–1973),
novelist and writer; leading figure of Greek letters (the generation of the 1930s)[74]

Aiolian Land is considered a Modern Greek classic, and by some a world classic. Variously described as an epic, a folk song, an ancient Greek drama, a hymn and symbolic lyric poetry, the story introduces us to the visible and invisible forces of nature through a series of childhood reminiscences set in the farmlands at the foot of the Kimindenia mountains of the Aegean. The author, Ilias Venezis, was born in Aivali, the Turkish name for the Greek Kydoniai in Asia Minor. Novelist, author of innumerable short stories and plays, and consummate storyteller, Venezis was a leading figure in Modern Greek letters, a member of the Academy of Athens and director of the Greek National Theater. The ethos of the land is at the heart of his universal and affecting tale about the last Greek inhabitants of Aiolia in the years prior to World War I. Venezis has composed a captivating song of things eternal at a time when people lived close to the earth and cherished it and children resonated with the natural world around them.

IT WAS IN THE COUNTRY, close to the land, that I began to learn of the secret life of trees and of the deep bond that exists between man and the sun, the soil, and water. . . .

So Uncle Joseph grew old on the land under the Kimindenia [he had come to earn enough money to return to Limnos and marry his sweetheart. But he did not go back]. He succeeded in only one of the farm tasks, and in that he became a specialist: grafting trees. He knew each of his trees well; he was their friend; he became one of them. He had at last found a goal in life, and he withdrew from men and from worldly things. He did not even care to learn of the world from which he had come. Only at night, in his dreams, did memories of the sea come to him, visions of the fishing boat that he had never bought. But, soon, the imaginary boats and sails would be transformed into trees and leaves. When the time came each year to graft the trees, Uncle Joseph would become very restless and excited. We were sent with him so that we could watch the procedure and so that each of us might choose a tree that would be grafted in his or her name. For Uncle Joseph, the grafting was a sacred ceremony and we, too, were carried away by the atmosphere, even though we could not understand the reason why.

And since, in this way, Uncle Joseph had taught me to love trees, I cried when the old walnut tree on the farm died. My mother, who instinctively wanted to protect me for as long as possible from the knowledge of death, explained to me the "story" of the tree, of how it had been planted and of how it would continue to live through its offspring. That afternoon, I brought Artemi to the old tree and tried to retell the story to her. We lay down on the ground to try to hear the sound of the tree's blood in the young roots, just as Uncle Joseph had done when he had grafted his trees. After a while, the miracle happened: we heard the tree's heart beating—or so at least we believed, for in fact we heard the beating of our own hearts. That evening, Artemi overheard Grandfather ask Uncle Joseph if he wanted to plant the new walnut tree the next day; if he were not afraid to plant it. Questioned later by Artemi, Uncle Joseph explained to her that some people—though not he—believed that anyone who planted a walnut tree would die when it bore its first fruit. So the next morning, when Uncle Joseph arrived at the site of the tree, he found Artemi awaiting him. When he took the seeds out of his pocket, she grabbed them from him and threw them into the ground herself. She did not know why she had done it, but she felt that by so doing she would perhaps learn another of the secrets of the world.[75]

The following passage from Pericles Yannopoulos' *The Greek Line* (published in Athens in 1961, fifty years after its author's tragic death) reveals a mind at large in nature, breathing in all the morning dew of holy Greece. The author takes on the heartbeat of the Greek landscape as he absorbs the harmonic proportions of Hellas' horizon, respectfully probing the impenetrable sanctuaries of the Hellenic tradition.

THE SUN FALLS behind the city of Syra. . . . Silence reigns over all, not a single breath of air stirs; over all an indolent warmth spreads and the sea, drowned, is still. Sailing ships rest where they happen to be with folded wings, like birds resting on the water.

When the wind-blown, wave-rocked, deep-sounding current of the Aegean, whose mood directs the life and expression of the islanders, quietens, everything takes on another look, a new look. Then at all points, clear, large, rising up and approaching in silence, the islands which circle the horizon appear, as if some mass were performed, something great consummated in nature.

Unpaintable, unsingable, inexpressible then is the dance of the Nymphs of the Aegean, crown of flowering passion. Tinos, a warm, violet pile, copying the inimitable Hymettos during the most intense moments of its life, the last caresses of the Sun. A joining blue line of sea links Tinos and Mykonos. Mykonos, a most gentle pink, like a faded April rose. Another, more open joining line of sea and then Naxos, velvet, dark red burning fire. Holy Delos swimming in motionless water. A wonderful necklet of flowers circling the sky with its central flower the small isle of Pharos, a gold branch of an acacia. . . .

Here everywhere and on all sides, from the depths of the Aegean, from the bowels of those magic soils, crumbled as if ready to be shaped into many forms, rises to the light the race of men, created under the maternal caresses of these holy dwellings of the Gods. Here only skies and earth and winds and sea and colour forever caress the senses, like a mother a beloved child; they nourish the mind with tenderness like a natural flower, flower above the visible animal world of earth. Body and soul, heart and mind open like beautiful flowers and like a bunch of flowers give out rich perfume. . . .

O God of Greece. Once only have my lips moved in prayer, once only have they uttered a petition, that such be the hour and such the sight when my worshipping eyes close, when but one way of expressing this holy enchantment remains, to bend and kiss the native soil, to rise up and cross myself in deep reverence, worshipping the soil and the waters and the colour and the sky of holy Greece.[76]

The body of man inclines towards the soil
leaving behind his unfulfilled love;
like a stone statue touched by time,
he falls naked on the rich
breast which softens him little by little.

GEORGE SEFERIS (1900–1971),
poet and essayist[77]

The wisdom of the ancients in all its aspects streams through the numinous imagination of George Seferis, whose words exhibit a finely honed sensitivity to the moods of Nature. Perceived by many as the leading figure of the modernist movement, Seferis often points out that a Modern Greek folk song may throw light on a passage of

Homer or of Aeschylus. He has written that if we are to understand the ancient Greeks "it is always into the soul of our own people that we should look."

Essayist, diarist, poet, Greek ambassador to London, recipient of the Nobel Prize for Literature (1963), George Seferis, through his many works, conveys a quiet humility about everything. He gives the impression that he is simply flattered to be alive. His gratitude is rooted in the natural world—his delight in just being alive.

> THE DAY BEFORE YESTERDAY under my northern window I saw two shy little blossoms on an almond tree—the first almond tree in blossom. On the mountain the cyclamen turn to leaves; in the sea, the dark blue fluttering of the kingfisher.
> I give thanks.[78]

As a child, Seferis lived in a world peopled by trees that "smiled" at him and upon him. Trees were his only dreams in childhood. He tells us he "was very fond of the green leaves" and admits half seriously he may have "learned a little at school simply because the blotting paper on my desk was also green." Tree trunks were another matter. They played a decisive role as he began to grow. Their roots "tormented" him "when in the warmth of winter they'd come and wind themselves around [his] body." The poet quietly confides: "That's how I got to know my body." Trees introduced Seferis to himself.

The influence of trees persisted. Seferis sought the regenerative powers of his arboreal teachers throughout his adult life.

> I KNOW A PINE TREE that leans over near a sea. At mid-day it bestows upon the tired body a shade measured like our life, and in the evening the wind blowing through its needles begins a curious song as though of souls that made an end of death, just at the moment when they begin to become skin and lips again. Once I stayed awake all night under this tree. At dawn I was new, as though I had been freshly quarried.[79]

Coming down from the mountain of "obscure verses," Bashō's teaching to Kikakou suddenly took hold of the thoughts of poet George Seferis.

WE SHOULDN'T ABUSE God's creatures. You must reverse the haiku, not:

> A dragonfly;
> remove its wings—
> pepper tree.

but:

> A pepper tree;
> add wings to it—
> dragonfly.[80]

This holiness of Nature is a fragile thing: it wilts in proportion as her own virginal purity is tampered with, her modesty pried into, her austere exuberance "tamed," as the brutal saying goes. "Avoid tampering" is a spiritual maxim the Taoist sages made into the keynote of their teaching; the world's busybodies have gone on neglecting it to their own and our great peril. Under the continual measuring and delving and lumping together which now has reached its climax, the face of the Great Mother is becoming so disfigured that soon it may be unrecognisable, with all its eminences "conquered," its furrowing dales "brought under the discipline of a map" (as another blasphemy hath it), its underwater—sky even—contaminated, the whole so blotched and flayed and carved up and reshuffled that only the all-seeing Intellectual Eye will still be able, across the wreckage of a dishallowed world, to perceive the Motherly Presence there where she subsists. . . .

> MARCO PALLIS,
> *entomologist, mountain climber*
> *and music teacher*[81]

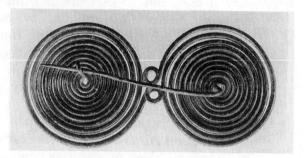

TOP LEFT: *Gold pendant,* Crete, ca. 1600 B.C. TOP RIGHT: *A coin from Knossos,* Crete, home of the "original labyrinth," second century B.C. BOTTOM: *Bronze Wire Fibula* (or Brooch), Greece, tenth century B.C. This ancient fibula is one flowing bronze wire. The double spiral shows the two halves of the spherical vortex; the winding and unwinding, without beginning or end, continuously renewing itself; the symbol of rebirth in nature and humankind.

Make us find ourselves again in our love for you, brotherly earth!

MINAS DIMAKIS *(1916–1980),*
poet and essayist[82]

No place is as precious as one's homeland.

THEOGNIS
*(fl. second half
of 6th century B.C.),
elegiac poet*[83]

*In the modern Greek no region of his homeland calls forth
a disinterested quiver of aesthetic appreciation. The region
has a name; it is called Marathon, Salamis, Olympia, Ther-
mopylae, Mistra, and it is bound up with a memory . . .*

NIKOS KAZANTZAKIS,
novelist and poet[84]

THE GREEK HOMELAND

Another aspect of earth in Greek thinking revolved around a deeply patriotic attitude toward country that was essentially inseparable from sense of self.

The ancient Greeks believed their homeland to be an extension of their bodies and spirit. The ground and self were considered one, a belief that sprang from deep love of country and the hallowed ancestral imperative that rooted and nourished the Greek spirit. "[O]ur ancestors . . . deserve praise," said Pericles (ca. 495–429 B.C.) in his famous Funeral Oration, for "[t]hey dwelt in the country without break in the succession from generation to generation, and handed it down free to the present time by their valor."[85] In the *Panegyricus* (an address to the Hellenic nation), Isocrates (436–338 B.C.), teacher and founder of a prominent school in Athens to foster rhetorical skills, upholds the value of *autochthony,* that is, being born of the soil, and states its unique significance to an understanding of what it means to be Greek.

> [W]E DID NOT BECOME DWELLERS in this land by driving others out of it, nor by finding it uninhabited, nor by coming together here a motley horde composed of many races; but we are of a lineage so noble and so pure that throughout our history we have continued in possession of the very land which gave us birth, since we are sprung from its very soil and are able to address our city by the very names which we apply to our nearest kin; for we alone of all the Hellenes have the right to call our city at once nurse and fatherland and mother.[86]

The bond with homeland—the sacred soil of one's natal roots—

is a mystical attachment that has vital power. It fuses the primary elements of Nature with the true nature of the inhabitants and their ancestors. Lilika Nakos (1899–1984) was one of the first women writers of Modern Greek prose and for many years the only woman in Greek journalism. In these passages from two of her novels, the nature of the Greek earth is explored and revealed.

A commitment to the ancestral mandates that saturate the Hellenic tradition is expressed by the protagonist of *Boetian Earth* (1955).

SHE FELT DEEPLY BOUND TO THIS LAND. She had deep roots in the earth she walked on, and the more it suffered, the more she loved it! The Greek soil wasn't like any other. It was made of the dust of our grandfathers who freed it from the Turk, it was made of the Ancient ancestors who illuminated and gave shape to matter with their spirit . . . It was made even of the dust of our own beloved dead . . . How can anyone, then, without wrenching, leave for good, uproot himself thus to distant foreign countries? Doesn't each of us have a duty to do something to better life in this unhappy land?[87]

In *Ikarian Dreamers* (1963), the principal character, Kosmos, listens in on a conversation in a hired car as another Greek traveler is reminded of the home he was forced to leave after the Asia Minor disaster.

WAY OVER THERE could be seen the mountains of Asia Minor and Samos next to them. A traveler waved his hand in that direction . . . , "Over there is Cesme. Holy soil, blessed land . . . We had our fields there," he said and sighed with grief. It was apparent that he was from Asia Minor. The other travelers, who weren't refugees, but natives, also sighed. Before the Catastrophe, Ikarians and Samiotes went and worked in Smyrna. They were all still leaning psychologically toward Asia Minor. It was a second homeland to them.[88]

O shining city, festooned in violets, draped
in song,
you are the marble strength of all Hellas,
glorious Athens, sacred citadel.

PINDAR *(ca. 518 b.c.–ca. 438 b.c.),*
prince of choral lyric poets[89]

Heracleides of Crete (first century B.C.) wrote a delightful evocation of Athens that reads like a modern travelogue and displays his own admiration of the city's grandeur in a surge of patriotic pride.

THE ROAD TO ATHENS is a pleasant one, running between cultivated fields the whole way. The city itself is dry and ill supplied with water. The streets are nothing but miserable old lanes, the houses mean, with a few better ones among them. On his first arrival a stranger could hardly believe that this is the Athens of which he has heard so much. Yet he will soon come to believe that it is Athens indeed. A Music Hall, the most beautiful in the world, a large and stately theatre, a costly, remarkable, and far-seen temple of Athena called the Parthenon rising above the theatre, strike the beholder with admiration. A temple of Olympian Zeus, unfinished but planned on an astonishing scale; three gymnasiums, the Academy, Lyceum, and Cynosarges, shaded with trees that spring from greensward; verdant gardens of philosophers; amusements and recreations; many holidays and a constant succession of spectacles—all these the visitor will find in Athens.

The products of the country are priceless in quality but not too plentiful. However, the frequency of the spectacles and holidays makes up for the scarcity to the poorer sort, who forget the pangs of hunger in gazing at the shows and pageants. Every artist is sure of being welcomed with applause and of making a name; hence the city is crowded with statues. . . .

In short, Athens as far surpasses all other cities in the pleasures and conveniences of life as they surpass the country. But a man must beware of the courtesans, lest they lure him to ruin. . . .[90]

Long ago, the Mountain Mother
Of all the gods . . .

EURIPIDES *(ca. 480–406 B.C.),*
Helen[91]

. . . the shore and the mountains with all their voices. . . .

DIONYSIOS SOLOMOS *(1798–1857),*
national poet of modern Greece[92]

MOUNTAIN WORLDS OF GREECE

Kostas Pasagianis (1872–1933) was one of Greece's first modern travel writers, with a Hellenic twist. He devoted himself entirely to the geographical terrain of Hellas—the region of Messenia, and Peloponnesos in general. In *Greek Travels,* Pasagianis unfolds the mountain world of Greece, its subliminal character so redolent of *illo tempore* (Mircea Eliade's term, conveying the notion of primordial time). The commanding and dazzling presence of "these high blue solitudes," reflects, in a sense, the character of Greek ideals more than any other single element of Hellas' physical makeup. Experiencing the heights is an altogether transcendent experience that summons up another world—the vast realm of the imagination that illumines the continuum of the Hellenic tradition.

FROM DELVINO ONWARDS the road rises abruptly from mountain to mountain, from ridge to ridge, ribbon-like, over-hanging, with steep climbs.

All round, the mountain-sides supporting the bare, treeless peaks are green with wild ilex and oak.

Lower down, thick shady plane-trees cover the ravines.

Crystal waters utter their cool song sweetly in the deep valleys.

From bush to bush, in white-flowering myrtle and in the thick wild shrubs the playful speech of the stonechat fills the quiet mountain dawn with joy.

At each new bend, as the road climbs higher, the sky opens wider; eyes embrace beautiful, ever-expanding worlds.

Plains and mountains, rivers and seas dream in the

blue light. They level out in the distance. They mingle with the boundless sky.

High, terribly high. The great contentment which the sensitive traveller experiences in these high blue solitudes is doubled by the secret feeling of delight that no ugliness of the human crowd reaches here.

The motionless mountain silence prompts with a certain secret pleasure in the soul the happiness of complete isolation. Something which seems outside life. Something therefore like the longing for eternal peace. The thrice-blessed non-existence! . . .

One embraces life more completely on the heights. Perhaps because one comes closer to God.

We go on.

Now we cross a sun-dazzled stretch with open, limitless horizon above the mountain-mass.

We turn back and descend into a small green valley.

Then we climb once more into the mountains. To other mountains and to other sun-dazzled stretches, and to other sharp peaks.

A mountain-world. And only mountain. And again mountain. The mountains dominate to the horizon beneath us.

Ravine, valley, are lost, are assimilated in the boundless, many-branched mountain-mass.

High mountains, shadowing mountains, wooded mountains, mountain-shapes like petrified waves in space, in a blue, mystical light.

Somewhere round here was the religion of ancient Greece born. Dodona, Io, Zeus the Thunderer. . . .

One experiences more deeply the mystery of the world's birth, seeing from these heights the god-created crown of the mountains of Epiros waving bluely and dipping up and down in space.

A poor little mountain-village to our left, upon a projecting rock. Thatched huts. Small houses covered with grassy tiles which shine silver in the sun.

The village of Garthikaki.

Such a caressing sound has the name of this isolated little mountain-village that one would say it takes something from the call of the partridges which fill the surrounding rocks with joy.

At the foot of the mountain-village, goat-folds. He-goats and she-goats. Bleatings and bells. Kitsos and the shepherdess Mosco. Daphnis and Chloe. Pan, the Great Pan, who never dies up here. Deathless, incorruptible Life. . . .[93]

Throughout his years of mountaineering, Marco Pallis sought among the mountains—both on "home crags and in the greater ranges abroad"[94]—the symbolism of Wayfaring and the enlightenment that accompanies it. "[I]t should surprise nobody," he once wrote, "that there is a metaphysical doctrine of wayfaring and also one of climbing, each carrying with it its appropriate symbolism."[95] The symbolism of Wayfaring, in almost all cultures, is marked by the symbolic *journey,* which has come to signify a quest for unity, a return to a state of wholeness and, ultimately, self-knowledge. The Way, itself, contains an organic invisibility that will yield only to true insight—"the true Olympus," in the words of entomologist and teacher of music Pallis.

In *The Way and the Mountain,* Pallis considers some aspects of that correlation (namely, the symbol of the Way and its corresponding symbol in the Mountain) which, he proposes, has universal significance and is an unconditional and transcendent reality.

[T]HE WAY ITSELF is indefinable apart from the wayfarer. Without a way there can be no wayfaring but it is the wayfarer's presence in it which in effect makes it possible to speak of a way at all. The "realizing" of the Way is therefore, for the wayfarer, nothing other than the "pilgrimage of his own Self" (as an Indian sage once described it) and it is the unseen Way which itself makes its own various stages and incidents real according to their kind and degree. . . .

[A] complementary symbolism [to the symbolism of Wayfaring is] that of the Mountain. Here we have an almost bewildering wealth of examples to draw upon. Sacred mountains, symbolising the exaltation of Divinity, are to be found in every corner of the globe. The Grecian Olympus will be the first to spring to mind, only here it is important to expose the common error of thinking that the ancients believed their gods to be physically resident on the actual Mount Olympus, that glorious peak. . . .

[T]he true Olympus is only discernible by those "who have eyes to see," and it can only be scaled by a true wayfarer, while the earthly mountains that have been given that name (for there are several of them) are themselves so called in order to turn them into reminders, or symbols, of the heavenly Olympus. The taking of such a symbolism too literally by the ignorant, among whom many professional scholars must be included, is but an example of how a doctrine can degenerate in times of decay into a "superstition," by the literal survival of its symbols after their deeper meaning has been lost sight of.

The way to the Mountain is nowhere and everywhere; it therefore cannot be specified in rational language, but it becomes immediately apparent to those who have earned that knowledge by paying the required price. That price is the renunciation or denial of self in its separative individual sense, in order to realise true Selfhood in the universal sense. Middle English possessed a most concise and expressive term for this sacrificial abandonment: it called it "self-noughting" (which is the same as Self-knowing), and this it is which furnishes the principal theme for many a Gospel and for all the fairy-tales. . . .

[E]very being, whether aware of it or not, is born a potential wayfarer, and . . . his true destiny is to realise all that is implied in such a status by searching for and ultimately arriving at the Goal. . . .

It would be impossible in a small space to enumerate one half of the mountain peaks that are traditionally associated with this kind of symbolism; some mention should however be made of the practice of going on a pilgrimage to a sacred mountain, since the ritual act assuming such a form is one in which the ideas of the Way and the Mountain are closely linked together. In quite a general sense, the rite of pilgrimage is always an imitation of the Way, while the place of pilgrimage itself, whether this be some natural landmark, or a shrine, represents the Goal. Pilgrimage to Mecca for the Moslem or to Jerusalem for the Jew are well-known examples.

Many pilgrim routes exist in which the centre in question takes the form of a mountain; one of the most famous of these, a familiar feature in Japanese art, is the conical summit of the volcanic Mount Fuji up the slopes of which thousands of pilgrims make their way annually to the edge of the crater. Among pilgrim ways having this character there is one, however, which, to the mountaineer, is more than ordinarily suggestive, and that is the track leading across the main Himalayan chain to the Kailas, a high peak situated in Tibet near the sources of the rivers Brahmaputra and Satlej. This mountain is particularly sacred to both Hindus and Buddhists. The former regard it as the symbolical abode of Shiva, which is the name attached to the divine function of Transformation, or passage beyond individual forms and their distinction into the indistinction of formless Knowledge. The long and arduous journey through the mountains of Garhwal, with their indescribably glorious scenery, is well calculated to awaken, in the mind of one coming from the plains, an aspiration to enter that supreme and inward Way which is thus outwardly prefigured.[96]

Marco Pallis has some experience of the irresistible attraction of the summit of mountains. He addresses the metaphysical dimensions of achieving the heights. Arrival bespeaks self-realization. There is no art to getting there. The peak exists in the knowing and that knowledge requires purity of heart.

[O]NLY HE WHO HAS ATTAINED THE SUMMIT and made himself one with it knows the solution of the mystery, for as between any stage or step, even the most exalted, and the supreme realization there is an absolute discontinuity which it would be idle to try and bridge by word or thought. So long as there yet exists a step to be taken there are alternatives and hence there are possibilities of comparison, but at the summit all alternative routes become one; every distinction between them, and therefore every opposition, is spontaneously reconciled. The summit itself not only occupies no space, although the whole mountain is virtually contained in it, but it is also outside time and all succession, and only the "eternal present" reigns there. It is utterly inexpressible in its uniqueness; silent is the Knower of the Summit and the whole Universe strains its ears to catch the accents of his speechless eloquence.[97]

What is fundamental in the work of George Seferis is the transcendent and universal nature of the Greek landscape. In his unique world, a rare imagination flourishes. A strange ubiquitous beauty effloresces. In "A Letter to a Foreign Friend," Seferis continues his journey to a remembered oneness; he writes, "at times you cannot discern whether the mountain opposite is a stone or a gesture. The *Logos* in its disembodied form is something which transcends our powers."[98]

THE MOUNTAINS, each inside the other, are bodies hugging each other, flowing into each other; they proceed and *complete* you. The same with the sea. This amazing thing *happens*. It is impossible for me to express this revelation in a better way. After this, whether or not you are a person has no significance. Or, the person is no longer *you*, the person is *there*. If you can, you complete it. If you can, you perform a sacred act. At this point, happiness or unhappiness mean nothing; it is a struggle that takes place elsewhere.[99]

All men by nature reach out their hands for the light which will lighten their going to and fro in the world.

ARISTOTLE (384–322 B.C.),
Physics[100]

The factor which renders Greece's mountains, villages and soil buoyant and immaterial is the light. In Italy the light is soft and feminine, in Ionia extremely gentle and full of oriental yearning, in Egypt thick and voluptuous. In Greece the light is entirely spiritual. Able to see clearly in this light, man succeeded in imposing order over chaos, in establishing a "cosmos"—and cosmos means harmony.

NIKOS KAZANTZAKIS,
Report to Greco[101]

I believe it's really the light. There must surely be something about the light that makes us what we are. In Greece, one is more friendly, more at one with the universe.

GEORGE SEFERIS[102]

SHADES OF LIGHT

I n his *Observations on the Climate of Athens* published in 1841, poet and writer Konstantine Mavroyannis (1816–1861) describes the exceptional and illusory nature of the light that clothes the Greek landscape, displaying its endless variety of foibles and conjuring tricks; at once a fluidity of softness, an infinity of angles.

THE BEAUTY OF GREEK NATURE seems to be due above all to two particular characteristics. The first is variety combined with extreme simplicity: the simplicity in the formal elements, the lines of the horizon; the variety being due to the light which, especially at sunrise and sunset, changes the scene magically every moment, as though clothing it in a different dress. Our attention is thus always held by this gradual transformation, the image before us being renewed through the play of light and shadows. The facade in itself is of extreme simplicity: clear sky, attractive and gentle horizon, streams and the sea's inlets. But the colours of the mountains, the surface of the sea, the tones of the sky, are always changing according to the state of the atmosphere. This happens also elsewhere, but as it is above all the light that gives this perpetual variety to the scene, and as the light is exceptional in Greece, these compelling alternations are more perceptible and manifold.

The other characteristic is the feeling of calm and repose. Rarely does the atmosphere grow forbidding, and when it does it soon clears up again: its disturbance is as a passing cloud of anger. The vibrant light of the stars, the waves of scent-laden breezes are so gentle, so calm, that it seems that the elements become rarified and are diffused into the harmony of that image of His own beauty in which God created them. . . .[103]

Light radiates from the Greek earth and has magnetized the imaginative worlds of both ancient and modern Greece. In *this* light —enduring, transcendent and inescapable; a light that has dominated the experience of the Greek landscape since time immemorial—another side to living existed. "[T]his essential . . . this foundation of life," wrote George Seferis in his diary; "I know I must live with the light. I know nothing further." Elsewhere, he observed: "The most worthless playthings leap and dance in the light; you watch it transforming them, turning them into other things . . . Greece is merciless."[104] In the poetics of Constantine Cavafy, the unrelenting light is approached differently but with similar impassioned reflection. In "The Windows," Cavafy enters his own heartbeat as he ventures knowingly but warily, "Perhaps the light will prove another tyranny," and then proceeds to ask, "Who knows what new things it will expose."[105] Nikos Kazantzakis, perhaps Greece's most famous modern writer, suggests that the challenge of the Greek landscape lies in the regenerative power of the light. He experiences the light as a metaphor for human potential; it bestows opportunities as it floods the soul with the terror of its bounty. Kazantzakis was haunted by the exacting nature and profound beauty of this "entirely spiritual light."

That light did not escape Homer, "the great leader and teacher," in Plato's words. His poems became the cornerstone of Greek literature and education. Homer was the great molding force of Greece. It appears that the famous Homeric Question—who was Homer and how much of the *Iliad* and *Odyssey* did he write?—continues to elicit elaborate guesswork. Herodotus places him in the ninth century before Christ ("four hundred years before my time and not more"), while Hellanicus, an early Ionian writer, suggests the twelfth century (closer to the fighting at Troy that Homer so vividly describes). A number of modern historians favor the eighth and seventh centuries B.C. Fortunately, the conundrum of Homer's genesis has taken a back seat to what he has come to represent, not only in antiquity but throughout the ages. One ancient writer says of Homer that "he touched nothing without somehow honoring and glorifying it."[106] George Seferis has confided that he returns time and again to the "vibrating chord" of Homer where he experiences a "harmonious sound." "[I]n Homer," he writes,

> EVERYTHING MESHES, the whole world is a woof of organic "umbilical cords"; the earthly, the heavenly world, animals, plants, elements, the hearts of men, good, evil, death, life—that ripen, vanish, and flower again. The *mechanism* of the gods performs nothing supernatural, nothing ex machina; it retains coherence, nothing else.[107]

In the *Odyssey*, the great epic poem attributed to Homer, Anticlea's last words, sung to her son, acknowledge the nourishing gift of light:

> And the soul takes flight like a dream
> Now quick as you can
> Go back to the light, and remember all these things . . .[108]

> Come see, come marvel on the sun's upleaping,
> how morning star outglows and how it lights
>   the world.
> Come see, my hero, how the sun upleaps,
> how dawning crowns the mountains, how the gorges
>   shine.
>
>   Mourning song of Greek women
>   urging dead sons back to life
>   *(18th–19th century)*[109]

> Desperately I move
> out of the subject
> toward the object
> which is eternal
> and shines, its navel
> in the middle
> like an enormous lamp.
> Not that I'm not afraid
> but if the night is obliging
> the ropes open
> I go in and out of the body and see
> my heart
> a lump of earth
> leaning on the light
> light incomparable

light concrete as water
smiling at the dead one
which it knew
long before me.

KATERINA ANGHELAKI-ROOK,
poet and translator, "My Heart at Night"[110]

The whole sees, the whole perceives, the whole hears.

XENOPHANES (b. ca. 580 B.C.),
moral philosopher[111]

I have found that the eye which sees the whole circle expresses our soul simply and perfectly.

NIKOS KAZANTZAKIS[112]

ONE FROM MANY

(E PLURIBUS UNUM)

Pericles Yannopoulos (1869–1910) was a much admired prose writer who took his life by riding on horseback to his grave beneath the sea of Salamis, near Eleusis, at the age of forty-one. Yannopoulos spent his short life "painting" the different faces of Attica with a delicate fervor and "a quick and limpid laughter," in the words of a friend. His thought and style inspired the great modern poet Angelos Sikelianos, who wrote that this tormented and gifted soul was possessed of a "rhythmical strength which declares beauty effortlessly."[113] Another modern Greek writer, Ion Dragoumis, was equally influenced by Yanno-poulos' work and upon hearing of his death wrote: "It appears to me, now that he is gone, that I must assume all the burdens he carried on his shoulders . . . I must not lose a single minute of my life."[114]

In his book about the interior landscape of Attica, *The Greek Line,* Pericles Yannopoulos presents "a whole world," woven from the soil of one Greece, that refuses to separate from its diverse compo-nent parts. A geographical scale of tones and forms derived from the Greek earth itself makes up the essential fabric of Yannopoulos' Hellenic universe. Through a magnifying of the sacred landscape of Athens and its environs, a world of "distinct personalities" emerges to forge a cosmic expression of earthly joy and sorrow, tinged with "a certain modest . . . melancholy thoughtfulness."

> STAND IN AN OPEN PLACE of Athens. At the Zappeion, at Patissia, where you like. Climb a small slope, a hill, Ar-dettos, Lycabettos, Philopappus, the Acropolis, wherever you like. Go if you prefer up to the small church of St. Demetrios, beneath the Acropolis, and turning to the right where a road has been cut out for you continue on a few paces until all opens out before you. There is best, for then your head is one with the line of all the hills and mountains and you are neither too high nor too low.

Go there either one dry cloudless red-dawn of a day, or at a bright noontime, or better, three hours before sunset, when all is more clear and simple to the uninitiated eye. Stay there, two, three, four, five hours. Nothing will happen to you at once. It is so good, so pleasant, to sit down on the ground and to stroke the grass and the stones, with which so soon you will be one. Sit without thought, without purpose; allow yourself to be bewitched by what is visible and in your mind's dark-room photograph hills, mountains, shores, waters, smoke, colours, whatever there is.

What do you see?

A whole world.

And each thing of this world delicate, dry, coloured. Follow with your eyes your fingers stroking the earth. Dry earth, fine, crumbled, hollow, fragments of many-coloured stone, often fragments of vases from a crumbled world. Look more carefully: a plant, just discernible, just protruding above the surface, minute, very delicate, many-coloured—you can just tell whether it is dead or living. Observe what is more visible, the stones beside you, the grass. Each pebble, each stone, each blade of grass, perfectly set, shaped most distinctly, imposing its features like an individual, like a person. Each blade of grass, from its root to its crest, to its final ray, all most beautiful to see. Each stone, grass-blade, little flower, plant, bush is outlined so clearly, is so distinct, so different, with such intensity proclaims its existence, its individuality, that each pebble, blade of grass is like a Mr. A., a Mr. B. Observe the nearby flowers of the asphodel: one by one like human faces they gaze at you; observe the least stripe of its petals: in a large one you can make out all its globular seeds. Expand your gaze to the flowering asphodels which dress the slopes of the hills opposite, their pink shimmering lights breathing a gentle delight. Wherever you look you see, one by one, asphodels, you have the sense of the air and light between them. Observe, observe carefully each solid stone, each bulk, each protrusion of earth, each blue-grey rocky outcrop. . . .

All the rocks, the hills, the mountains sit one by one like beautiful women of the people, dreaming modestly, like mothers holding in their arms fine children, like Byzantine Madonnas bending their head slightly with deep love; the small hills sit at the feet of the big hills like girls leaning their heads on the knees of their lovers, caressed and meditative. . . .

It is a single waving line. Everywhere a most simple, a most delicate curve moist and elusive as the huge quiet breathings of the sea, like the huge quiet waves, giving deep sensual delight. The straight line, the upright line of the one-boned Englishman, of the lance-like English-woman, is a line which produces strength, has resistance, it is a line that repels. A hill's curving line, the softly curv-ing throat of a woman, is a line creating sympathy, desire to caress, it attracts the kiss; the line of a woman or of a hill is what attracts, what asks for the caress. And it is strange that the curves of the Parthenon are thought to be so marvellous, for it is obvious that the true artist having to raise lines on a hill of Attica will but seek to harmonize his lines with those curves that surround him. . . .

It is this same line whose likeness we find in all ancient statues and works of art, in Byzantine Madonnas and the saints, in the demotic songs, in the young men and in the village lad, the village girl of today: of all these the body is a delicate line, all the movements and gestures are delicate, and the face has that intoxicated look of melancholy, ex-presses that strange mixture which we are of light festivity and of a certain modest and melancholy thoughtfulness.

A single waving line, circular and most musical. Be-side all the other impressions the most powerful is that of music. It is like that of our circling dance of beautifully dressed, lightly joined bodies of young men and women, waving rhythmically and singing of the desires and sor-rows of mortal life. Watching it one thinks that one hears always, from the circle of earthly lines, the friendliness and love of the song's joy and sadness which comes from the dance; and that music, changed from sight into sound, is like the long cry of passionate Aphrodite for the wounded Adonis, the highest poetical expression of the Greek earth.[115]

In his short life, Pericles Yannopoulos seems to have studied everything. His passion for country and the Greek landscape is the mighty stream that nourishes his work. Experience, imagination, art and history are his vehicles of transport. Yannopoulos renders a vision of perfection in his portrait of the Greek Ideal as he reaches for a renewal of the ethos of Hellas:

> EVERYWHERE LIGHT, everywhere day, everywhere charm, everywhere ease. Everywhere order, symmetry. Everywhere purity of lines, the versatility of Odysseus, the melodiousness of the *palikare* [ideal modern Greek hero]. Everywhere gentleness, grace, smiles. Everywhere the sport of Greek wisdom, the desire for laughter, the Socratic irony. Everywhere philanthropy, sympathy, love. Everywhere a passion for song, for embracing. Everywhere a desire for the material, the material, the material. Everywhere a Dionysiac pleasure, a desire for intoxication through light, a thirst for beauty, a cherishing of felicity. Everywhere a breath of air full of war songs, a vitality, a gallantry and an ardor everywhere, and, simultaneously, a breath of air of melancholy beauty, a sadness of beauty, a lamentation of a dying Adonis. And everywhere the air of a bright war song, and at the same time the air of the flute softening the body with a voluptuousness. And everywhere a breath of air, everywhere the lamentations of Aphrodite, and simultaneously, a very strong acid satire.[116]

I woke with this marble head in my hands; it exhausts my elbows and I don't know where to put it down . . . so our life became one and it will be very difficult for it to separate again.

> GEORGE SEFERIS,
> *evaluating the weight of tradition*[117]

Memory functions as a "rich injunction" and expresses itself organically in the natural forms of George Seferis' ancestral universe. There, it is wholly alive, teeming with soul and spirit and ready to provide nourishment and completion for the seeking human spirit.

Seferis has written that "memory has one horizon—whether the days of 200 B.C. or A.D. 340 or 1911." He suggests that fundamentally memory is not a fragmented experience despite the gaps or disruptions. Rather, continuity persists because it insists; it is, *au fond*, an organic umbilical cord. "We separate it into compartments," he says, "because our thoughts are paratactical [linear] and we place them paratactically. . . . The question is not one of retrospection as one reads in the chapter of a history book, or various 'intellectual' conveyances, as some would say. It is a question of an emotional agent that I do not know if we are at this moment trained enough to discern."[118]

> *The olive trees with the wrinkles of our fathers*
> *The rocks with the wisdom of our fathers*
> *And our brother's blood living upon the earth*
> *Were a robust joy a rich injunction*
> *For the souls who understood their prayer.*[119]

> *. . . the earth and the heavens are one*
> *and our own thought is the world's hearth and center,*
> *since we also say that earth may mingle with the stars*
> *as a field's subsoil with its topsoil, so that*
> *the heavens too may bring forth wheat . . .*

> *ANGELOS SIKELIANOS*
> *(1884–1951) "Daedalus"*[120]

> *The sea's sound floods my veins,*
> *above me the sun*
> *grinds like a millstone,*
> *the wind beats its full wings,*
> *the world's axle throbs heavily.*
> *I cannot hear my deepest breath,*
> *and the sea grows calm to the sand's edge*
> *and spreads deep inside me.*

> *ANGELOS SIKELIANOS*[121]

What would this Helen have been if Homer's breath had not passed over her? . . . it is to Homer that this tiny riverbed, Eurotas, owes its immortality.

NIKOS KAZANTZAKIS [122]

Seeking and learning are in fact nothing but recollection.

SOCRATES (to Meno) [123]

POETRY, PHILOSOPHY AND THE LANDSCAPE OF LIFE

An intimate connection between literature, philosophy and life existed in ancient Greece. The poets' and philosophers' task was to reveal and express "the inner movement and operation of cosmic powers."[124] Their function was to speak of the essentials of knowledge, the things of utmost importance for humankind to know. They addressed the spiritual and physical landscapes of life holistically.

The mission of the person with true knowledge—the prophet, the sage, the visionary poet—writes Greek scholar Edmund Keeley, is "to restore . . . lost unity and to reconcile natural with supernatural, visible with invisible, first in his [or her] life and then by making others aware of their divided state."[125]

Another function of the poet and philosopher is to summon up and recapitulate the essential wisdom of the ages that is indispensable to the present and future generations: how to live life's lessons, endure suffering, battle against wrong, triumph wisely in victory, and bring harmony and goodness into all aspects of living.

Sappho, one of the first known women poets (fl. ca. 610–580 B.C., in Lesbos, an island in the Aegean off the coast of Asia Minor), launched a thousand lyric poets with her laughter, talk, eroticism, insults, irony, despair and, most importantly, her astonishing insight into the world of sensuality, beauty and nature.[126] Only two hundred or so fragments (about seven hundred lines) of her work survive (of perhaps more than five hundred poems) and they are pieced together from many ancient sources, including damaged and worn papyrus strips, the commentaries of the early scholars and the mummy wrappings in Egyptian tombs.[127] We are told that "ancient commentators praised the smoothness of Sappho's style, the 'euphony' of her language" ("Come, my lovely tortoise-shell lyre; / my music will give you speech"). She was also known "for her skilful and innovative use of metre."[128] Sappho was called "the Tenth Muse" by Plato,[129] "the fair Sappho" by Socrates[130] and "a marvel" by the geographer Strabo.[131] The ancient Greeks (sometime after her death) engraved her face on coinage, painted her portrait on vases and cast her in marble. A fourth-century A.D. bishop and a medieval pope, however, considered her influence so subversive that they ordered all copies of her poems burned. A distinctive presence, uncompromising in her directness, Sappho presents the "biography of a voice," in the words of one Greek scholar,[132] through her often unrelentingly candid internal dialogues and passionate observations of the universe around her and in her.

Sappho's images reflect a mutuality between woman and the natural world. In the absence of a friend, she describes "gentle Atthis" as "shining brighter than all the stars; its light / stretches out over the salt-filled sea and fields brimming with flowers: / the beautiful dew falls and the roses / and the delicate chervil / and many-flowered honey-clover bloom."[133]

Nature sings with bird life in the lyric poetry ("lyric" means, literally, "accompanied by the lyre") of Sappho. Nightingales, crickets, doves, pigeons, the honey bee and sheep roam the landscape of her mind:

> When sun dazzles the earth
> with straight-falling flames,
> a cricket rubs its wings
> scraping up a shrill song.[134]

> The nightingale is
> the harbinger of Spring
> and her voice is desire

> Hesperus [the evening star], you bring
> everything that
> the light-tinged dawn has scattered;
> you bring the sheep, you bring the goat, you
> bring
> the child back to its mother.[135]

Sappho's song is hard to surpass. She is able to convey a sense of the sublimity of the natural world with the ease and wonder of quicksilver as she aptly demonstrates in the following communion under the moon, in a grove of apple trees. (Some consider this to be a part of a simile "which compares the beauty of a woman who surpasses her companions to the moon outshining the stars.")

The glow and beauty of the stars
are nothing near the splendid moon
when in her roundness she burns
silver about the world.

Leave Krete and come to this holy temple
where the graceful grove of apple trees
circles an altar smoking with frankincense.

Here roses leave shadow on the ground
and cold springs babble through apple branches
where shuddering leaves pour down profound sleep.

In our meadow where horses graze
and wild flowers of spring blossom,
anise shoots fill the air with aroma.

And here, Queen Aphrodite, pour
heavenly nectar into gold cups
and fill them gracefully with sudden joy.[136]

Sappho is said to have been the first to use the *pectis*, a kind of harp. A prescient voice sings out in one of the fragments of her poems, certain of its place in the varied prospect of memory.

> I tell you;
>> in time to come,
> someone will remember us.[137]

Euripides (ca. 480–406 B.C.), whom the ancients were fond of calling "the philosopher upon the stage,"[138] entertained his audiences with the fusion of poetry and philosophy in his plays. The convergence of these two streams of thought illumined his writings and became the most striking feature of what is regarded as an extraordinary body of work, which includes the *Hippolytus*, *Medea* and *Elektra*, the *Alcestis*, and the mysterious *Bacchae*, a haunted work that, in part, explores the eruptive force of nature and man.

In a remaining fragment from one of his lost dramas, Euripides calls Earth the "mother of all things" and couples her with all-embracing heaven, "the ether of Zeus" (supreme Sky-god), to produce humankind and all that lives. They are the universal parents, the universal womb.

Earth the mighty and the ether of Zeus,
He is the begetter of men and gods;
And she, when she has caught the rain's moist drops,
Gives birth to mortals,
Gives birth to pasture and the beasts after their kinds.
Whence not unjustly
She is deemed mother of all things.
But that which has been born of earth
To earth returns;
And that which sprouted from etherial seed
To heaven's vault goes back.
So nothing dies of all that into being comes,
But each from each is parted
And so takes another form.[139]

Very little is known for certain about the life of Heraclitus, beyond the fact that he lived in Ephesus. According to chronographer Apollodorus, Heraclitus prospered in the LXIX Olympiad (504–501 B.C.). In addition, one distinguished scholar suggests that "he came of an old aristocratic family, and that he was on bad terms with his fellow citizens."[140] Renowned even in antiquity for his impenetrability and called the "riddler" by third-century B.C. satirist Timon of Phlius, it is said that the often cryptic pronouncements of Heraclitus irritated his contemporaries. Diogenes Laertius, ancient biographer and compiler, reports that Heraclitus was the author of a book entitled *On Nature*, and that it was divided into three discourses: On the Universe, Politics, Theology. He maintains that some say Heraclitus wrote "rather obscurely so that only those of rank and influence should have access to it, and it should not be easily despised by the populace." He says "[t]he work had so great a reputation that from it arose disciples, those called Heracliteans."[141] Historians of philosophy and science G. S. Kirk and J. E. Raven remind us on the other hand that "ancient biographers and historians assumed that all the pre-Socratics wrote one or more books," and that the rubric "On Nature" was regularly assigned to the works of the "natural philosophers."[142] In many cases, the provenance and veracity ascribed to material of antiquity are unverifiable. Nonetheless, the surviving fragments of Heraclitus' teachings are considered to be important oral apothegms.

Heraclitus taught that there was an underlying unity of all things. The moving force of his philosophy was the belief that man's life is inseparably bound to everything else that exists. Understanding of the *Logos*—the true and shared constitution of all things, according to Heraclitus—was necessary for a person to become wise and fully effective. *Logos* was the unifying element, the experience of truth common to all things. Heraclitus also emphasized the continuity of change ("all things are in flux") and the stability that persists through it: everything is in perpetual flux like a river. What follows is a brief reconstitution of some of Heraclitus' provocative thoughts and oracular pronouncements, based on extant fragments and translated from the Greek by Thomas Merton, poet and Trappist monk.[143] Heraclitus' legacy is one of cosmic midair triple somersaults with unexpected turns of language, puns, assonance, epigram and explicit verbal contradictions that added a new dimension to philosophy. One enterprising modern philosopher likens Heraclitus to Bashō, a Japanese Zen Buddhist monk and poet, in his use, sense and *experience* of paradox in a "world of transient individuality."[144] Heraclitus saw both sides of the paradox of truth, showing us that it is not an abstract, simple, or meaningless cosmos of which we are all a part.

> WISDOM IS ONE THING: it is to know the thought by which all things are steered through all things.
>
> The wise is one only. . . .
>
> Nature loves to hide.
> It rests by changing.
>
> The way up and the way down are one and the same.
>
> In the circumference of a circle the beginning and the end are one.
>
> You cannot step twice into the same stream; for fresh waters are ever flowing upon you.
>
> We must know that conflict is common to all, and strife is justice, and that all things come into being and pass away through strife.
>
> Homer was wrong in saying: "Would that conflict might perish from among gods and men." He did not see that he was praying for the destruction of the universe; for if his prayer were heard, all things would pass away. (Men do not know how what is at variance agrees with itself. It is a

harmony of opposite tensions, like that of the bow and lyre.)

Every beast is driven to pasture with blows!

It is wise to hearken not to me but to my Logos, and to confess that all things are one.

Those who speak with understanding must hold fast to what is common as a city holds fast to its law, and even more strongly. For all human laws are fed by the one divine law.

Thought is common to all.
So we must follow the common,
yet though my Logos is common the many
live as if they had a wisdom of their own.
They are estranged from that with which
      they are in constant contact.
The waking have one common world, but the
sleeping turn aside each into a world of his own.

One is as ten thousand to me, if he be the best. And it is law, too, to obey the counsel of one.

The lord whose oracle is at Delphi neither speaks nor conceals, but indicates with a sign.[145]

Plato, the son of Ariston and Perictione, was born, it is generally thought, in Athens (ca. 427–ca. 347 B.C.). An aristocrat by birth, he grew up during the Peloponnesian War (431–404 B.C.) and witnessed the decay of Athenian democracy, as the political climate of general decline moved more and more toward imperialist rule. In Athens, at the age of forty, he founded the Academy, the first university—a center of research and instruction where scholars and younger students could come to pursue serious studies in the mathematical, scientific, philosophical and artistic disciplines. The Academy did include a few women but higher education for women was unheard of for the most part and considered silly at best. The most powerful influence on Plato's life was his teacher, Socrates, who communicated to him the value of philosophy as a means to self- and soul-discovery, and whose insights were the subject of Plato's dialogues. The nature of knowledge, and of good and evil, preoccupied Plato throughout his life. He never lost sight, however, of the ideals of beauty, goodness and truth, which he believed existed and, in fact, thought necessary for an inspired and full life. Plato soared to heights of poetic, metaphysical and moral idealism as he strove to construct a system of philosophy that illumined the reasons for humankind's existence and examined the intrinsic nature of society. Diogenes Laertius (fl. ca. early third century A.D.), author of *Lives and Opinions of Eminent Philosophers*, relates a story about Socrates and his prospective young student. Diogenes reports "that on the night before Socrates met Plato for the first time, [Socrates] dreamt that a young swan rested for a moment on his knees, and then suddenly grew wings and flew aloft, uttering a sweet cry." This story, writes one eminent Greek scholar, "illustrates . . . the relation in which [Plato] stood to the master whom he so greatly loved and honoured."[146]

Plutarch, Greek biographer and moral philosopher, explained Plato's relevance in this way: "Plato is philosophy and philosophy is Plato."[147] A. N. Whitehead, philosopher and social scientist of our own times, once characterized Western philosophy as "a series of footnotes to Plato."[148] The humanist Plato, through his own "speculative vision," writes another historian of philosophy, "gave the West a tradition it has never lost and a goal it has never realized."[149]

In the *Laws,* the longest of the dialogues, and his last written work, Plato forges a noble theology in which education is the primary occupation of the Athenian citizen and the minister of education is the most important official in the state; the arts are ethical touchstones and the poet espouses the good and is a moral exemplar of universal truths. Socrates is not present at the conversation contained in the *Laws.* The chief speaker, an "Athenian Stranger," represents the views of Plato; he is walking and discoursing with Cleinias, a Cretan, in this passage in which Plato outlines some of his prophetic intentions and human ideals.

ATHENIAN: . . . I seek to distinguish the patterns of life, and lay down their keels according to the nature of different men's souls; seeking truly to consider by what means, and in what ways, we may go through the voyage of life best. Now human affairs are hardly worth considering in earnest, and yet we must be in earnest about them —a sad necessity constrains us. And having got thus far, there will be a fitness in our completing the matter, if we can only find some suitable method of doing so. But what do I mean? Some one may ask this very question, and quite rightly, too.

CLEINIAS: Certainly.

ATHENIAN: I say that about serious matters a man should be serious, and about a matter which is not serious he should not be serious; and that God is the natural and worthy object of our most serious and blessed endeavours, for man, as I said before, is made to be the plaything of God, and this, truly considered, is the best of him; wherefore also every man and woman should walk seriously, and pass life in the noblest of pastimes, and be of another mind from what they are at present.

CLEINIAS: In what respect?

ATHENIAN: At present they think that their serious pursuits should be for the sake of their sports, for they deem war a serious pursuit, which must be managed well for the sake of peace; but the truth is, that there neither is, nor has been, nor ever will be, either amusement or instruction in any degree worth speaking of in war, which is nevertheless deemed by us to be the most serious of our pursuits. And therefore, as we say, every one of us should live the life of peace as long and as well as he can. And what is the right way of living? Are we to live in sports always? If so, in what kind of sports? We ought to live sacrificing, and singing, and dancing, and then a man will be able to propitiate the Gods, and to defend himself against his enemies and conquer them in battle. The type of song or dance by which he will propitiate them has been described, and the paths along which he is to proceed have been cut for him. He will go forward in the spirit of the poet.[150]

In the *Phaedrus,* we are told that a fundamental principle of Hippocratic physiology is the dogma that an understanding of the body is impossible without an understanding of Nature as a whole. Ancient Greek medicine and the name Hippocrates are synonymous. Called "the Great Hippocrates" by Aristotle, he was a force in ancient medical practice. Born in Cos, ca. 460 B.C., Hippocrates belonged to the guild of physicians called Asclepiadae and was a professional trainer of medical students. Plato refers to the significance of his work in two of his dialogues, the *Protagoras* and the *Phaedrus*. Hippocrates transformed the best tendencies of Greek medicine with his diligent application of a truly scientific spirit of inquiry combined with philosophic theory. In the collection of writings that bear his name (some seventy in all), the work called *Nutriment* recognizes the medical importance of the pulse. Its spirit is strikingly reminiscent of Heraclitus while at the same time it maintains its own refreshingly eclectic and challenging nature. Hippocrates contributed much to freeing Greek medicine from superstition and questionable hypotheses. The great physician also showed that there was an art of medicine and this affinity is reflected in the following passages from the *Nutriment*, where a philosophic element predominates over the scientific (a primary characteristic of this work).

THE THINGS ALSO THAT GROW in the earth all assimilate themselves to the earth.

Loud talking is painful. Overwork calls for gentle dissuasion. A wooded district benefits.

A crisis is the riddance of a disease.

The beginning of all things is one and the end of all things is one, and the end and beginning are the same.

Conflux one, conspiration one, all things in sympathy; all the parts as forming a whole, and severally the parts in each part, with reference to the work.

The great beginning travels to the extreme part; from the extreme part there is travelling to the great beginning. One nature to be and not to be.

Nature is sufficient in all for all.[151]

IV

AFRICA

Africa is not only a geographical expression; it is also a metaphysical landscape—it is in fact a view of the world and of the whole cosmos perceived from a particular position.

CHINUA ACHEBE (1930–   ),
Nigerian novelist and poet[1]

Bushman rock painting of double-headed snake, South Africa

[T]he whole earth is sacred. . . . And since the whole earth is sacred, every part therefore is sacred in a general way and is treated as such. So literally the people lived in the midst of the sacred.

COSMAS OKECHUKWU OBIEGO,
Nigerian scholar[2]

Deeply felt silences might be said to be the core of our Kofon religion. During these times, the nature within ourselves found unity with the nature of earth. This is not "closeness to nature" but rather an immersion in the common nature which pervades all life—plants, animal, human.

PRINCE MODUPE,
Sousou, Guinea,
(West Africa)[3]

Wealth is dew.

Azania proverb,
(South Africa)[4]

Janus Headdress, Nigeria or Cameroon, nineteenth to twentieth century. Eight dramatic spirals decorate this wooden double-faced head, thought to be an artifact of the Ekoi peoples of the Cross River State of Nigeria. They may originally have represented heads of enemies slain in intramural wars.

INTRODUCTION

In a country of nearly 500 million where there are about 3,000 different peoples, approximately 2,100 dialects and languages and three dominant religious systems (Islam, Christianity and Traditional Beliefs), the idea of coherence of any sort might appear preposterous. A commonality of interest in the form of African humanism and the expectation of some level of unity (not uniformity) in the midst of this dynamic diversity does, in fact, exist and is growing. Kwame Anthony Appiah, a politically engaged Ghanaian intellectual, considers the paramount endeavor of African philosophers, poets and writers to be primarily a *human* enterprise that will enrich "the one race to which we *all* belong." Mr. Appiah rejects any thought of a definition of an "African world-view," stating: "Whatever Africans share, we do not have a common traditional culture, common languages, a common religious or conceptual vocabulary . . . We do not even belong to a common race."[5]

The bond with the land, however, affirms the living social, historical and spiritual identity of the people. African philosopher and writer John S. Mbiti points out that the land provides African peoples with "the roots of existence as well as binding them mystically to their departed," adding,

> PEOPLE WALK ON THE GRAVES of their forefathers, and it is feared that anything separating them from these ties will bring disaster to family and community life. To remove Africans by force from their land is an act of such great injustice that no foreigner can fathom it. Even when people voluntarily leave their homes in the countryside and go to live or work in the cities, there is a fundamental severing of ties which cannot be repaired and which often creates psychological problems with which urban life cannot as yet cope.[6]

Jomo Kenyatta, ethnologist and father of the modern nation of Kenya, insists that land tenure is the most important factor in the lives of the Gikuyu people. In Gikuyu society, the soil is revered for a whole spectrum of reasons not the least of which being that the Gikuyu are agriculturalists. Land is the foundation of well-beingness that entwines all created things, living and dead. In the words of Kenyatta,

> ... THE GIKUYU PEOPLE depend entirely on the land. It supplies them with the material needs of life, through which spiritual and mental contentment is achieved. Communion with the ancestral spirits is perpetuated through contact with the soil in which the ancestors of the tribe lie buried. The Gikuyu consider the earth as the "mother" of the tribe, for the reason that the mother bears her burden for about eight or nine moons while the child is in her womb, and then for a short period of suckling. But it is the soil that feeds the child through its lifetime; and again after death it is the soil that nurses the spirits of the dead for eternity. Thus the earth is the most sacred thing above all that dwell in or on it. Among the Gikuyu the soil is especially honoured, and an everlasting oath is to swear by the earth *(koirugo)*.[7]

In Ethiopia, the soil of the country exerts a similar influence, often dramatic. A father who had just buried his child—dead of famine—cupped in his hand some excavated burial earth and *breathed* life into the earth as a symbolic gesture of continuity of life for his child—to help him over into the next state of consciousness. It was a compelling instance of the earth as the only true currency.[8]

"Earth is thought of as a living being," writes Malian theorist and sage Amadou Hampâté Bâ; hence "work in the fields," he says, "is seen as a process of procreation." Therefore, "[w]e sacrifice to the earth because the fruitfulness of the entire universe depends on that of the earth."[9]

The umbilical link many African societies experience with the Earth is expressed through the customs surrounding the disposal of the placenta and cord of a newborn. In a large number of the traditional cultures both cord and placenta are immediately reconnected to the Earth. For example, the Yansi of Zaire throw them into the river. The Gikuyu of Kenya will place the placenta in an uncultivated field and cover it with grain and grass, the elements symbolizing fertility. Among the Ingassana of Ethiopia the placenta is put in a calabash (gourd) and hung on a special tree *(gammeiza)*. Prince Modupe, a Sousou from Guinea, north West Africa, recalls the life-sustaining significance of the burial ceremony of the placenta:

> THE PLACENTA MUST BE BURIED with ceremony in the compound with the witch-doctor present. As the navel cord ties an unborn child to the womb, so does the buried cord tie the child to the land, to the sacred earth of the tribe, to the Great Mother Earth. If the child ever leaves the place he will come home again because the tug of this cord will always pull him toward his own.
>
> When I go home I shall stand on the spot where the waiting ones stood that night [of my birth] in the storm and I shall speak these words: "My belly is this day reunited with the belly of my Great Mother, Earth!" [10]

Jomo Kenyatta relates his ambivalent attachment to West Hampstead in London, his home base for two years and the birthplace of his daughter. Disheartened by the news that the hospital had burned his daughter's placenta yet emotional about the actual place of her birth, Kenyatta speaks of the impact of the absence of traditional ritual that would have linked his child with the ancestors and the land: "I felt sad to leave the birthplace of my daughter. In fact, I still feel sentimental about it because it was there that the placenta of my daughter was disposed of as soon as she was born; if she had been born in Kikuyu Country, the placenta would have been buried near our gate by the old woman who acted as midwife. At the hospital I was told that it had been burned. I wished it had been buried instead of being burned." [11]

The physical landscape of Africa is of profound symbolic significance to African nations. As the states achieved independence, the mountain world of Africa responded and contributed to the revitalization of her soul. When Tanganyika declared its independent status in 1961, its first prime minister, and later president, Julius Nyerere, proclaimed:

> WE WILL LIGHT A CANDLE on top of Mount Kilimanjaro which will shine beyond our borders, giving hope where there is despair, love where there is hate, and dignity where before there was only humiliation. [12]

In 1963, on the day Kenya attained her independence, native climbers ascended the peak of Mount Kenya and at midnight illuminated the mountain in a blaze of light, announcing to the world the birth of a nation.[13]

In a letter written to his own children, former Zambian president Kenneth Kaunda describes a commonality of feeling about being African:

> THE *AFRICAN-NESS* which has its roots in the soil of our continent rather than the lecture rooms of Western universities is basically a religious phenomenon; we are who we are because of our attitude to the mysterious depth in life, symbolized by birth and death, harvest and famine, ancestors and the unborn.[14]

Akwanshi stone carvings representing former chiefs, southeastern Nigeria. The three carvings—two standing and one fallen—are thought to have been sculpted over a period of three centuries ending about 1900. The height of the nearest boulder is forty-eight inches. These monoliths, often phallic in form with protruding navels, are believed by the inhabitants of the region to have grown "out of the ground like trees." Most of these artifacts were created from basalt, though sandstone and limestone were also used. Engraved spirals and concentric circles are recurrent motifs. The word *akwanshi* means literally "dead person in the ground."

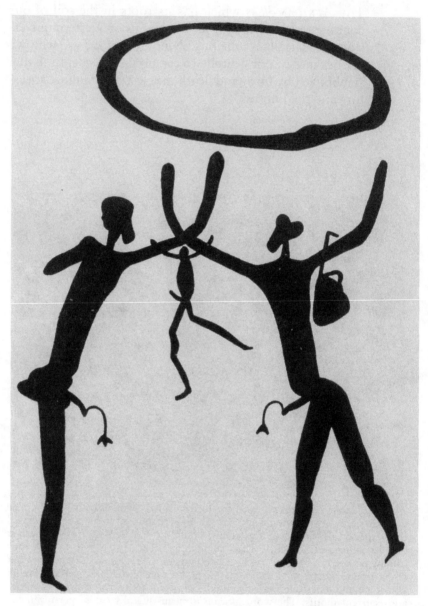

Ancient Bushman Rock Painting, Ceremonial Dance, Zimbabwe.

We are born from the womb of our mother; we are buried in the womb of the earth.

Ethiopian proverb[15]

Whenever a person breaks a stick in the forest, let him consider what it would feel like, if it were himself that was thus broken.

Nigerian proverb[16]

"But who are we?" asks Ghanaian poet, Kofi Awoonor.
"We are those whose hands fertilize the womb of the earth," declares Senegalese-Cameroonian poet David Diop.[17]

"And what, you ask, is the use of the paintings?" said Ogotemmêli. "It is this: they help the plants to grow, they promote germination. The day before the sacrificer wets his brushes, the ears for the sowing are spread out on the roof, the symbol of the primal field.

"In this way, at the start of the cycle of vegetable growth, the still unfertilized seeds are taken and incorporated in the universal cycle, in the general movement of clouds and men."[18]

THE RHYTHMS
OF THE EARTH

It was desirable to be on good terms with the spirit of the Earth," K. A. Busia tells us, of the Ashanti of Ghana. "Kinship, reverence for the ancestors and belief in the spiritual power of the Earth have combined to give land tenure in Ashanti its peculiar character," says the much-respected Ghanaian sociologist.[19] Although there were no priests or priestesses of the Earth amongst the Ashanti, it was believed the Earth was godlike and possessed a power or spirit of its own that was depended upon by the Ashanti for the fertility not only of their fields but also of their whole tribe. The land was alive and regarded as the property of the ancestors.

The strength of the bond between living and dead in Ashanti society determines the well-being of the tribe. The maintenance of good relations with the ancestors is crucial to the good fortune of the entire community. The ancestors are always watching, sending help and protection, and punishing misbehavior when necessary. Therefore the Ashanti say they have their ancestors constantly in mind.

"The power in the Earth was conceived as a female principle, *Asase Yaa* (Earth)," writes Busia, "whose natal day is Thursday."[20] Offerings are frequent and intended for propitiation and to ensure continuity of the people. For example, at every *Adae* ceremony ("those ceremonies at which the spirits of departed rulers of the clan are propitiated, their names and deeds recalled, and favours and mercy solicited"),[21] the drummer honors the Earth as he addresses it humbly and respectfully.

> *Earth, condolences,*
> *Earth, condolences,*
> *Earth and dust,*
> *The Supreme Being*
> *I lean upon you.*
> *Earth, when I am about to die,*

I lean upon you.
Earth, while I am alive,
I depend upon you.
Earth that receives dead bodies,
The Creator's Drummer says:
From wherever he went,
He has roused himself,
He has roused himself.[22]

Joy, praise and thanksgiving for the beneficence of the Earth is another dimension of African religious expression. A wide variety of names exists for the All Powerful One. To the Zulu and Nanyarwanda, he is known as "the Wise One"; to the Akan, as "He Who Knows or sees all"; to the Barundi he is "the Watcher of everything"; the Yoruba believe "Only God is wise" and that he is "the discerner of hearts." To other peoples he is "the Great Eye" and "the Sun" which beams its light everywhere and from Whom nothing is hidden.[23] The eternal and intrinsic attributes of the Supreme Being are expressed in this Shona (Zimbabwe) song of praise to the "Great Spirit," who manifests his grace in all aspects of the natural world. The Great Spirit heaps the rocks into mountains, calls forth the branching trees, causes the land to be filled with humankind and is most gracious and merciful.

Great Spirit!
Piler up of the rocks into towering mountains!
When thou stampest on the stone,
The dust rises and fills the land.
Hardness of the precipice;
Waters of the pool that turn
Into misty rain when stirred.
Vessel overflowing with oil!
Father of Runji,
Who seweth the heaven like cloth:
Let him knit together that which is below.
Caller forth of the branching trees:
Thou bringest forth the shoots
That they stand erect.
Thou hast filled the land with mankind,
The dust rises on high, oh Lord!
Wonderful One, thou livest

In the midst of the sheltering rocks,
Thou givest of rain to mankind:
We pray to thee,
Hear us, Lord!
Show mercy when we beseech thee, Lord.
Thou art on high with the spirits of the great.
Thou raisest the grass-covered hills
Above the earth, and createst the rivers,
Gracious One.[24]

A pattern of piety toward the Earth pervades the New Year's rites of a Sudanese clan. The sanctification of the forest and the friendliness and fertility of the earth were prayed for prior to the year's commencement of the tilling of the soil. The Keeper of the Clan Lands "makes right" the Earth as he stretches his arms out toward the forest and rivers, beseeching their goodness and grace and honoring their spirit:

O EARTH, wherever it be my people dig, be kindly to them. Be fertile when they give the little seeds to your keeping. Let your generous warmth nourish them and your abundant moisture germinate them. Let them swell and sprout, drawing life from you, and burgeon under your fostering care; and soon we shall redden your bosom with the blood of goats slain in your honor, and offer to you the first-fruits of your munificence, first-fruits of millet and oil of sesame, of gourds and cucumbers and deep-meshed melons.

O trees of forest and glade, fall easily under the axe. Be gentle to my people. Let no harm come to them. Break no limb in your anger: crush no one in your displeasure. . . .

O rivers and streams, where the woodman has laid bare the earth, where he has hewn away the little bushes and torn out the encumbering grass, there let your waters overflow. Bring down the leafy mould from the forest and the fertilizing silt from the mountains. When the rains swell your banks, spread out your waters and lay your rich treasures on our gardens.

Conspire together, O earth and rivers: conspire together, O earth and rivers and forests. Be gentle and give us plenty from your teeming plenty. For it is I, Lominga-moi of the clan Idoto, who speak, Keeper of the Clan Lands, Warden of the Forest, Master of the Clan.[25]

At a hand-washing ceremony that is part of the ritual celebrating the birth of a child, the Igbo of Nigeria pray for the fertility of crops, animals and children. The refrain "Earth Goddess, hear" is repeated by all present as they "drum" their hands lightly on the earth and alert the Earth Goddess to the emergence of a new life. After the blessing of the child and the giving of thanks, four large kola nuts are broken, split into small bits, dipped into ground pepper mixed with melon, crayfish and groundnuts and passed around.

> *Fellow men, we shall all live.*
> *Earth Goddess, hear.*
> *Whoever plants, let him dig up and eat.*
> *Earth goddess, hear.*
> *We shall give birth to sons.*
> *Earth Goddess, hear.*
> *We shall give birth to daughters.*
> *Earth Goddess, hear.*
> *We shall train them.*
> *Earth Goddess, hear.*
> *When we are old they will feed us.*
> *Earth Goddess, hear.*
> *Whoever sees us with an evil eye,*
> *When he plants may the floods sweep his mounds*
>   *away.*
> *Whoever wishes us evil,*
> *May he break his fist on the ground.*
> *We are broody hens, we have chicks.*
> *We do not fly up,*
> *We look after our brood.*
> *We do not eye others with an evil eye.*
> *This big-headed thing [child] that came home*
>   *yesterday,*
> *He is yet a seed.*
> *If you wish that he germinates*
> *And grows to be a tree,*
> *We shall be ever thankful.*
> *Earth Goddess, hear;*
> *He will grow to be like his stock.*[26]

Amadou Hampâté Bâ, Malian humanist and sage, describes the giving heart of the earth, its "feminine and maternal power" and its cosmic function as a "receptacle of the universal power." The source of the force, he says, is "heaven" and its intermediaries are water (*ji*), light (*yeelen*) and even darkness (*dibi*).

EARTH IS THE MOTHER OF BEINGS; the sky is her husband, the moon her star, the sun her polestar. She is the lap, back, and maternal breast for mankind. . . .

We sacrifice to the earth, because the fruitfulness of the entire universe depends on that of the earth. Each village has its sacrificer, or "minister of the earth."

The farmer does not sow or plant without asking the earth first to accept, then to watch over the seed which he entrusts to her. He asks her pardon before he cuts into her with his hoe so that she will accept this wound without anger. Since work in the fields is seen as a process of procreation, in certain places it is the men who plow the soil, while only the women, because of their analogical kinship with her, are allowed to bury the seeds in the heart of the earth as in a womb.

In fact, the deepest secrets of life are hidden in the bowels and tunnels of the earth. Myth tells us that life began in a grotto, grew in a well, and burst forth from a crevice.

Because the mother and the earth both manifest the mystery of germination, fruitfulness, and life, they are of utmost importance in the animist tradition. Although the father is considered to be the cosmic agent of contact on the level of the sacred he steps aside for the mother. He begets the child and he makes him legitimate, but it is the mother who perfects the child's being. One could not be without a mother, though one's father might well be unknown.

Earth is thought of as a living being.[27]

Ana, the Earth-Spirit, is perhaps the most beloved of all spirits in Igbo life in Nigeria. The Igbo say *Ana* brought forth everything as we know it today. Reverence for the Earth-Spirit extends to their attitude about land. The Igbo are ideologically opposed to the sale of any land. If such a transaction should take place, shame and guilt

C-1: Simon Ngumbe, *Rainbow Snake and Children*, ca. 1972. A depiction of Kunmangurr, the creator-being, as rainbow snake. The serpent's presence in water holes that contain the spirits of unborn children (wreathing the reptile's head) is reflected in the spiraled shape of the body.

C-2: *Whirling Snakes or Whirling Mountain*. A sand-painting of the Navajo Shooting Chant, 1930s.

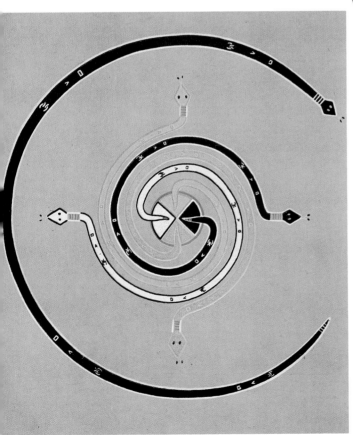

C-3: *Great Serpent Mound,* near Peebles, Ohio. The celebrated serpent effigy is thought to have been built by Adena-related people who lived in the area between 800 B.C. and 400 A.D. It is presumed to be an aspect of the belief system of its creators. If outstretched, the snake's body would measure about a quarter of a mile in length; thus it can only be interpreted from the air. There is an egg-shaped object in the open jaws of the serpent. The shape of this extraordinary earthwork is accentuated by clay from the region. A dowser, Sig Lonegren, discovered veins of water under each curvature of the winding body that concludes at its tail in a snug spiral.

C-4: Mineo (Katô) Okabe, *Oribe Ware Round Dish,* ca. 1960. Oribe ware was originated by a famous tea master, Furuta Oribe (late sixteenth, early seventeenth century). It is characterized by a largely greenish glaze with tinges of blue. Okabe's piece is unusual and nontraditional in that it has a low-relief sculptural spiral with an inward-slanting raised edge.

C-5: *Athena.* Marble. ca. 525 B.C. From the gable surmounting the facade of Gigantomachia, a detail of the old temple of Athena in the Acropolis of Athens. Athena, originally a Cretan goddess, was protectress of hearth and town. She holds a snake of many heads, a symbol here of fertility and renewal. She is the revered goddess of wisdom, the arts, and sciences. She is said to be the originator of the spiral pattern, which she formed from the clay of the Earth. A "garland" of coiled serpent heads wreathes the crown of her head.

C-6: Pansy Napangati, *Rainbow Serpent at Pikilli,* 1989. Wanampi, the Rainbow Serpent, is pictured stretched out in the sun at a spring, which is represented by a roundel. The background colors suggest vegetation.

C-7: *Tairona Figure Pendant.* Extravagant headdresses made up of stylized birds and other animals, plus prominent spirals—a feature of Tairona metalwork—are the most distinctive characteristics of these pendants. The flamboyant ornaments are faithful miniatures of personal adornments excavated in Tairona burial grounds. The figure may be a Tairona warrior, or perhaps a culture hero or a god.

C-8: *Gold Breastplate,* Mycenae period, ca. 1300 B.C. Covered with continuous double spirals that wind through the rounds of existence, this piece of armor was found in the tomb of King Agamemnon.

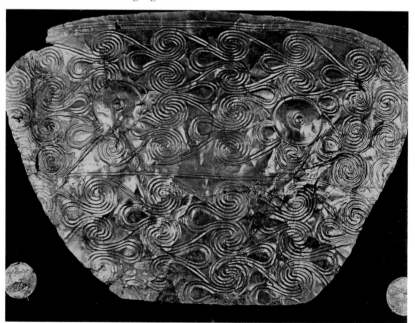

C-9: Hiroshige (1797–1858). *Crane and Wave*, mid-1830s.

C-10: *Cameroon Calabash*, West Africa, twentieth century. Serving palm wine is proper etiquette for greeting a guest in West Africa. Such an exquisitely crafted container, covered in imported glass beads and cowrie shells, was customarily owned only by the Fon, or chief, of the Bamileke people.

C-11: Charlie Egalie Tjapaltjarri, *Corroboree Dancing,* ca. 1972. The patterns of the corroboree dancing (social or ritual festivities) are inscribed by the spiraling lines that enclose ceremonial fireplaces. The horseshoe shapes represent figures seated in their prescribed places.

C-12: *Tairona Nose Ornament.* Typical Tairona braids and coils distinguish this nose ornament, one of the most popular forms of jewelry in pre-Hispanic Colombia.

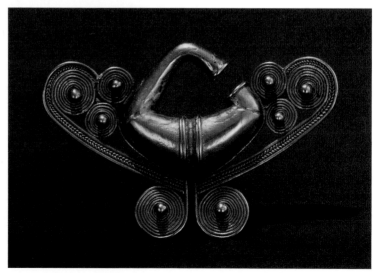

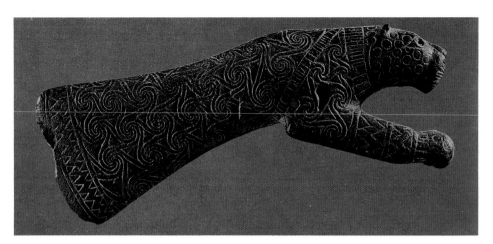

C-13: *Leopard* (slate). Minoan Civilization, 1700–1500 B.C. A part of the King's scepter displays a whole array of double spirals, one of the most ancient symbols known to man, the symbol of eternity.

C-14: *Kosode with Snow-Laden Orchids,* Mid-Edo period, mid-eighteenth century. Delicate red orchid blossoms flourish amid gold-embroidered spiraling leaves and stems bent under the weight of fresh snow in an unusual airy and free-wheeling depiction of Nature on this *kosode,* or "small sleeved robe," the forerunner of Japan's national dress, the kimono.

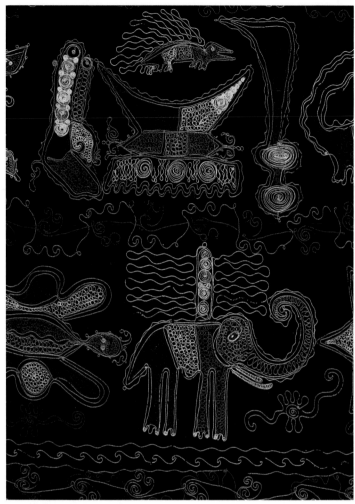

C-15: *Cloth of the Great.* Fante group, Akan peoples, Ghana, twentieth century. Only chiefs were allowed to wear costly fabrics called "cloths of the great" which were woven of imported textiles. Akan proverbs, which refer to the power of elders and chiefs, were often the subject matter of the embroidered images.

C-16: Goyce Kakegamic (Cree). *A Nest of Birds,* ca. early 1970s. The umbilical-like cords are life lines joining the forces of nature and a family of four to the power of life. The connectedness of Creation is conveyed by the circular imagery evoking a central Cree belief that "all is one."

accompany it. In order to complete a sale successfully, the Earth-Spirit must be ritually appeased. While the Igbo recognize the whole earth as one mighty spirit in general, the Earth-Spirit is the great Earth Mother and is honored continually as such.

ANA, THE EARTH-SPIRIT, is regarded as the "nearest" and "dearest" to the Igbo.

She is the great mother-goddess, the spirit of fertility —the mystic power of which every body stands in awe. She is a merciful mother who intercedes for her children with God and the other spirits; a mother whom the other spirits ask to "warn" her children on earth before they take action against them; but a mother when she has decided to punish, no other spirit may intercede or intervene; a mother, nevertheless, who does not punish in haste but quite reluctantly, after a series of warnings had gone unheeded; the great mother of all: of plants, animals and men both quick and dead. Hence the Igbo call her *Ana Nwe Mmadu Nine! Ana Nwe Anyi!*, *Ana*, the owner of all mankind, yes *Ana* is the owner.

As the spirit of fertility, she is believed to be responsible for increase of fertility both of man and of the land. Without her, life would be impossible. Public sacrifice is made to her before hoeing and planting the land; and at harvest, the Igbo offer her their first fruits. Her role in Igbo socio-religious life is such that the Igbo do nothing without first asking for her help.

Ana is the queen of the underworld. As such she is connected with the cult of ancestors. She is the unseen president of each Igbo community, the "parochial" symbol of the common origin and solidarity of the community—a common bond of humanity. . . .

Ana is believed to have helped the ancestors . . . to found the land—i.e. towns or villages. She is believed to have got the laws from God and handed them on to the ancestors. The ancestors "made" all subsequent laws under her direction, as did their descendants. Hence Igbo laws are always socio-religious laws and are believed to derive their sanction primarily from *Ana*. They are called *Omen-Ana*, that which obtains in the land. The ancestors were responsible for the erection of the first *Ana*-shrine (of course under her direction). That is why each Igbo community is incomplete without an *Ana*-shrine [place of worship for the localized social group]. This *Ana*-shrine is normally a tree with a pottery dish in which offerings are placed. This tree is in a great part of Igbo land, Ogirisi (a dolichandron tree).[28]

In his first novel about an Ibo village, *Things Fall Apart,* the prominent Nigerian novelist, Chinua Achebe (1930–   ), writes about the interrelationship of forces associated with humans, nature, the gods and the ancestors. It is a highly personal, profoundly spiritual energy field that must be cared for in all seasons of the spirit. His novel has an incident that captures the synergy between humankind and earth, and the community's obligation to maintain it. Okonkwo, the protagonist, is a successful but stubborn man with a quick temper. During the annual sacred Week of Peace (honoring the earth goddess *Ana*), he batters one of his wives. Consequently, he is visited by Ezeani, the priest of the earth goddess, who reproaches him for defiling the earth and his ancestors.

YOU ARE NOT A STRANGER IN UMUOFIA. You know as well as I do that our forefather ordained that before we plant any crops in the earth we should observe a week in which a man does not say a harsh word to his neighbor. We live in peace with our fellows to honor our great goddess of the earth without whose blessings our crops will not grow. You have committed a great evil . . . The evil you have done can ruin the whole clan. The earth goddess whom you have insulted may refuse to give us her increase, and we shall all perish.[29]

So now I come back home to Earth
I will remake my little peace with death
   sink my fingers deep and deeper still
   in this early morning dampness of our soil
I'll take my sandals off
   plant my feet among these ashes
   left by the season's many bushfires

My skin again shall feel
  the wet nuisance of dawn and dew
I'll hurry me up those old bush paths
    down those farms where once there grew
    the foods on which we grew to life's fullness
    even in those times of storm

They say our land has lost her joys
to seasons of teething pains and aches
that stupid elders and wild hunters
took and hid our hopes in foreign caves
and our offspring die of kwashi ork oric *[infant*
      malnourishment] dreams

But against the distant gleam of shooting stars
I chose and will choose again and again
The Homing Call of Earth
I am Earthchild turned to ghost
at festivals of Moonchildren
my voices heard only as distant calls of other
      worlds
my steps uncertain trods of alien feet

There is no sure motion
            Except
In the orbit of our own minds
So I must reject the honeyed call of distant dreams
I come back home to ragged hopes of Earth
The wealthy child's wardrobe may not outmatch
The earthy elder's termite-eaten wooden box of
      rags

Our Earth survives recurring furies
  of her stomach pains and quakes
From the bleeding anger of her wounds
  volcanic ash becomes the hope
    that gives rebirth to abundance of seedtimes.

Kofi Anyidoho, *Ghanaian poet,*
"The Homing Call of Earth"[30]

When we are the Children of the Forest, what need have we to be afraid of it? We are only afraid of that which is outside the forest.

A Pygmy of the Belgian Congo (Zaire) [31]

The Forest is Good.

MAKUBASI, *Pygmy father, rocking his infant son, singing his praises to his beloved forest home* [32]

THE POWER OF GREEN

I f you ask a Pygmy why his people have no chiefs, no lawgivers, no councils, or no leaders," writes Colin Turnbull, "he will answer with misleading simplicity, 'Because we are the people of the forest.' The forest, the great provider, is the one standard by which all deeds and thoughts are judged; it is the chief, the lawgiver, the leader, and the final arbitrator."[33]

The Pygmies of the Congo have a profound belief in the goodness of the forest. An intimate communion exists between these people and their forest world. For them, this ancient universe, with all its hardships, is a wonderful thing, full of joy. Their frequent singing and dancing, through the mysterious ritual of *molimo*, express an intense love for that world and a commitment to its happiness. Songs of devotion, praise and gratitude to their forest home honor its life-giving forces, contribute to its fecundity and ensure its continuing grace. Speaking of his good friend Kenge, one of his Pygmy teachers and guides, Turnbull reports: "what he liked best was to take me through the forest, as though he owned it personally, showing it to me with infinite pride."[34]

Kind, quiet old Moke describes just how the Bambuti Pygmies—people of the Ituri forest in Zaire (formerly the Belgian Congo) for thousands of years—trust the inherent benevolence of their rain-forest universe.

THE FOREST IS A FATHER AND MOTHER to us, and like a father or mother it gives us everything we need—food, clothing, shelter, warmth . . . and affection. Normally everything goes well, because the forest is good to its children, but when things go wrong there must be a reason.

Normally everything goes well in our world. But at night when we are sleeping, sometimes things go wrong, because we are not awake to stop them going wrong.

Army ants invade the camp; leopards may come in and steal a hunting dog or even a child. If we were awake these things would not happen. So when something big goes wrong, like illness or bad hunting or death, it must be because the forest is sleeping and not looking after its children. So what do we do? We wake it up. We wake it up by singing to it, and we do this because we want it to awaken happy. Then everything will be well and good again. So when our world is going well then also we sing to the forest because we want it to share our happiness.

[And when they are enveloped in darkness, they sing this one great song to awaken the forest:] "There is darkness all around us; but if darkness *is*, and the darkness is of the forest, then the darkness must be good."[35]

 Some learned scholars who have studied the language of my people say that the word "Kikuyu" or "Gikuyu" means "The People of the Fig Tree." It is true that as long as anyone can remember our people have loved trees and our sacred spots are always groves of trees. . . .

There were, and still are, very many sacred trees all over the Kikuyu country. The places where these trees grow are equivalent to churches in the Western world or shrines or temples in the Middle East and Asia. They could not be cut down. The ordinary people were not even supposed to go near them or to clear the bushes near by.

MUGO GATHERU,
Kikuyu, Kenya[36]

The Twi language of the Akuropon of Ghana is filled with references to leaves and trees which suggest a whole range of useful applications such as medicine, clothing, palm wine, ceremonial ritual, solace and supernatural power. The properties of trees and plants are associated with human characteristics. For example, one will say a person's dour expression is "like *kankuwa*"—an herb sour to the palate and often used as an arthritis remedy. "A large tree has fallen" is a commonly acknowledged metaphor for the death of a king.[37]

Despite the Christian influence of several centuries, beliefs about mystical powers and their sources continue to be widely held amongst the Akuropon. Although between two thirds and three quarters of Akuropon people are Christian, credence in the wisdom and might of the ancestors and other non-Christian deities is a fundamental aspect of Akuropon interpretations of existence. The power inhering in trees, animals and other elements of Creation is considered real, but the number of elders acquainted with its secrets has dwindled dramatically. An Akuropon elder expresses a palpable yearning for some of these gifts long forgotten and perhaps lost.

> IN THE OLD DAYS, if people tried to get hold of a chief in times of war or crisis, he could turn himself into a tree so that people would pass him by. The chief was powerful: because they believed it, it became true. . . . Many chiefs could turn into cats. One could touch a wall with his body and then you would see him behind the house. A very old chief in Amanokrom could do that: if he wanted to run away, he just leaned against the wall. . . . In those days, if you wanted to go to the king and were arrogant or came with an air of pride, he would put his foot on the ground and say: "Behold, what are you doing?" and then you would fall down. Today, this kind of belief has gone away. In the old days, the palace was a fearful and a wonderful place.
>
> In the old days, if someone fired a gun all you would see was water coming out of the gun. People could collect the bullets with their right or left hand. In those days, you could cut someone with a cutlass and the cutlass would break into pieces. In the old days, things happened which were fearful and wonderful.[38]

In the closing years of the last century, Prince Modupe, the son of a Yoruba trader and a Sousou daughter of royalty, was raised as heir to the chieftainship in the Sousou tribe. Prince Modupe recalls a life in French Guinea (now Guinea), West Africa, untouched by the ways of an outside world and directed by a feeling for the poetry and unity of life that was to be found in the wisdom of the Earth itself.

THE PLANT LIFE around any village is highly important to the community. Our food, clothing, the roofs of our shelters, the medicines, the spices, the well-being of the people derive largely from the things that grow in the earth. A medicine-man may be thought of as a specialist in roots and herbs and plants, but every individual must know the commoner uses of plants. Therefore a great emphasis was placed in the Bondo schooling on botany. [The word *Bondo* means strength].

We also learned the names our people have given the stars and the constellations, and the stories about them. We learned to track and to hunt game, to identify and to imitate the sounds of the jungle creatures. We learned that silences as well as sounds are significant in the forest and how to listen to the silences.

It seems to me now that this insistence upon the deep silences in order to become attuned to the rhythms of earth was one of the most distinguishing phases of our Bondo training. . . . Deeply felt silences might be said to be the core of our Kofon religion. During these times, the nature within ourselves found unity with the nature of earth. This is not "closeness to nature" but rather an immersion in the common nature which pervades all life—plants, animal, human.[39]

O weaving reeds, may you never be poverty stricken
May you never be taken for sale in the market
May none be ignorant of your maker
May no unworthy man ever tread on you

> *Women's work*
> *song, Somalia (East Africa)*[40]

This grass in my hand before it was cut
Cried in the wind for the rain to come:
All day my heart cries in the sun
For my hunter to come.

> *Bushman "Grass song"*[41]

Apart from its obvious ecological significance the vegetation cover [of Maasailand] plays an extremely important role in the social life of the Maasai community. From a very early age, children are expected to distinguish between the various plants and grasses and their uses. Grass is, for instance, used in the building of houses, for grasping in the hand as a sign of peace, as well as for blessings during rituals. Trees and shrubs provide traditional medicines and herbs, some of which have special ritual value. According to a popular myth, it was the folk of the forest, the hyena, who taught the Maasai the medicinal uses of various plants. It is significant to note that the Maa word for tree is the same as that for medicine (olcani; *pl.* ilkeek), and that every ailment has a traditional treatment, if not a cure, obtained from leaves, bark or the fruit of plants. The importance of trees and plants is also noted during rituals, when some of them are symbolically associated with certain notions of cosmology. The **Oreteti** tree (Ficus nalalensis), "bark cloth fig," is one of these. Its size, shape, sturdiness and long life epitomize the ideal in life, hence it is sung about and invoked in prayers and blessings.

NAOMI KIPURY,
Maasai educator,
Kajiado, Kenya[42]

Without green plants, all living things would perish, and the Earth would revert to its original barren state. Mankind survives on the Earth only because green plants grow here. Indeed, "all flesh is grass" (Isaiah 40:6).

The old adage, We are the microcosm of the macrocosm, suggests that everything which exists in the universe also exists in the human body. This supports the fact of the interrelationship of all things, both physical and spiritual. This appears to extend beyond the racial, religious and cultural boundaries and alludes to a common origin of all knowledge and all life.

ANTHONY K. ANDOH,
Ghanaian ethnobotanist[43]

Throughout the history of humankind, botany and medicine have been natural allies, "synonymous fields of knowledge," in the words of ethnobotanist R. E. Schultes.[44] Ethnobotany embraces the knowledge and wisdom derived from traditional and herbal medicine. The exploration, preservation and validation of the medicinal, spiritual and religious properties of plants have long been the work of ethnobotanist, horticulturalist and taxonimist Anthony K. Andoh. Born in the rain-forest belt of West Africa, in Kumasi, Ghana, Andoh is dedicated to enhancing the respectability of Ghana's traditional doctors within their own nation and throughout the world. Andoh investigates this age-old, yet vital, reciprocal relationship between man and plants in his remarkable book *The Science and Romance of Selected Herbs Used in Medicine and Religious Ceremony.* He documents 446 species in 75 families of plants occurring around the world, setting forth the theoretical, practical, medicinal, spiritual, legendary and romantic characteristics of each plant family. At a young age, he apprenticed to his father, Joseph Andoh, a forest botanist par excellence who trained at the Royal Botanic Gardens of Kew in England. Anthony Andoh eventually trained at Kew as well. He believes many modern scientific advances are simply a "re-discovery" of ancient Egyptian knowledge and that much of recent pharmacology "is simply an application of the profundity of the ancient civilizations."[45]

Andoh writes that Africans knew their physical environment intimately and were well versed in astronomy. In *The Science and Romance of Selected Herbs,* he reveals aspects of the ancient Africans' unique insights.

> OUR FOREFATHERS were true naturalists. They lived close to the earth and the elements of their environment, and they were meticulously observant of the cycles of birth, growth and decay of the ambient vegetation. Because they understood the interdependence between man, the surrounding flora and fauna and the seasonal changes, they were able to group herbs into categories which these ancient peoples claimed were governed by certain natural phenomena, including spiritual and planetary forces.
>
> In the human cultures of antiquity, the reverence for plants has always formed the link between the physical and the spiritual worlds. Our ancestors intuitively understood the Biblical verse, "*To everything there is a season, and a time to every purpose under the heaven. . . .* "[46]
>
> Since time immemorial, the ancient people have always used plants as a guide to the perpetuation of their

species and for their philosophical and spiritual development. Knowledge of the environment has always correlated with the level of civilization. Thus, we find scattered throughout literature of the ancients, how the total sum of the ecosystem of any given civilization was preserved and held in awe as a monument to the benevolence of Nature.

Because of the importance which the ancients attached to the natural world, and again on their pointed observation of the growth, behavior and usage patterns of certain plants, some selected plants gained a place of worship and high esteem within the society. Consequently, the worship of certain trees, shrubs, herbs and grasses, supposed to possess spirits, has at all times been practiced throughout the world. These practices still remain a part of all societal and religious activities, from the so-called "*primitives*" of the darkest Amazon and the Congo to the modern temples and cathedrals of Europe, including the Vatican.

In the Old World, especially Africa and India, there abound numerous such plants which are regarded as objects of veneration or esteemed as emblems of some special virtue. Thus, the myrrh, belonging to the family **Burseraceae,** genus **Commiphora,** with approximately 160 species, all of which, with the exception of perhaps a dozen, occur in Africa, was so highly regarded that it was one of the three gifts from the Wise Men to the Baby Jesus at the event of the Savior's birth.

Other plants are said to be possessed of a soul or the spirits of ancestors. An example here is the *"up-side-down"* tree—the Baobab tree, known botanically as **Adansonia digitata,** endemic to the dry veldt of Africa. This particular tree has many uses also. The leaves, pulp, seeds and oil extract are edible, the shells are used as containers, the bark is used for making ropes and baskets, the roots, bark and leaves are used as medicine. It should be borne in mind that not all sacred trees possess great utility. Some are used to erect shrines (the Cedars of Lebanon) for offering of prayers, while others such as the Bo-tree of India (**Ficus religiosa**) is used as a canopy under which devotees sit to pray and meditate for enlightenment; Gautama Buddha himself received his calling while meditating under a Bo-tree.

It is generally believed in the scientific world that the Plant Kingdom consists of no less than 500,000 species. This figure, though incomplete, because of our lack of knowledge of the entire plant world, still represents a bewildering array of complex organisms, each of which is a different chemical factory. Of these plant species, only a fraction of a percentage plays any part in our economic lives, and hardly more than a thousand have any financial significance in international markets. But most astonishing, only 15 species of plants and nine species of animals provide almost all the food for the world's population . . . The 15 staple food plants are: rice, wheat, maize, barley, sorghum, sugar cane, sugar beet, potato, sweet potato, cassava, bean, peanut, soybean, coconut, and banana, the forage grasses and legumes, the fiber and forest plants. The nine principal domestic animals are cattle, swine, sheep, goats, water buffaloes, chickens, ducks, geese and turkeys. . . .

[T]he fact that all animals depend upon a food chain which contains plant products as its fundamental link renders the study of vegetation a basic necessity in relation to all questions affecting animal nutrition.

Green plants, by the miracle of photosynthesis, capture a tiny fraction of the Sun's awesome physical energy and convert it into enough chemical energy to support all life on this planet.[47]

Respect for nature is inseparable from the world's cultural perceptions, from education in the fundamental values of life, from philosophy and from imagination and mythology.

GASTON KABORE (1951–   ),
film director and writer,
Burkina Faso (West Africa)[48]

Obscurity knows Nature will light the lamps.

Dahomean proverb[49]

[T]he urgency of our task . . . is to clear away the rubbish and excavate nature. This is a noble task. If we allow ourselves to be convinced that all we need is to acquire the West's mastery of the material world, we will fail. For the West has become a world of things, not people.

CHEIKH HAMIDOU KANE,
Senegalese novelist[50]

Yoruba, *Mask (Gelede)*, Republic of Benin, West Africa. Two coiled snakes, forming interlocking spirals, attack a quadruped atop this dramatic wooden mask. Imagery of this sort functions to edify, instruct and delight the community. Snakes as symbols of sacred truths are an artistic reference common to masquerade performances honoring the spiritual powers of elderly women.

NATURE:
THE GREAT TEACHER
AND HEALER

After the Sharpeville massacre in South Africa and the banning of the African National Congress and the Pan-Africanist Congress in 1960, most of the black writers left the country. Threat of arrest led many into exile, including Bessie Head (1937–1986), a teacher and novelist, who took up life as a refugee in Botswana, the setting for three of her novels. During her ten-year stay in the traditional African village of Serowe in Botswana, she produced a stunning and intimate portrait of one of Africa's largest villages (population 35,000), home to the Bamangwato tribe. Bessie Head credits Banmangwato country with the restoration of her being, a place where, as she put it, "the shattered bits began to grow." In her poetic account of the intensity of life in *Serowe: Village of the Rain Wind,* she also gives us a poignant self-portrait—perhaps inadvertently—of her own re-connection to life as she struggled for clarity with her own creative powers.

ALL TIME STANDS STILL HERE and in the long silences the dancing of birds fills the deep blue, Serowe sky. Serowe people note everything about nature: "The birds are playing," they say, more prosaically.

And indeed there seems to be no sense at all in the bird activity in the sky, other than playing and dancing. . . .

During my ten-year stay here, the two or three seasons when it rained for a whole month in one long, leaden downpour were so exceptional and stunning that I cannot even describe them. I am more familiar with the rain pattern of drought years. It rains sparsely, unpredictably, fiercely and violently in November, December and January. Before the first rains fall, it gets so hot that you cannot breathe. Then one day the sky just empties itself in a terrible downpour. After this, the earth and sky heave alive and there is magic everywhere. The sky becomes a huge backdrop for the play of the rain—not ordinary rain but very peculiar, teasing rain.

A ring of low blue hills partly surrounds the village; at least, they look blue, misty, from a distance. But if sunlight and shadow strike them at a certain angle, you can quite clearly see their flat and unmysterious surfaces. They look like the uncombed heads of old Batswana men, dotted here and there with the dark shapes of thorn trees. It is on this far-off horizon that all through December and January, the teasing summer rain sways this way and that. The wind rushes through it and you get swept about from head to toe by a cold, fresh rain-wind. That's about all you ever get in Serowe most summers—the rain-wind but not the rain.

Even so, summertime in Serowe can be an intensely beautiful experience, intense because with just a little rain everything comes alive all at once; over-eager and hungry. A little rain makes the earth teem with insects, tumbling out of their long hibernation. There are swarms of flies, swarms of mosquitoes, and swarms of moths—sometimes as big as little birds. Crickets and frogs appear overnight in the pools around the village: there is a heavy, rich smell of breathing earth everywhere. . . .

There is a sense of wovenness, a wholeness in life here; a feeling of how strange and beautiful people can be —just living. People do so much subsistence living here and so much mud living; for Serowe is, on the whole, a sprawling village of mud huts. Women's hands build and smooth mud huts and mud courtyards and decorate the walls of the mud courtyards with intricate patterns. . . .

Serowe is a traditional African village with its times and seasons for everything; the season of ploughing, the season for weddings, the season for repairing huts and courtyards and for observing the old moral taboos. In the traditional sense, it is not really a place of employment but almost one of rest. The work areas are at the lands and cattle-posts miles away. . . .

[T]he construction of Serowe intimately involved its population. They always seem to be building Serowe with their bare hands and little tools—a hoe, an axe and mud—

that's all. This intimate knowledge of construction covers every aspect of village life. Each member of the community is known; his latest scandal, his latest love affair. At first glance it might seem nearly impossible to give travel directions in the haphazard maze of pathways and car tracks. Everything goes in circles; the circular mud huts are enclosed by circular yards and circular pathways weave in and out between each yard. . . .

Although we live by such an ancient pattern, no other village in Botswana is as dynamic as Serowe and no other has seen so much tangible change.[51]

In her third novel, *A Question of Power,* Bessie Head explores the naked "bleak, arid barrenness of soul [that] had broken down"[52] after she fled South Africa and was forced to confront her own state of exile. It is a haunting account of her near-insanity which eventually leads to a "freedom of heart."[53] The story is about the roots of identity gone amuck. Head's writing has been described as "hav[ing] a way of soaring up from rock bottom to the stars, and [being] very shaking."[54] Breakdown and breakthrough are recurring themes. They surface in a remarkable piece of short fiction she calls *The Green Tree.* The interior landscape of her immediate physical environment becomes a macrocosm of her world of struggles and provides a sanctuary of hope. Head describes the Green Tree, or Rubber Hedge (*Tlharesetala*), as "a rather unattractive plant commonly used for hedging." She speaks with wonder of its amazing properties not only to reproduce itself but also to ward off any incipient danger to its survival. What's more, the plant is highly democratic in nature. It is available to anyone! "From planted cuttings, with little or no water, the Green Tree," she writes, "sends out new roots and starts a new life for itself. A waxy coat effectively prevents water-loss by evaporation and milky sap gives it a bad enough taste to deter goats from eating it. The sap congeals on exposure to air, so water losses through damage to stems and leaves are kept to an absolute minimum."[55]

The Green Tree is a metaphysical journey into at-one-ment; a quest for re-embodiment. It is a powerful metaphor for the resilience, resourcefulness and, above all, the courage of the human spirit. While acknowledging the fear of terra incognita, Bessie Head expresses "the passion [she] feel[s] for this parched earth"[56] as she struggles to regain equipoise.

THIS SMALL HILL of my village in Africa abounds with the song of birds. The birds are small and brown and seem bound up in the thick profusion of dark brown branches. The green leaves of the trees are so minute that the eye can hardly see them. Everything that is green in my country is minute and cramped for my country is semi-desert.

From this hill you may think the village below a fertile valley. It is shrouded and hidden in tall greenery. But that greenery is unproductive, contained and drawn into itself, concerned alone with its silent fight for survival. We call it the green tree. It came here as a stranger and quickly adapted itself to the hardness of our life. It needs no water in the earth but draws into itself the moisture of the air for its life. We use it as a hedge. It also protects us from the sandstorms that blow across our desolate and barren land.

If you tell my people that there are countries with hills and hills of green grass where no cattle graze, they will not believe you. Our cattle graze on parched grass that is paper-dry. Our goats eat the torn shreds of windscattered papers and thrust their mouths into the thorn bushes to nibble at the packed clusters of leaves that look like pin-points of stars farflung in the heavens. That is our life. Everything is jealously guarded. Nothing is ever given out. All strength and energy must be contained for the fight to survive tomorrow and tomorrow and tomorrow. . . .

The powdery dust of the earth, the heat, the cattle with their slow, proud walk—all this has fashioned our way of life. Our women with their tall thin hard bodies can drive a man to the depths of passion. All this is ours. Few are they, strangers, who like the green tree are quickly able to adapt themselves to our way of life. They are to be most feared for the adaptation is merely on the surface, like a mask, while underneath they are new and as strange as ever. They cause a ripple on the smooth pond of life that cannot be stopped from spreading from one thing to another. . . .

Just as our cattle would go insane at the unaccustomed sight of a hill covered with greenery; so do I live in fear of the body of a woman that has been transplanted by upheaval and uncertain conditions into harsh and barren soil. Sometimes I feel it beneath me; cool, like the depths of night when the moon brings the pale light of heaven to earth and makes the dust shimmer like gold. Then my hands reach out to crush the life out of the thing that torments me.[57]

In his novel *L'aventure ambiguë* (*Ambiguous Adventure*), the Senegalese writer Cheikh Hamidou Kane, a Fulani, embarks on a mystical quest to re-member himself. In this work, described as a "philosophical autobiography,"[58] Hamidou Kane's characters espouse a range of philosophic possibilites and then contemplate their influences. Like Bessie Head's work, Hamidou Kane's writing is also about loss of unity of being when separated from his essential nature. *Ambiguous Adventure* enters mind and spirit as a means to a rediscovery and re-memberment of Nature and self-Nature. Cheikh Hamidou Kane suggests that such a metaphysical "adventure" is risky, even dangerous. "It may be," he writes, "that we shall be captured at the end of our itinerary, vanquished by our adventure itself."[59] Kane seeks, ultimately, reconciliation and re-union with a lost world—the life-sustaining spirit of Africa—as he searches for the significance of his country, his history, his blackness—himself. *Education,* at the expense of leaving "human" Africa for "seductive" Paris, is the dilemma of the horn. Samba Diallo, Kane's autobiographical hero, summons his spiritual and ancestral foundation to "preserve" himself from a friend's proletarian, proselytizing efforts. In so doing, he experiences a shock of recognition of singular truth.

YOU HAVE NOT ONLY RAISED YOURSELF above Nature. You have even turned the sword of your thought against her: you are fighting for her subjection—that is your combat, isn't it? As for me, I have not yet cut the umbilical cord which makes me one with her. The supreme dignity to which, still today, I aspire is to be the most sensitive and the most filial part of her. Being Nature herself, I do not dare to fight against her. I never open up the bosom of the earth, in search of my food, without demanding pardon, trembling, beforehand. I never strike a tree, coveting its body, without making fraternal supplication to it. I am only that end of being where thought comes to flower. . . .

It might be said that I see less fully here than in the country of the Diallobé. I no longer feel anything directly. . . .

It seems to me, for example, that in the country of the Diallobé man is closer to death. He lives on more familiar terms with it. His existence acquires from it something like an aftermath of authenticity. Down there, there existed between death and myself an intimacy, made up at the same time of my terror and my expectation. Whereas here death has become a stranger to me. Everything combats it, drives it back from men's bodies and minds. . . . It still seems to me that in coming here I have lost a privileged mode of acquaintance. In former times the world was like my father's dwelling: everything took me into the very essence of itself, as if nothing could exist except through me. The world was not silent and neuter. It was alive. It was aggressive. It spread out. No scholar ever had such knowledge of anything as I had, then, of being. . . .

Here, now, the world is silent, and there is no longer any resonance from myself. I am like a broken balafong [a Senegalese xylophone], like a musical instrument that has gone dead. I have the impression that nothing touches me any more.[60]

Tepilit Ole Saitoti, a Maasai, describes a journey home to observe the rites of burial of a dead brother. Consoling a younger brother, and accompanied by a cousin and an elder, they drive a large donkey caravan through the deep gorges and ravines of his native highlands. Saitoti's own anguish is mitigated by the magnificence of Serengeti.

BELOW US IN THE DISTANCE was the plain of the Serengeti, now golden and dry. The breathtaking beauty of this land continued to console me, and it helped lift my spirits.

The distant peaks far away appeared like pillars supporting the heavens. The trees were as attractive as the flame lilies, which seemed to be everywhere. The trees reminded me of elders addressing meetings in ancient times. I paid closer attention to the rocky hill ahead of me, shaded at one point by a candelabra tree. Under the tree was a cave. I thought of the many lion cubs it must have sheltered from the rain, the wind, and the heat of the sun.

The area was uninhabited and cicada sounds echoed persistently. Cicada noises symbolized loneliness and isolation for the Maasai, and before I could ask myself where the people had gone to, I saw a flash of light like lightning. Soon I saw the silhouette of a figure. He turned out to be a warrior heading in the opposite direction. We met and greeted each other and talked for a while. He mentioned that there were many settlements not far away. I crossed a gully and found a beautiful herd of cattle grazing on the lush green. The sound of their bells was echoed by the nearby trees. The silhouette of the lone warrior in the distance made me think of the first man who ever trod the tawny plain.[61]

The unitive truths of the political philosophy of Kenneth D. Kaunda (1924–   ), former president of the Republic of Zambia, included responsibility for one's community and country; ministering to human need as the criterion of progress; and developing human dignity and potential. These principles are grounded in the soil and in the natural world of the African continent.[62] Nature as a creative force is a fundamental source for this knowledge. In his book *A Humanist in Africa*, Kaunda examines African traditional community life in order to draw from it tenets for community living in modern African countries.

I BELIEVE THAT THE UNIVERSE IS BASICALLY GOOD and that throughout it great forces are at work striving to bring about a greater unity of all living things. It is through cooperation with these forces that Man will achieve all of which he is capable. Those people who are dependent upon, and live in closest relationship with Nature are most conscious of the operation of these forces: the pulse of their lives beats in harmony with the pulse of the Universe. They may be simple and unlettered people and their physical horizons may be strictly limited, yet I believe that they inhabit a larger world than the sophisticated Westerner who has magnified his physical senses through invented gadgets at the price, all too often, of cutting out the dimension of the spiritual. . . . I am not denying the importance of the scientific method. But my point is that people in close relationship with Nature are forced to ask *big* questions however crude their answers might be. I could entertain you for hours retelling the traditional stories of my people I first heard in my childhood, many of which offer ingenious, if somewhat fanciful, explanations of the great riddles of life to which the world's great thinkers have sought solutions.

It is easy, of course, to romanticize Nature, but this is an error more likely to be made by those comfortably protected from it than by people like myself who have experienced its cruellest moods in disease, blight, famine and drought. To be exposed to Nature and to have to live your life at its rhythm develops humility as a human characteristic rather than arrogance. Men are more companionable and take the trouble to live harmoniously together because they know that only by acting together can they reap the benefits and try to overcome the hardships of Nature.

Was it not the Luddites in England who went around smashing the new machines of the Industrial Revolution because they could not face the future? I am no Luddite! I welcome all the advantages which Western science and technology have brought to Africa. I even welcome the fact that technology reduces our dependence upon the uncertainties of Nature, in spite of all that I have said. Yet my question is this: Is there any way that my people can have the blessings of technology without being eaten away by materialism and losing the spiritual dimension from their lives? I suppose the answer is that, however intensely we industrialize, the vast majority of the peoples of Africa will still live in close contact with Nature and so keep alive this element in our culture.[63]

Birago Diop, a Senegalese writer (1906–   ), declares in his poem "Breaths" that "the dead are not dead" but breathing in all of nature:

> Listen more often
> To things than to beings;
> The fire's voice is heard,
> Hear the voice of water.
> Hear in the wind
> The bush sob:
> It is the ancestors' breath.
>
> Those who died have never left,
> They are in the brightening shadow
> And in the thickening shadow;
> The dead are not under earth,
> They are in the rustling tree,
> They are in the groaning woods,
> They are in the flowing water,

They are in the still water,
They are in the hut, they are in the crowd:
The dead are not dead.

Listen more often
To things than to beings;
The fire's voice is heard,
Hear the voice of water.
Hear in the wind
The bush sob:
It is the ancestors' breath,
The breath of dead ancestors
Who have not left,
Who are not under earth,
Who are not dead.
Those who died have never left,
They are in the woman's breast,
They are in the wailing child
And in the kindling firebrand.
The dead are not under earth,
They are in the fire dying down,
They are in the moaning rock,
They are in the crying grass,
They are in the forest, they are in the home:
The dead are not dead.[64]

In *Tell Freedom*, Peter Abrahams, a South African writer, relives the joys of childhood where the world of nature was his first teacher.

IN THE LONG SUMMER AFTERNOONS, after my day's work, I went down to the river. . . .

Often, with others or alone, I climbed the short willows, with their long drooping branches. The touch of willow leaf on the cheek gives a feeling of cool wonder. Often I jumped from stone to stone on the broad bed of the shallow, clear, fast-flowing river. Sometimes I found little pools of idle water, walled off by stones from the flow. I tickled long-tailed tadpoles in these. The sun on the water touched their bodies with myriad colours. Sometimes I watched the springhaas—the wild rabbit of the veld—go leaping across the land, almost faster than my eye could follow. And sometimes I lay on my back on the green grass on the bank of the river and looked up at the distant sky, watching thin, fleecy white clouds form and re-form and trying to associate the shapes with people and things I knew. I loved being alone by the river. It became my special world.

Each day I explored a little more of the river, going farther up or down stream, extending the frontiers of my world. One day, going farther downstream than I had been before, I came upon a boy. He was on the bank on the other side from me. We saw each other at the same time and stared. He was completely naked. He carried two finely carved sticks of equal size and shape, both about his own height. He was not light brown, like the other children of our location, but dark brown, almost black. I moved nearly to the edge of the river. He called out to me in a strange language.

"Hello!" I shouted.

He called out again, and again I could not understand. I searched for a place with stones, then bounded across. I approached him slowly. . . .

Joseph and I spent most of the long summer afternoons together. He learned some Afrikaans from me; I learned some Zulu from him. Our days were full.

There was the river to explore. . . .

There was the hot sun to comfort us. . . .

There was the green grass to dry our bodies. . . .

There was the soft clay with which to build. . . .

There was the fine sand with which to fight. . . .

There were our giant grasshoppers to race. . . .

There were the locust swarms, when the skies turned black and we caught them by the hundreds. . . .

There was the rare taste of crisp, brown, baked, salted locusts. . . .

There was the voice of the wind in the willows. . . .

There was the voice of the heavens in thunderstorms. . . .

There were the voices of two children in laughter, ours. . . .

There were Joseph's tales of black kings who lived in days before the white man. . . .[65]

In *Comes the Voyager at Last,* a journey of mythic consciousness and profound vision, Kofi Awoonor somersaults into the life-affirming realm of consoler of the people and metaphysician of the sacred word. It is Awoonor's belief that through immense love the enduring good-heartedness of black Africa will bring about "a return to a humane society, free and unfettered." He calls up that primeval time when "in the forest of [his people's] abandonment," there flourished "in our hearts an eagled desire which knew no bounds."[66]

In Kofi Awoonor's mythic forest, trees are cathedrals of the spirit. They teach humankind how to re-ascend to the loftiest heights through an unfolding of the levels of consciousness present in each earthly being.

NIGHT WAS UPON US when we entered the forest only to be assailed by a thick impenetrable darkness thickened by tall trees whose canopies covered our skies and the eyes of the heavens. Beneath our weary feet was a soft carpet of rotting leaves. A magic smell of mould and decay rose everywhere.

We camped near the first giant tree for the night. The night was a whining long moan of trees as they whispered in the periodic winds that rushed through the few lingering patches of cleared ground. We managed a few fitful winks of sleep punctuated by neighborly nightmares of screams and wild speech. It had been the same every night of our journey. . . .

The giant trees reached almost to the heavens. Tall, erect their bases were large ominous temples of marching feet that supported shrines and homes of gods and spirits. From the heavens their crowns dropped occasional dew and twigs. Several climbers clung upon their bodies like beads on the devotees of a god. Lichens and epiphytes were the thoroughfare of squirrels and the mouse-faced woodpecker that flit from under tree to under tree. The sacred Logo tree stood guard over the forest at legendary intervals humming with all the supervisory deities long known chants of ancient rites. Birdsong and dirge for the dead days of our lives everywhere, life above and around, beneath, putrefaction, decay to nurture life and the tree. The trees would swoon now with a solemnity that was the signal of distress in their heavens high above our sorrow. It seemed they have been called upon by their very nature to share and hearken unto our inner sorrows swaying, in

giddy waves in a melancholy jubilee in the heart of the
forest and our souls.[67]

We have been told that we must go from our land, from the land of our ancestors. But it is a very difficult thing to uproot an old oak of many years. The roots of such a tree are very deep. Certainly one can take an axe and cut down such a tree, that is easy, but the roots remain and are very hard to dig up. So you see, the tree really remains. The tree goes on.

ALEX LAGUMA,
Time of the Butcherbird *(1979)*[68]

. . . to anyone who wants to understand Gikuyu problems, nothing is more important than a correct grasp of the question of land tenure. For it is the key to the people's life; it secures for them that peaceful tillage of the soil which supplies their material needs and enables them to perform their magic and traditional ceremonies in undisturbed serenity, facing Mount Kenya.

JOMO KENYATTA,
Facing Mount Kenya *(1938)*[69]

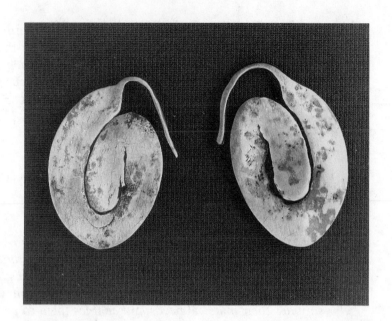

Turkana, *Earrings*, Kenya. Spirals of flattened metal—either silver or brass—are worn by many east-central African peoples.

Coiled Wire Bangle, Kenya. In the northern desert of Kenya, spiraled brass armlets are worn on the lower arm by Rendille women upon marriage. It shifts to the upper arm when the first son is circumcised. In other African societies, the coil is a dynamic symbol of Creation worn as a protective talisman.

"FROM LAND CAN I
NEVER BE BANNED"

For the Kikuyu of Kenya, the land supplies the roots of their existence, linking the dead, unborn and living into one organic whole. A vital mystical bond exists with their departed; the Kikuyu depend on this communion with their ancestral spirits for their reason for being. A passionate regard of country and a deep and abiding love of its living presence reflect the sanctity in which the land is held. In *My People of Kikuyu*, Jomo Kenyatta, unquestionably still the most interesting figure of African ethnology, addresses the sacral and beloved nature of his homeland. Kenyatta evokes the umbilical link the Kikuyu experience with the land and the gratitude they feel for its Source of being.

IN SPEAKING OF THEIR COUNTRY the Kikuyu never forget to give thanks for Mwene-Nyaga, or Ngai, the High God, for they say that when he was putting into shape the country that he gave them he was not in a hurry but took great care to make the country beautiful and fertile. He set mountains and hills in their proper places. He made the forests grow in abundance to beautify their slopes, and provided numerous birds to sing soothingly in the trees. He also provided grass lands for domestic and wild animals to graze in contentment. From hills and mountains he made rivers and springs to flow forth and supply people and beasts with pure clear water. When Mwene-Nyaga had done these things, he said: "My heavenly glory will always remind you of my greatness and generosity towards you; I will command the sun to shine over you to give you light and warmth in the day, while you go about your various activities, and the moon and the stars will shine over you in the night to give you fresh cool air that you may rest in comfort after your toil."

In remembrance of what Mwene-Nyaga has given them, the Kikuyu address him thus in their prayers:

"O our heavenly Great Elder, we are thankful for the natural gifts which you have bestowed upon us, unlike the lands of our neighbours, some of which you passed over in a hurry, and threw one river here and another there, leaving the rest of the country dry and in many places unforested. Remembering this, we surely believe that even as you gave us all the good things of life, you will no doubt always give us wisdom to make good strong spears and sharpen them well. O Mwene-Nyaga, the Greatest Elder, you will give us knowledge to make strong bows and arrows that shoot well and to the mark, so that we may keep our enemies at bay, who seek to take our cattle and therefore starve our women and children and make the tribe weak. O Mwene-Nyaga, who dwelleth on Kere-Nyaga, you will give us strength so that when our enemies come to close quarters we will be able with your guidance and our strong muscles to drive our spears right through their hearts, and prevent them from depriving us of the gifts which you the Lord of Nature have bestowed upon us. We pledge to you, O Mwene-Nyaga, that we shall not sit idle and let anyone snatch away what you have promised to our forefathers, to be our children's birthright for ever."[70]

The vitality of Kikuyu society of central Kenya lies in the sanctuary of the Kikuyu soil itself. Jomo Kenyatta, author of the classic ethnographic work *Facing Mount Kenya,* discusses the critical issue of land tenure as the visible symbol of social cohesiveness and cultural continuity. It represents both the unborn as well as the living's "partnership in the common life of generations," explains Kenyatta.[71] That system can only be understood through the ties of kinship that bond all members of the Kikuyu community. Land, writes Kenyatta, is "the material symbol that holds family and tribe together."[72]

IN STUDYING THE GIKUYU[73] tribal organisation it is necessary to take into consideration land tenure as the most important factor in the social, political, religious, and economic life of the tribe. As agriculturists, the Gikuyu people depend entirely on the land. . . .

In Gikuyu life the earth is so visibly the mother of all things animate, and the generations are so closely linked together by their common participation in the land, that agricultural ritual, and reverence for ancestral spirits, must naturally play the foremost part in religious ceremonial. . . .

Land . . . is the key to the people's life; it secures for them that peaceful tillage of the soil which supplies their material needs and enables them to perform their magic and traditional ceremonies in undisturbed serenity, facing Mount Kenya. . . .

When the European comes to the Gikuyu country and robs the people of their land, he is taking away not only their livelihood, but the material symbol that holds family and tribe together. In doing this he gives one blow which cuts away the foundations from the whole of Gikuyu life, social, moral, and economic. When he explains, to his own satisfaction and after the most superficial glance at the issues involved, that he is doing this for the sake of the Africans, to "civilise" them, "teach them the disciplinary value of regular work," and "give them the benefit of European progressive ideas," he is adding insult to injury, and need expect to convince no one but himself. . . . As it is, by driving him [the African] off his ancestral lands, the Europeans have robbed him of the material foundations of his culture, and reduced him to a state of serfdom incompatible with human happiness.[74]

The symbol of land dominates every phase of Kenyan novelist Ngugi wa Thiong'o's (James Ngugi) novel *Weep Not, Child*. His protagonist, Ngotho, is a farmer on his own beloved ancestral land, but like thousands of other Africans, he is now obliged to till it for a stranger. The British proprietor is Mr. Howlands, whose sense of the land is quite different from the old African's. Ngotho, who is in Howlands' pay, caresses his natal soil, honoring the spirit of it.

[HOWLANDS] JUST LOVED TO SEE Ngotho working in the farm; the way the old man touched the soil, almost fondling, and the way he tended the young tea plants as if they were his own. . . . Ngotho was too much of a part of the farm to be separated from it. Something else. He could manage the farm-labourers as no other person could. Ngotho had come to him at a time when his money position was bad. But with the coming of Ngotho, things and his fortune improved. . . .

They went from place to place, a white man and a black man. Now and then they would stop here and there, examine a luxuriant green tea plant, or pull out a weed. Both men admired this *shamba* [farm]. For Ngotho felt responsible for whatever happened to this land. He owed it to the dead, the living and the unborn of his line, to keep guard over this *shamba*. Mr. Howlands always felt a certain amount of victory whenever he walked through it all. He alone was responsible for taming this unoccupied wildness. They came to a raised piece of ground and stopped. The land sloped gently to rise again into the next ridge and the next.[75]

Ngotho knows the ways of the land and the hidden things of the tribe. He possesses such a profound love for his ancestral fields that sometimes he cannot even bear the thought of disturbing the tea plants by walking through them.

NGOTHO LEFT EARLY FOR WORK. He did not go through the fields as was his usual custom. Ngotho loved the rainy seasons, when everything was green and the crops in flower, and the morning dew hung on the leaves. But the track where he had disturbed the plants and made the water run off made him feel as if, through his own fault, he had lost something. There was one time when he had felt a desire to touch the dew-drops or open one and see what it held hidden inside. He had trembled like a child but, after he had touched the drops and they had quickly lost shape melting into wetness, he felt ashamed and moved on. At times he was thankful to Murungu [the Creator] for no apparent reason as he went through these cultivated fields all alone while the whole country had a stillness. Almost like the stillness of death.[76]

In his monumental study of modern Africa and its literature, *The Breast of the Earth,* Kofi Awoonor, Ghanaian poet, novelist, teacher and diplomat, reveals essential aspects of the African quest for cultural self-discovery. He describes its significance as "an umbilical link with the aboriginal literatures of our people," stating, "That is how it should be, for as we say, 'you weave the new rope where the old one left off.'"[77] Awoonor's own "mythical meeting point with [his] eternal earth and sea mother" dwells in both geographical and cultural realities, one being the African's conception of land. "Landscape," he once wrote, "intertwines with the most fundamental framework of our existence."[78] In fact, the symbol of the land has dominated the mental landscape of the African world since time immemorial. Moreover, it is considered a "sacred force" that has unfailingly ensured the continuity and renewal of a race. Awoonor attests to its symbolic, unitive and creative power.

> LAND WAS NOT MERELY AN ECONOMIC COMMODITY, it was, more importantly, a sacred entity. The earth represents in most African myths the mother principle which is central to the survival and continuity of the group. That is why land is still communally held in most parts of Africa and not regarded as a commodity that can be parceled out and sold at will. In the pantheon of African gods, the Earth Goddess is an important benevolent spirit upon whom man depends for food and sustenance and to whom he returns at death. Her sanctity as the natural principle is recognized in a number of taboos and abominations which cannot be committed against her. The sanctity of the earth is recognized in ceremonies that mark the clearing of virgin forests for farming and the preparation of new plots for building. Land, thus, is the center of the community's life. The numerous first-fruits ceremonies constitute homage to the Earth Goddess, who blesses crops and yields the abundance of her bosom for her children. All human beings, the African believes, are all children of the earth; but the earth of our native soil, of our village or town, becomes the bond of the community's cohesiveness. It is for this we fight when strangers want to dislodge us. It is the place where our umbilical cord is buried, and our link stretches through her to our ancestors who were buried in her womb. It is this great sacred force that . . . informed every fierce act of heroism and bravado.[79]

This is a Kipsigi song of pleasure from Kenya. The singer is much enamored of his natural roots, serenading the beauty of the landscape where he lives. The intense admiration and love felt by the oral poet for his home soil is vocalized almost entirely through color, sound and animals, particularly cattle. "Kiboney" is said to be the name of a hill.

> *We live at the field of Kagipsirich,*
> *We live where the calf, the calf plays with the*
> > *calabash:*
> *We live at that hill the colour of sandy-sided cattle,*
> *That hill where the grass is burned until only a*
> > *patch remained where the rabbit sleeps:*
> *I love that stone, stone of Kiboney*
> *Which rolls into the shade and rests there like a*
> > *man purging himself:*
> *I love the salty water at Pirar, where the cattle*
> > *drank until the pebbles showed:*
> *We live at this hill where the blue-grey bulls, the*
> > *blue-grey bulls are grazing.*[80]

As a schoolboy on his many visits to the tiny village of Tindican in Guinea, Camara Laye participated in the rice harvest festival and later, in his twenties, composed a lyrical reminiscence of the experience. In reaping the bounty of the soil, the workers felt an at-oneness with the land and each other. "It was as if the same soul bound them," wrote Laye.

DECEMBER, DRY AND BEAUTIFUL, the season of the rice harvest, always found me at Tindican, for this was the occasion of a splendid and joyful festival, to which I was always invited, and I would impatiently wait for my young uncle to come for me. The festival had no set date, since it awaited the ripening of the rice, and this, in turn, depended on the good will of the weather. Perhaps it depended still more on the good will of the genii of the soil, whom it was necessary to consult. If their reply was favorable, the genii, on the day before the harvest, were again supplicated to provide a clear sky and protection for the reapers, who would be in danger of snakebite.

On the day of the harvest, the head of each family

went at dawn to cut the first swath in his field. As soon as the first fruits had been gathered, the tom-tom signaled that the harvest had begun. . . .

Once the signal had been given, the reapers set out. With them, I marched along to the rhythm of the tom-tom. The young men threw their sickles into the air and caught them as they fell. They shouted simply for the pleasure of shouting, and danced as they followed the tom-tom players. . . .

When they had reached the first field, the men lined up at the edge, naked to the loins, their sickles ready. My uncle Lansana or some other farmer—for the harvest threw people together and everyone helped everyone else —would signal that the work was to begin. Immediately, the black torsos would bend over the great golden field, and the sickles begin to cut. Now it was not only the morning breeze which made the field tremble, but also the men working.

The movement of the sickles as they rose and fell was astonishingly rapid and regular. They had to cut off the stalk between the last joint and the last leaf at the same time that they stripped the leaf. They almost never missed. This was largely due to the way the reaper held the stalks so as to cut them. Nonetheless, the speed of the sickle was astonishing. Each man made it a point of honor to reap as regularly and as rapidly as possible. As he moved across the field he had a bundle of stalks in his hand. His fellows judged him by the number and size of these bundles.

My young uncle was wonderful at rice-cutting, the very best. I followed him proudly, step by step, he handing me the bundles of stalks as he cut them. I tore off the leaves, trimmed the stalks, and piled them. Since rice is always harvested when it is very ripe, and, if handled roughly the grains drop off, I had to be very careful. Tying the bundles into sheaves was man's work, but, when they had been tied, I was allowed to put them on the pile in the middle of the field. . . .

The tom-tom, which had followed as we advanced into the field, kept time with our voices. We sang as a chorus, now very high-pitched with great bursts of song, and then very low, so low we could scarcely be heard. Our fatigue vanished, and the heat became less oppressive.

On such occasions, if I happened to stop work for a moment and look at that long, long line of reapers, I was always impressed and carried away by the infinite love and kindliness of their eyes, as they glanced here and there. . . .

The long line of reapers hurled itself at the field and hewed it down. . . . They sang and they reaped. Singing in chorus, they reaped, voices and gestures in harmony. They were together!—united by the same task, the same song. It was as if the same soul bound them.[81]

"Where is the *Muntu* (human being) that we should be?" asks K. Kia Bunseki Fu-Kiau in his absorbing book *The African Book Without Title*. It's a work about his Kongolese roots and traditional African legal concepts. A dynamic world of cultural history emerges which, in his words, "give[s] rise to authentic and original African constitutions." Real African life is met in the countryside, writes Fu-Kiau, "where most critical African problems are lived, and above all, where cosmologies that generate all African thought (philosophy) [are] still alive."[82] The genuine lessons of life lie in "the deepest understanding of all of our regional cultures which symbolize ourselves," says Fu-Kiau. The life force and preservation of this powerful cultural matrix rests in the identity of the land itself.[83] Land is the spiritual, physical and social link between the community, its ancestors and its deities. It is part of "the eternal root." The potentiality for regeneration blooms through it. Fu-Kiau ponders the nature of the land's inalienability, succinctly summed up by the Kôngo proverb, "To sell community land is to carry a mortal yoke."[84]

INSIDE YOU ARE YOU; outside you are not. You only are a tiny part of a huge and coherent body, the community within the universal totality. . . .

The community land is untouchable, it is considered taboo . . . because it belongs first to the eternal community roots, the ancestors (the real living gods) as well as to the people in the living community. . . .

The defence of the land was and still is the cornerstone of oral, and unwritten legislation. One who knows the Kôngo land-holding system, knows its social organization, and therefore its concept of law and crime in the past as well as the present.

One of the essential characteristics of the Kôngo system of property is its inalienability. There is no valable condition that could change this inalienability of the ancestral land. . . .

[A Kôngo proverb advises:] If the community lacks the land, the door for survival, its members will disperse. The community land, its availability to all members, is the symbol of security and of togetherness within the community. A community leader as well as a national one must know that community/national land is the first property of the society that should be protected, even at the price of blood. A leader that sells or alienates the land of the community/society is a murder[er], because he prevents the community/society from having access to its first source of all possibilities for survival.[85]

"May you endure like Kibo."
"As Kibo moves not, so may life not be removed from you."
"As Kibo ages not, so may you never be old."

Chagga salutations.
Kibo is the highest peak of
Mount Kilimanjaro in Tanzania

You are not a full human being if you don't come from Kilimanjaro. In fact, the higher up the mountain you live, the more fully human and blessed you are.

Chagga belief[86]

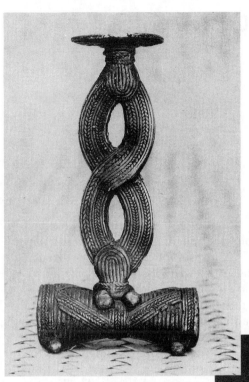

Tiv Brass Ring, Nigeria. This elaborate ring of bronze or brass is actually a platform for taking snuff, which is offered to distinguished figures by the elders.

Tiv-carved wooden spoon, Nigeria. The most arresting feature of this wooden implement is a human form rendered as a figure eight, which appears to be unique in the region, or even in all of Africa. It was used by the Tiv for offering food to important visitors.

MOUNTAINS OF MAGIC

Mircea Eliade, scholar of world religions, once observed that "the symbolic and religious significance of mountains is endless."[87] The multiplicity of images through which mountains are viewed all seem to evoke a profound sense of the sacred. Following in this tradition, the Kikuyu—the largest tribe in Kenya with more than 2 million members—revere Mount Kenya, the heavenly abode of their Supreme Being, Ngai. Mount Kenya is Africa's second highest peak with its tallest summit, Batian, reaching an altitude of 17,058 feet (Mount Kilimanjaro is the first with its immense dome, Kibo, rising to 19,340 feet).[88] It is the only peak in the world to have a country named after it. The Kikuyu refer to Mount Kenya as *Kere-Nyaga,* the "mountain of brightness." In their prayers and sacrifices, they turn north toward their sacred mountain and address Ngai—who is believed to dwell upon its holy peak—as *Mwene-Nyaga,* the "possessor of brightness." In fact, the Kikuyu insist that the light and the realm of light are one and the same. In *Facing Mount Kenya,* Jomo Kenyatta writes that "it is taboo to look toward the heavens during a thunderstorm." The Kikuyu believe, he says, "the noise of the thunder . . . to be that of Ngai 'cracking' his joints (. . . as a warrior limbering up for action)." Thunder and lightning are a clear signal to make way "for Mwene-Nyaga's movements from one sacred place to another." It is said that "when a man happens to be stricken by the lightning . . . [it is] for daring to look upwards to see Mwene-Nyaga stretching himself and cracking his joints in readiness for his active service to chase away or smash his enemies."[89]

Ngai's divinity is manifested through all aspects of the natural world, sun, moon, earth, stars, rain. The blessings of Ngai are beseeched at all public assemblies in Kikuyu country with such ceremonial phrases as: "Say ye, the elders have wisdom and speak with one voice [an elder]; Praise ye Ngai. Peace be with us [community voice]. Say ye that the country may have tranquillity and the people may

continue to increase; Praise ye Ngai. Peace be with us."[90] When the
first seeds of the season are to be planted, a "planting ceremony" is
arranged to ensure good crops and the bountiful fertility of the fields.
The honored elder who recites the prayers faces Kere-Nyaga, raises
his hands, holding one of the seed-calabash offerings, and calls out:

> MWENE-NYAGA, you who have brought us rain of the sea-
> son, we are now about to put the seeds in the ground;
> bless them and let them bear as many seeds as those of
> *gekonyi* [a very prolific creeper].[91]

One of Africa's most esteemed keepers of the word, Amos Tutuola has been described as a "natural mythologist" whose work, in the
words of Ghanaian poet Kofi Awoonor, "is a recapitulation in the
written form of what is essentially the great common soil of literature
[the oral tradition]."[92] As a novelist, Tutuola's use of folklore and
mythology derived wholly from the African tradition. They form
(along with "felicitous accidents of language"[93]) the drive and core
of his story-telling and set him apart from all other African writers.
Tutuola is a Yoruba (of a nation of several million people in the
western part of Nigeria) who is deeply rooted in that tradition of
story-telling. His fusion of an idiosyncratic and rudimentary English
with numerous Yoruba folktales creates what Awoonor describes as
"a unified cosmic territory." That technique has earned him wide
admiration both at home and abroad. His novels include *The Palm-
Wine Drinkard, My Life in the Bush of Ghosts, The Brave African
Huntress* and *Simbi and the Satyr of the Dark Jungle*.

In the Yoruba world of Amos Tutuola, hills and peaks are repositories of sacred energies, conduits of power and loci of hallowed
ancestral spirits. In a rare piece of short nonfiction, Tutuola harnesses
this mighty energy to explain the genesis of his own people and to
demonstrate how the physical and metaphysical universes coexist. He
writes,

> [I]N MY TOWN, which is Abeokuta, one of the biggest Yor-
> uba towns in the west of Nigeria, and which is about sixty
> miles away from Lagos, the federal capital, we have strong
> belief that many mighty hills are the homes of spirits.
>
> In Abeokuta town, one mighty hill is in the heart of
> the town. This hill is called Olumo. Several shrines are on
> top of it. The people sacrifice to the spirits who dwell in
> this hill and many people worship these spirits in a certain

period of the year. But of course, in the past days or several years ago, human beings were included in the sacrifices such as goats, rams, cows, costly clothes, cola nuts, plenty of palm oil, and many other valuable things they were giving to the spirits of Olumo, the hill.

The first people who came to Abeokuta had no other place to live but in the cave which is in this hill. At last they found out that the hill was the homes of spirits. But as they had no other god to worship, they started to worship the spirits of the hill. Of course as time went on the people were increasing in large number until the cave could not accommodate them. They began to spread to the surroundings of the hill, Olumo. It was like that, they spread on and on until a large town was formed and then the Olumo hill was then in the heart of the town.

In those days, whenever the neighboring people beseiged them, the devotees of the hill spirits would sacrifice immediately to the spirits. They would ask the spirits to help them conquer their enemies, and unfailingly their enemies would be conquered right out. Not only that, when one was seriously ill, that person would certainly be well as soon as the sacrifice was given to the hill spirits. When one was in great burdens, his or her burdens would be eased as soon as the sacrifice was given to the spirits. When there were epidemics of such the sicknesses as smallpox, etc., etc., and that people were dying in large number or more than it should be, the devotees would not waste time to give the right sacrifices to the hill spirits in order to help to get rid of all these things. When one woman was barren more than it should be, she would become the mother of children soon after the sacrifices were given to the spirits. When the rain kept too late to fall on crops in the year, then the sacrifice would be given to the spirits in order to help them to cause the rain to fall, and in fact the rain would start to fall as soon as the sacrifice was given to them. Furthermore, special sacrifices were given to them when the people of the town wanted to choose a new ruler.

For all these reasons, the Yoruba people still respect the spirits who are dwelling in this hill, Olumo, till present time, and the devotees are still sacrificing to them.

Again, to bring more light to the belief which we the Yoruba people have that there are spirits in certain hills.

Ibadan, the largest town in West Africa, and which is forty-eight miles from my town, Abeokuta, also has a mighty hill which is at the outskirt of the town. The people here also have strong belief that spirits are in their hill which is called Oke-Ibadan, meaning Ibadan Hill. The spirits helped them greatly in the past days to conquer their enemies, to help them to overcome all their difficulties, etc.

From the children and to the very old age, people join together to worship the spirits in the month of March every year. They all dance about in the town with great joy for about two days.

The people of Ibadan are doing so every year in remembrance of the great help which their hill spirits rendered to them in the past days and which they are still rendering to them at the present days.[94]

Mugo Gatheru is a Kikuyu from Kenya, East Africa, the firstborn son of a known *mundumugo* (medicine man). He comes from a long line of highly respected men who bore the name Mugo, which means, he says, "Man of God," a lineage "stretching far, far back into time."[95] Here he comments on the significance of Mount Kenya in the lives of his people.

I HAVE SEEN the beautiful pictures the Japanese paint of a mountain in their homeland called Fujiyama. These Japanese remind me much of the Kikuyu, for they, too, are people in love with a mountain. We live in a very beautiful part of east Africa, some 5000 feet above sea level, among rolling hills, where for many hundreds of years the Kikuyu have planted and reaped and tended their sheep and goats and cattle.

When the first Europeans came to explore these highlands they saw a beautiful snow-capped mountain rising up from the low hills high into the cloud-filled blue skies. They asked my people what it was called in their language, and they were told that it was *Kere-Nyaga* which meant "white stripes." The word was strange to their ears, and as some of our people pronounce it, it sounded to the Europeans like "Kenya." So in the geography books it is "Kenya," but we still call it *Kere-Nyaga*. The early Europeans left, never knowing how important the mountain was to the people, who believed that high up on its snow-capped peak lived Ngai, the great and powerful unseen god who made all things. Then, and even now, when a most solemn prayer is being made for help, the people turn their faces towards the mountain. And it was to Mt. Kenya that my father turned when he was healing people. Many are the times I have seen him do it. It was from Mt. Kenya, too, that Ngai spoke, in the beginning of time, and called the first man into being.[96]

All you big things, bless the Lord
Mount Kilimanjaro and Lake Victoria
The Rift Valley and the Serengeti Plain
Fat baobabs and shady mango trees
All eucalyptus and tamarind trees
Bless the Lord
Praise and extol Him for ever and ever.

All you tiny things, bless the Lord
Busy black ants and hopping fleas
Wriggling tadpoles and mosquito larvae
Flying locusts and water drops
Pollen dust and tsetse flies
Millet seeds and dried dagaa
Bless the Lord
Praise and extol Him for ever and ever.

African canticle[97]

They call it simply the Mountain. It soars in the near distance, rises above their small Tunisian village in North Africa as a symbol of continuity and tradition. It is the sacred dwelling of their ancestors. A reassuring presence, it provides solace, strength and a sense of the sublime to the village inhabitants. They are reminded of its centrality in their lives when the future of their village is called into question in a short novel by Tunisian writer, Mustapha Tlili.

THAT HORIZON, where our ancestors suddenly appeared one day, gave this village its name.

Lion Mountain.

Everything here is imbued with the legend of those founding fathers, those learned warrior-lords, the Ouled El-Gharib. . . .

Opposite Horia's house looms the Mountain. It makes an imposing and unusual boundary. . . .

Seen from Horia El-Gharib's house, with its view unobstructed by the slightest natural or artificial obstacle, the Mountain was inexhaustibly beautiful.

A geography more than physical or human: sacred. . . . Yes, that's the way it really was for the villagers. In their vision of the world—and above all in the eyes of the imam, that vigilant guardian of the Law—the natural order of things was profoundly at one with the moral and judicial orders. In this mystical topography, landmarks determining the rights of each and every individual were perfectly clear. And so on the eve of the events that would abruptly call into question a good many truths, everyone knew that the rise of land sweeping from Horia's house up to the mountain was the legitimate realm of the old woman, as it had been for her family before her, and for their ancestors from time immemorial. No one needed to discuss or prove this, for it had always been so. . . .

Sitting before her home, her kingdom on this earth, she never tires of this marvelous view, like a gift offered to delight a lonely old woman who no longer expects much from this life. She admires that pure and perfect line, so perfect it renders unthinkable the slightest change, which could spoil it. The horizon of Lion Mountain. The Mountain. . . .

At any time after the first light of dawn, or at twilight, our ancestors might appear in the distance, swarming out of the wilderness beyond the Mountain. This land is their land; it is their place of refuge and redemption. They claim it for their own, as it claims them in return. It is theirs and always has been. . . .

Land of our ancestors. Ancestors of this arid earth, poor yet so beloved, yes, so beloved by Horia. Ancestors of that venerated Mountain over there.[98]

*Man's whole life unfolds according to a set of rules trans-
mitted by the ancestors and dictated of old to one of them
by a god. Religious life, craft, marriage, family, eating—
everything is regulated by precise rules. Nothing is left to
chance. . . . [T]here is no such thing as the sacred on one
side and the profane on the other. Everything is connected,
everything brings the forces of life into play. These forces
are the manifold aspects of Sé, the sacred primordial force,
which is itself an aspect of God.*

AMADOU HAMPÂTÉ BÂ,
Malian writer and sage[99]

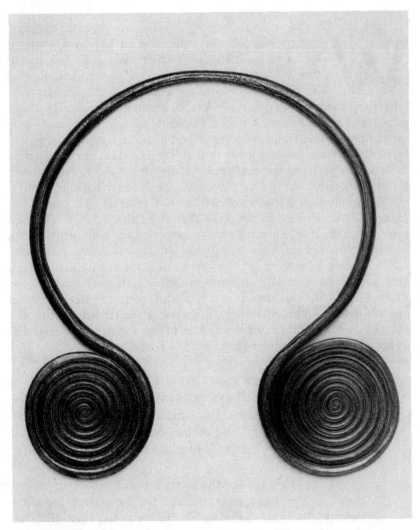

Mongo Necklace (iron), Zaire.

THE SACRED FORCE

West Africans call him "the Sage of Marcory," after a district in Abidjan, Ivory Coast, where he has settled after a life of journeying throughout Africa, Europe and beyond. Revered for decades in the francophone African community and known for his voluminous writings about Africa and its traditions, Amadou Hampâté Bâ is virtually unknown in the English-speaking world. A teacher, novelist, theorist and global humanist, Bâ was born in 1901 in Bandiagara, Mali. He has worked tirelessly to preserve the oral tradition in Africa and is best known for his aphorism "An old man dying is like a library burning."[100]

Symbolism in African culture "is not abstract or mental, but concrete," writes Bâ, "in the sense that an earthly symbol is like an echo or a concrete expression of an aspect of the primordial force. Things below are reflections of higher principles—living reflections which contain a Presence."[101] Crafts-making, for example, is considered sacred work and not just simply a utilitarian, domestic or income-producing pastime. It is a recapitulation of a primordial act inspired by the infinite Master. Bâ describes the transformative element of crafts, and traditional activities in general, as a manifestation of holy knowledge and the One Creative Force.

> THE THIRTY-THREE PARTS OF THE LOOM are not cut at random, but according to a sacred formula. It was necessary to get permission from the Force-Source in order to transform his initial and divine work into human work—tools. The use of each tool likewise is preceded by a prayer of incantation.
>
> The "language" of the loom is a great lesson in philosophy. Everything speaks: the shuttle, the pedals, the warp thread, the beater, the roller, the cylinder, the rails, etc. Each element represents an aspect of the play of cosmic

life: the creative Word, dualism, the law of cycles, the past, the present, the future, the passing of time, etc. As he handles each part, the weaver sings or recites a precise litany, for he knows that he is in contact with one of the mysteries of Life, or with its symbol, which for him is the same thing.

The same is true for every traditional activity: the arts of the blacksmith, the shoemaker, and the potter (pottery is traditionally reserved for women, since symbolically all that is hollow and is consequently a receptacle represents the feminine).

The farmer never allows himself to open the bowels of the earth without first saying the appropriate and consecrated words. He buries the seed only after having blessed it and commended it to the Force-Source, which watches everywhere and over everything at the same time, so that nothing is disturbed and so that cucumbers should not begin to grow on the branches of a *baobab* tree. The shepherd does not take his flock into the bush without having asked the place "to open its good mouth and to close its bad mouth."

Most of the rites performed by traditional people are thought of as being the repetition of a primordial act which was inspired by *Masa-Dembali* (the uncreated, infinite Master), and which has been transmitted through the chain of ancestors-initiates. . . . It was always an elder, or an ancestor, of each clan or tribe who was the first to enter into relationship with the "forces" of nature, the agents of God. This generally took place by the intermediary of a fabulous being (a spirit, an animal, or an atmospheric or astronomic phenomenon), from whom the elder received a certain knowledge which he then transmitted to his descendants. . . .

For the ancient traditional societies, the principle of all real knowledge, of whatever order, always comes from above. "We can do nothing unless it comes to us from *Masa-Dembali* and at the moment chosen by him." Thus one does not say that man "invents" something, but that he "discovers" it or "rediscovers" it. The thing existed before man, who merely discovers or unveils it at the time chosen by *Masa-Dembali.*

The ancestors of farmers, of the two kinds of hunters

(animal hunters and fishermen), and of the three kinds of herdsmen (of cattle, goats, and sheep) entered into relationship with the hidden forces that live in the bosom of the earth, in trees, and in water. It is thanks to the transmission of this knowledge, by way of initiation, that they could accomplish their traditional activities.[102]

In a seminal work, *Aspects de la civilisation africaine,* Amadou Hampâté Bâ addresses the notion of the "One Force"—"the All-Powerful Source of existence," the sacred Presence in all things—that permeates African thinking and being. The intermediaries for the Sacred Force range from the venerated ancestors and tribal elders to the four fundamental elements of nature—water, earth, air and fire, with their corresponding and enormously varied pantheon of African gods. Bâ is quick to point out that "in discussing the traditional relationship of African man with God, one must avoid premature generalizations, for there is not an "African man" who represents the whole continent." To proceed correctly, "one must focus on a particular ethos," says Bâ.[103] Thus the religious traditions of the Bambara, Peule, Dogon and Malinké tribes of Mali ("the country I know best") are central to his thought and writing.

> BLACK AFRICAN MAN IS BORN A BELIEVER. He does not need books of revelation to make him believe in the existence of the One Force, the All-Powerful Source of existence and the prime mover of the activities and motions of beings. He does not consider this Force to be outside of creatures—it is inside each being. It gives him life, and it watches over his development and his eventual procreation.
>
> Surrounded by a universe of the tangible and the visible—men, animals, plants, stars, and so forth—African man has always perceived that in the depth of these beings and of these things there dwells an indescribable power which animates them.
>
> This perception of the sacred force in all things is the source of numerous beliefs which take various forms. . . .
>
> In the belief of the Bambaras, the Bozos, and others, the notion of the Sacred is essentially ambiguous: the same term is used to designate both the Sacred itself and its manifestation. The words *nyama* and *do* designate the Sa-

cred in itself. They also designate everything which resembles a quality or an attribute of the divine, which therefore becomes the receptacle or the special place where this divine quality is manifested.

Thus, advanced age gives to a man or a woman something of *nyama*. The transcendent God particularly is of a very great age, having been present at the beginning of time. It is believed that he lives in the body of every aged being, and age becomes therefore a sacred privilege. Among the Bambaras, the oldest person in the tribe is the trustee of sacred powers; he is the one who officiates at sacred rituals. . . .

Man's whole life unfolds according to a set of rules transmitted by the ancestors and dictated of old to one of them by a god. Religious life, craft, marriage, family, eating—everything is regulated by precise rules. Nothing is left to chance. . . .

When a man takes his meal in the bush, he begins by throwing some morsels to the four cardinal directions before putting anything into his mouth. He has to know an entire ritual procedure. He must respect the middle of the dish, which is the spot where the divine power descends to give the food its nutritional value—the center of each thing is like its heart and belongs to the gods.

It can be seen that there is little or no room for a profane life, in the modern sense of the word: there is no such thing as the sacred on one side and the profane on the other. Everything is connected, everything brings the forces of life into play. These forces are the manifold aspects of *Sé*, the sacred primordial force, which is itself an aspect of God.[104]

Wood is the most widely utilized material in African religious art, "sharing with metals a high degree of spirituality," according to Kofi Awoonor.[105] Preservation of the organic shape of the trees in African carvings, for instance, is a fundamental principle in traditional sculpture. In the act of creation, respect for the integrity of the original medium—combined with poetic awareness and a deep communal and ceremonial sensibility—assume an essential spiritual importance. The abundance of ritual and its practice express the cosmology of the African world, where the natural and supernatural realms point the way. Through the ceremonies of supplication, conciliation and thanksgiving, the vital interplay between man, spirits and the mysterious forces of nature is acknowledged, honored and vivified. Trees are one aspect of that multifaceted bursting reciprocity. Awoonor addresses the nature of their life force.

> BEING PART OF THE DYNAMIC UNIVERSAL FORCE that reposes in all natural objects, the tree has always represented a powerful symbolic element expressive of the life force itself. A carver or sculptor who goes into the forest to cut down a tree must go through a ritual and make an offering to the tree spirit, whose pardon and help he must seek in his venture. An egg is broken against the trunk and the following prayer, with variants from place to place, is offered:

> *I am coming to cut you down and carve you, receive this egg and eat, let me be able to cut you and carve you. Do not let iron cut me; do not let me suffer in health.*[106]

According to the Akan of Ghana, musicians, craftsmen, artists and poets are the linguists, the spokespersons for the Creator, the Supreme Deity. Thus they become "interpreters of the eternal truth of creation and of joys, sorrows, needs and destinies of man," says Ghanaian writer A. A. Y. Kyerematen.[107] Their skills are of a sacred nature and therefore must display the corresponding qualities of imagination, originality, a sense of beauty and inspiration. A sense of humour, adds Kyerematen, is paramount. Drums, horns and flutes communicate a tonal system of language that is unique to Africa. The "talk" of these musical instruments has captivated and confounded the world. It is nonoral poetry used to transmit messages, recount history, sing the praises of the natural world, provide solace, and convey traditional wisdom and proverbs. Inspired verbal and musical versatility are necessary in order to produce this incomparable poetic tradition that continues to animate modern African poetry and writing. Here is an example of the famous Akan drum prelude, called the *Anyaneanyane (Awakening)*, played at the Adae festival in Kumasi, the Ashanti capital:

> *The path has crossed the river.*
> *The river has crossed the path.*
> *Which is the elder?*

We made the path and found the river.
The river is from long ago,
the river is from the ancient creator of the universe.[108]

The principal horn of Togbui (head of the Mafi State of Tongu, Volta Region) alludes to a story of migration in the following way:

"Mighty land, mighty land,
Send me away if you will.
A dweller of some land shall I be still,
From land can I never be banned."

To this the drum, agblovu, *responds:*

"Stand up and shout Yeve!
I retreat: but not to run away;
There is a purpose to my flight."[109]

I should say river. I should say tornado. I should say leaf.
I should say tree. I should be wet by all rains, made damp
with all dews. . . . Whoever would not comprehend me
would not comprehend the roaring of the tiger.

AIMÉ CÉSAIRE (1913–   ),
poet, Martinique[110]

In his famous book *L'enfant noir* (*The Dark Child*), a work of immense beauty and radiant vision that describes his halcyon childhood memories in narrative form, Camara Laye, a Malinké from Guinea, re-creates the wonder of that ideal world of endless grace when "miracles took place before our eyes."[111] In his recollection of childhood in the African town of Kourassa, Camara Laye reenters, through memory and art, a unified world where incompleteness and ambiguity are unknown, and where the "omnipresence of mystery" reigns.[112]

Camara Laye's father was a much admired jeweller who worked in gold. The sacred métier of a goldsmith was exacting, from "the microscopic delicacy of the work" to the "intense heat of the forge."

The craftsman who works in gold must be in a state of ritual purity before he enters his workshop and remain in a state of purity while working the gold. At the moment of the melting of the gold, alchemy of assorted dimensions takes place, recalls Camara Laye: "The operation that was going on before my eyes was simply the smelting of gold; but it was something more than that: a magical operation that the guiding spirits could look upon with favour or disfavour; and that is why there would be all round my father that absolute silence and that anxious expectancy. I could understand, though I was just a child, that there was no greater craft than the goldsmith's. I expected a ceremony, I had come to be present at a ceremony, and it really was one." [113]

The praise-singer, or the "go-between," recounts Laye, was an essential ingredient in the success of the whole process of transformation. The praise-singer was a reliable vehicle for the favourable ear of a sought-after goldsmith. Singer of the goldsmith's praises, the go-between assisted in the unfurling of ancestral traditions and in the rhythmic spinning and shaping of golden treasures. Camara Laye perceives a "fine careless rapture" in his father's unique, creative universe.

> OF ALL THE DIFFERENT KINDS of work my father performed, none fascinated me so much as his skill with gold. No other occupation was so noble, no other needed such a delicate touch; and, moreover, this sort of work was always a kind of festival: it was a real festival that broke the monotony of ordinary working days.
>
> So if a woman, accompanied by a go-between [official praise-singer], crossed the threshold of the workshop, I would follow her in at once. I knew what she wanted: she had brought some gold and wanted to ask my father to transform it into a trinket. . . .
>
> The praise-singer would install himself in the workshop, tune up his cora, which is our harp, and would begin to sing my father's praises. This was always a great event for me. I would hear recalled the lofty deeds of my father's ancestors, and the names of these ancestors from the earliest times; as the couplets were reeled off, it was like watching the growth of a great genealogical tree that spread its branches far and wide and flourished its boughs and twigs before my mind's eye. The harp played an accompaniment to this vast utterance of names, expanding it and punctuating it with notes that were now soft, now shrill. Where

did the praise-singer get his information from? He must certainly have developed a very retentive memory stored with facts handed down to him by his predecessors, for this is the basis of all our oral traditions. Did he embellish the truth? It is very likely: flattery is the praise-singer's stock in trade! Nevertheless, he was not allowed to take too many liberties with tradition, for it is part of the praise-singer's task to preserve it. But in those days such considerations did not enter my head, which I would hold high and proud; for I used to feel quite drunk with so much praise, which seemed to reflect some of its effulgence upon my own small person.[114]

Life to a tribal African is synonymous with religious living. His beliefs come into play in the smallest detail of his life. We believe in one Supreme Being but we do not visualize this Being in the image of man. We feel this Being as soul-force or spirit-energy manifesting itself in all life. We believe in life after death, an active life, in which the spirits of ancestors participate in all important tribal affairs. This has been called ancestor worship, but we do not deify our ancestors, or any human. We venerate their memories and feel their influence active among us as long as they are remembered. In the Bondo, we were taught that by emptying our minds, by making our minds void of all sensation, the spirit-force of the Supreme Being could fill us.

PRINCE MODUPE,
Sousou, Guinea[115]

There exists a wealth of African prayers traditionally ascribed to the ancestors and heroes of Africa's enduring heritage. These texts include prayers for consolation, harmony, wealth, peace, blessings, protection, fertility and abundance; prayers of supplication, thanksgiving, praise and joy. Through them and their accompanying rituals, a person's life and the community's is sanctified. Prayers are the yarn that weave the physical and metaphysical worlds together, rubbing the physical dimension with the spiritual and the spiritual with the physical. In the following two prayers, offered upon the occasions of the sowing and harvesting of the earth's fruits, the unitive power of the universe is invoked and praised.

DEDICATING THE SEEDS BEFORE SOWING

O *nyambe*, you are the creator of all. Today we your creatures prostrate ourselves before you in supplication. We have no strength. You who have created us have all power. We bring you our seed and all our implements, that you may bless them and bless·us also so that we may make good use of them by the power which comes from you, our creator.

GREETING GOD AT SOWING TIME

Oh God! Receive the morning greetings!
Ancestors! Receive the morning greetings!
We are here on the chosen day,
We are going to sow the seed,
We are going out to cultivate.
Oh God! Cause the millet to germinate,
Make the eight seeds sprout,
And the ninth calabash.

Give a wife to him who has none!
And to him who has a wife without children
Give a child!
Protect the men against thorns,
Against snake-bites,
Against ill winds!

Pour out the rain,
As we pour water from a pot!
Millet! Come![116]

An Xhosa man from southwest Africa responds to the news that Christians were bringing God to his people. He reproves the missionary for his assumption that the traditional ways and beliefs of his people are merely superstitions and of no real value.

WE HAD THIS WORD before the missionaries came; we had God (*Utikxo*) long ago; for a man when dying would utter his last words, saying, "I am going home, I am going up on high." For there is a word in a song which says:

Guide me, O Hawk!
That I may go heavenward,
To seek the one-hearted [sincere] man,
Away from the double-hearted men,
Who deal in blessing [giving gifts]
and cursing [witchcraft].

we see, then, that those people used to speak of a matter of the present time which we clearly understand by the word which the missionaries teach us.

The God who is now, is the one who was from everlasting, before the missionaries came. Before they came we spoke of *Kamata* [God], and we spoke of *Tiko* [Utikxo (God)]; the word *Kamata* means Tiko. We trust that there were some of our people in heaven before the missionaries came. We had righteousness and evil; there were men-destroyers and there were good men; the men-destroyers were wicked men; we had life and death; and the graves which are now, were long ago. So we say there is no God who has just come to us. Let no man say The God which is, is the God of the English. There are not many Gods. There is but one God. We err when we say, "He is the God of the English." He is not the God of certain nations; just as man is not English and Kosa; he is not Fingo and Hottentot; he is one man who came forth from one God.[117]

Humor governs the world well.

Dahomean proverb,
West Africa[118]

THE PROVERBIAL RIDDLE

P roverbs provide valuable clues to ways of thinking and feeling, to philosophical systems. Every African society has its proverbs. The eternal verities are a major component of these far-reaching insights. Almost all proverbs contain a code of ethics for the community. Some proverbs are a record of actual historical events but most are inspired, imaginative teachings of truth, handed down orally and indispensable to the smooth functioning of the society. Some entertain, others instruct, while still others encourage aesthetic values by the very nature of their own literary merits. Proverbs also convey sharp wit, humor, rhetoric and sarcasm. According to one Akan (Ghana) proverb, wise men speak and are spoken to not in ordinary language but in proverbs. The proverb is the horse of conversation, say the Dahomeans (West Africa), so we shall canter ahead and sample the sagaciousness of a number of African nations.

> Without proverbs, the language would be but a skeleton without flesh, a body without soul.
>
> Zulu proverb
> (South Africa)[119]

> Lizard says, "If a man were to achieve everything he would lose his mind."
>
> Ashanti proverb
> (Ghana and Ivory Coast)[120]

> The world is a marketplace [we visit], the otherworld is home.
>
> Yoruba proverb
> (Nigeria)[121]

We will all be dead if the forest [the substructural ground of our system of survival] is exterminated.

Bambuti (Pygmy) proverb
(Zaire) [122]

The clan is just like the cluster of trees. (If one is far away from a cluster of trees, he sees all the trees as huddled or massed together. It is when he goes near that he recognizes the trees in fact stand *individually*.)

Fante proverb [123]
(Ghana)

Be careful about what you throw into the "pond of life" because of the waves it is bound to create! (If you throw in a little pebble, the wave will not go far; but if you throw in a big piece of wood, the waves will not stop until they have crossed the pond and reached its banks. Not only will the waves do damage to the banks, but they will also return to the starting point and meet the waves going in the opposite direction, which could produce a shock with disastrous and unforeseeable consequences.)

Bambara proverb [124]
(Mali)

Faults are like a hill: You stand on your own and talk about those of other people.

Hausa proverb
(Nigeria) [125]

Cattle are born with ears, their horns grow later.

Azania proverb
(South Africa) [126]

The past teaches us. It makes the desert bloom.

Gabra proverb
(Northern Kenya) [127]

The earth is mother of all.

Ugandan proverb [128]
(Central East Africa)

Life is like a palm tree.
The fronds go this way and that.

Dahomean proverb
(West Africa) [129]

Tradition endures.

Akan proverb
(Ghana) [130]

The forest has ears.

Kenyan proverb [131]
(East Africa)

Cattle lick each other because they know each other.

Azania proverb
(South Africa) [132]

Hearts cannot be lent.

Azania proverb
(South Africa) [133]

"Nsi mfinda"—nations are forests—says a Kôngo proverb. A "forest" of one type of trees is not a forest, it is a
"ndima" no matter how large it is, for a forest always is
an ensemble in diversity.

Here is what the kongolese-cosmology taught me: I am a
going-and-coming-back-being around the center of vital
forces. I am because I was and re-was before, and that I
will be and re-be again.

Man is a second sun rising and setting around the earth.
He has to rise as the sun does in order to Kala (to be, to
become, to [ignite] fire).

K. KIA BUNSEKI FU-KIAU,
Kôngolese writer (Zaire) [134]

K. Kia Bunseki Fu-Kiau believes that in the provenance and providence of the proverb lies the key to understanding the African Mûntu (person). "Proverbs," writes Fu-Kiau, "are regarded as the warehouse of the ancient African wisdom."[135] Fu-Kiau is a member of the Kôngo culture (a Bântu ethnic group in the center of west Africa), a citizen of Zaire, an author and a dedicated "pioneer" of Kôngo culture. He urges the study of proverbs as a rich source of African thought and a repository of all that was and is. Proverbs "are very meaningful by themselves," says Fu-Kiau, "and, paramount, in historical, philosophical, legal, religious and theoretical information about African schools of human knowledge."[136] Proverbs are used within the community, are about the community and explain the ideal of community (*Kânda*). They are lively, wise and provocative instruments! They are essential tools for living correctly. Fu-Kiau states that "in debates, in ceremonies, in judgements, in joy as well as misery, proverbs are frequently used to reprimand, to criticize, to compare, to segregate, to encourage and to punish . . . to teach [and] to explain. . . ."[137] In his fascinating account of Kôngo cosmology and the African traditional legal system, *The African Book Without Title*, Fu-Kiau reveals the great significance of the world of the proverb in sustaining African culture and guiding its destiny.

> PROVERBS, IN AFRICAN CONTEXT, are laws, reflections, theories, customs, social norms and values, principles, and unwritten constitutions. They are used to justify what should be said or what has been said. Proverbs play a very important ethical role in story telling, legends, etc. Very often parents as well as griots (*n'samuni*), and story tellers end their tales by [a] very fitting proverb.
>
> African proverbs are numerous and diverse. They deal with people, God, ancestors, animals, forests, goods, money, ideas, wars, sun, moon, time, social problems, education, food, life . . . traditions (*kinkulu*), history (*kikulu*), plants, insects. . . .
>
> Our ancestors did not have dictionaries/encyclopedias, but by their experiences, proverbs, and their sincere autocritiques they did maintain and save the national and community security. . . .
>
> The proverbs below are excerpted from the unpublished "*Dingu kia Nkumbu ye Ngana Zeto*" (Dictionary of nouns and proverbs Kôngo). . . . [They show] us how strong the concept of "*Kânda*" [community] is among the Bântu people in particular and among African people in general.[138]

Tell me the old principles/theories in order to understand the new ones. All educational process is gradual. Don't reverse the historical truth. History accumulates itself. One can only build on old materials.

As long as there is a female "shoot" within the community, it cannot be annihilated. The presence of a female in the community is the symbol of continuity of life in that community, and, on the contrary, her absence is the symbol of its end.

The community is the union of the ancestors and of the living people. The community is an accumulation of the living unity of the physical and spiritual elements.

There are no boundaries (of land) within the community land. The freedom of land use by all community members is warranted within the community. There is no privacy on land issues; its ownership is public for no one came in this world with a piece of land in his/her hand. Therefore it cannot be sold, bought or alienated.

If the concept of community is annihilated/destroyed the world is destroyed. If principles, concepts, norms and values that make world communities alive are violated, weakened or completely destroyed [the] human being will easily destroy his world.

The initial community capital (bându, from "bânda," to start) is its human resources and the land. Life would be impossible within the community without land and without valid people in it. The community must pay a particular attention for its youth as well as for its land, the fundamental capitals of a society.[139]

Riddles exist in most cultures and are not for the weak of mind. Africa is a veritable cornucopia of riddles. In Dahomean society of West Africa, for example, riddles are so important that they have become a key element of Dahomean everyday communication. In *Dahomean Narrative*, Melville J. Herskovits suggests that the appeal of the riddle "lies not only in the hidden meaning of the solution, but more especially in its double entendre." Punning is a skill that is highly valued, so much so that "a period of riddling prefaces all storytelling sessions," writes the ethnologist.[140]

What follows is a Zulu riddle (South Africa) of the greatest skill, a witty and mysterious conundrum of universal significance.

> THE QUESTION: Guess you: a pumpkin plant; it is single, and has many branches; it may be hundreds; it bears many thousand pumpkins on its branches; if you follow the branches, you will find a pumpkin everywhere; you will find pumpkins everywhere. You cannot count the pumpkins of one branch; you can never die of famine; you can go plucking and eating; and you will not carry food for your journey through being afraid that you will find no food where you are going. No; you can eat and leave, knowing that by following the branches you will continually find another pumpkin in front; and so it comes to pass. Its branches spread out over the whole country, but the plant is one, from which springs many branches. And each man pursues his own branch, and all pluck pumpkins from the branches.

> THE ANSWER: A village and the paths which pass from it are the branches, which bear fruit; for there is no path without a village; all paths quit homesteads, and go to homesteads. There is no path which does not lead to a homestead. The pumpkins are villages from which the paths go out.[141]

We praise the landscape and the cattle and the beauty of it all.

TEPILIT OLE SAITOTI,
Maasai (Tanzania)[142]

"AN OX NEVER
LETS YOU DOWN"

For the Shona of Zimbabwe in southern Africa, the zebra is regarded as one of Earth's great treasures, a symbol of unfathomable mystery, stellar character and a metaphor for the qualities of an entire community or a whole clan system. In this lively, glowing Shona Praise-Poem (a Clan Praise), an intimate knowledge of animals is revealed and celebrated. Gratitude for the Zebra's incomparable beauty, "Creature that makes the forests beautiful," is also expressed in unique bursts of transcendent imagery.

> Thank you, Zebra,
> Adorned with your own stripes,
> Iridescent and glittering creature,
> Whose skin is as soft as girls' is;
> One on which the eye dwells all day, as on the
>   solitary cow of a poor man;
> Creature that makes the forests beautiful,
> Weaver of lines
> Who wear your skin for display,
> Drawn with lines so clearly defined;
> You who thread bead in patterns,
> Dappled fish
> Hatching round the neck of a pot;
> Beauty spots cut to rise in a crescent on the
>   forehead,
> A patterned belt for the waist;
> Light reflected,
> Dazzling the eyes.
> It is its own instinct, the Zebra's,
> Adorned as if with strings of beads around the
>   waist as women are;
> Wild creature without anger or any grudge,

Lineage with a totem that is nowhere a stranger,
Line that stretches everywhere,
Owners of the land.[143]

Animals are a part of the human lineage in Ghanaian society. "There is no division between us and the animal world," says Kofi Awoonor. Animals partake in the living myth that animates the living community. "We respect and revere them as part of ourselves," continues Awoonor.[144] They are a component of the entire religious frame of reference of the community. The following folktale demonstrates the interdependency of humans and the animal world.

ONE DAY, A HUNTER was wandering in the forest looking for game.

After many weary hours of fruitless search, he decided to return home. His path went through a thick bush that soon changed into a wide Savannah, with little hills and clumps of bushes here and there. Evening was fast approaching and he was hurrying to reach home before the night falls. The sun was far away, low at the end of the world, red before it disappeared into its house where folks believe it too will go to sleep until tomorrow.

Suddenly, the hunter's eye caught a creature several yards away on a little hill. It was a gazelle. Slim with an exquisitely well framed neck with beautiful rings of folds. Its eyes were deep brown, cool quiet like a little pool in a hidden place under the trees of the forest.

The hunter, his heart beating fast, aimed his spear at the gazelle.

Just at that moment, the animal turned round and stared with its soft melancholy eyes at the hunter. The hunter lowered his spear as he looked intensely at the gazelle.

"What a beautiful creature! No creature on earth is as beautiful as this gazelle," he murmured to himself.

"I heard you," the gazelle said distinctly in a quivering feminine voice. The hunter stepped back. "I will turn into a woman if you promise to marry me and take me home," the gazelle said.

The hunter knelt in the grass and exclaimed, "Oh,

what a great joy will it be. I will marry you and take you home."

"But first," replied the gazelle, "you must swear never never to reveal the secret of my origin to anyone."

Trembling with joy, the hunter swore all the ancestral oaths that he would never never tell anyone the origins of the gazelle soon to be the woman he would marry.

Long stories are tedious. So we will make our own tale short.

The hunter and his wife lived happily for many years. She bore him five children, three girls and two boys, as handsome and beautiful as their parents. The hunter became successful; with success he felt he needed to marry another wife. But he married a quarrelsome and difficult woman who soon bore him two boys, rowdy unruly brats who respected nothing or nobody.

One day the hunter was away. A little quarrel between two children of the co-wives turned into a terrible row. Neighbors hung onto the fence to witness the disgraceful squabble as the two women and their children hurled insults at one another. The second wife screamed at the top of her voice the ultimate insult, "You mere gazelle from the forest, an animal like you, how dare you," she said.

The gazelle woman, stung for a moment, not by the insult but by the fact that her husband had revealed her origins, stood still. Then she dashed to the room, went straight to the rafters where her gazelle skin was hidden, and took off with it out of the compound.

When the husband came home and heard the news, he gave chase. He arrived panting at the spot where he first met his wife. And lo, on the same little hill was standing his wife, now a gazelle looking away into the far horizon. It turned round, looked at the hunter, and then slowly descended into the valley and vanished among the trees.

Her great great grandchildren are still in our village. It would be an offence against the ancestors to reveal their true identity, because who knows, it may be that I too am descended from the gazelle-woman.

Such are the ways of our earth.

It may seem an odd juxtaposition, but has to be faced—
"people and cattle are one." Mention of either invariably
provokes thought of the other; and did so now in the
car, for is not a right-minded right-living man traditionally
surrounded by stock and offspring? Cattle spelt prestige,
children continuity, happiness. The delight of Xhosa men
in their babes, toddlers and young has to be seen to be
appreciated. They are his calves, his diamonds. . . .

NONI JABAVU,
Xhosa author[145]

"Where are you going?"
"We follow the cattle."

A Wodaabe, breaking camp in Niger
(to director Werner Herzog)[146]

In her graceful, delicate and profoundly observant works about her people, the Xhosa of South Africa, Noni Jabavu has a sense of things: that life is one large grand observance of ceremony, a sometimes wry—but always seriously intense—performance of ritual and, in the words of James Olney, "a continual drawing and redrawing of the delicate network of human relationships out of which individual existence gradually defines itself."[147] Life is a finely woven net in which all worlds are joined—ancestors, spirits, humans, animals and the natural universe—bonded by the timeless eternal spirit of that which has always been and is, and the compelling mystical force of "that which has always been done." In *The Ochre People*, Noni Jabavu writes about her re-discovery of "the mirror of ancestral conditions and 'umbilical' attitudes,"[148] best summed up here by the phrase "an ox never lets you down!" In a charmed moment of suspended lightness and humor, Jabavu returns to her ancestral fields (*veld*) to re-acquaint herself with her people's highly valued and idiosyncratic cattle. It is a point of pride that a Xhosa, when in possession of his cattle, knows complete happiness. In fact, a vast vocabulary exists for cattle that reflects their important symbolic wealth as well as their virtual weight in gold.[149] Jabavu's teacher is Long Ear, a teenage youth who coddles his cattle like a mother hen.

HE WAS LOOKING towards the trees below the kraal and whistling, drew breath, whistled again. Presently an ox ambled up. He praised it. Then whistled again, and another came, again in a leisurely manner. He praised it too. Finally both stood still, near by but aloof and distant, sometimes turning their faces towards him then away as if looking at the view.

"Does each one know his whistle call?" I asked.

"Oh yes, cattle have brains," he said proudly. "You can single one out from the middle of the herd. Of course to teach them you have to persevere. Sometimes they delay coming because they don't feel like being disturbed. But the herd turns to look at the disobedient one, so in the end he thinks: 'Ag! There'll be no peace until I obey,' he pushes his way out of the crowd and comes. . . ."

"I had no idea cattle were clever," I said. . . .

"Cattle are clever, all right," he laughed.
"To teach them tricks when we are out herding, oh, that is real fun! . . ."

Pointing at the animals jogging along before us, he said, "Some of those chaps are absolutely mad about racing. They know which ox runs fastest and fix their eye on him, not bothering about the rest. Sometimes they try to gore the best challenger; go out of their way to eliminate him, oh, they are too good these fellows," and he chuckled. Then he talked of the fun of teaching oxen to lie down on a prescribed spot and stay in it unsupervised.

"When you want time off for a bit, say you have 'an appointment,' " giving a sly look for he meant meeting a sweetheart. "You can *instruct* an ox to stay put whereas a horse would have to be hobbled. But an ox never lets you down. You can be absent for hours trapping eatables for the pot. . . ." And [he] started to tell me about the birds that "helped with the herding," especially the fork-tailed shrike. I smiled because Long Ear was unwittingly confirming the old saying: "The cattle of him who lacks a herdsman are herded by the shrike. *Indoda engena malusi inkomo zayo zaluswa yintengu.*" [150]

V

SOUTH AMERICA: THE KOGI

You are uprooting the Earth and
We are divining to discover how
to teach you to stop. . . .
We work to take care of the world. . . .
We are all here to give a warning. . . .

Kogi Mamas, 1990[1]

Colombian ornament

The clothing of the Indians of the diocese and state of
Santa Marta consists of shirts and painted cotton blankets;
they wear gold earrings, bits of gold in their nostrils, gold
plaques and eagles on their breasts, with pebble bracelets
and gold pieces on their wrists and insteps.

VAZQUEZ DE ESPINOSA,
writing about the Tairona,
the Kogi ancestors (1629)[2]

We once had golden bowls for divination. Gold images.
Gold oracles. All these things. We prophesied with gold.
We had many things. Younger Brother took it all. So now
we're sorrowful, we're weak. You see the Earth is decaying. It's losing its strength because of your greed. You
take gold and all the minerals out of the Earth.

Kogi priest,
1990[3]

Tairona pendant. Tiny delicate spirals lift the wingspan of
this elegantly sculpted example (2⅜ inches high) of Tairona craftsmanship.

INTRODUCTION

Who are these astounding people called the Kogi? While the world outside this last functioning pre-Columbian civilization has changed or "advanced" over the last four hundred years, Kogi society has not. It is both ancient and modern. It is also astonishingly evolved in ways that are essential to the world's understanding of itself. For this reason, I have chosen this tiny society to represent the South American continent, to the exclusion of other admittedly rich and far better-known cultural traditions. The reason is their message.

The Kogi live on an isolated dome-shaped mountain mass, described by a historian as "a copy of the whole planet in miniature." The Kogi, however, call their remote retreat "the heart of the world."[4]

The Sierra Nevada de Santa Marta in Colombia, South America, only twenty-six miles inland, is the highest coastal mountain in the world. It rises nearly 19,000 feet above the sea. The mountain is home to approximately 11,000 Kogi, people who call themselves the Elder Brothers of humanity.

The Kogi call us their Younger Brothers.

The Kogi represent the most complete surviving culture of pre-conquest America. They claim to be the direct descendants of the Tairona, a civilization whose engineering techniques and resourcefulness were openly admired by the Spanish. Kogi fields and villages have been cultivated and inhabited for thousands of years. The Kogi perceive the universe in a radically different manner from us. It is their fundamental belief that they are the guardians of life on Earth. That is what it means to be an Elder Brother.

The Kogi spend most of their time on scattered homesteads spread over the mountainsides at different altitudes. They sometimes own five or more houses. The Kogi refer to their frequent moves between homesteads as a "weaving." Throughout their peregrinations, every hill, valley and mountainside "becomes a loom" on which they live out the pattern and fabric of their existence. Kogi families are in perpetual motion, rotating their work from field to field, where they weed, tend and harvest each plot. Kogi agricultural pursuits include the harvesting of potatoes, onions, squash, plantain, bananas, pineapple, beans, sweet manioc, sugarcane and some maize. They also grow cotton.

Sacred patterns of movement permeate Kogi daily routine. Crossing from one valley to the next, walking up or down the steep slopes and rocky trails, traversing rivers and streams, and moving from one field to the next are activities that respectfully acknowledge and vivify the spirit paths of their ancestors. The steady crisscrossing of their environment reflects not merely a roaming but a profound networking and intimate knowledge of what the Kogi consider to be a sacred legacy bequeathed to them by the Ancient Ones; a legacy that lays claim to guardianship of the Earth, and a cosmic spirituality of remarkable dimensions. These endless journeys through the hidden folds of the mountain are marked by life-sustaining agricultural pursuits, trade relationships, ritual observance of the sanctity of the natural environment and meditation upon ultimate realities.

The Kogi believe deeply in the sacredness and purity of life. They also believe they are here today to restore harmony to a shattered world.

Everywhere in the Sierra Nevada de Santa Marta there exist reminders of an ancient past; a landscape animated by remembered events and ancestral spirits, and kept alive through the work of the *Mamas,* the custodians of Kogi cosmological thought. "These men," writes Gerardo Reichel-Dolmatoff, the great figure of Colombian anthropology and the pioneering authority on the Kogi, "are not shamans, or curers, but constitute a class of tribal priests who are highly respected."[5] They are, in effect, the government of the people.

The *Mamas* possess a profound knowledge of the workings of the universe, a knowledge developed from early childhood through years of specialized and rigorous training in the esoteric wisdom of their tribal traditions. A Kogi will explain that the *Mama* "sees the world in a different light," as in the Kogi adage: "You have learned to see through the mountains and through the hearts of men. Truly, you are a *mama* now!"[6] The Kogi claim that the *Mamas* are clairvoyant and omniscient. Their education embodies a system of progressive illumination, the power and range of which depend upon the purity of their minds. Their whole way of life is dedicated to the health of the planet and, in particular, to the spiritual and worldly welfare of their own people. The *Mamas* are the teachers and exemplars, specialists in the transmission and implementation of religious principles. They are masters of the Law of the Mother, the body of ethics to which their entire life is dedicated.

Kogi learning embraces a wide range of teachings about ancient ecological canons, topography, astronomy, anatomy, physiology and tribal history, and an intimate familiarity with animal and plant life. Most critically, the Kogi believe they possess a highly developed communications system with other spheres that is essential to the well-ordering of the universe. All of this knowledge has a single purpose: to find and strike a balance between the creative and destructive energies experienced throughout one's life. It is called *yuluka*, "to be in agreement with," "to be in harmony with."[7] A standard Kogi response to "How are you?" reports Alan Ereira, is "I am well seated"—even though the speaker may be walking at the time. What he means, explains Ereira, "is that he is at ease, in his proper place, and in balance and harmony with the world."[8]

In the Kogi world, there exists a relationship among all things. The Kogi acknowledge and respect the mutual presence of all life. Consider the following statement by a Kogi *Mama*:

> YOU CAN'T JUST CUT BANANA TREES. You can't cut them because banana trees are like your father, like your mother. You have to respect them as much as any person. You must be respectful. You shouldn't cut down mango trees, or avocado trees. Any growing tree is like a human being, and they hurt too, just like you are cutting off your own leg. Nor should you disturb stones.[9]

The Kogi put a great deal of emphasis on how to think, behave and "feel the world" correctly. They are concerned that Younger Brother is engaged in questionable activities. They say he is actually provoking the universe, that he has lost his perspective. They also say we are doing great damage to the earth and wounding the Mother. That is why they have decided to break their silence of many centuries and convey their message to the world. In 1990, they chose a British historian, Alan Ereira, to be their intermediary. In his extraordinary account of his contact with the Kogi, Ereira presents their message, their teachings and what they have to say about us. *The Elder Brothers* is a desperate plea to Younger Brother to stop mining Mother Earth's minerals and blasting her resources. These gentle yet austere and profoundly religious people believe such ignorance and greed will shortly bring an end to life on Earth, as we know it. From their isolated mountaintop, the Kogi *see* a universe in wrenching labor and they *hear* the Earth groan. Furthermore, they firmly feel if we do not change our ways, the planet will cease to be fertile. Ereira informs us that they will not speak again.

"GOLD WAS HUNG FROM THE TREES"

Gold is of special significance to the Kogi. It is equated with the fertility of the universe. They say it "has its own thought" and "is a living being."[10] The Kogi word for gold (*niuva*) means "sunny,"[11] and "the sun sees everything."[12] In sacred places, gold was hung from the trees. Gold possessed a transcendent quality. Immortal gold carried the mystery of life into the land of *aluna* (the world of spirit).[13] Hence gold was its own communications system ("it can speak") and was, and still is, of great import in Kogi divination ritual. For the Kogi, it is also a powerful metaphor for much of what is wrong with the world. The Kogi say Younger Brother is "taking gold and all the minerals out of the Earth" and "killing it by what [they] do."[14] The Kogi believe that *all* minerals in the earth play an important part in its life. They *know* the planet is a living creature dependent on its own blood and water: "The earth has its blood and it has its water. When we bleed we die. When they dig things out of the earth, when they take stones out, they are bleeding this world and it could die. Taking the gold out of the earth like this it can die."[15]

In a recent plea to all of humankind, the Kogi have stepped forward, after centuries of concealment, to give a warning from "the heart of the world."

> WE WORK TO TAKE CARE OF THE WORLD.
>
> We respect the Mother Earth. . . . [W]e know that the land is our Mother Earth.
>
> If we plant an orange tree or any type of tree and then pull it up by the roots it will die. Digging out the earth's gold is the same thing. It could die. We've all heard many stories that the world is dying. Why is it dying? It is because they have robbed so many tombs.[16] The world is like a person. Robbing tombs, stealing its gold, it will die. We

don't take out the earth's gold. We know that it is there but we do not take it. We know from our divinations that the advice of the Mother is not to take the gold. We know where it is but we decide only to make offerings to it.

How is it that we are able to live? Without blood we cannot live and without bones we cannot walk. Here all the *Mamas* are in agreement about what it is we are going to say and how to speak. If I cut my foot off I cannot walk. When they [the Younger Brothers] dig into the earth and take its gold it is the same thing. . . . Gold has its own thought and it can speak. It is a living being. They must stop stealing it.

If they take all the gold the world will end. The Mothers of the banana trees, of all the trees and of all the birds, they have all been stolen. They are cutting off the flesh of the Mother's body. They have taken everything. They have stolen the spirits of all things from the Mother. They are stealing the very spirit and thought of the Mother. . . .

It is the mountains which make the waters, the rivers and the clouds. If their trees are felled they will not produce any more water. We do not cut down the trees that grow by rivers, we know that they protect the water. We do not cut down huge areas of forest like the Younger Brother does, we cut small clearings for our fields. The Mother told us not to cut down many trees, so we cut very few, tiny patches.

If the Younger Brother keeps cutting down all the trees, there will be fires because the sun will heat the earth. . . . We are the Elder Brothers so we have to think clearly. . . .

Younger Brother, stop doing it. You have already taken so much. We need water to live. Without water we die of thirst. We need water to live. The Mother told us how to live properly and how to think well. We're still here and we haven't forgotten anything.

The earth is decaying, it is losing its strength because they have taken away much petrol, coal, many minerals. Younger Brother thinks "Yes! Here I am! I know much about the universe!" But this knowing is learning to destroy the world, to destroy everything, all humanity. . . .

The Mother is suffering. They have broken her teeth

and taken out her eyes and ears. She vomits, she has diarrhoea, she is ill.

If we cut off our arms, we can't work, if we cut off our tongue we can't speak, if we cut off our legs, we can't walk. That is how it is with the Mother. The Mother is suffering. She has nothing.

Does the Younger Brother understand what he has done? Does he?[17]

"WEAVING ON
THE LOOM OF LIFE"

From a cosmic perspective, the Kogi "conceptualize the earth as an immense loom on which the sun weaves the Fabric of Life," writes anthropologist Reichel-Dolmatoff.[18] The loom—with its complementary counterpart, the spindle, as world axis—is the preeminent symbol of Kogi society, and like gold, may be viewed as a powerful communications system.[19] The loom is also a map for daily living. The Kogi say that "weaving is putting things in accord with each other" and that "the crossed stakes of the loom hold the world."[20] Careful weaving keeps the world well and it is always supervised by a *Mama* (Enlightened One). According to Kogi teaching, "the Loom represents all the worlds," and those worlds "must never be weakened."[21] Historian Alan Ereira describes the first Kogi loom—conceived of in *aluna*—as an *idea* "making order thinkable" and "granting a shape to possibilities."[22] It is, he writes, "a model for the frame of the universe," and it embodies "a basic concept of order."[23] It is also an instrument provided by the Mother to assist the Kogi in achieving their goal of purity of mind and unity of spirit. "When we look at the Kogi world," observes Ereira, "we do not see what they see. Men and women are not simply people, they are the embodiment of principles [to the Kogi]. . . . The harmony and balance of the world is constructed out of the partnership of masculine and feminine, the dynamic process of weaving on the loom of life."[24]

The dress a Kogi wears *is* the Fabric of Life, so beautifully expressed in the following words to a tune that is hummed while he is "weaving his life."[25] The textile has two sides, and the sun, "spiraling back and forth . . . weaves day and night on both sides of the cloth, a dayside and a nightside, light and darkness, life and death."[26]

> *I shall weave the Fabric of my Life;*
> *I shall weave it white as a cloud;*
> *I shall weave some black into it;*

I shall weave dark maize stalks into it;
I shall weave maize stalks into the white cloth;
Thus I shall obey divine Law.[27]

The loom, then, is symbolically a memory bank, a framework of relationships, a code of ethics. As one Kogi put it, "it is life's wisdom that envelops us like a cloth."[28] In the act of weaving, a Kogi is spinning his thoughts into an integrated way of being that encompasses the whole society. The quality of life depends on a man's thoughts. "Thoughts," the Kogi say, "are like threads: cotton thread is white, 'good' thought, and the act of spinning represents the act of thinking."[29] And a strong and good heart is essential to the fulfillment of a worthy, sincere and happy life.

When the heart thinks, it weaves.
Thoughts make a textile.
   To spin is to think. When one sits
and twists the thread on one's thigh,
one thinks a lot; one thinks about
one's work, one's family, one's neighbors,
everything. The yarn we spin is our
thoughts.
   And when the men gather, ceremonially, at
night in the nuhue *(temple), they sing:*
"Alone one weaves one's Fabric of Life."[30]

The Mother told us to look after all mountains. They are ceremonial houses. We know that all the mountains we see are alive.

MAMA BERNARDO[31]

This is the Land of the Mother; the lagoons are the openings of her body. This is why we should not look at them.

Kogi Mama[32]

There is a holy mountain of the Kogi called *Uasuloa*. Unassuming in height (only 2,000 meters), it lies to the northeast of the Kogi heartland. Reichel-Dolmatoff reports that he did not understand the great significance that the Kogi attached to this sacred site until he saw an aero-photographic map of it. "I was immediately struck by the perfect X-shaped and solstice-oriented contours of the mountain," he says.[33] The crossroads, cross-poles, X-shaped cross is a geometric configuration that is imprinted upon the Kogi spirit. It is a life force and it is best understood when related to Kogi thinking.

Kogi thought functions chiefly through the use of analogy. Chains of associations, correspondences and images constitute a constellation of resonating symbols. Nothing in the Kogi worldview is unrelated. Hidden connections abound everywhere. For example, the cosmos is a womb—the divine uterus of the Mother Goddess—as is the earth, a *nuhue* (temple), every mountain, tomb, cave and all of the Sierra Nevada. "The land is conceived as a huge female body that nourishes and protects," observes Reichel-Dolmatoff, and each feature of the terrain corresponds to some anatomical detail of the vast mother-image.[34] Ramon Gil, a Kogi interpreter, once told Alan Ereira, "I know that the world is round, as an eye is round and a head is round and a house is round."[35] Another example is the pot—it begins with a spiraling motion, as does the spinning of wool or cotton into yarn; indeed, the Kogi perceive the spindle as a model of the universe.

In like fashion, the X-shape pattern *insinuates* its organic form upon all aspects of Kogi life. "It stands for deliverance, for the fate of the souls, for obedience to what the Kogi call "The Law of the Mother," writes Reichel-Dolmatoff. "It is found," he says, "in nature and culture, in artifacts and gestures, in fleeting shapes, and in firmly traced lines . . . [not to mention], in a most spectacular way, in cloud formations during the season when the trade winds blow from the northeast."[36] The cotton bags that all Kogi men wear, when crossed over the chest and back, are conceived of as "a replica of the loom and of the crossroads of the soul."[37] The loom, with its simple wooden cross and cardinal points, is considered by the Kogi to be the fundamental structure of the world. Reichel-Dolmatoff relates a conversation with a Kogi priest who elaborates upon the ubiquitousness and the importance of this motif.

> WE MUST HAVE THIS LOOM constantly before our eyes. It is to remind us always, everywhere, day and night, of the need to live well, so that our souls will go into the right direction. We must think of this all the time.[38]

The Kogi traditional greeting upon meeting a stranger is reflective of the ever-present fear of pollution of their life by undesirable and disrespectful outside influences. A comparable statement from Bhutan, a country in the Himalayas, exhibits the same concern. A vice president of the World Wildlife Fund and regular visitor to Bhutan since 1986 once encountered a village *gomchen*, a lay priest, on a valley path, who approached him and said: "I always pray to the local deities for snow when you outsiders come to our valley, so you will go away. You use all our firewood and show little respect for our traditions."[39] A similar impetus—more often than not stated as a demand—is apparent in the Kogi custom of "welcoming" an unexpected outsider with these words:

WHEN are you leaving?[40]

They keep coming up here, they keep coming, why do they keep coming? Is it that they've lost their own law?

Kogi Mama,
questioning incursions
by outsiders[41]

Only one thought
Only one Mother
Only one single word reaches upward
Only one single trail leads heavenward.

Kogi prayer (mulkuakve),
to encourage equanimity
in all things and purity
of mind and heart[42]

VI

NATIVE
NORTH AMERICA

In the beginning we were told that the human beings who walk upon the Earth have been provided with all things necessary for life. We were instructed to carry a love for one another, and to show a great respect for all beings of this Earth. We were shown that our life exists with the tree life, that our well-being depends on the well-being of the vegetable life, that we are close relatives of the four-leggeds. In our way, Spiritual consciousness is the highest form of politics.

Statement by representatives of
the Diné (Navajo), Lakota (Sioux) and
Haudenosaunee (Iroquois Confederacy),
1978 [1]

Hopi pottery design

374

Within and around the earth, within and around the hills, within and around the mountains, your authority returns to you.

A Tewa prayer[2]

We are of the soil and the soil is of us. We love the birds and beasts that grew with us on this soil. They drank the same water we did and breathed the same air. We are all one in nature. Believing so, there was in our hearts a great peace and a welling kindness for all living, growing things.

LUTHER STANDING BEAR,
Lakota author[3]

The Creator made man able to do everything—talk, run, look, and hear. He was not satisfied, though, till man could do just one thing more—and that was: LAUGH. *And so man laughed and laughed and laughed. And the Creator said: "Now you are fit to live."*

Apache myth[4]

When we pray we raise our hand to the heavens, and afterwards we touch the earth, for is not our Spirit from Wakan-Tanka, and are not our bodies from the earth? We are related to all things: the earth and the stars, everything, and with all these together we raise our hand to Wakan-Tanka and pray to Him alone.

BLACK ELK[5]

David B. Williams (Ojibwa), *Untitled*, 1980. The life cycles of nature are the subject of many of David B. Williams' paintings. His original line format is almost a template that joins everything and provides unity to his pictures. The white egret, a water bird, stands on a scroll that is a wave, the second scroll being air. A water lily with a large, flat, oblong-shaped leaf grows in the water in the lower left corner. The three oblongs in the left frame are bulrushes flourishing. To the right, the oblongs may be earth, rock, and water, out of which spring two trees.

INTRODUCTION

Sacred geography is a fundamental ingredient of Native North American religious beliefs and practices. The idea of the sacred is founded upon a profound knowledge, understanding and conviction of the inherent sanctity of all things. Entering sacredness is the universal goal of all American Indian ritual. Their ceremonies are inextricably tied to the natural world. Portals to the sacred are the holy sites that dominate the spiritual and physical landscape of Native American life. "You cannot think of Indian people without their sacred places," observes Tewa poet and scholar Alphonso Ortiz. "They are always joined together."[6] The cosmic and cultural significance of Ortiz's remark is reflected in a statement that was issued more than two decades ago by the Taos people of New Mexico, toward the end of their successful sixty-four-year struggle to regain their inviolable Blue Lake:

> OUR TRIBAL GOVERNMENT is responsible to this land and to the people. We have been on this land from days beyond history's records, far past any living memory, deep into the time of legend. No man can think of us without also thinking of this place. We are always joined together.[7]

Sacred sites are sources of communication with the spirit world; they are holy maps that provide direction to life and ensure tribal continuity and identity. They are natural law. In accessing their sacred power through ritual, order is conferred upon the universe. Above all else, sacred sites are alive, imbued with vast currents of energy and power. Their effective activation depends on the earnestness of the seeker and the observance of appropriate rituals which are tied to seasonal rhythms, the sun and the moon.

Mountaintops, waterfalls, origin and burial sites, medicine wheels or Sun Dance arbors, lakes, rock art sites of pictographs and petroglyphs and unusual geological formations are just a few of the holy sites of prayer, pilgrimage, vision quests and medicinal cures. The Black Hills in South Dakota, for example, are the locus for virtually every kind of ritual, including the Sun Dance; their peaks, in particular, are favored for vision quests. Sixty years ago, Luther Standing Bear, a Lakota, described the collective symbolic and spiritual importance of the Black Hills:

> OF ALL OUR DOMAIN, we loved, perhaps, the Black Hills the most. The Lakota had named these hills *He Sapa*, or Black Hills, on account of their color. The slopes and peaks were so heavily wooded with dark pines that from a distance the mountains actually looked black. In wooded recesses were numberless springs of pure water and numerous small lakes. There were wood and game in abundance and shelter from the storms of the plains. It was the favorite winter haunt of the buffalo and the Lakota as well. According to a tribal legend these hills were a reclining female figure from whose breasts flowed life-giving forces, and to them the Lakota went as a child to its mother's arms. The various entrances to the hills were very rough and rugged, but there was one very beautiful and easy pass through which both buffalo and Lakota entered the hills. This pass ran along a narrow stream bed which widened here and there but which in places narrowed so that the tall pines at the top of the cliffs arched their boughs, almost touching as they swayed in the wind. Every fall thousands of buffaloes and Lakotas went through this pass to spend the winter in the hills. *Pte ta tiyopa* it was called by the Lakotas, or "Gate of the buffalo." Today this beautiful pass is denuded of trees and to the white man it is merely "Buffalo Gap." . . .
>
> [O]ur legends tell us that it was hundreds and perhaps thousands of years ago since the first man sprang from the soil in the midst of these great plains. The story says that one morning long ago a lone man awoke, face to the sun, emerging from the soil. Only his head was visible, the rest of his body not yet being fashioned. The man looked about, but saw no mountains, no rivers, no forests. There was nothing but soft and quaking mud, for the earth itself was still young. Up and up the man drew himself until he freed his body from the clinging soil. At last he stood upon the earth, but it was not solid, and his first few steps were

slow and halting. But the sun shone and ever the man kept his face turned toward it. In time the rays of the sun hardened the face of the earth and strengthened the man and he bounded and leaped about, a free and joyous creature. From this man sprang the Lakota nation and, so far as we know, our people have been born and have died on this plain; and no people have shared it with us until the coming of the European. So this land of the great plains is claimed by the Lakotas as their very own.[8]

American Indian religious practices are land-based theologies whose effectiveness is dependent upon access to specific sacred sites. Consequently, dispute over land has become, undoubtedly, the most significant and pressing dilemma facing Native North Americans today. Sacred geography is the essential feature of that struggle. Tourism and accelerated mineral exploration by the U.S. government over the past three decades have heightened the ongoing battle by Native Americans for land rights. The essence of Native American religious freedom is the land. (That conviction found concrete expression in the Native North American Freedom–Exercise of Religion Act of 1993, introduced by Senator Daniel Inouye.) Native peoples, however —alone among American citizens—are effectively denied their constitutionally guaranteed rights by reason of being denied access to their sacred sites. "Our land is a living church—it is our Jerusalem, our Mecca, our Machu Picchu," states a Navajo teaching.[9] "The earth and myself are of one mind. The measure of the land and the measure of our bodies are the same," explained the great Nez Perce leader Chief Joseph more than a hundred years ago. The plain of Oklahoma is described by Kiowa novelist N. Scott Momaday as a vital wellspring of inspiration where "[y]our imagination comes to life, and this, you think, is where Creation was begun."[10]

A 1980 Supreme Court Decision affirmed that Congress had illegally confiscated the Black Hills from the Lakota people in 1877 (for the express purpose of the exploitation of gold in the hills and the granting of rights of passage to the railroad companies). Bear Butte, the most sacred ceremonial site in the Black Hills for the Lakota and Cheyenne peoples, now a state park, is one of the many sites across the country that is involved in the continuing controversy. Joe Little Coyote describes the significance of Bear Butte to his people:

IT'S ALWAYS BEEN OUR DESIRE to try to [re]secure Bear Butte. . . . Bear Butte belongs to our people. That was our birthplace. Bear Butte. That was where the Creator first made a man and a woman. And all of our spiritual history surrounds Bear Butte. Our point of origin as a people. And also it is a reference point for our existence as a people in this land. It's a symbol and a physical thing that substantiates our existence as a people. We can point to that and say, "this is living proof, physical proof that we as a people were given our birth here. And we have rights to this land." We have received our most important covenant with our Creator at Bear Butte. *Nohawus.* And that Covenant, that Arrow Covenant was made between our people and the Creator. And we carry that Covenant with us today. . . . [T]he instructions. The spiritual traditions, the concepts and the values are all encompassed in the Covenant. And along with that he gave the ceremonies . . . [t]o renew our universe. To renew our world and the life of the people. All of our identity as a people is encompassed within these ceremonies. Our origin.[11]

The power of the sacred embedded in the Native American landscape is poignantly demonstrated in a story by Tewa poet Alphonso Ortiz. Ortiz describes a journey he made with an old Tewa Pueblo Indian friend through the country of the Utes in southwestern Colorado. As they approached the town of Pagosa Springs, both men experienced an epiphany of cosmic dimensions:

So IT WAS that by the time we neared the town . . . it was no longer July 1963, but another time, a time in and out of time. This place is called Warm Sands in Tewa, for there are sands which are kept warm by the hot springs which gave birth to the town; sands which by themselves are said to be able to melt snow and moderate the mid-winter cold; sands for the obtaining of which our religious men in other times made winter pilgrimages. My companion and I both silently recalled ancestors who were among these religious men. He wanted to stop, to gather some of the warm sand from nearby the springs, as did I. When we came to the sands, he knelt before the land, then he ran the sand through his fingers. And then he wept. He had never been here, but then had never really left. He remembered his own grandfather and the other grandfathers who had preceded him here. He had heretofore never journeyed here, but now it was as if he had come home.[12]

INTRODUCTION *379*

[W]e are taught that everything is alive. It is hard to teach somebody else that the land is alive. If we pray and there is rain, the grass starts waking up, it starts growing, and then you hear the wind whispering in the trees and the plants—they are talking to each other. That is how we are. We are like plants. That is how we are; we are like plants.

ROBERTA BLACKGOAT,
Navajo elder[13]

As I get older, I burrow more and more into the hills. The Great Spirit made them for us, for me. I want to blend with them, shrink into them, and finally disappear in them. . . . All of nature is in us, all of us is in nature. That is as it should be.

PETE CATCHES,
Sioux medicine man[14]

Petroglyph exhibiting labyrinthine spiral with unique stylized body. Formerly a high-noon solstice marker. Dinnebito Wash, Arizona.

As Native American peoples, we come from land-based cultures. Our identities and well-being are intricately linked to our lands. As we think about the future of our communities, many of us worry that the proper, productive use of our lands has diminished as a priority. In our culture, even today, to work with the land, with our Mother Earth, is among the most honorable of activities.

RON LaFRANCE,
Iroquois traditionalist,
1991[15]

"We listen to the piñon and watch the ways of the spiders," say the old Navajo men. "From the ancient creatures came our life and our love of the land."[16]

I will never leave the land, this sacred place. The land is part of me, and I will one day be part of the land. I could never leave. My people are here, and have been here forever. My sheep are here. All that has meaning is here. I live here and I will die here. That is the way it is, and the way it must be. Otherwise, the people will die, the sheep will die, the land will die. There would be no meaning to life if this happened.

KATHERINE SMITH,
Navajo elder, protesting
relocation; Big Mountain,
northern Arizona, 1972[17]

THE NATURE OF LAND IN NATIVE AMERICAN THOUGHT

The Onondaga sachem Canasatego (ca. 1685–1750), was considered the preeminent orator of the Six Nations of the Iroquois Confederacy. Benjamin Franklin, then a government printer, was impressed with his oratorical gifts. Author Ronald Wright writes that "anyone who reads the minutes and transcripts of conferences involving the Six Nations will be impressed by the way Europeans were forced to adopt Amerindian protocol. They had to acquire a rich metaphorical language . . . reciprocity [exchange of goods] being the key to all discourse."[18]

At a conference in the early 1740s, Canasatego demonstrated his famous diplomacy as he reprimanded the British for their continuing illegal encroachments onto Iroquois lands.

> WE KNOW OUR LANDS are now become more valuable. The white people think we do not know their value; but we are sensible that the land is everlasting, and the few goods we receive for it are soon worn out and gone. . . . Besides, we are not well used with respect to the lands still unsold by us. Your people daily settle on these lands, and spoil our hunting. We must insist on your removing them . . . for they do great damage to our cousins the Delawares. . . .
>
> It is customary with us to make a present of skins whenever we renew our treaties. We are ashamed to offer our brethren so few; but your horses and cows have eaten the grass our deer used to feed on.[19]

Brothers, you see this vast country before us, which the Great Spirit gave to our fathers and us; you see the buffalo and deer that now are our support. Brothers, you see these little ones, our wives and children, who are looking to us for food and raiment; and you now see the foe before you, that they have grown insolent and bold; that all our ancient customs are disregarded; the treaties made by our fathers and us are broken, and all of us insulted; our council fires disregarded, and all the ancient customs of our fathers; our brothers murdered before our eyes, and their spirits cry to us for revenge. Brothers, these people from the unknown world will cut down our groves, spoil our hunting and planting grounds, and drive us and our children from the graves of our fathers, and our council fires, and enslave our women and children.

> KING PHILIP, *celebrated warrior and Pequot leader,*
> *"father" of Pequot country and*
> *son of Pokanoket sachem Massasoit, 1675*[20]

Makataimeshekiakiak, better known as Black Hawk (1767–1838), leader of the Sauk Nation, declared war on white settlers who streamed into Illinois country—old Sauk and Fox territory—after the War of 1812. Here he ponders the significance of land to the Sauk and Fox Nation.

MY REASON TEACHES ME that *land cannot be sold.* The Great Spirit gave it to his children to live upon, and cultivate, as far as is necessary for their subsistence; and so long as they occupy and cultivate it, they have the right to the soil—but if they voluntarily leave it, then any other people have a right to settle upon it. Nothing can be sold, but such things as can be carried away.

In consequence of the improvements of the intruders on our fields, we found considerable difficulty to get ground to plant a little corn. Some of the whites permitted us to plant small patches [of corn] in the fields they had fenced, keeping all the best ground for themselves. Our women had great difficulty in climbing their fences (being unaccustomed to the kind) and were ill-treated if they left a rail down.

One of my old friends thought he was safe. His corn-field was on a small island of Rock river. He planted his corn; it came up well—but the white man saw it!—he wanted the island, and took his team over, ploughed up the corn, and re-planted it for himself! The old man shed tears; not for himself, but the distress his family would be in if they raised no corn.[21]

In 1867, at the Council of Medicine Lodge Creek, the Comanche Indian Ten Bears questions the efficacy of white ways as a viable substitute for the laws of nature and its systems and the incomparable procreative energies of the land.

YOU SAID that you wanted to put us upon a reservation, to build us houses and make us medicine lodges. I do not want them. I was born upon the prairie, where the wind blew free and there was nothing to break the light of the sun. I was born where there were no enclosures and every-thing drew a free breath. I want to die there and not within walls. I know every stream and every wood between the Rio Grande and the Arkansas. I have hunted and lived over that country. I live like my fathers before me and like them I live happily. . . . [W]hy do you ask us to leave the rivers, and the sun, and the wind, and to live in houses? Do not ask us to give up the buffalo for the sheep. The young men have heard talk of this, and it has made them sad and angry. . . . [T]hat which you now say we must live in is too small. . . . The whites have the country which we loved, and we only wish to wander on the prairie until we die.[22]

Abiding love for the soil and respect for its sacred places and holy associations reside at the center of Native American belief systems. They are the predominant impulses for all action. The following words—recorded ca. 1910—are the anguished thoughts of an old Omaha man who remembers a time that nourished his soul and enriched his life in a place along the western bank of the Missouri River (now Nebraska).

WHEN I WAS A YOUTH, the country was very beautiful. Along the rivers were belts of timberland, where grew cottonwood, maple, elm, ash, hickory, and walnut trees, and many other kinds. Also there were various kinds of vines and shrubs. And under these grew many good herbs and beautiful flowering plants.

In both the woodland and the prairie I could see the trails of many kinds of animals and could hear the cheerful songs of many kinds of birds. When I walked abroad, I could see many forms of life, beautiful living creatures which Wakanda [the Great, Spirit] had placed here; and these were, after their manner, walking, flying, leaping, running, playing all about.

But now the face of all the land is changed and sad. The living creatures are gone. I see the land desolate and I suffer an unspeakable sadness. Sometimes I wake in the night, and I feel as though I should suffocate from the pressure of this awful feeling of loneliness.[23]

The interaction of beliefs and the ground upon which they flourished and beneath which they originated is an integral part of Native American thinking about the nature of reality. The natural unity of Creation embraces life and death in a reciprocal creative flow that accounts for the proper place of all things. Lee Marshall, Havasupai Tribal Council chairman, whose people live in what is now a National Park Service zoo—the Grand Canyon—once responded to U.S. Forest Service officials' discussions on the significance of the Grand Canyon to the Havasupai tribe: "I heard all you people talking about the Grand Canyon. Well, you're looking at it. I *am* the Grand Canyon."[24] In 1912, sixty years before Marshall's declaration, Curley, a Crow Indian, describes in similar fashion the inherent makeup and function of land as a ground of being, as a vital and unifying element of Native American existence.

THE SOIL YOU SEE is not ordinary soil it is the dust of the blood, the flesh and the bones of our ancestors. We fought and bled and died to keep other Indians from taking it, and we fought and bled and died helping the Whites. You will have to dig down through the surface before you can find nature's earth, as the upper portion is Crow.

The land as it is, is my blood and my dead; it is

consecrated; and I do not want to give up any portion of it.[25]

I will tell you first that in old times, before any white men came, [my] people were a mighty race and their land went from the plains east of the mountains to the Snpoilshi [Columbia] River. This is no boast about something that never was. When we made a treaty with the Government they saw how it was, and that was the country we owned. We had a strong nation and those who later became our greatest enemies, the Blackfeet and their kinsmen, and the Crows too, they respected us. We went twice a year to hunt on the Missouri and there were few who dared invade our hunting ground. It had been that way for longer than any man can say.

MODESTE,
blind Salish chief, 1920's[26]

Mary José Hobday grew up in the Southwest, close to the Navajo and Ute Mountain Indians. Her own Seneca-Seminole natal roots focused her interests early on in life on Native American literature, theology, architecture and engineering. She has lived and worked, as a Sister of St. Francis of Assisi, with the Sioux and Assiniboine peoples of Montana, and the Papago tribe of Arizona. She teaches at the Institute of Culture and Creation Spirituality in Oakland, California and lectures extensively on Native American issues, ecology and spirituality. Hobday suggests that America needs a blood transfusion to strengthen her heart, a heart that has lost its tenderness and capacity to feel. It is time "to seek a moist heart," she says, and this can be achieved by submitting to the needs of the land. Honor and respect for the sacred principles of nature and therefore human nature will restore an animating and humane force to the body, soul and spirit of the country.

THE TRADITION OF THE TRIBE is that each person, and the entire tribe have a moral, an ethical, relationship with the land. The land is the Mother. The grass is her hair. She is fertile and generous with her gifts, yielding life and beauty in abundance. She provides nourishment for the living and a welcoming embrace for the dead. She is not prejudiced, for she treasures the so-called weeds as readily as the more resplendent flowers. Not only do Indians love the land because it mingles with the dust of the dead, but because it is vital and alive, and is part of the life of each person. . . . They cultivate the ways that the land can transport them, can teach them the secrets and mysteries of nature. The land is not only the soil. It is the four-leggeds, the winged creatures, the growing plants and trees. It is the directions which teach courage, birth, warmth, and death, as well as what in life is up, what is down, and what is inside. The land can be touched and heard, smelled and brushed against. It can be inhaled and rubbed into the skin. It can be caressed and admired. . . .

Indians have always had a more accommodating spirit toward the land, because they believe the land shares the Great Spirit. The white mentality has been to conquer, to dominate: *Make* the land fit! *Force* the land to yield! Indians feel white people do not know how to obey what is holy and reasonable in nature, and this is partly why white culture has such little patience and reverence for the land. The land has its own needs, apart from humans.

If the American people do not want to be treated as strangers, even as enemies, by the land, they must grow in wisdom and respect for the balance of nature.[27]

 "It is The Way," he said softly. "Take only what ye need. When ye take the deer, do not take the best. Take the smaller and the slower and then the deer will grow stronger and always give you meat. Pa-koh, the panther, knows and so must ye."

And he laughed, "Only Ti-bi, the bee, stores more than he can use . . . and so he is robbed by the bear, and the 'coon . . . and the Cherokee. It is so with people who store and fat themselves with more than their share. They

will have it taken from them. And there will be wars over it . . . and they will make long talks, trying to hold more than their share. They will say a flag stands for their right to do this . . . and men will die because of the words and the flag . . . but they will not change the rules of The Way."

I trotted behind Granpa and I could feel the upward slant of the trail.

    I could feel something more, as Granma said I would. Mon-o-lah, the earth mother, came to me through my moccasins. I could feel her push and swell here, and sway and give there . . . and the roots that veined her body and the life of the water-blood, deep inside her. She was warm and springy and bounced me on her breast, as Granma said she would.

LITTLE TREE,
Cherokee[28]

Although the respected Abenaki scholar and poet Joseph Bruchac calls *The Education of Little Tree* "one of the finest American autobiographies ever written,"[29] a wealth of controversy surrounds the question of whether the book is fact or fiction or a mélange of both.[30] *The Education of Little Tree* has the force of a cyclone and the soft touch of a sweet, gentle springtime wind that rushes upon you just after the Indian violets have emerged in late March. In its tone and telling, a fresh yet very old spirit is at play through the alchemy of inspiration from the Great One, *Mon-o-lah,* the Mother. Taken in by his Cherokee grandparents at the age of five, Forrest Carter, the narrator, goes to live with them in the 1930s on their farm among poor people, deep in the mountains of Tennessee. They call him "Little Tree" and he learns their ways. An entire way of living, seeing and understanding is offered to Little Tree; a model of being that includes respect for the land and all its living creatures and a sense of humor that is gentle, persistent and wise. The story, first published in 1976, "is a necessary book," writes Bruchac, "one which if read and understood and acted upon can change people's lives." He equates the story to "one of the great myths which reflect human experience so well that they offer new messages for each stage of life on the great journey."[31]

Irrespective of its provenance, *The Education of Little Tree* contains beguiling insights into a Native American sensibility. From his new home in the woods, perched high in the hills, Little Tree describes the birthing of the world around him.

> FOLKS WHO LAUGH and say that all is known about Nature, and that Nature don't have a soul-spirit, have never been in a mountain spring storm. When She's birthing spring, She gets right down to it, tearing at the mountains like a birthing woman clawing at the bed quilts.
>
> If a tree has been hanging on, having weathered all the winter winds, and She figures it needs cleaning out, She whips it up out of the ground and flings it down the mountain. She goes over the branches of every bush and tree, and after She feels around a little with Her wind fingers, then She whips them clean and proper of anything that is weak.
>
> If She figures a tree needs removing and won't come down from the wind, She just *whams!* and all that's left is a torch blazing from a lightning stroke. She's alive and paining. You'll believe it too.
>
> Granpa said She was—amongst other things—tidying up any afterbirth that might be left over from last year; so Her new birthing would be clean and strong.
>
> When the storm is over, the new growth, tiny and light, timid-green, starts edging out on the bushes and tree limbs. Then Nature brings April rain. It whispers down soft and lonesome, making mists in the hollows and on the trails where you walk under the drippings from hanging branches of trees.
>
> It is a good feeling, exciting—but sad too—in April rain. Granpa said he always got that kind of mixed-up feeling. He said it was exciting because something new was being born, and it was sad, because you knowed you can't hold onto it. It will pass too quick.
>
> April wind is soft and warm as a baby's crib. It breathes on the crab apple tree until white blossoms open out, smeared with pink. The smell is sweeter than honeysuckle and brings bees swarming over the blossoms. Mountain laurel with pink-white blooms and purple cen-

ters grow everywhere, from the hollows to the top of the mountain, alongside of the dogtooth violet that has long, pointed yellow petals with a white tooth hanging out (they always looked to me like tongues).

Then, when April gets its warmest, all of a sudden the cold hits you. It stays cold for four or five days. This is to make the blackberries bloom and is called "blackberry winter." The blackberries will not bloom without it. That's why some years there are no blackberries. When it ends, that's when the dogwoods bloom out like snowballs over the mountainside in places you never suspicioned they grew: in a pine grove or stand of oak of a sudden there's a big burst of white. . . .

Granpa said the woods would feed you, if you lived with the woods, instead of tearing them up.[32]

N. Scott Momaday, a Kiowa novelist, essayist, poet and painter, spent his childhood on Indian reservations in the Southwest. He is a Pulitzer Prize–winning novelist for his story-telling in *House Made of Dawn*. He is also a member of the Kiowa Gourd Dance Society and a Fellow of the American Academy of Arts and Sciences. Momaday has written about the different notions that surround the American Indian attitude toward land and has approached these beliefs metaphysically: "[T]he native American ethic with respect to the physical world is a matter of reciprocal appropriation: appropriations in which man invests himself in the landscape, and at the same time incorporates the landscape into his own most fundamental experience." The relationship requires two visions, simultaneously, he adds; one that is "physical" and another that is "imaginative."[33]

In an essay entitled "The Man Made of Words," Momaday reflects upon the boundless resources of man's inner world. He suggests yielding to the infinite landscape of the imagination as a source of renewal and a mode of consciousness that has significance for the entire human community. Momaday proposes a shift in thinking— from the human world to the natural world—for greater clarity and awareness and a transcendent sense of one's place in the structure of the universe.

ONCE IN HIS LIFE a man ought to concentrate his mind upon the remembered earth, I believe. He ought to give himself up to a particular landscape in his experience, to look at it from as many angles as he can, to wonder about it, to dwell upon it. He ought to imagine that he touches it with his hands at every season and listens to the sounds that are made upon it. He ought to imagine the creatures that are there and all the faintest motions in the wind. He ought to recollect the glare of noon and all the colors of the dawn and dusk.

The Wichita Mountains rise out of the Southern Plains in a long crooked line that runs from east to west. The mountains are made of red earth, and of rock that is neither red nor blue but some very rare admixture of the two like the feathers of certain birds. They are not so high and mighty as the mountains of the Far West, and they bear a different relationship to the land around them. One does not imagine that they are distinctive in themselves, or indeed that they exist apart from the plain in any sense. If you try to think of them in the abstract they lose the look of mountains. They are preeminently an expression of the larger landscape, more perfectly organic than one can easily imagine. To behold these mountains from the plain is one thing; to see the plain from the mountains is something else. I have stood on the top of Mt. Scott and seen the earth below, bending out into the whole circle of the sky. The wind runs always close upon the slopes, and there are times when you can hear the rush of it like water in the ravines.

Here is the hub of an old commerce. A hundred years ago the Kiowas and Comanches journeyed outward from the Wichitas in every direction, seeking after mischief and medicine, horses and hostages. Sometimes they went away for years, but they always returned, for the land had got hold of them. It is a consecrated place, and even now there is something of the wilderness about it. . . . It was here, the Kiowas say, that the first buffalo came into the world. . . .

I am interested in the way that a man looks at a given landscape and takes possession of it in his blood and brain. For this happens, I am certain, in the ordinary motion of life. None of us lives apart from the land entirely; such an isolation is unimaginable. We have sooner or later to come to terms with the world around us—and I mean especially the physical world; not only as it is revealed to us immediately through our senses, but also as it is perceived more truly in the long turn of seasons and of years. And we must come to moral terms. There is no alternative, I believe, if we are to realize and maintain our humanity; for our humanity must consist in part in the ethical as well as the practical ideal of preservation. And particularly here and now is that true. We Americans need now more than ever before—and indeed more than we know—to imagine who and what we are with respect to the earth and sky. I am talking about an act of the imagination essentially, and the concept of an American land ethic. . . . I doubt that any of us knows where he is in relation to the stars and to the solstices. Our sense of the natural order has become dull and unreliable. Like the wilderness itself, our sphere of instinct has diminished in proportion as we have failed to imagine truly what it is. And yet I believe that it is possible to formulate an ethical idea of the land—a notion of what it is and must be in our daily lives—and I believe moreover that it is absolutely necessary to do so.[34]

I do not believe
we go up to the sky
unless it is
to fall again
with the rain.

A warmth which holds us
to the Earth, an umbilical cord
that neither life nor death
can ever break.

Nothing fertilizes,
strengthens more
than long decades
of love for this Earth.

I find reminders
of the soil which shaped
the bones of my lineage.

From four poems by *JOSEPH BRUCHAC,*
Abenaki poet and writer[35]

We planted corn, beans, squash, cotton, having received these gifts from the earth. The plants provided for us over generations and generations as long as we also provided for their care and gave back to the earth what it had given us. And we gave back, in work, song, prayer, replanted seed, a system of thought and practice that spoke and acted upon the responsibility that we had learned we must have for the land and its fertility and for the People and their vital health. The land is not just dirt, stones, clay; over generations and generations, our People learned they must care for it because it provides food, clothing, and shelter, and we know we are part of the land; and we are responsible for ourselves in caring for the land. . . .

SIMON ORTIZ,
poet and writer,
Acoma Pueblo, 1979[36]

Native North Americans have varying objectives in mind with regard to the valuation and disposition of their land. Some, when pressed by industry and government, have been willing to compromise and cooperate with land developers such as oil and gas interests as well as cattle ranchers. Many lived to regret those transactions, after being bilked unscrupulously of their birthrights. Others knew just what they were doing, and were satisfied to accept the short-term gains. While still others have steadfastly refused to forge agreements with speculators of any stripe. And some continue to seek redress for deceptive contractual agreements. Such is the case with the Nishnawbe-Aski (better known as the Cree and Ojibway) and Inuit peoples of northeastern Canada. In 1975, they signed the James Bay and Northern Quebec Agreement, ceding much of their traditional homeland to the Province of Quebec and its utility company, called Hydro-Quebec. The three phases of Hydro-Quebec's plan would involve the construction of three dozen dams and hundreds of dikes that would reshape irrevocably a land mass roughly the size of France. The Crees and the Inuits claim they were misled about the ecological, cultural and sociological effects of the James Bay project. As phase one was under way, the waters became seriously contaminated with highly toxic methyl mercury, which poisoned the fish, an important staple of the Cree and Inuits' traditional diet, which in turn led to abnormally high levels of methyl mercury in the local population. Later, ten thousand migrating caribou drowned when waters released from the reservoirs on the Caniapiscau River became raging torrents.

At approximately the same time, the Cree-Ojibway bands of Northern Ontario (North of the 50th parallel) were faced with a massive deforestation threat by the Reed Paper Company—which already had inflicted appalling mercury pollution on the English-Wabigoon river system.

On July 7, 1977, the Nishnawbe-Aski treaty chiefs delivered a declaration of independence to the Premier of Ontario, William Davis, and his cabinet, reasserting their claim to their birthright, demanding compensation for their exploited natural resources, and announcing their sovereignty, using—ironically—the American Revolutionary experience as their model. The Nishnawbe-Aski cannot and are not willing to think of themselves as separate from their traditional lands.

> WE, THE PEOPLE AND THE LAND, declare our nationhood. We, of the Cree and Ojibway nation who come from within your boundaries of Ontario, Manitoba and Quebec, and who live in the Ontario North at the height of land known as the Arctic Watershed, declare ourselves to be a free and sovereign nation. We bring you a declaration of independence.
>
> We say to you that we have the right to govern our own spiritual, cultural, social and economic affairs.... You are the only people who have ever questioned our sovereignty. Our rights and entitlements to this land were inherited from our forefathers. Unlike you, we have no memory of an existence in other lands across the sea. We have prior rights to the custody of this land, which precede and supersede all of your claims.
>
> This custody must remain with us. It is our sacred duty to pass it on to our unborn children. We do not accept the illegal seizures of our land by the Europeans, and their descendants. We will protect these custodian rights by whatever means necessary....
>
> You took most of our land, outlawed our religious beliefs and practices, destroyed much of our animal life and forest, restricted our movements, stopped us from using our languages, and tried to convince us that our music, dances, and arts were barbaric....
>
> Your cultural genocide is about to end. In order to

regain our freedom we must establish our own control, and return to our traditional philosophy of life. We recognize only one ruler over our nation—the Creator. He made us part of nature. We are one with nature, with all that the Creator has made around us. We have lived here since time immemorial, at peace with the land, the lakes and the rivers, the animals, the fish, the birds and all of nature. We live today as part of yesterday and tomorrow in the great cycle of life.

Unlike you, we have a sacred respect for the land. You have alienated life and land by the exploitation of the natural resources. As a result of your greed there is a real possibility that our environment will be destroyed. If it is, we also will be destroyed because we are part of nature. . . .

In your rush for materialistic gain, you are threatening nature's very limits. Now, it is our sacred duty to slow you down before she is destroyed.

In Chief Emile Nakogee's statement of 1977 he said, "I am not against employment, it is a good thing. But the most important thing we must take into consideration is the land around us. It is also our income and we must not make decisions that might destroy it."

We are here with another unalterable principle: "Nishnawbe-Aski are not for sale!" We remember the legacy of Old Joseph, as he spoke to his son Chief Joseph in 1871: "My son, my body is returning to my Mother Earth, and my spirit is going very soon to see the Great Spirit Chief. When I am gone, think of your country. You are the chief of these people. They look to you to guide them. Always remember that your father never sold his country . . . this country holds your father's body. Never sell the bones of your father and your mother."

We can no longer permit the progressive rape of our mother earth, and its life-giving forces. We have our children to save. The continued existence of our race is a sacred mandate passed on to us by our ancestors. . . .

Our nationhood itself is sacred and cannot be negotiated.[37]

I recall with startling clarity and longing every detail of the land, the river, the people . . . Alaska mesmerizes my spirit, and I finger the thoughts like beads of prayer. I still feel the crush of the last bed of wild violets in the Aleutian hills where one day I flung myself down in a rapture, knowing who I was, what the wild violets meant. Alaska is my talisman, my strength, my spirit's home. Despite loss and disillusion, I count myself rich, fertile, and magical.

I tell you now. You can go home.

MARY TALLMOUNTAIN,
Koyukon Athabascan writer
and poet[38]

Audrey Shenandoah, Onondaga elder of the Eel Clan of the Six Nations, says there is no word for nature in her language. "Nature in English," she points out, "seems to refer to that which is separate from human beings. It is a distinction we don't recognize."[39]

I REMEMBER MY GRANDMOTHER telling me that we were rich because we had such good land to grow our crops on, that we had such good fish to eat. Now . . . [t]he fish are not fit to eat, the waters are so polluted. And I can remember my grandmother saying now how rich we were that we could have this fish, so fresh. This is what made us prosperous. It was right out of the water and onto our table. I can never remember my grandmother saying we were poor because we had all this. We had the hills to appreciate, you know, and in those times when she was still alive, there were people coming to our nation with these [grand] ideas about how wealthy we could be if we would allow them to put a ski resort at the top of our beautiful hill. And I can remember, especially that time, my grandmother saying we would be poor if we allowed them to take that hill and make it into a ski resort because we would lose everything that's on that hill. . . . It would twist our minds.[40]

My name is Karonienhawi. I am of the Wolf Clan of the Mohawk Nation. The Original Instructions that were given to us, direct that we who walk about on the earth are to express a great respect, affection, and gratitude toward all the spirits who create and support life. So, we give a greeting and a thanksgiving to the many supporters of our own lives: the corn, the beans, the squash, the winds and the sun. When people cease to respect and to express their gratitude for these many things, then all life will be destroyed and human life on this planet will come to an end. Our roots are deep in the lands where we live. We have a great love for our country, for our birthplace is here. The soil is rich from the bones of thousands of our generations. Each of us have been created in our lands and it is our duty to take care of them, because from these lands there will spring the future generations of the Real People. We walk about with a very great respect, for the Earth is a very sacred place. We are not a people who demand or ask anything of the Creators of Life, but instead we give greeting and thanksgiving that all the forms of life are still at work. We deeply understand our relationship to all living things. To this day the territories we still hold are filled with trees, animals and the other gifts of the Creators. In these places we still receive our nourishment from our Mother the Earth.[41]

"Osage is my tribe of enrollment on my father's side," says George Tinker. "My mother was a Lutheran." These days he is putting to good use both lines of his heritage as an associate pastor of Living Waters, a joint Episcopal-Lutheran parish, and assistant professor of cross-cultural ministries at Iliff School of Theology in Denver, Colorado. Tinker has spoken about the concern of marginalized people "that the ecology movement has detracted from justice issues."[42] The following comments by him focus upon the Native Americans' conviction that they and the land are intrinsically inseparable.

INDIAN PEOPLE LOOK AT THE LAND as generative. It is where we come from. It's not something we possess or own. Land ownership is a Western European philosophical notion that's become rooted in political and economic systems. . . .

There were consistent efforts in the 19th century to teach Indians private ownership of property because it was considered the civilized way of existing. Of course, what it did was destroy the structure of Indian society and culture and meant that Indians were reduced to levels of existence that forced co-dependent relationships upon the U.S. government. . . .

Indians believe that the Creator put them in a specific place and that is their place. To move to another place is a very hard thing to do, and people die when they move. The Osages did not thrive when we were moved out of Missouri and into Kansas. And when we were moved out of Kansas and into Oklahoma it became even worse. That's the story of many, many tribes that were relocated in Indian territory, where they had to learn to live in relationship to a new land.

The relationship to a land is not only a spiritual relationship; it's one of physical economy as well. You know the land; you know the sacred sites; you know the medicines, the herbs, the foods that grow there and where they grow.

When you are moved to a new place you suddenly don't have access to those things anymore, so that many of your patterns for religious ceremonies and observances are broken. How can you have a ceremony if you don't have access to the various things of the land that you need to conduct that ceremony? . . .

I would argue that the European intellectual tradition is fundamentally temporal, with spatial aspects being subordinate to this primary category of time. But Indian people are just the opposite. We're spatial, rooted in the land. . . .

A proper relationship recognizes that I am simply a part of the creation, one of God's creatures along with other two-leggeds, the four-leggeds, the wingeds, and the other living, moving things—including the trees, the grass, the rocks, the mountains.

All those things are relative. That's the universal Indian notion of the interrelationship of all things in creation. Human beings are a part of creation—not apart from it and somehow free to use it up or abuse it.[43]

The lineal descent of the People of the Five Nations shall run in the female line. Women shall be considered progenitors of the Nation. They shall own the Land and the Soil. Men and Women shall follow the status of their Mothers. . . . We turn our attention now to the senior women, the Clan Mothers. Each nation assigns them certain duties. For the People of the Longhouse, the Clan Mothers and their sisters select the chiefs, and remove them from office when they fail the people. The Clan Mothers are the custodians of the Land, and always think of the Unborn Generations. They represent Life and the Earth. Clan Mothers! You gave us Life—continue now to place our feet on the right path.

Kaianerekowa, *the Great Law of Peace, and the original instructions given to the Iroquois People of the Longhouse in the beginning*[44]

When the child is born, the afterbirth is taken and offered to a young tree or to a greasewood bush. The child becomes rooted in the Earth, and when it is born the roots are like a little string. Our rootedness to the Earth is like tying a string to yourself and the other end to your mother. The string thickens with each Offering, with each ceremony, each member of the family, each generation.

LENORA HATATHLIE HILL, *Navajo*[45]

Lolita Concho, *Canteen*, ca. 1983, Acoma pueblo, New Mexico. A prominent double spiral surrounded by hatched motifs is reminiscent of the work of twelfth and thirteenth century Anasazi artists. Traditional designs continue to provide inspiration for contemporary Pueblo potters.

The symbolic importance of the umbilical cord and its talismanic influence upon the lives of indigenous peoples across the planet is richly conveyed through the ritual observances of the umbilicus in Native American cultures. For example, the Havasupai of the Grand Canyon still color a child's dried umbilicus with natural red ochre paint and apply it in traditional patterns to the child's body (at the age of one) as a way of imprinting, symbolically, strong ancestral ties.[46] A Chippewa mother places the dried cord in a small beaded buckskin bag that she then buries. A father, on the other hand, might take his son's bag on a hunting trip and drop it wherever he killed the first animal. His boy would then be blessed with the attributes of a good hunter. Cords often were buried in the trunks of trees. If a mother was neglectful and "put the bag anywhere," her child could develop a knack for "get[ting] into things." People would then say, the child "is searching for his navel cord."[47]

In Navajo country, with the elders on the land where the umbilical cords are buried, a physical and spiritual foundation of native cultural identity is established and ensured. The cord is a magnet assuring an enduring bond to the home grounds. Roberta Blackgoat, a Navajo elder, describes this connection between herself and the land where "my old ancestors were born and buried" as a "real deep spot where I am . . . [m]y place in the order of Creation. . . ."[48] In fact, the Navajo introduce their children to the Earth *before* they are brought into the world by means of a "Planting of the Spirit," through a Blessing Way ceremony, which marks "the first tie of the fetus to the universe," explains Navajo interpreter Lenora Hatathlie Hill.[49] Later on, the umbilical cords of female infants are buried under a loom outside the hogan, and in the cornfields or sheep corrals in the event of a male child.

Alvin Clinton, Navajo elder and medicine man, speaking out in defense of thirteen years of resistance against a federal policy of relocation and out of a conviction that "our children and our children's children [should] know what happened and why," states that in accordance with the Navajo Way "the land is part of us, and we are part of land." There is no harmony unless the Navajo maintain their connection to their sacred places and the world of the Holy Beings. "The people are crying for the land, and I use the Navajo Ways to heal them," says Clinton. "There is a responsibility to stay on this Land—this place, our Mother. . . . We would be violating our religious laws that have been handed down to us for generations from the Gods if they take us away from here."[50] Clinton describes this rootedness as an unending circle of connectedness that begins before birth, continues through birth and cycles back through rebirth.

WHEN YOU WERE BORN, that little piece of cord comes off and it is tied. Then it is buried here. Every Navajo family that has kids, children, they have that umbilical cord and they keep it here and they bury it in the corral or here at the homesite and that is where it is kept. Their being is right here. Not in some other place. That is why the Navajo always comes back to where they live. This is one of the natural laws that we live by.

Their cord is buried at the corral, at the sheep corral, and from that time on this person will always think of that place where their umbilical cord has been buried. They will always think of where they were born and they will return. They always do, they always return.[51]

An Indian needs his river, his mountain, wherever he prays, so when he comes back from wherever he's been, there's a place to go. At least I have a river I can sit by. A lot of Indians don't have a river.

BILLY FRANK, JR.,
*Nisqually activist, recipient
of the Albert Schweitzer Prize
for Humanitarianism, 1992*[52]

LEFT TOP: *Pima Basketry Tray*, Sacatón, Arizona, 1900–1915. Pima (ákĭmel ó ›odham) legends from the American Southwest feature a supernatural being whose home is represented by a maze design called *Siuhü Ki*. An identical design popularly called "Man in the Maze" is both painted and woven by their neighbors the tóhono ó ›odham (Papago). These creations are made primarily for sale. LEFT BOTTOM: *Diegueño Basket*, Southern California. Known for their fine basketry, pottery and elaborate ritual, the Yuman-speaking Diegueño featured the coiled serpent design on some of their woven plaques. BELOW: Gelineau Fisher (Ojibwa), *Untitled*, 1984. The undulating and swirling motion of the natural world is at work in this unique and graceful painting of dancing bird-flowers at play in a fusion of petals, feathers, and beaks. To the left and center is the emblem for the Great Spirit who presides over all Creation.

ENCOUNTERS
WITH THE SACRED

For the Oglala Sioux, all manifestations of life in the universe share a dimension of the sacred, and within this sacredness lies a sense of the holy "mystery." The way sacred power works to create unity between humans, nature and the spirit world depends on a flow of creative continuity. In a remarkable reference to the surge of creation, an old Dakota wise man in the 1880s explains the workings of the cosmic order in terms of an ongoing genesis. All the varied forms of life—physical and metaphysical—have their place, are equally important and mutually inter-dependent.

> EVERYTHING AS IT MOVES, now and then, here and there, makes stops. The bird as it flies stops in one place to make its nest, and in another to rest in its flight. A man when he goes forth stops when he wills. So the god has stopped. The sun, which is so bright and beautiful, is one place where he has stopped. The moon, the stars, the winds, he has been with. The trees, the animals, are all where he has stopped, and the Indian thinks of these places and sends his prayers there to reach the place where the god has stopped and win help and a blessing.[53]

Lone Man, a Teton Sioux, was active in tribal warfare and took part in the Custer massacre. In 1918, he explained how—through a vigilant scrutiny of the natural world—his spirituality began to burgeon. His pithy account of this experience reveals the way sacred power works through Nature.

> WHEN I WAS A YOUNG MAN I went to a medicine-man for advice concerning my future. The medicine-man said: "I

have not much to tell you except to help you understand this earth on which you live. If a man is to succeed on the hunt or the warpath, he must not be governed by his inclination, but by an understanding of the ways of animals and of his natural surroundings, gained through close observation. The earth is large, and on it live many animals. This earth is under the protection of something which at times becomes visible to the eye. One would think this would be at the center of the earth, but its representations appear everywhere, in large and small forms—they are the sacred stones. The presence of a sacred stone will protect you from misfortune." He then gave me a sacred stone which he himself had worn. I kept it with me wherever I went and was helped by it. He also told me where I might find one for myself. *Wakan Tanka* [The Great Spirit, Bïg Holy] tells the sacred stones many things which may happen to people. The medicine-man told me to observe my natural surroundings, and after my talk with him I observed them closely. I watched the changes of the weather, the habits of animals, and all the things by which I might be guided in the future, and I stored this knowledge in my mind.[54]

Arthur Amiotte, Lakota writer, teacher and artist, describes the worldview of the Lakota in which the transcendent dimension of the sacred takes precedence over the linear dimension of the world of appearances.

IN THE MYTHIC BEGINNING of the Lakota world, its sacred and temporal dimensions were one, and the Lakota still recognizes himself as a microcosmic reflection of the macrocosm. If he can live in concert with the holy rhythm of that which causes all life to move, he is then assisting in the ongoing process of creation. To maintain his participation in this process, he needs annually to make the journey to the Center of the World, which is the place of his beginning and the origin of all things. There he can renew his relation with the sacred rhythm in the ceremony known as the Sun Dance.

[T]he Lakota sacred traditions have remained uninstitutionalized as "organized religion." Today, they formally and consciously reject permanent sacred architecture as suitable or as having any lasting significance. The transparency of the world of matter and the transmutability, birth-lifetime-death, of all things including the earth itself, precludes the thought that material permanence has very much to do with sacred space. Rather, by not being in a structure, one is in the sacred temple—*templum*—which is the world itself, with the actual dirt of the earth as the floor and the vast blue dome of the actual sky as the ceiling. Any material representation could potentially be a profanation of that which already exists in a sacred manner and is readily available around one. Thus, once a year at the height of the life cycle of the earth and sun, the temple is replete. The re-creation of the world at this time appears visible in the temporary Sun Dance lodge, which can never be used again, and serves only as a *temporary device* to assist men to realize that there is a sacred world whose center is everywhere, including inside himself; and that our whole life is the journey towards it.[55]

*I am blind and do not see the things of this world; but when the light comes from Above, it enlightens my Heart and I can see, for the Eye of my Heart (Chante Ishta) sees everything: and through this vision I can help my people. The heart is a sanctuary at the Center of which there is a little space, wherein the Great Spirit (*Wakantanka) dwells, and this is the Eye. This is the Eye of* Wakantanka *by which He sees all things, and through which we see Him. If the heart is not pure,* Wakantanka *cannot be seen, and if you should die in this ignorance, your soul shall not return immediately to* Wakantanka, *but it must be purified by wandering about in the world. In order to know the Center of the Heart in which is the Mind of* Wakantanka, *you must be pure and good, and live in the manner that* Wakantanka *has taught us. The man who is thus pure contains the Universe within the Pocket of his Heart (Chante Ognaka).*

BLACK ELK[56]

N. Scott Momaday offers a compelling interpretation of the ways of sacredness and the range of its animating and vital power. Encounters with the sacred are transforming experiences that elevate the human spirit. But it is the recognition and cultivation of the sacred that is of profound importance. Sacred places are but one dimension of the mysterious and the holy. These spiritual centers of the earth are distinctive in their sacredness but all are drawn together in their rootedness in the land. Sacred sites are engaged in the "drama of *being*," says Momaday, and therefore must be carefully protected. They are also timeless paths to the very heart of human existence.

THERE IS A PLACE, a round, trampled patch of the red earth, near Carnegie, Oklahoma, where the Kiowa Gourd Dances were held in the early years of the century. When my father was six or eight years old, my grandfather, who was a member of the *Tian-paye,* or Gourd Dance Society, took him there. In one of the intervals of the dance there was a "give-away," an ancient Plains tradition of giving gifts as a public expression of honor and esteem. My grandfather's name was called, and he let go of my father's hand and strode out upon the dance ground. Then a boy, about my father's age, led a black hunting horse, prancing and blowing, into the circle. The boy placed the reins in my grandfather's hand, still warm with my father's touch. The great muscles of the horse rippled in light, and bright ribbons were fixed in its mane and tail. My father watched in wonder and delight, his heart bursting with excitement and pride. And when he told me of that moment, as he did a number of times because I craved to hear it, I could see it as vividly as if I had been there. The brilliant image of that moment remained in my father's mind all of his life, as it remains in mine. It is a thing that related him and relates me to the sacred earth.

To encounter the sacred is to be alive to the deepest center of human existence. Sacred places are the truest definitions of the earth. They stand for the earth immediately and forever; they are its flags and its shields. If you would know the earth for what it really is, learn it through its sacred places. At Devils Tower or Canyon de Chelly or the Cahokia Mounds you touch the pulse of the living planet, you feel its breath upon you. You become one with a spirit that pervades geologic time, that indeed confounds time and space. When I stand on the edge of Monument Valley and behold the great red and blue and purple monoliths floating in the distance, I have the certain sense that I see beyond time. There the earth lies in eternity.

Sacred ground is in some way earned. It is consecrated, made holy with offerings—song and ceremony, joy and sorrow, the dedication of the mind and heart, offerings of life and death. The words "sacred" and "sacrifice" are related.

And acts of sacrifice make sacred the earth. Language and the sacred are indivisible. The earth and all its appearances and expressions exist in names and stories and prayers and spells. North American place names are a sacred music: Medicine Wheel, Bear Butte, Bobaquiveri, Chaco, Sleeping Ute, Lucachukai, Wounded Knee.

Sacred ground is ground that is invested with belief. Belief, at its root, exists independent of meaning. That is, its expression and object may escape what we can perceive as definable meaning. The intrinsic power of sacred ground is often ineffable and abstract. I behold a particular sacred place, the great gallery of rock paintings at Barrier Canyon, Utah, for example. There on the massive wall are large, sharply delineated works of art, anthropomorphic figures in procession. They image ceremony in its ultimate expression: humans, or human-like gods, engaged in the drama of *being,* the essential act of being itself. They perform the verb *to be.* They reflect the human condition; they signify humanity in all places at all times. They proceed from the depths of origin, from a genesis nearly beyond the reach of the imagination.

The figures in the eternal procession at Barrier Canyon are related to us in story. We do not know the story, but we see its enactment on the face of the earth, that it reaches from the beginning of time to the present to a destiny beyond time. We do not know what the story means, but far more importantly we know *that* it means, and that we are deeply involved in its meaning. The sacred is profoundly mysterious, and our belief is no less profound.

A prayer from the Night Chant of the Navajo begins with homage to *Tsegi,* "place among the rocks," place of origin. It would be impossible to imagine an invocation of greater moment or power, or a word or concept more elemental.

> *House made of dawn,*
> *House made of evening light,*
> *House made of dark cloud,*
> *House made of male rain,*
> *House made of dark mist,*
> *House made of female rain,*
> *House made of pollen,*
> *House made of grasshoppers,*
> *Dark cloud is at the door.*
> *The trail out of it is dark cloud.*
> *The zigzag lightning stands high upon it.*

But where there is the sacred there is sacrilege, the theft of the sacred. To steal the sacred is to rob us of our very selves, our reason for being, our being itself. And sacrilege is a sin of which we are capable. Look around. . . .

The sacred places of North America are threatened, even as the sacred earth is threatened. In my generation we have taken steps, small, tentative steps, to preserve forests and rivers and animals. We must also, and above all, take steps to preserve the spiritual centers of our earth, those places that are invested with the dreams of our ancestors and the well-being of our children.

It is good for us to touch the earth. We, and our children, need the chance to walk our sacred earth, this final abiding place of all that lives. We must preserve our sacred places in order to know our place in time, our reach to eternity.[57]

Black Mesa begins in us. The Four Sacred Mountains are our laws. Navajo people emerged from the previous worlds, here, between our Four Sacred Mountains, and this is where we must remain to live in the Dineh-Navajo *Way.*

> *Navajo response to enforced*
> *relocation from their sacred ground, 1985*[58]

Asa Bazhonoodah, a Navajo elder, was born and raised at Black Mesa. She and her husband cleared the land and planted a cornfield nearby. Her husband, her mother and her relatives are all buried here. Specific sacred places on the land represent parts of the body bonding the individual with the soil. Asa Bazhonoodah's grandson, Kee Shay, relates some of his grandmother's teachings: "My grandmother told us that the coal at Black Mesa near Cactus Valley is the lungs. And Navajo Mountain is the head of 'she' mountain, and Big Mountain, the most prominent on Black Mesa, is the liver to that female mountain, and where the fingernails are, that's the Hopi mesas. The head of the male mountain is at Ganado, where the rock sits and there is a stand of trees that look as though they are tied together. Then, on the road to Page is a tall, narrow rock—that rock is a child, and where the road turns in a long, narrow curve, it is Mother Earth's arm holding her grandchild. The waterways connect the mountains. They run in a circle, clockwise from east to west . . . all these rivers form the boundaries of our sacred universe. The rivers are intertwined with each other, and like a young couple they flow—laughing and twisting and turning—linking the mountains into a communication system that is the Navajo Way."[59]

The resistance of the Diné (Navajo) and Hopi traditionalists to the Peabody Coal Company's open-pit mining on top of Black Mesa in the Arizona desert in the early seventies was especially well organized. The stakes were high: Beneath the Mesa lay 20 billion tons of high-grade low-sulphur coal. The Diné and the Hopi objected to the sacred mesa being cut open and to their water being used to transport the smashed coal to the Mohave electrical plant, 273 miles away. It is their belief that when mineral resources are disturbed or excavated, all life is affected. David Monogye, Wu'wuchim priest at Hotevilla, member of the highest religious society among all Hopi traditional leaders, says that "these mineral resources should be left in the ground . . . left in a natural state and taken out only after human beings learn how to live in peace and harmony . . . [and] to use these mineral resources in a peaceful way. Even then there must be a purification before they can be removed."[60]

Asa Bazhonoodah describes an unnatural state of affairs: "[T]he holy elements have been tampered with. . . . [O]ur prayers and healing have been tampered with." The plants are no longer growing, she laments. The animals are dying, water and other holy elements are being taken from the veins of the earth, cedar trees are turning red and her relatives' graves are being disturbed. She urges full recognition of the ruin caused by the reckless mining of the land and a reconciliation with the Holy Elements which allow her people to flourish and to care for the planet. This is her testament to the inviolate nature of the Earth; it is also her testimony given during the spring 1971 Senate hearings in Washington, against the misguided strip-mining operations on Black Mesa that are tearing up the Earth and scarring the Mother of All. (Twenty-three years later, little has changed. The Peabody Coal Company continues to expand its mining activities on Black Mesa.)[61]

IN ENGLISH THEY CALL ME "Kee Shelton's Mother." In Navajo my name is Asa Bazhonoodah, "woman who had squaw dance." I am 83 years old.

I am originally from Black Mesa. I was born and raised there. My parents and grandparents were all from that same area. . . .

I strongly object to the strip mining for many reasons. . . .

A long time ago the earth was placed here for us, the people, the Navajo, it gives us corn and we consider her our mother.

When Mother Earth needs rain we give pollen and use the prayer that was given us when we came from the earth. That brings rain. Black Mesa area is used to ask for rain. And afterward (after the mining) we don't know what it will be like. We make prayers for all blessings for Mother Earth, asking that we may use her legs, her body and her spirit to make ourselves more powerful and durable. After this the pollen is thrown into the water.

Air is one of the Holy Elements, it is important in prayer. Wooded areas are being cut down. Now the air is becoming bad; not working. The herbs that are taken from Mother Earth and given to a woman during childbirth no longer grow in the cut area. The land looks burned.

The Earth is our mother. The white man is ruining our mother. I don't know the white man's ways, but to us the Mesa, the air, the water, are Holy Elements. We pray to these Holy Elements in order for our people to flourish and perpetuate the well-being of each generation.

Even when we were small, our cradle is made from the things given to us from Mother Earth. We use these elements all of our lives and when we die we go back to Mother Earth.

When we were first put on Earth, the herbs and medicine were also put here for us to use. These have become part of our prayers to Mother Earth. We should realize it for if we forget these things we will vanish as the people. That is why I don't like the coal mine.

How much would you ask for if your Mother had been harmed? There is no way that we can be repaid for the damages to our Mother. No amount of money can repay, money cannot give birth to anything.

Black Mesa is to the Navajo like money is to the Whites. Our Mother gives birth to the animals, plants, and these could be traded for money. Black Mesa is my bill-fold. Black Mesa gives life to animals and these animals give us money. . . .

The Whites have neglected and misused the Earth. Soon the Navajo will resemble the Anasazi ruins. The wind took them away because they misused the Earth.

The White men wish that nothing will be left of us after this is over. They want us like the Anasazi. . . .

Our Mother is being scarred. This is what I am saying, how much would you ask if your Mother was harmed.

Mother Earth is like a horse. We put out hay and grain to bring in the horse. So it is when we put out pollen to bring life from Mother Earth. We pray to Mother Earth to ask blessings from the water, the sun, and the moon. . . .

I don't think they (Peabody Coal Company) can re-plant. There is nothing but rocks, no soil. I don't see how they could replant. The soil is underneath. It won't be replanted, no possible way. They advocate that the place will be beautiful when they finish. I don't believe that this place will be beautiful when they finish. If they replant, they will not replant our herbs. Even now our herbs are vanishing.

I have gone three times looking for herbs. I couldn't recognize the place where we find them. Finally I found some plants but they were scorched. I couldn't find my way around the mountain because it was so distorted. The mining operation is near by.

We have herbs that cure diseases that white medicine doesn't cure. Sometime the people come here to find medi-cine when the Public Health Service doesn't cure them. They pray and give Mother Earth something for curing them. This the white people do not know about.

Our prayers and healing have been tampered with and they don't work as good anymore. How can we give something of value to Mother Earth to repay the damages that the mining had done to her. We still ask for her blessings and healing, even when she is hurt. . . .

I want to see the mining stopped.[62]

I work with little children . . . and one time I asked—I was trying to understand if these children knew the word "sacred" and its meaning—so I asked them, "What does sacred mean to you? What do you know in your life that is sacred?" And most of them said, "My mother." "And how do you treat something that is sacred to you?" And their answers were really, really something . . . [they] almost brought tears to my eyes because they talked about protecting their mother, not letting their mother get hurt and loving their mother. And this was from little children . . . kindergarten and first grade. So when I talked about the Sacred Mother Earth, I wanted to be sure that they knew what the word sacred meant and they said that their mother was sacred to them.

AUDREY SHENANDOAH,
Onondaga elder,
Eel Clan, Six Nations,
Iroquois Confederation[63]

Henrietta Mann is a full-blood Cheyenne enrolled with the Cheyenne-Arapaho tribes of Oklahoma. Professor, writer and human rights activist, Mann was the first woman to serve as director of the Office of Indian Education Programs, Bureau of Indian Affairs, in 1986. She has been accorded many honors, including National Indian Woman of the Year in 1987. In 1990, *Rolling Stone* named her one of the ten leading professors in the nation. Until recently, she was director of the Association on American Indian Affairs' Religious Freedom Coalition Project. Currently, she is professor of Native American Studies at the University of Montana in Missoula.

"Indians understand that our spirituality is the core of our culture and identity," states Mann. "Therefore, if one destroys Indian

spirituality or religion, the people are simultaneously destroyed."[64]
The varied ways of experiencing sacredness in the Cheyenne tradition
are recapitulated in the following meditation by a woman who is not
only a scholar and author, but also a close participant in the ceremonial life of her people.

> IT IS APPARENT FROM THEIR ACCOUNT of creation that
> Cheyennes look upon the earth as their mother, referring
> to her as grandmother, a beloved kinship term indicating
> her timeless status as the first and oldest of all women.
> Equally important, earth is viewed as a woman, who has
> the sacred responsibility of giving life to maintain the continuity of the people. She must, therefore, maintain a stable, solid state so as to support the feet of her many
> children as they walk their life journeys on earth. She also
> has to provide for her children's physical needs by nurturing the plants with her body, thereby, providing the necessities to keep famine away. She does this either directly or
> she does so indirectly by nourishing the birds and animals,
> who in turn sustain us as human beings. This concept of
> earth as giver of life, therefore, is a sacred relationship of
> a mother to her child or as children to their mother. In
> return for her gift of life, we keep her alive through our
> ceremonies, and we return time and again to our sacred
> sites to renew and strengthen our spirits and the spirit of
> the earth.
>
> Since earth is mother, she is treated with the unconditional respect, reverence, consideration, and love that we
> as individuals feel for and give to our mothers. If we understand this special relationship, we can further understand
> the need for Indians to live in harmony and interdependence with this land.
>
> According to Indians, the earth is not only compositionally balanced, but the earth also is sacred. She is physically alive and spiritual and human beings must walk with
> her in goodness, harmony, beauty, and interdependence.
> Cheyennes are aware of their sacred mission in life which
> is to maintain their history and continuity as a people
> and to be the keepers of the earth, as their prophet Sweet
> Medicine taught them. He brought their Arrows [the four
> sacred Arrows symbolize the collective identity of the
> Cheyenne people] and accompanying ceremony [Arrow

Renewal Ceremony] from out of Bear Butte, their sacred ground, located northwest of the Black Hills in South Dakota.

Looking far into the future, Sweet Medicine sadly prophesied what would happen to the Cheyenne people and to their land. He stated that they would meet some white, good-looking strangers, who would follow their own ways, which would be in conflict with those the Grandfather had given them. He further said that despite their knowledge, the strangers would eventually overpopulate the world, pollute the air, contaminate the water, and kill the earth. He reassured the Cheyenne, however, that so long as they maintained their sacred ways and spiritual beliefs, they would retain their unique identity as a people and endure into eternity.

We confronted our destiny as a people and one day just as our prophet had predicted, we acquired that fleet, nervous animal with its huge eyes, long tail, and flowing mane. That animal, the horse, changed our way of life and transformed us into the horsemen of the plains. . . . We valued the horse, counting our wealth by the number we owned.

Accordingly, the tribe held doctors of horses in great respect. My great-grandmother was a doctor of horses. . . . She possessed powerful horse medicine and like others of her profession, she never ate its flesh. After performing her healing ritual, she knew with certainty that a horse was going to recover if it fell to the ground and rolled in the dirt. This was its way of rubbing and brushing away its illness by coming into contact with the healing powers of the soil by laying its "wounds to the earth." The four-leggeds have not lost their sacred intimacy with the earth that we as Indians strive to maintain despite alienating external forces.

Seattle, venerated Dwamish chief, to no avail, tried to explain this attachment to the land by stating, "to us the ashes of our ancestors are sacred and their resting place is hallowed ground." Cecilio Blacktooth, too, spoke for her tribe saying they preferred death to leaving their ancestral homelands. "If we cannot live here, we want to go to the mountains and die."

American Indians were baffled by the ruthless intensity of Manifest Destiny. Christians had inherited this land from their God, and Indians were disinherited. They were confused by white zealousness to "civilize" them by confining them to reservations and small individual land allotments. . . . They were expected to think, talk, dress, act, and live like white people, which in this instance meant to become farmers. Smohalla, a dreamer prophet from the Pacific Northwest voiced his antipathy for farming by stating:

You ask me to plow the ground.
Shall I take a knife and tear my mother's breast?
Then when I die she will not take me to her bosom
      to rest.
You ask me to dig for stone.
Shall I dig under her skin for her bones?
Then when I die I cannot enter her body to be born
      again.
You ask me to cut grass and make hay
And sell it and be rich like white men.
But how dare I cut off my mother's hair?

Government policy legislated that in order for Indians to become "civilized" they had to individually own land. The church decreed that in order for Indians to be Christianized, they had to give up their ancient, sacred beliefs and ceremonies. The education system directed children away from their origins as Indians. The entire thrust was to change, replace, alter, and to negate Indian culture and values, especially as those values related to land.

Like many other Indians, I remember the earth and always will, just as I remember some special feast days from my childhood. There were always relatives and friends present. Weather permitting, the women spread a large canvas or blankets on the ground under the trees. They then arranged an oil cloth in the center upon which they placed the food. We all sat down, an elder prayed over the food, and with much talk and laughter the family ate together. My grandfather said it was good to sit on the ground and to feel the purifying, energizing, healing, and loving power of our mother, the earth. We, thus, periodically renewed ourselves by sitting close to the ground, and touching the soil.

My great-grandmother taught her son and grandson, and through them she passed on to me her profound respect for the earth. She said that we come from the earth, that we belong to her, and that we return to her to rest when our life journeys are over. Because of her, I know the earth as a wise, loving, generous, and powerful woman, who will continue to sustain us as a people so long as we continue to revere her and maintain a balance in life. A stable, solid earth, fresh air, continuing heat from the sun, and clear water are important to us because they were important to our beloved ancestors.

As American Indians we are fortunate in having been the first to love the earth woman. She is enduring, as White Antelope's death song at Sand Creek attests: "Nothing lives long, only the earth and the mountains."

To Indians, the land is much more than a commodity to be purchased, sold, exploited, or desecrated; she is our beautiful mother, both in reality and myth.

Today we are engaged in a spiritual conflict with the descendants of the very people who fled to this land 500 years ago to escape religious persecution. They have diminished our land base and left us with very little. We must guard what little remains, particularly our sacred sites. Today we, too, must act on the prayers of some Northern Cheyenne traditional leaders who ask the Creator "to always safeguard some earth for us so that we can continue to send our prayers up to you."[65]

Every society needs . . . sacred places. They help to instill a sense of social cohesion in the people and remind them of the passage of the generations that have brought them to the present. A society that cannot remember its past and honor it is in peril of losing its soul.

> VINE DELORIA, JR.,
> Standing Rock Sioux,
> scholar, writer and professor of law[66]

The horizon is one of the most important things in our lives. When we get up in the morning, we look that way. We look to the sun that gives us light and gives us wisdom. If we don't see the horizon anymore, it becomes very demoralizing. That's what we're faced with.

BILL TALLBULL,
Northern Cheyenne spiritual leader, objecting to railroad development in the sacred valley of the Tongue River, 1991[67]

Bill Tallbull is a Northern Cheyenne spiritual leader and teacher at the Dull Knife Community College in Lame Deer, Montana. The Tongue River Valley in Montana, which forms the eastern boundary of the Northern Cheyenne Indian Reservation, is a landscape of considerable religious importance. The Cheyenne people have long thought it to be a holy site for vision quests, children's afterbirth rituals, cloth and tobacco offerings and the growing of medicinal herbs. It's also the setting of important burial grounds. A proposed extension of the Tongue River Railroad has threatened the valley with air, water and sound pollution, and has created the dread of greater deforestation and strip-mining for coal in southeastern Montana. Bill Tallbull has objected to the encroachment that he feared would desecrate sacred land and forest. The entire enterprise endangered the vital relationship his people hold with the hills. It imperiled the horizon line which has great import for the Northern Cheyenne. Tallbull urges the Forest Service to show proper respect for the trees that they purportedly "manage."

WE TALK ABOUT SACRED PLACES and things to regenerate spirits as well as the physical body. They come hand in hand. I have talked many times with the Forest Service. They are dealing with the other part of our lives which has been very important to us. I have said we are dealing with spiritual things now. Each one of us has a spirit. Do you know yours? How well do you know yours? I said I bet you wouldn't know a spirit if it kicked you. . . .

When Indian people walk down the valley, they have had a spiritual relationship, a spiritual tie with the area.

They lived within these areas because they were spiritually compatible with that area. And these relationships are very strong.

I'm running into the same thing that all tribes run into from time to time—it's [land] development. I'm to talk about the railroad that is being planned for Southeast Montana, along Tongue River, which is just across the river from the Reservation. I have great difficulty in expressing the Tribe's concerns about the area across the river. Over the years people have developed those spiritual relationships with the plant life and animal life across the river. There's graves over there, ceremonial places over there. There are powerful things people have done. An archaeologist is going to note whatever he can find on the ground. And five o'clock comes along and he hangs up his boots. This is the time of the day when the spiritual part of the valley comes alive, in the evening and in the darkness. There are many things that a person can find in the valley. A lot of the spirits don't come out until the sun sets. That's when the valley comes alive.

There was a rock wall that was cut into the mountainside to make a road. Out of this rock wall stepped a wolf. No one saw it but me. Now, at this point in time, I was wondering if they would believe my report if I had to write that.

Sometimes, you don't want to tell of these [sacred] places. Then it becomes a point of interest. They put it on a map. Some people find out about it, and then people begin to converge on the area. . . .

Are they [the Forest Service] going to listen to any of our concerns? They've already made up their minds. There's going to be a railroad.

As we all know, at the beginning of time, when the earth was created, it had a spiritual beginning as well as a physical beginning. When the plants appeared and flourished, plants also had a spiritual beginning. When animals appeared and flourished on plant life, animals also had a spiritual beginning. When man appeared, he also had a spiritual beginning. And since that time, there has been a very strong relationship between the animals, plants, and the earth. And we've maintained that relationship.

It is difficult to express these concerns to people who

have very little understanding of other parts of our life. I often wonder. It's hard to understand why major religions do not go to see some of the powerful places like the Medicine Wheel, Bear Butte—some of these places. Is there something wrong with their teaching? They know that in their Bible, Moses went and received the covenant on the mountain. And when Moses got there he was told to take off his shoes. That ground was *sacred*. God makes ground sacred, not Forest Service or anybody else. . . .

I have made an attempt many times to try to talk to the Forest Service so they can begin to understand a little about the Indian—to understand a little bit about the plant life, animal life. And that since animal life, plant life have spirits, at their passing their spirits go into the hills— they go into the mountains. This is where we go to appease them, to continue the spiritual harmony that we have created over the years, over the generations.

So all our hills have spirit life of animals, plants. The water people that live in the water, their spirits in the water. So if you ask an elder about God, he will say: "God is an everywhere-spirit." If you look at a stone, he's there. If you look at a tree, he's there. Everywhere you look, he's there. I would try to understand that people would take that stone, and really look at a stone, and say, "Stone, you are the oldest person that I know; although you don't have eyes and legs, and all of those things. . . ."

It is these things that we know. That when trees have a relationship with us, who are very strong spirit people, we go and offer tobacco. As I come down into this county, I will stop and offer tobacco. It's always been a special place for my people.

I don't know what we must do to convince the people who are the caretakers of these places that perhaps we could be part of that. Who could be the stewards of these parts? Who would make atonements for all the mistakes that have been made by people?—not knowing that they are making these mistakes. The Forest Service does not need to try to be an Indian, but at least should have some respect for the very trees that they manage. . . .

I'm not gonna' talk much about the railroad. They're going to build a railroad. It's difficult to change the minds of those who want to open up the Powder River Country.

Thirteen massive coal mines are in this plan, and these railroads are gonna' be carrying coals. There are going to be 100-car trains, 10, 15, 20 moving coal out. This threatens the relationship these people have had with the hills to the east. The horizon is one of the most important things in our lives. When we get up in the morning, we look that way. We look to the sun that gives us light and gives us wisdom. If we don't see the horizon anymore, it becomes very demoralizing. That's what we're faced with.[68]

John Trudell was the cofounder of the American Indian Movement. In the summer of 1980, in the *Paha Sapa* (Black Hills) of South Dakota, he delivered a remarkable address to an international audience of indigenous peoples and their supporters who had come from such widely separated locales as Nicaragua, Northern Europe, South America and North America. It was called the Survival Gathering and was organized by the Black Hills Alliance, a coalition of whites and Native Americans, set up to organize workshops on land use, indigenous peoples' self-determination, corporate control and political oppression. The natural, sacred elements of the earth, Trudell said, were the principal sources of power for all indigenous peoples.

I WOULD LIKE TO TALK tonight in honor of all of us in the Struggle who have lost our Relations to the Spirit World. I would like to talk in honor of the Wind, one of the Natural Elements. This is a Survival Gathering. And one of the things I hope that you all learn while you are here is that you learn to appreciate the Energy and Power that the Elements are—that of the Sun, the Rain, and the Wind. That you go away from here understanding that this is Power—and this is the only true, real Power. This is the only true real connection we will ever have to power . . . our relationship to the Mother Earth. . . .

We are a natural part of the Earth. We are an extension of the Earth; we are not separate from it. We are a part of it. The Earth is our Mother. The Earth is a Spirit, and we are an extension of that Spirit. We are Spirit. We are Power. They [the white power structure] want us to believe that we have to believe in them and depend upon them, and we have to assume these consumer identities, and these political identities, these religious identities, and these racial identities. They want to separate us from our Power. They want to separate us from who we are—genocide. . . . [T]hey have limited our ability to see the necessity for our survival because they want us to believe that genocide just means the physical extinction. We must consider the Spiritual genocide that they commit against us. The spiritual genocide that the white people [themselves] have been victimized by for thousands of years, the Spiritual genocide that told them not to respect the Earth, not to respect the Life that is Earth, but to pay all of their tribute through the Churches to God and heaven, that the heaven would take care of it in the afterlife. They tried to take and suppress our natural identity, our natural Spiritual connection to the Earth. . . .

We see the physical genocide that they are attempting to inflict upon our lives, and we understand the psychological genocide that they have already inflicted upon their own people, and that is the trade-off that they want us to make for survival, that we become subservient to them, that we no longer understand our real connection to Power, our real connection to the Earth.

Power. They can't stop the Wind and they can't stop the Rain. They can't stop the Earthquake and the Volcano and the Tornado. They can't stop Power. We are a Spiritual connection to the Earth. As individuals we have Power and collectively, we have the same power as the Earthquake, the Tornado, and the Hurricanes. We have that potential. We have that connection. . . .

We will not allow you to smash us. This is our obligation to the Earth. Only by fulfilling our obligation to the Earth, can we fulfil our obligation to the People. Only by understanding our connection to the Earth can we create a fair system that's going to be good to the People. . . .

Let us struggle for a Purpose. Let us struggle for the purpose of freeing the Earth, because only by freeing the Earth from those who would attack the Earth can we be free ourselves. . . .

The people have risen before. The people have spoken before. The people have tried before. But somewhere they did not put it all together, and the reason was because they had always attempted to change the social conditions in

America without addressing the issue of our relationship to the land. They cannot create a . . . repressive military regime without the land. They cannot exploit the economics without the land. But we must not be arguing with them. We must not take them on just the fact that we are going to own the land, turn into one of them. Our concern has got to be for the land as well as for ourselves. . . .

We must put the foolishness out of our mind that man is going to destroy the Earth because man is not that powerful. Man may be stupid enough to destroy his ability to live on the Earth, but man will not destroy the Earth. The Earth will purify itself if it takes a billion years. The Earth has the time to do that. The Earth will come through this all right. It's us. It's us. . . . [W]e are a Natural Part of the Earth. Because we are a natural part of the Creation Earth, because we were here, the Earth did not put useless things here, we are a natural part of the Creation. . . .

And All Our Ancestors, All Our Relations who went to the Spirit World, they are here with us. They have power. They will help us. They will help us to see if we are willing to look. We are not separated from them because there is no place to go. This is our place, the Earth. This is our Mother. We will not go away from our Mother. No matter what they do to us—no matter how they ever strike at us . . . everytime they do it, we must never become reactionary. The one thing that has always bothered me about revolution, everytime I have seen the revolutionaries, they have reacted out of hatred for the oppressor. We must do this for the Love of our People. No matter what they do to us, we must always act with the Love of Our People, and the Earth. We must never react out of hatred against those who have no sense.[69]

Few people of the world were more devoted to art than the Haida of the Queen Charlotte Islands (called the "Canadian Galapagos") on the rim of Canada's Pacific continental shelf, a hundred kilometers out from the coast of British Columbia. Their cultural achievements are unique to the world. Their totem poles, says master Haida carver Bill Reid, radiated "a terrible vitality that only decay and destruction could end." The Haida constructed their material culture from the great cedars of the forest, a treasure trove Reid calls "incalculably valuable"—and not only economically. "There is no dollar-and-cents equivalent with which to measure the sacred," he wrote.

OH, THE CEDAR TREE!

If mankind in his infancy had prayed for the perfect substance for all material and aesthetic needs, an indulgent god could have provided nothing better. Beautiful in itself, with a magnificent flared base tapering suddenly to a tall, straight trunk wrapped in reddish brown bark, like a great coat of gentle fur, gracefully sweeping boughs, soft feathery fronds of gray green needles.

Huge, some of these cedars, five hundred years of slow growth, towering from their massive bases.

The wood is soft, but of a wonderful firmness and, in a good tree, so straight-grained it will split true and clean into forty foot planks, four inches thick and three feet wide, with scarcely a knot.

Across the grain it cuts clean and precise. It is light in weight and beautiful in color, reddish brown when new, silvery grey when old.

It is permeated with natural oils that make it one of the longest lasting of all woods, even in the damp of the Northwest Coast climate.

When steamed it will bend without breaking. It will make houses and boats and boxes and cooking pots. Its bark will make mats, even clothing. With a few bits of sharpened stone and antler, with some beaver teeth and a lot of time, with later on a bit of iron, you can build from the cedar tree the exterior trappings of one of the world's great cultures.

Above all, you can build totem poles, and the people of the Northwest Coast built them in profusion: forests of sculptured columns between their houses and the sea, proudly announcing to all the heraldic past of those who dwelt there.[70]

Popovi Da (1921–1971) was a prominent Pueblo potter and the son of Maria Poveka Martinez, considered the most famous of Native American potters for her innovative black-on-black ware. Her son,

"Po," was also an innovator who developed new finishes and techniques, such as those used to produce the popular gunmetal ware, and introduced the use of turquoise in his work. Po was an active ceremonial leader and six times governor of his Pueblo, San Ildefonso. He was also an eloquent speaker and frequent lecturer. Two years before his death, he gave a talk addressing the indissoluble, sacred link between creative activity and life itself. In the act of creation—whether it be a pot or a Pueblo dance—humans commingle with the spirit world; they enter sacred space and move in a sacred manner. The same can be said, Po suggests, of the very experience of being alive in the world. In fact, all of life is considered a manifestation of the sacred, where sacred time fuses with linear time.

WE BELIEVE we are the first conservationists. We do not destroy or disturb the harmony of nature. To us this is beauty; it is our sense of esthetics. We care for and husband our environment, trying to be all-forbearing like Mother Earth. We feel ourselves trustees of our environment and of our creative values. And this gives us a union with all existence, all the creatures which live in the world: wild animals, little crawling things, and even men.

We have multitudes of symbols—corn blossom, squash blossom, eagle and deer, rainbow and fire, and storm cloud; the design of plants, of all living things; the underworld which gave forth man and all the creatures— symbols whose secret meanings are only secret because they are within and cannot be easily expressed. This symbolism is perpetuated through memory alone, because we have no written language. But to be able to use our symbols and keep in harmony with our world we must work by fasting, continence, solitary vigil, and symbolic discipline. Out of the silences of meditation come purity and power which eventually become apparent in our art: the many spirits which enter about us, in us, are transformed within us, moving from an endless past not gone, not dead, but with a threshold that is the present. From this time sense, from this experience deep within, our forms are created. Even our smaller children sense this, and consequently create beautiful designs. Our simple lines have meaning. . . .

Our symbols and our ceremonial representations are all expressed as an endless cadence, and beautifully organized in our art as well as in our dance.

A pueblo dance is a sacred drama and a tremendous religious experience to us. You behold a masterpiece of color, form and movement, sound, rhythm, a slow sequence of chants, beat of feet. This ceremony combines our spiritual and our physical needs. The dance expresses the union we feel between man and the whole of humanity or the union of all living things. At the same time, the dance gives to man, in his trustee-ship of the corn, the health of the plant. The dance encourages the corn to grow. . . .

Fine art within our lives has been balanced and directed in a positive sense by the forces about us. If life is unbalanced, as it is now, by the pressure of mechanical things all about us, life seems to lose man in a cold world of steel where we are frustrated and afraid. This frustration will be reflected in our art. . . .

But the best in pueblo life is reflected by paintings and designs which tend to be four-dimensional. They point to rhythm and the motion in the dance, the action of the horse, the speed of the antelope, the heat of the desert. We have a form of art which is distinctively North American Indian, and we must preserve our way of life in order for our art to continue. From this part of us comes our ability to create, as can be seen from the thousands of designs found on ceremonial and cooking pots from prehistory, dating back to time immemorial. I doubt that the designs improved the cooking, but they were created because they had to be created; it is our role to create.

Except for our ritualistic dances and our way of life, our efforts are related to the care of our environment and what we create. Our pueblo people eat gently, recognizing with inner feelings that the corn or the squash were at one time growing, cared for, each a plant alive, now prepared to become part of us, of our bodies and our minds, quite sacred. We reflect on the plant. . . .

There is a design in living things; their shapes, forms, the ability to live, all have meaning. We must cling to our Indian traditions which exalt beauty. To the white man, religion is a method, a system which he can employ . . . when necessary. But to us there is no word in our language for an isolated dogma: all we can say is that we have a way of life, and that this is life itself. If we fill our minds with pure materialism and accept a convenient religion, then the backbone of our way of life, of our perception of beauty, will be broken and we will disappear as unseen winds, gone. . . .

The State government will try to gain our land through condemnation. The Federal government will try to take land for parks and forest services. There will be no feeling for the great trust we have in the land. What will happen to Blue Lake and other sacred areas? [After a sixty-four year struggle, Blue Lake was returned to Taos Pueblo in 1971.]

Our values are indwelling and dependent on time and space unmeasured. This in itself is beauty. Our first great value is our trusteeship of nature, and this is beauty also. Then there is an order and direction of our lives, a unity, the ability to share the joy of sharing, creativeness and minimum competition. This too is beauty.

Come to our dances or our homes; we share our meals with you. We feel then that we can be part of each other, confluent human forces, sharing giving. It is not the disease known as obligation, but exists because it exists and that is enough.[71]

Manfred Susunkewa, a traditional kachina carver from the Hopi village of Shungopavi, explains the spiritual essences of the kachina and how his identity as a Hopi is bound to the ancient tradition of carving these cottonwood figures.

FOR ME, THE KACHINA has always been a means of communication with the spiritual world for the Hopi. In order for this to happen, natural resources, not man-made chemical materials, should be used. How can there be a line of communication using unnatural materials?

Each character has certain design elements. There are symbols for earth, man, plants, animals, the Creator, stars, and others. The cottonwood root is a natural thing, and if it was bent or had a flaw, it was still used. The first carvers were not looking for a perfect cottonwood root. They were not artists. Sometimes the natural shapes "tell" the carver what person is to be carved. A bent root with a big bump, for example, may become a Humpback Kachina. There was a primitiveness and simplicity in their appearance. When you look at them, you don't have to talk about them like they do with art; they were just there. The bulky form is not art in the *western* sense—they were a spiritual thing.

The [old-style] dolls don't stand on bases; they had a string around the neck, either to be hung from the wall or used to hold them. The string is tied before the base coat of clay whitewash is applied. Then it is painted over with the rest of the doll, so the string does not show—it becomes part of the character. . . .

The word "kachina" comes from the Pueblo culture. It is a Hopi, or Zuni, or other Pueblo deity that doesn't exist in any other culture. For them [non-Pueblo people], it is just merchandise. . . .

Even other Hopi are not aware of the uniqueness of the Hopi culture. The word "Hopi" is valuable. The translation of the word Hopi means "blameless." To be blameless, we never wrong another or create conflict with mother earth or anything that comes from the earth, including fellow humans. This is maybe why we were called the "peaceful ones."

We are not born Hopi; Hopi is earned. The newborn infant is like a foreign element. As it grows, it is taught about Hopi culture, Hopi life, Hopi traditions. The child goes through different stages of initiation. At the last initiation, the child must decide on its own if it wants to be Hopi. It is a choice, and it is a commitment. There are values to live by, and everyone needs something to believe in.

Our simple primitive ways helped us to survive in a desolate land somehow. Our elders were scientists, doctors, meteorologists, and visionaries—they had it all. I wish I could meet them, but the only way I can is through carving their kachinas the way they did. I hope they are seeing what I am doing. If they are, I would like them to accept me as part of them—to be called Hopi.[72]

Linda Hogan (1947–   ) is a Chickasaw novelist, poet and essayist. She is the author of a collection of short fiction and several books of poetry. She teaches creative writing at the University of Colorado.

Her novel *Mean Spirit* (1992) is set in eastern Oklahoma in the 1920s, when oil was discovered on Osage lands and unscrupulous whites used every means possible to defraud Indians and the new settlers of their land. In this passage, near the end of the novel, Hogan (through her character Belle Graycloud) returns to a remembered, sacred site for courage, solace and inspiration.

UP THROUGH THE BACK WAY, above the Blue River, Belle made her way toward the caves that were on the other side of Sorrow. . . .

There was nothing to do. The world had turned under and over, and now they were left, left to go on, to survive.

She stopped a moment, standing in the open mouth of the cave, and looked down over the river. Below her, the world stretched on, curved around the horizon. And then it was night, and the smell of the land was rich and fertile with the dank odor of grasses and herbs.

Then she went inside the cave that was behind Sorrow. There were four chambers there, like a heart. Some of the bats still lived there, and for this Belle was grateful. They would always be there, she knew, living in the borderland between worlds.

She sat in the open mouth of the cave and thought of the fallen world, the fallen houses and the fallen people.

That night, the moonlight was an entrance into still another land. She went out from the cave and stood before it, in the light of earth's reflected face. She raised her head and looked up at the sky. It was beautiful and enormous, the world that lived far beyond theirs, beyond the stars, and beyond even the constellations of buffalo and deer.

She slept on the ground of the cave that night, feeling the land, feeling it move up through her. She saw her own self lying there, a white-haired woman, a strong woman, part of earth's terrain. In the cave she remembered how there was hope in the land, hope and tomorrow living in the veins and stones of earth.

She remembered that the river was going to the sea, had been rain clouds and lakes. It had been snow. Now it was on its journey back to the great first waters of life.[73]

Michael Horse, a diviner in Linda Hogan's novel *Mean Spirit,* discovers oil on the land while seeking water. As his wife goes into labor, he is inspired to complete the writing of *The Book of Horse.* He confides that he has "added" what is missing from the Bible and begins by setting forth "the simple rules for life" on this "sacred" earth.

HONOR FATHER SKY AND MOTHER EARTH. Look after everything. Life resides in all things, even the motionless stones. Take care of the insects for they have their place, and the plants and trees for they feed the people. Everything on earth, every creature and plant wants to live without pain, so do them no harm. Treat all people in creation with respect; all is sacred, especially the bats [for their ancient powerful medicine].

Live gently with the land. We are one with the land. We are part of everything in our world, part of the roundness and cycles of life. The world does not belong to us. We belong to the world. And all life is sacred.

Pray to the earth. Restore your self and voice. Remake your spirit, so that it is in harmony with the rest of nature and the universe. Keep peace with all your sisters and brothers. Humans whose minds are healthy desire such peace and justice. . . .

This is the core of all religion. It is the creator's history, the creator who spoke to a white man as clearly as he spoke to me, and said to him, "As you do unto the least of these, my brothers, you do unto me." The creator said this and we abide by it.

Now, Horse continued, the people will go out of their land. They, like the land, are wounded and hurt. They will go into the rocks and bluffs, the cities, and into the caves of the torn apart land. There will be fires. Some of them will be restored to the earth. Others will journey to another land and merge with other people. Some will learn a new way to live, the good way of the red path. But a time will come again when all the people return and revere the earth and sing its praises.[74]

[P]erhaps you have noticed that even in the very lightest breeze you can hear the voice of the cottonwood tree; this we understand is its prayer to the Great Spirit, for not only men, but all things and all beings pray to Him continually in differing ways.

BLACK ELK[75]

Here nature knows us. The earth knows us. We make our offerings to certain trees, certain rocks, to natural water springs, on top of hills. This is where we make our Offerings. We have Songs and prayers. Our history cannot be told without naming the cliffs and mountains that have witnessed our people.

RUTH YINISHYE,
Navajo[76]

To us, each object is imbued with invisible fibers of light that reach out into the universe and are connected and related to all things and all times, and the song that the maker sang when making the object still hangs in the air.

ALEX JACOBS,
Iroquois artist[77]

You asked about the line that goes to the heart. It leads to the spirit which resides in all things—the spirit of life and hope. When we show respect for the spirits around us, they respect us. From this comes good. We show respect in prayer and ceremony—in all things. We demonstrate this by showing that all animals, even snakes, possess souls.

Hopi artist[78]

ABOVE: *Redware Bowl,* Mogollón; Gila County, Arizona, 900–1000. A hole was deliberately struck in such bowls prior to burial to exorcise the spirit within it.

BELOW: *Black-on-White Ware Bowl,* Anasazi; Coconino County, Arizona, 1250–1300. Four distinct spiral designs ornament this bowl from the ancestors of the present-day Pueblo peoples of the Southwest.

VOICES OF CREATION

T he very old story of Sky Woman is "more than a beautiful myth," writes Abenaki poet and storyteller Joseph Bruchac. "It is," he says, "a legend to live by.

"To some," continues Bruchac, the story "is as new and real as if it happened yesterday." It reminds the Abenaki that all of nature and humankind are interconnected, that the earth beneath their feet is alive. Modern scientific theories of continental drift and tectonic plates, says Bruchac, validate the ancient concept of a "living land on the back of a great slow animal."[79] Turtle Island is the Native American expression for North America.

ONCE, THE STORY GOES, a woman fell from the land in the sky. She fell through a hole made by the uprooting of a great tree and as she fell she grasped in her palm a handful of seeds. Down she fell, a long long way. Below her there was no Earth, only the ancient waters and in those waters birds and animals swam.

"Look," they said, "Someone is coming." Then some of the birds—Swans or Geese—flew up to catch her on their wings. Below the other creatures held council.

"There must be a place for her to stand," they said. "We must bring up Earth."

So, one after another, they dove down to try to bring up some mud from below that ancient sea. All of them failed but the last one—Muskrat. It brought up a tiny pawful of wet dirt.

"Now where shall we place it?" they said. "Place it on my back," a deep voice answered. It was the Great Turtle swimming up from the depths. When they placed the earth on Great Turtle's back it grew larger and larger until it became this continent on which we stand, this

Earth on Great Turtle's back. There Sky Woman was placed by the birds. There she dropped the seeds which grew into the good plants. So that story of Creation begins.[80]

I was given the following Cheyenne creation myth by Henrietta Mann, a full-blood Cheyenne scholar and teacher. It is a greatly condensed version of the original, which is preserved in the two major tribal ceremonies of the Cheyenne (the Arrow Renewal and the Sun Dance ceremonies). It is exemplary in its capacity to create "a basis for understanding the American Indian peoples' ancient and intimate relationship with the land," says Mann. "I make this statement," continues Mann, "while simultaneously recognizing the fact that Indians are diverse, that their creation myths are tribal specific, and that they, consequently, have evolved varying views of the world."[81] The Cheyenne creation myth has much in common with the Abenaki creation myth in the preceding passage. The key image in both is the turtle as the progenitor of the North American continent.

THE WISE CHEYENNE OLD ONES say that in the far distant past, generations upon generations ago, the Creator made this universe. With his awesome power and supreme knowledge, he created four spiritual beings to witness the sacred act of creation. He created a world using sinew, buffalo fat, sweet grass, and red earth paint, to which he gave sacred life by breathing upon it four times. Following this, he made the water; the beings that live on or in the water; the light and flaming heat of the sun; and the air in its boundless blue sky.

In response to their request, the Creator gave the water beings the ability to fly. They, however, not only wanted to be able to swim, to dive, and to fly, but to live and rest upon what they described as a dry solid place. The Creator, subsequently, requested that one of them had to bring up some mud from the depths of the salty water. After three of them failed, a small coot successfully swam down to get some red earth.

Since there was only water and air all around him, the Creator decided to place this mud upon the back of one of the water beings. All proved unsuitable, however, except for Grandmother Turtle. He placed mud upon her back, which under his power expanded to become this sacred land. Because a grandmother holds up this island, the Creator decreed that the earth, too, is to be known as our grandmother. He, thereafter, continued to create everything else in the universe and ordered it into a complete, harmonious, interdependent but delicately balanced ecosystem.[82]

The gods and the spirits of the Sacred Mountains created *Man. He was made of all rains, springs, rivers, ponds, black clouds, and sky. His feet are made of earth and his legs of lightning. White shell forms his knees, and his body is white and yellow corn; his flesh is of daybreak, his hair darkness; his eyes are of the sun. White corn forms his teeth, black corn his eyebrows, and red coral beads his nose. His tears are of rain, his tongue of straight lightning, and his voice of thunder. His heart is obsidian; the little whirlwind keeps his nerves in motion, and his movement is the air. The name of this new kind of being was "Created from Everything."*

Navajo origin legend[83]

The Keepers of the Wisdom in Native American cultures are wholly aware of the illusory character of the cosmos. Black Elk, a holy man of the Oglala Sioux Nation, tells of his vision of the real world, "the shape of all shapes."

I SAW MORE THAN I CAN TELL and I understood more than I saw; for I was seeing in a sacred manner the shapes of all things in the spirit, and the shape of all shapes as they must live together like one being. . . . Crazy Horse dreamed and went into the world where there is nothing but the spirits of all things. That is the real world that is behind this one, and everything we see here is something like a shadow from that world. . . .

I knew the real was yonder and the darkened dream
of it was here.[84]

*The earth was once a human being; Old-One made her
out of a woman. "You will be the Mother of all people,"
he said.*

*Earth is alive yet, but she has been changed. The soil
is her flesh; the rocks are her bones; the wind is her breath;
trees and grass are her hair. She lives spread out, and we
live on her. When she moves, we have an earthquake.*

*After changing her to earth, Old-One took some of
her flesh and rolled it into balls, as people do with mud or
clay. These balls Old-One made into the beings of the early
world. They were the ancients. They were people, and yet
they were at the same time animals.*

*In form, some of them were like animals; some were
more like people. Some could fly like birds; others could
swim like fishes. In some ways the land creatures acted like
animals. All had the gift of speech. They had greater powers and were more cunning than either animals or people.
And yet they were very stupid in some ways. They knew
that they had to hunt in order to live, but they did not
know which beings were deer and which were people.
They thought people were deer and often ate them.*

*Some people lived on the earth at that time. They
were like the Indians of today except that they were ignorant. Deer also were on the earth at that time. They were
real animals then too. They were never people or ancient
animal people, as were the ancestors of most animals.
Some people say that elk, antelope, and buffalo also were
always animals, to be hunted as deer are hunted. Others
tell stories about them as if they were ancients or half-
human beings.*

*The last balls of mud Old-One made were almost all
alike and were different from the first ones he made. He
rolled them over and over. He shaped them like Indians.
He blew on them and they became alive. Old-One called*

them men. *They were Indians, but they were very ignorant. They did not know how to do thngs. They were the most helpless of all creatures Old-One made. Some of the animal people preyed on them and ate them.*

Old-One made both male and female people and animals, so that they might breed and multiply. Thus all living things came from earth. When we look around, we see everywhere parts of our Mother.

Okanogan creation of the
animal people[85]

The day was bright when I went into the planted field and *alone I wandered in the planted field and it was the time of the second hoeing.*

Suddenly a damsel appeared and threw her arms around my neck and as she held me she spoke, saying,

> *"When you leave this earth for the new world above it is our wish to follow you."*

I looked for the damsel but saw only the long leaves of corn twining about my shoulders. And then I understood that it was the Spirit of the Corn who had spoken, she the sustainer of life.

So I replied,

> *"O Spirit of the Corn do not follow me but abide on the earth, be strong and faithful to your purpose. Ever endure and do not fail the children of women. It is not time for you to follow for Gai'wiio' (the Good Message) is but in its beginning."*

Eniaiehuk. (It was that way.)

HANDSOME LAKE *(1735–1815),
Seneca prophet*[86]

In a speech entitled "Justice, Peace, and the Integrity of Creation," given to the World Council of Churches in Seoul, Korea, in 1991, George Tinker, an Osage-Lutheran scholar, addressed Native American notions of respect and reciprocity as necessary values to assist in the "fulfill[ment] of our responsibility as part of the created whole."[87] They are indispensable, he declared, to sustaining balance and interdependence in the world. Appropriate attitudes, he said, are essential to a harmonious and just cosmos.

AMERICAN INDIANS and other indigenous peoples have a long-standing confidence that they have much to teach Europeans and North Americans about the world and human relationships in the world. They are confident in the spiritual foundations of their insights, confident that those foundations can become a source of healing and reconciliation for all creation. A couple of simple examples come from an Indian perspective.

My Indian ancestors had a relationship with God as Creator that was healthy and responsible long before they knew of or confessed the gospel of Jesus Christ. This relationship began with the recognition of the Other as Creator, the creative force behind all things that exist, and long predated the coming of the missionaries.

In all that they did, our Indian ancestors acknowledged the goodness of the Creator and of all creation, including themselves. That was the point of the stories, the focus of their prayers, and the purpose of the ceremonies. They recognized the balance and harmony that characterized all of the created universe: Winter and summer were held in balance with one another. So also were hunting and planting, sky and earth, hot and cold, sun and moon, female and male, women and men. Our ancestors recognized all this as good, just as God does at the end of the sixth day (Genesis 1:31).

All American Indian spiritual insight, hence Indian theology, begins with creation, and this is reflected in the basic liturgical posture of Indians in many North American Indian tribes. Our prayers are most often said with the community assembled into some form of circle. In fact, the circle is a key symbol for self-understanding in these tribes, representing the whole of the universe and our part in it.

We see ourselves as co-equal participants in the circle, standing neither above nor below anything else in God's creation. There is no hierarchy in our cultural context, even of species, because the circle has no beginning or ending. All the createds participate together, each in their own way, to preserve the wholeness of the circle.

When a group of Indians form a circle to pray, all know that the prayers have already begun with the representation of a circle. No words have yet been spoken and in some ceremonies no words need be spoken, but the intentional physicality of our formation has already expressed our prayer and deep concern for the wholeness of all of God's creation.

The Lakota and Dakota peoples have a phrase used in all their prayers that aptly illustrates the Native American sense of the centrality of creation. The phrase, *Mitakuye oyasin,* "For all my relations," functions somewhat like the word "Amen" in European and American Christianity. As such, it is used to end every prayer, and often it is in itself a whole prayer, being the only phrase spoken.

Like most native symbols, *Mitakuye oyasin* is polyvalent in its meaning. Certainly, one is praying for one's close kin—aunts, cousins, children, grandparents. And "relations" can be understood as tribal members or even all Indian people.

At the same time, the phrase includes all human beings, all two-leggeds as relatives of one another, and the ever expanding circle does not stop there. Every Lakota who prays this prayer knows that our relatives necessarily include the four-leggeds, the wingeds, and all the living-moving things on Mother Earth. One Lakota teacher has suggested that a better translation of *Mitakuye oyasin* would read: "For all the above-me and below-me and around-me things: That is for all my relations." . . .

The Indian understanding of creation as sacred, of Mother Earth as the source of all life, goes far beyond the notion of such Western counterinstitutions as Sierra Club or Greenpeace. It embraces far more than concern for harp seals or a couple of ice-bound whales. It embraces all of life, from trees and rocks to international relations. And this knowledge informs all of the community's activity, from hunting to dancing and even to writing grant proposals or administering government agencies.

It especially concerns itself with the way we all live

together. Perforce, it has to do with issues of justice and fairness, and ultimately with peace.

Indian peoples have experienced and continue to experience endless oppression as a result of what some would call the barbaric invasion of America. And we certainly suspect that the oppression we have experienced is ultimately linked to the way the immigrants pray and how they understand creation and their relationship to creation and Creator.

Moreover, we suspect that the greed which motivated the displacement of all indigenous peoples from their lands of spiritual rootedness is the same greed that threatens the destiny of the Earth and the continued oppression of so many peoples. Whether it is the stories the immigrants tell or the theologies they develop to interpret those stories, something appears wrong to Indian people.

But not only do Indians continue to tell the stories, sing the songs, speak the prayers, and perform the ceremonies that root themselves deeply in Mother Earth, they are actually audacious enough to think that their stories and their ways of reverencing creation will some day win over the immigrants and transform them. Optimism and enduring patience seem to run in the life blood of Native American peoples.

Mitakuye oyasin! For all my relatives.[88]

Wisdom of Nature calls at all seasons,
When will you learn from her instruction,
Understanding speaks aloud and gives sound reasons,
When will you listen, hear and take discretion.

At the entrance of the forests wisdom hails,
At the entrance of the prairies she is at hand,
At the heights beside the mountain trails,
And in the valleys she takes her stand.

Stoney beliefs[89]

Chinook Invocation

We call upon the earth, our planet home, with its beautiful depths and soaring heights, its vitality and abundance of life, and together we ask that it

Teach us, and show us the Way.

We call upon the mountains, the Cascades and the Olympics, the high green valleys and meadows filled with wild flowers, the snows that never melt, the summits of intense silence, and we ask that they

Teach us, and show us the Way.

We call upon the waters that rim the earth, horizon to horizon, that flow in our rivers and streams, that fall upon our gardens and fields and we ask that they

Teach us, and show us the Way.

We call upon the land which grows our food, the nurturing soil, the fertile fields, the abundant gardens and orchards, and we ask that they

Teach us, and show us the Way.

We call upon the forests, the great trees reaching strongly to the sky with earth in their roots and the heavens in their branches, the fir and the pine and the cedar, and we ask them to

Teach us, and show us the Way.

We call upon the creatures of the fields and forests and the seas, our brothers and sisters the wolves and deer, the eagle and dove, the great whales and the dolphin, the beautiful Orca and salmon who share our Northwest home, and we ask them to

Teach us, and show us the Way.

We call upon all those who have lived on this earth, our ancestors and our friends, who dreamed the best for future generations, and upon whose lives our lives are built, and with thanksgiving, we call upon them to

Teach us, and show us the Way.

And lastly, we call upon all that we hold most sacred, the presence and power of the Great Spirit of love and truth which flows through all the Universe . . . to be with us to

Teach us, and show us the Way.[90]

So in the form of these Sacred Mountains was our Mother made for us. Blanca Peak is our Mother. . . . In accordance with it we live. In the midst of these four Sacred Mountains that were placed, there we live. With that, we who are The People are the heart of the world.

Navajo origin legend[91]

*There are whole weeks
when I dream of mountains
sometimes climbing them
sometimes being the mountain
being climbed. . . .*

JOSEPH BRUCHAC,
*Abenaki poet, teacher,
novelist and wrestler*[92]

Eunice Carney, *Dance Boots,* ca. 1986. Kutchin Athapascan; Alaska. Mrs. Carney says of her work with moosehide and glass beads, "We Athapascans yet do floral designs with stems and hair-stems done in white beads. The Indians called these mouse tracks and the five-petaled flowers they called dog paws . . . what an array of beautiful footwear when they did their Indian dances."

"LOOK TO THE MOUNTAINTOP"

In his essay "Look to the Mountaintop," Tewa scholar and poet Alphonso Ortiz describes widespread notions shared by most Native Americans of the Southwest about tribal space and place of origins. "We have a complex mosaic of overlapping tribal worlds defined by mountains," writes Ortiz, adding it "is the belief that human life began, on a plant analogy, within the earth, usually beneath a lake or deep in a canyon."[93] According to Ortiz, "the undulating rhythms of nature govern . . . [the] whole [of Pueblo] existence from the timing and order of ritual dramas to the planning of economic activities."[94] Nothing is inconsequential and everything—animate and inanimate—has its proper place in the universe.

The locus of mountains in the human psyche as beams of revelation and knowledge is a distinctive feature of Native American reality.

[M]OUNTAINS ARE MORE, much more, than boundary markers defining the tribal space within which a people lives and carries on most of its meaningful, purposeful activities. The Pueblo peoples, for instance, believe that the four sacred mountains are pillars which hold up the sky and which divide the world into quarters. As such they are imbued with a high aura of mystery and sanctity. And this sacred meaning transcends all other meanings and functions. The Apaches, the most recent mountain dwellers among all southwestern Indians, believe that mountains are alive and the homes of supernaturals called "mountain people." They further believe that mountains are protectors from illness as well as external enemies, that they are the source of the powers of shamans as well as teachers of songs and other sacred knowledge to ordinary humans, and that finally, mountains are defenders as well as definers of tribal territory. . . .

The Pima, a desert people occupying the great valley of the Gila and Salt Rivers in Arizona, stress, in addition, the harmful potential of the high mountains for those who have not ritually purified themselves prior to embarking on expeditions to these places and for those who stay too long. Mountain air, they assert, will cause a person's hair to turn white and make him age prematurely. Mountains will also cause one to have bad dreams and lose his strength. In Pima tradition the high mountains are not places where the young or ritually ignorant may safely trespass, and those who must go into the mountains must purify themselves ritually before and after each journey. At that they may stay only long enough to carry out a given task.

Both the Pima and their Yuman-speaking neighbors, the Maricopa, Quechan, and Mojave, believe further that specific mountains and other high places are the homes of individual, named, supernatural teachers who may transport them there on dream journeys to give them specific kinds of knowledge and teach them specific skills. . . .

The Pueblos and other farming Indians explicitly recognize, in addition, that mountains are also the sources of precious moisture and other life-sustaining blessings which may be appealed to and tapped by those who are eligible and who undergo ritual preparations. . . . Among many of the Pueblos only the medicine men are eligible to ascend to the very summits of the sacred mountains, and then only at dawn after they have shorn all their clothing and spent a whole night at the base praying and otherwise purifying themselves. The idea involved here—and it is one profoundly revealing of the meaning of sacred mountains to the Pueblo people—is that one may approach the pure sacra or divinity represented by the mountaintop only after first attaining a state as close to pure innocence and purity as possible. . . . These or similar conceptions are found all over aboriginal North America, wherever there are high places to be contemplated and climbed.

It is by now anticlimactic to say that sacred mountains may not be owned or fought over; they can belong to no one, so they cannot be subjects of dispute. *Tsikomo,* which is an eastern sacred mountain of the Navajo, was once the destination of regular pilgrimages by members of this tribe as well as by their enemies the Tewa. Yet the Tewa say that this is the one place they would never fight with the Navajo if they encountered them, however tempted they might be. And they quickly add that the Navajo felt the same way. . . .

One might generalize by saying that mountains and other sacred high places are alternately symbols and metaphors of and for the Indian's most exalted yearnings and accomplishments, as well as his deepest fears. Throughout the Southwest . . . mountains are sacred sources of knowledge and life-sustaining blessings, the homes of the gods, definers and protectors of group space, dangerous for those uninitiated and unprepared, and not subject to claims of ownership or dispute by any people.[95]

The people walk over me.
The old men all say to me, I am beautiful. . . .

Navajo Chant of the Beautiful
Mountains of the East and West[96]

Some day the Great Chief Above will overturn the mountains and the rocks. Then the spirits that once lived in the bones buried there will go back into them. At present those spirits live in the tops of the mountains, watching their children on earth and waiting for the great change which is to come. The voices of these spirits can be heard in the mountains at all times. Mourners who wail for their dead hear spirit voices reply, and thus they know that their lost ones are always near.

Yakima tradition[97]

The people in the Tewa villages of Tesuque, Nambe, San Ildefonso, Santa Clara and San Juan in New Mexico live in a geographic and metaphysical landscape that stretches in all directions, six to be exact—the four cardinal directions, plus above and below. The point of intersection of the six directions is the *Center* of the cosmos (sometimes called the seventh direction), represented by the entire village or, symbolically, by the *sipapu,* an earth navel and the place of emergence. All space is therefore considered sacred. The Pueblos believe that there are three cosmic levels within the universe: the sky, earth and the underworld (the latter sometimes being subdivided). They have developed their way of life, their beliefs and their ceremonies in accordance with the patterns and events in these triune dimensions.

Pueblo dances, songs, poetry and ornamental designs reflect the physical, cultural and spiritual geography of the land. Each pueblo has its special sacred hills and peaks which hold their shrines and medicine plants. All the pueblos have sacred lakes of the four cardinal directions. The most progressive Tewa profess a deep love of homeland and tradition and they continue to practice their sacred ceremonies. Pueblo metaphysics sees the human life cycle "as a slowly revolving giant cylinder on which are imprinted the generations," writes Alphonso Ortiz, distinguished Tewa scholar and poet. "Thus to die in a pueblo," he continues," is not to become dead but to return to the only real life there is; one 'changes houses' and rejoins the ancestors, but one can come back later." Life is lived out in a "relentlessly interconnected universal whole," states Ortiz, where sacred knowledge is essential for control.[98]

Ortiz turns to a Tewa expression, *Pin pe obi,* "look to the mountaintop," for a guiding vision of life. He believes, he says, that life for a Tewa, "in the most basic, transcendental sense," is a journey in search of the meaning of these words.

A WISE ELDER among my people, the Tewa, frequently used the phrase *Pin pe obi,* "look to the mountaintop," while he was alive. I first heard it 25 years ago when I was seven years old, as I was practising for the first time to participate in relay races we run in the Pueblo country to give strength to the sun father as he journeys across the sky. I was at one end of the earth track which ran east to west, like the path of the sun. The old man, who was blind, called me to him and said: "Young one, as you run look to the mountaintop," and he pointed to *Tsikomo,* the western sacred mountain of the Tewa world, which loomed off in the distance. "Keep your gaze fixed on that mountain, and you will feel the miles melt beneath your feet. Do this and in time you will feel as if you can leap over bushes, trees, and even the river." I tried to understand what this last statement meant, but I was too young.

On another occasion a few days later, I asked him if I really could learn to leap over treetops. He smiled and said, "Whatever life's challenges you may face, remember always look to the mountaintop, for in so doing you look to greatness. Remember this, and let no problem, however great it may seem, discourage you nor let anything less than the mountaintop distract you. This is the one thought I want to leave with you. And in that dim coming time when we shall meet again, it shall be on the mountaintop." Again I wondered why he was telling me these words and what they meant. I did not have long to wonder why, for the following month, when the cornstalks were sturdy on the land, he died quietly in his sleep having seen eighty-seven summers. . . .

In accordance with our beliefs, the ancestors were waiting for him at the edge of the village that day he died, waiting to take him on a final four-day journey to the four sacred mountains of the Tewa world. . . .

I have come to understand that this old Tewa saw the whole of life as consisting of the dual quest for wisdom and for divinity, and he anchored his aspirations and his vision firmly onto that greatest, most immovable, and most enduring of the earth's natural monuments. He recognized clearly that to live is simply to seek knowledge and fulfillment on the one hand, and redemption on the other. That is all. And these twin quests proceed apace, along the way to the mountaintop, one of the most ancient of all metaphorical journeys of mankind. They are the same journey. He recognized, too, that a man has problems in this life only when he forgets that these two quests must be kept in balance and harmony, when he sacrifices the search for divinity for the sake of knowledge. . . .

For my people generally, the phrase *pin pe obi,* look to the mountaintop, also means look to the north, for *pin* means both north and mountain, and look to the north means look to the beginning of the beginning of all beginnings, for we began life in the north. So you see, all paths rejoin in the end, and the end again becomes the beginning. . . .

To be alive and to be a son or daughter of the mountains and the deep canyons, then, is to be the living embodiment of a tradition which extends from deep within the good earth to the mountaintops where the earth meets the sky. It is to be the repository of a spiritual heritage which draws from each of these, and from everything between. It is to be a thousand years old, a part of the beginning. . . .

To be a child of the mountains and deep canyons is also to need, periodically, to return from wherever one may be, to re-enact the odyssey which renews the ties to a place and a time. This odyssey may take many forms. It may be to go to a Snake Dance, a Squaw Dance, a Bear Dance, or a Corn Dance. It may be to stand on the rim of Canyon de Chelly at sunrise, watching creation unfold anew with the changing of colors as the light moves down through the many layers of the far canyon wall. It may be to peer deep within this innermost being of the remembered earth at sundown to watch the lights and the colors reverse themselves, as the earth prepares to sleep, enshrouded in darkness. It may be to sit on the shore of a mountain lake to watch for *Poseyemu,* the Creator, to arise as mist to mediate, as he has always done, between the heaven and the earth. It may be something else, but always it is an odyssey, and always it renews. To those without roots of their own on this land, the odyssey beckons more insistently in our time than ever before.[99]

The Stoney way of life begins with reverence for the Great Spirit and gratitude for the sacred mountains created by Him for Himself and His children. In the mountains we find many truths. As we cast our eyes toward them they seem to be different each day, and yet we know that they have always been the same, strong and unchanging. . . . The man who learns well the intricate pattern of nature will live a good life and a useful one to his people.

CHIEF JOHN SNOW,
Stoney teacher and writer [100]

She continued walking down the trail until she came to Patu, the mountain. He spoke to her. "Look at me very closely. This is the way I am, like a design. The outlines of my peaks are designs." She looked at his peaks and thought, "These peaks would be beautiful on my basket."

Legend of the First Cedar Basket[101]

These Mountains Are Our Sacred Places is an autobiographical account of Chief John Snow's people, the Stoneys, who are native to the Saskatchewan River country in what is presently known as Southern Alberta in Canada. He explains the unending cycle of connectedness that links the natural world with all aspects of Stoney society—political, economic, social, religious and metaphysical—and permeates all Stoney reasoning. "Our philosophy of life sees the Great Spirit's creation as a whole piece," points out Snow.[102] The metaphorical significance of mountains as illimitable and unalterable sources of ancient truth and prophecy is the motivating motif in Stoney life in Chief John Snow's illumined recounting of his people's traditions. "A man must seek to emulate the mountains," writes Snow, "[to be] strong in body and will and resolve, unchanging in his faith, yet flexible in his relations with his fellow men, compassionate with those who suffer, relentless with those who would stupidly abuse their authority, warm with his brothers and sisters."[103]

LONG AGO MY ANCESTORS used to go to the mountain tops to pray. They were a deeply religious, sincere, and tradition-oriented people who followed, observed, and upheld the teachings, customs, and beliefs of our forefathers, respected the creations of the Great Spirit, and lived in harmony with nature. They were Stoneys—members of the Great Sioux Nation who spoke a dialect of the Nakota [sic] branch of the Siouan language family. Today we, their descendants, speak the same tongue. . . .

In order to understand the vital importance the mountains had—and still have—to my people, it is necessary to know something of our way of life before the coming of the whiteman. It is not enough to say the mountains were the Stoneys' traditional place of prayer because our life was not a fragmented one with a compartment for religion. Rather, our life was one in which religion (and reverence for nature, which revealed religious truth) was woven throughout all parts of the social structure and observed in conjunction with every activity. Our forefathers were a proud people because they knew they had been selected by the Creator to receive a precious gift of special understanding and they have handed that gift down to us as a sacred trust. . . .

The eagle held a very sacred place in our society. Ceremonies, prayers and fasting took place and visions had to appear before an eagle was killed. The hunters were taught that the eagle is a sacred messenger created by the Great Spirit. Therefore, no Indian hunter was to kill the eagle unless the feathers were required for a ceremonial occasion. So even the feathers of the birds were used in our way of life.

Truly, our people respected the Creator's beings, and as a result, in our long history of dominance on this continent, none of the animals we hunted ever became extinct. . . .

Human kindness was imprinted in our hearts, and the law of the Great Spirit, the Creator, was the only law that we observed. Our society was built around the concept that the Creator is the Supreme Being, the Great Mystery; recognizing Him as the One who provides all things was the very first step and beginning of our tribal society. The recognition of the Creator in all of life was essential for our survival here on earth and in the hereafter.

In this society there was no need to convince anyone that there was a Creator who made all things. . . . [T]he little crocus reminded us that there was a second life after death. Along the Rocky Mountain foothills the crocus is the first wild flower to blossom in the spring. It blooms beautifully for a while, then fades away. But in the autumn, when all the summer flowers have bloomed and gone, the little crocus comes out again. It appears and fades once more, as though to say: "So long for this summer, but I'll be the first one to return next spring." The appearance of the crocus twice in one summer revealed to us that there is more than one life.

So . . . from nature did my people garner much symbolism, which they used in formulating their principles, theories, philosophies and religion. . . . [A]ll the Stoney people were continually searching for the truth by observing the universe around them. The most sacred search was a special religious journey into the rugged mountains, seeking wisdom and divine guidance. This was known as the vision quest, a tradition handed down through the centuries and practised by us as a means of approaching the Great Spirit. If the seekers were favoured, the Great Spirit would deliver a revelation and thus give direction and guidance to our tribe.

Sacred ceremonies and rituals were observed by these seekers of truth before they journeyed into the rugged mountainous country. In this preparation they were guided and aided by many members of the tribe who spent much time fasting and praying in the sweat lodge. . . .

There are lessons hidden in creation that we must learn in order to live a good life and walk the straight path. Behind these lessons and teachings is the Creator. These things can only be understood through the Great Spirit.

Century after century the rugged Rocky Mountains sat there in majesty, and nature seemed to say: "Your thoughts must be as firm as these mountains, if you are to walk the straight path. Your patience and kindness must be as solid as these mountains, if you are to acquire understanding and wisdom."

The old Stoney medicine man [*Iktumni,* keeper of the medicine, teacher and prophet] had said: "You must continue to go to the sacred mountains. You must fast and pray for many days and nights, and perchance you will see a vision upon the mountains." Before he went to the beautiful land of the spirits beyond the sunset, the old man with a century of experience spoke these words: "You must search and search and you will find ancient truths and wisdom that shall guide you in the future." He continued: "My grandfathers told me these things when I was just a little boy and in my youth it was told to me over and over again by the campfire and in the tribal encampment, so it has been imprinted in my heart ever since that time."

And the medicine man stated further: "My grandchildren, you must search and continue to search in order to find them. When a revelation is open to you, you will become a special person to our tribe. It may be that you will gain courage and bravery and become a hero in many battles. It may be that you will be given understanding and wisdom and become a Chief amongst Chiefs. It may be that you will become a great hunter, knowing the paths and circling of the four winds, knowing where the animals roam and birds migrate at the seasons appointed for them by the Creator. It may be that you will be given the gift of prophecy, see into the future, and will advise and guide your people along the straight path."

Upon these lofty heights, the Great Spirit revealed many things to us. Some of my people received powers to heal. They could heal the physical body with herbs, roots, leaves, plants, and mineral spring waters. They could also heal the broken and weary soul with unseen spiritual powers. Others received powers over the weather. These gifted religious men and women could call for a great storm or calm the weather; they could call on the winds, rain, hail, snow, or sleet, and they would come. From these mountain-top experiences my fellow tribesmen and women were given unique tasks to perform to help the tribe prepare for things to come.

Therefore the Rocky Mountains are precious and sacred to us. We knew every trail and mountain pass in this area. We had special ceremonial and religious areas in the mountains. In the olden days some of the neighbouring tribes called us the "People of the Shining Mountains." These mountains are our temples, our sanctuaries, and our resting places. They are a place of hope, a place of vision, a place of refuge, a very special and holy place where the Great Spirit speaks with us. *Therefore, these mountains are our sacred places.*[104]

My words are tied in one
With the great mountains,
With the great rocks,
With the great trees,
In one with my body
And my heart.
Do you all help me
With supernatural power,
And you, Day
And you, Night!
All of you see me
One with this world!

Yokuts prayer[105]

I have always been a poor man. I do not know a single song.

Navajo interviewee, 1938[106]

The Sky blesses me, the Earth blesses me;
Up in the Skies I cause to dance the Spirits;
On the Earth, the people I cause to dance.

Cree round dance song[107]

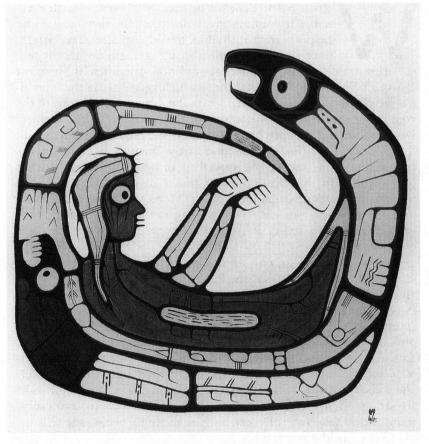

Roy Thomas (Ojibwa), *Serpent Man*, 1975. Ojibwa painter Roy Thomas portrays a human being inside the "womb of challenge" grappling with life's puzzles and obstacles and struggling to reach for solutions. Stretching is what it's about, says Thomas. "Challenges make you strong; they give you faith." The serpent (and there are two here) is a symbol of Creation, according to Anishnawbe teaching.

"SONGS KEEP THE WORLD GOING RIGHT"

When a society depends on memory," writes David Riesman, "it employs every device of the demagogue and the poet: rhyme, rhythm, melody, structure, repetition. Since we tend to remember best things most deeply felt, the memorable words in an oral tradition are often those most charged with group feeling and those which keep alive in the individual the childhood sense of dependence, the terrors and elations of the young and something of their awe for the old."[108] The tribal elders were and are the memory banks of experience, social custom and all that is holy. They, in fact, function as the *memory* of the tribe. As technicians of the sacred and specialists in mnemonics and in what one might term the recollection of things to come, they hold the integrity of the entire community intact. Moreover, virtually everyone in indigenous societies has some training in the oral tradition; each individual is, in a sense, a living repository of tribal wisdom and mythology.

In *The Autobiography of a Papago Woman*, Ruth Underhill states that "making songs is the Papago achievement *par excellence,* all outward acts being considered merely as a preparation for it. . . . [S]ong making is a *sine qua non* for success in life. . . . [It] is the spiritual crown conferred on one who has already achieved in the physical world."[109] Maria Chona, the ninety-year-old speaker, daughter of the former governor of Mesquite Root (an ancient Papago village, now abandoned) calls her father a great song-maker. She adds, "You see, I come of a singing family. It is natural for us to see strange things and to make songs. . . . [O]ur way to cure everything and to take care of everything, is to sing." Songs, she tells us, "keep the world going right."[110]

The impact of the spoken or sung word—its emotional force, its power to both shatter and bring alive energies of disparate natures, its intense beauty—is unforgettably conveyed in the following passage from Chona's autobiography:

Early in the morning, in the month of Pleasant Cold, when we had all slept in the house to keep warm, we would wake in the dark to hear my father speaking.

"Open your ears, for I am telling you a good thing. Wake up and listen. Open your ears. Let my words enter them." He spoke in a low voice, so quiet in the dark. Always our fathers spoke to us like that, so low that you thought you were dreaming. . . .

It was good at cactus camp. When my father lay down to sleep at night he would sing songs about the cactus liquor. And we could hear songs in my uncle's camp across the hill. Everybody sang. We felt as if a beautiful thing was coming. Because the rain was coming and the dancing and the songs.

> *Where on Quijotoa Mountain a cloud stands*
> *There my heart stands with it.*
> *Where the mountain trembles with the thunder*
> *My heart trembles with it.*

That was what they sang. When I sing that song yet it makes me dance. Then the little rains began to come. . . .

The men from all the villages met at Basket Cap Mountain, and there my father made them speeches, sitting with his arms folded and talking low as all great men do. Then they sang the war songs:

> *Oh, bitter wind, keep blowing*
> *That therewith my enemy*
> *Staggering forward*
> *Shall fall.*
>
> *Oh, bitter wind, keep blowing*
> *That therewith my enemy*
> *Staggering sideways*
> *Shall fall.*

Many, many songs they sang but I, a woman, cannot tell you all. I know that they made the enemy blind and dizzy with their singing and that they told the gopher to gnaw their arrows. And I know that they called on our dead warriors who have turned into owls and live in

Apache country to come and tell them where the enemy were. Facing the enemy they sat, while they sang, that they might bring darkness upon him. . . .

On winter nights, when we had finished our gruel or rabbit stew and lay back on our mats, my brothers would say to him: "My father tell us something."

My father would lie quietly upon his mat with my mother beside him and the baby between them. At last he would start slowly to tell us about how the world began. . . . Our story about the world is full of songs, and when the neighbors heard my father singing they would open our door and step in over the high threshold. Family by family they came, and we made a big fire and kept the door shut against the cold night. When my father finished a sentence we would all say the last word after him. If anyone went to sleep he would stop. He would not speak any more. But we did not go to sleep.[111]

Every person has a song to sing when the time comes to leave the earth. When a person is departing he must sing that song and continue to sing on his journey to the other world. They will do this who have repented and who believe in Gai'wiio' (the Good Message). So they said and he said. Eniaiehuk (It was that way).

HANDSOME LAKE (1735–1815),
Seneca prophet[112]

In 1923, Orpingalik, a great Netsilik hunter, famous shaman and poet, explained how songs are born in the human mind and their centrality in the lives of the Netsilingmiut peoples. "All my being is song," he began, "and I sing as I draw breath."[113] He continued:

SONGS ARE THOUGHTS, sung out with the breath when people are moved by great forces and ordinary speech no longer suffices.

Man is moved just like the ice floe sailing here and there out in the current. His thoughts are driven by a flowing force when he feels joy, when he feels sorrow. Thoughts can wash over him like a flood, making his breath come in gasps, and his heart throb. Something, like an abatement in the weather, will keep him thawed up.

And then it will happen that we, who always think we are small, will feel still smaller. And we will fear to use words. But it will happen that the words we need will come of themselves. When the words we want to use shoot up of themselves—we get a new song.[114]

On certain occasions, the Kwakiutl have reason to summon to their home a song-maker ("man of understanding") and a "lyricist" or "word-passer." The song-maker's task is musical composition and conducting singers. The word-passer puts words to the music, and acts as prompter to the singers. These two go into the woods, sometimes accompanied by a novice composer (referred to as "sitting-close-beside-the-head"). What follows is an intriguing account of the very act of musical creation, as related to ethnologist E. S. Curtis by a Kwakiutl Indian informant in 1915.

THE SONG-MAKER draws inspiration chiefly from the sounds of running or dropping water, and from the notes of birds. Sitting beside a rill of falling water, he listens intently, catches the music, and hums it to himself, using not words but the vocables *hamamama*. This is his theme. Then he carries the theme further, making variations, and at last he adds a finale which he calls the "tail." After a while he goes to the word-passer, constantly humming the tune, and the word-passer, catching the air, joins in, and then sets a single word to it. This is called "tying the song," so that it may not "drift away" like an unmoored canoe. Then gradually other words are added, until the song is complete. The novice sits a little apart from the master, and if he "finds" a melody, he "carries" it at once to the song-maker, who quickly catches the theme and proceeds to develop it. Many songs are obtained from the robin, some from a waterfowl which whistles before diving, and from other birds. An informant has seen a song-maker, after employing various themes, coil a rope and then compose a song representing it. On a certain occasion when the singers were practicing new songs in the woods, the song-maker lacked one to complete the number, and he asked the others if they had a song. The other composers present said they had none. One of them looked across at a visiting woman *nãkati* [song-maker] and said to the presiding song-maker, "I will ask her." She heard the phrase, caught the inflection of the rising and falling syllables, and began to sing *hamamama*. As the sound left her lips, those on the opposite side of the circle heard it and at once began to hum, and together they composed the necessary song. This manner of catching a melody is called "scooping it up in the hands."[115]

My shining horns.

A Chippewa Song of the Deer[116]

For we are the stars. For we sing.
For we sing with our light.
For we are birds made of fire.
For we spread our wings over the sky.
Our light is a voice.
We cut a road for the soul
for its journey through death.
For three of our number are hunters.
For these three hunt a bear.
For there never yet was a time
when these three didn't hunt.
For we face the hills with disdain.
This is the song of the stars.

"Song of the Stars,"
Passamaquoddy[117]

Every shaman has his or her own particular song which is sung when calling up helping spirits. This was the song of Uvavnuk, an Iglulik woman shaman, celebrating the joy of being moved by Nature. The purity and subtlety of the song defies full understanding by anyone unfamiliar with the Arctic landscape and the intensity of feeling that it evokes.

> The great sea
> Has sent me adrift
> It moves me
> As the weed in a great river
> Earth and the great weather
> Move me
> Have carried me away
> And move my inward parts with joy.[118]

The Omaha belief that each species of flower has its own song which expresses its particular nature is illustrated here in the "Song of the Twin-flower." The plant is called "twin-flower" because it usually bears just two flowering scapes. It is the first flower to bloom in the spring, often before the snow has melted, for which reason it is considered an "elder." When ripe, it exhibits a bushy white head, which accounts for the Omaha conviction that it is "wise." This is the song it sings:

> I wish to encourage the children
> Of other flower nations now appearing
> All over the face of the earth;
> So while they awaken from sleeping
> And come up from the heart of the earth
> I am standing here old and gray-headed.[119]

Sometimes I hear it [the earth] talking. The light of the sunflower was one language, but there are others, more audible. Once, in the redwood forest, I heard a beat, something like a drum or heart coming from the ground and trees and wind. That underground current stirred a kind of knowing inside me, a kinship and longing, a dream

barely remembered that disappeared back to the body. . . .
Walking, I can almost hear the redwoods beating. . . .
Walking, I am listening to a deeper way. Suddenly all
my ancestors are behind me. Be still, they say. Watch and
listen. You are the result of the love of thousands.

LINDA HOGAN,
Chickasaw poet and writer[120]

It is lovely indeed, it is lovely indeed.
I, I am the spirit within the earth . . .
The feet of the earth are my feet . . .
The legs of the earth are my legs . . .
The bodily strength of the earth is my bodily
strength . . .
The thoughts of the earth are my thoughts . . .
The voice of the earth is my voice . . .
The feather of the earth is my feather . . .
All that belongs to the earth belongs to me . . .
All that surrounds the earth surrounds me . . .
I, I am the sacred words of the earth . . .
It is lovely indeed, it is lovely indeed.

Song of the Earth Spirit,
Navajo origin legend[121]

The solid sky,
the cloudy sky,
the good sky,
the straight sky,
The earth produces herbs.
The herbs cause us to live.
They cause long life.
They cause us to be happy.

The good life,
May it prevail with the air.
May it increase.
May it be straight to the end.

Sweet Medicine's earth is good.
Sweet Medicine's earth is completed.
Sweet Medicine's earth follows the eternal ways.
Sweet Medicine's earth is washed and flows.

Cheyenne song[122]

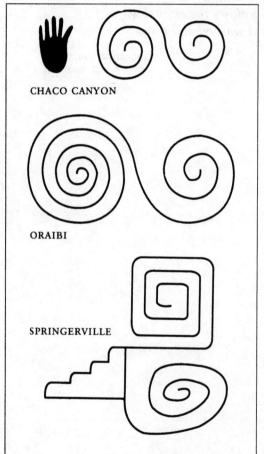

CHACO CANYON

ORAIBI

SPRINGERVILLE

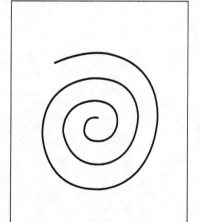

With all things, the Creeks were told, there must be a ceremony or ritual . . .

LOUIS LITTLECOON OLIVER [123]

A strict law bids us dance.

Kwakiutl teaching [124]

We do not believe our religion, we dance it!

Native American belief [125]

The object of all the ceremonies is to bring down the spirits from above, even their ancestors.

Li Chi *(Book of Rites)* [126]

TOP: The labyrinth embodies the image of Mother Earth for the Hopi. The symbol is also known as *Tapu'at,* Mother and Child. It expresses the meaning of Emergence of the Hopi people. In the *Book of the Hopi* it is written that "all the lines and passages within the maze form the universal plan of the Creator which man must follow on his Road of Life." FAR LEFT: The Hopi Migration Symbol. The Hopi clans' migrational track throughout America defined a four-directional spiral path from their point of Emergence "to the fourth world." These ancient symbols appear on rocks and pottery across the land. CENTER RIGHT: The Hump-back Flute Player, emblem of the Flute Clan, and a symbol of fertility and musical expression. BOTTOM RIGHT: The Great Coil, Mesa Verde, Colorado. A symbol of the Winds above the Square Tower House Ruin: "The great First Wind is the cyclone. He who travels around, but not the whirlwind. He is very great."

THE PRAYER OF CEREMONY

When asked why the rules of ceremony were of such urgent importance, Confucius replied, "It was by those rules that the ancient kings sought to represent the ways of Heaven and to regulate the feelings of men. Therefore he who neglects or violates them may be (spoken of) as dead, and he who observes them, as alive." [127] In "All My Relations," Linda Hogan, poet, writer and teacher of Chickasaw descent, addresses a larger world, most often unacknowledged, that makes itself known through ceremonial ritual. It includes, she says, "not just our own prayers and stories of what brought us to it," but also "the unspoken records of history, the mythic past, and all the other lives connected to ours, our family, nations, and all other creatures." [128] In this way, ceremony becomes a metaphor for the cosmos. It is the bond that holds us and "sets us back upright." [129] It is an event, whose closure is, in the luminous thought of Ms. Hogan, "as if skin contains land and birds." [130]

BY LATE AFTERNOON we are ready, one at a time, to enter the enclosure. The hot lava stones are placed inside. They remind us of earth's red and fiery core, and of the spark inside all life. After the flap, which serves as a door, is closed, water is poured over the stones and the hot steam rises around us. In a sweat lodge ceremony, the entire world is brought inside the enclosure. The soft odor of smoking cedar accompanies this arrival of everything. It is all called in. The animals come from the warm and sunny distances. Water from dark lakes is there. Wind. Young, lithe willow branches bent overhead remember their lives rooted in ground, the sun their leaves took in. They remember that minerals and water rose up their trunks, and birds nested in their leaves, and that planets turned above their brief, slender lives. The thunder clouds travel in from far regions of earth. Wind arrives from the four directions. It has moved through caves and breathed through our bodies. It is the same air elk have inhaled, air that passed through the lungs of a grizzly bear. The sky is there, with all the stars whose lights we see long after the stars themselves have gone back to nothing. It is a place grown intense and holy. It is a place of immense community and of humbled solitude; we sit together in our aloneness and speak, one at a time, our deepest language of need, hope, loss, and survival. We remember that all things are connected.

Remembering this is the purpose of the ceremony. It is part of a healing and restoration. It is the mending of a broken connection between us and the rest. The participants in a ceremony say the words, "All my relations," before and after we pray; those words create a relationship with other people, with animals, with the land. To have health it is necessary to keep all these relations in mind.

The intention of a ceremony is to put a person back together by restructuring the human mind. This reorganization is accomplished by a kind of inner map, a geography of the human spirit and the rest of the world. We make whole our broken off pieces of self and the world. Within ourselves, we bring together the fragments of our lives in a sacred act of renewal, and we reestablish our connections with others. The ceremony is a point of no return. It takes us toward the place of balance, our place in the community of all things. It is an event that sets us back upright. But it is not a finished thing. The real ceremony begins where the formal one ends, when we take up a new way, our minds and hearts filled with the vision of earth that holds us within it, in compassionate relationship to and with our world.

We speak. We sing. We swallow water and breathe smoke. By the end of the ceremony, it is as if skin contains land and birds. The places within us have become filled. As inside the enclosure of the lodge, the animals and ancestors move into the human body, into skin and blood. The land merges with us. The stones come to dwell inside the person. Gold rolling hills take up residence, their tall grasses blowing. The red light of canyons is there. The black skies of night that wheel above our heads come to live inside the skull. We who easily grow apart from the world are returned to the great store of life all around us and there is the deepest sense of being at home here in this intimate kinship. There is no real aloneness. There is solitude and the nurturing silence that is relationship with ourselves, but even then we are part of something larger.

After a sweat lodge ceremony, the enclosure is abandoned. . . . The prayer ties are placed in nearby trees. Some of the other people prepare to go to work, go home, or cook a dinner. We drive home. Everything returns to ordinary use. A spider weaves a web from one of the cottonwood poles to another. Crows sit inside the frame-work. It's evening. The crickets are singing. All my relations.[131]

Now let this be your ceremony when you wish to employ the medicine in a plant:

> *First offer tobacco. Then tell the plant in gentle words what you desire of it and pluck it from its roots. It is said in the upper world it is not right to take a plant for medicine without first talking to it. Let not one ever be taken without first speaking.*

So they said and he said. Eniaiehuk. (It was that way.)

HANDSOME LAKE,
Seneca Prophet[132]

An intimacy with the universe is invoked when an Omaha newborn is introduced to the cosmos, so that, in the words of physicist Brian Swimme, "the universe shivers with wonder in the depths of the human."[133] The ceremonial announcement of the coming forth of a new living being expresses the profound belief held by the Omaha in "the oneness of the universe through the bond of a common life-power that pervaded all things in nature, animate and inanimate."[134] The interdependence of all forms of life radiates throughout the ritual; so does gratitude to the teeming life of the world that is greeted.

The numinous invocation affirms the equal rights to life of all of earth's many children (other than humankind) and beseeches the powers of the heavens, the earth, and the in-between for the safety of the child from birth to old age. It is a grand metaphor for life's journey, pictured as an exacting road marked by four hills covering infancy, youth, adulthood and the evening of one's years. The entrancing supplication that follows brims with respect for the natural world. Alice C. Fletcher, who recorded it nearly a hundred years ago, writes that "it expresses the emotions of the human soul, touched with the love of off-spring, alone with the might of nature, and accompanied only by the living creatures whose friendliness must be sought if life is to be secure on its journey."[135] On the eighth day after birth, "The Introduction to the Cosmos of the Newborn" takes place and the priest *intones* the universe into alertness to the existence of a new life.

Ho! Ye Sun, Moon, Stars, all ye that
move in the heavens,
I bid you hear me!
Into your midst has come a new life.
Consent ye, I implore!
Make its path smooth, that it may reach
the brow of the first hill!

Ho! Ye Winds, Clouds, Rain, Mist, all ye
that move in the air,
I bid you hear me!
Into your midst has come a new life.
Consent ye, I implore!
Make its path smooth, that it may reach
the brow of the second hill!

Ho! Ye Hills, Valleys, Rivers, Lakes,
Trees, Grasses, all ye of the earth,
I bid you hear me!
Into your midst has come a new life.
Consent ye, I implore!
Make its path smooth, that it may reach
the brow of the third hill!

Ho! Ye Birds, great and small, that
fly in the air,
Ho! Ye Animals, great and small, that
dwell in the forest,

Ho! Ye Insects that creep among the
    grasses and burrow in the ground—
I bid you hear me!
Into your midst has come a new life.
    Consent ye, I implore!
Make its path smooth, that it may reach
    the brow of the fourth hill!

Ho! All ye of the heavens, all ye of
    the air, all ye of the earth:
I bid you all to hear me!
Into your midst has come a new life.
    Consent ye, I implore!
Make its path smooth—then shall it
    travel beyond the four hills.[136]

Men, animals, plants and spirits are intertransposable in a seemingly unbroken chain of being. A persistent relatedness determines every factor of the universe and casts its mandate upon every detail of living. Harmony is achievable when the natural laws are honored through the careful observance of ritual. When life is taken to sustain life, thanksgiving is offered and the hunter requests that his prey's great power be invested in himself. That custom is expressed in this Kwakiutl prayer to the slain black bear. The hunter sits down on the ground at the right-hand side of the bear and prays to it:

Thank you, friend, that you did not make me walk
    about in vain.
Now you have come to take mercy on me so that I
    obtain game, that I may inherit your power of
    getting easily with your hands the salmon that
    you catch.
Now I will press my right hand against your left
    hand
—says the man as he takes hold of the left paw of
    the bear. He says,
O friend, now we press together our working
    hands, that you may give over to me your
    power of getting everything easily with your
    hands, friend
—says he. Now it is done after this, for now he
    only skins the bear after this.[137]

[I]n the heyoka ceremony, everything is backwards, and it is planned that the people shall be made to feel jolly and happy first, so that it may be easier for the power to come to them. You have noticed that the truth comes into this world with two faces. One is sad with suffering, and the other laughs; but it is the same face, laughing or weeping. When people are already in despair, maybe the laughing face is better for them; and when they feel too good and are too sure of being safe, maybe the weeping face is better for them to see. And so I think that is what the heyoka ceremony is for.

BLACK ELK[138]

Soon after the sap begins to run, the Seneca people celebrate a "maple thanksgiving." They call the maple "the Chief of trees." The purpose of the ceremony is to thank all trees for their services to humankind and to ask for their benevolence in the year ahead. The following prayer is recited to the maple by a priest who sprinkles tobacco in a fire at the foot of the tree:

> TO THE TREE:
> *O partake of this incense,*
> *You the forests!*
> *We implore you*
> *To continue as before,*
> *The flowing waters of the maple.*
>
> TO THE CREATOR AND THE TREE:
> *It is the will of the Creator*
> *That a certain tree*
> *Should flow such water.*
> *Now may no accidents occur*
> *To children roaming in the forests.*
> *Now this day is yours*
> *May you enjoy it,—this day.*
>
> TO THE CREATOR:
> *We give thanks, oh God, to you,*
> *You who dwell in heaven.*

We have done our duty
You have seen us do it.
So it is done.[139]

The.sunflower root, eaten by the Thompson Indians of British Columbia, is considered a mysterious essence. As a result, women practice sexual continence while extracting or cooking the root. Men may not approach the oven while the root is being baked. A prayer is offered to the sunflower root by youths eating the first fruits of the season. Nonobservance of this ritual "would make the eater lazy and cause him to sleep long in the morning."[140]

> I INFORM THEE that I intend to eat thee. Mayest thou always help me to ascend, so that I may always be able to reach the tops of mountains, and may I never be clumsy! I ask this from thee, Sunflower-Root. Thou art the greatest of all in mystery.[141]

> *All along the Klamath River the baskets come out. We believe the baskets are alive and want to dance. That is why they were created, to help us fix the world.*

> JULIAN LANG,
> *Karuk tribal scholar,*
> *singer and dancer*[142]

The dance baskets of the Karuk, Hupa and Yurok of northern California are unique—cylindrical-shaped and nonutilitarian. They serve in the Jump Dance as conductors of physical and spiritual health to right the world. They are a life force, contributing to the energy of planetary renewal and assisting in balancing the great cosmic order.

Dance regalia serves a complementary function to dance baskets. It is "alive and feeling" and "cries to dance," relates Thomas Buckley. Native people say, "These feathers want to dance, so I'm going to let them go to Klamath" and "This headroll danced last year at

Hoopa."[143] Karuk tribal scholar, ceremonialist, author and artist Julian Lang describes the dynamic nature of the dance baskets, their "divine" origins, their contribution to collective illumination, and their crucial role in providing a foundation for Karuk, Hupa and Yurok cultural identities.

BY TODAY'S STANDARDS the task of weaving a basket must seem silly to some, compared to deep space exploration or the transmitting of data concerning the origin of the universe. After all, a basket consists of woven sticks, plaited together into containers. Some of us put our dirty clothes into a basket, but for the most part, basketry has fallen into disuse if not obsolescence. It seems the time has passed when basketry was marveled at for its utility and perfected design. In northwestern California, however, a uniquely-shaped, nonutilitarian basket is still essential to three local Indian tribes for conducting their ceremonies to "fix the world." Without the baskets the Hupa, Karuk, and Yurok would not be able to perform the highly important Jump Dance without solving extremely difficult problems and taking drastic measures.

I am a Karuk Indian and have held these dance baskets in my hands many times. Each possesses its own weight, shape, and danceability. Some of these baskets display the innovative mark of the artist, while others suggest strict adherence to traditional proportion and construction. Whatever the sensibility of the weaver, the baskets are known to the Karuk people as *vikapuhich;* the Yurok call them *e'gor;* the Hupa say *na'wech.* Their curious cylindrical shape suggests the feminine; their decoration, the sublime. These little baskets are found nowhere else in the world. Within our traditional culture and psyche, the baskets are like jewels.

In order for us to fully appreciate the role that baskets play in our ceremonies and life, it is necessary to look to our *pikva,* our stories, and also to the voices of our oldest generations. The stories give us a glimpse of the foundation of our cultural identity. When we saw the high regard in which the white man held the Bible, we translated it into our language as *apxantinihichpikva,* or "white man's myths."

One of many stories about basket weaving takes place

during the *pikvahahirak* ("myth-time-and-place"), when an Ikxaréeyav family (the Ikxaréeyav are the Spirit-beings of the *pikva* stories) lived in a good way until the father abandoned them in favor of a new wife, and their family life was disrupted. The jilted mother told the children they were going "a different way." They were going to be transformed. The father knew this was about to happen and returned to the house of his first wife, but it had already been abandoned. He caught up with his family on the hillside above the ranch and killed them in a fit of blind rage. Before dying, the wife cursed him, "You will be nothing once Human has arrived! Human will have nothing to do with you! We will be sitting in front of Human (at the annual World Renewal ceremonies). We will be beauty! The slain family then metamorphosed into the materials used to weave a basket: hazel, willow, bull pine, maidenhair fern, and woodwardia fern. Thus, basketry materials are to us not just natural fibres, but gifts of divine origin.

The three local tribes perform the Jump Dance as part of the ceremony to fix the world. This dance is a ten-day ceremony that is held to rid the earth of sickness and other potential natural catastrophes. It is solemn, ecstatic, and beautiful in its simplicity. The songs are slow and sonorous. Each song begins quietly but is repeated at a higher pitch and intensity as it continues. In steady cadence a line of male dancers stamps the earth to rid it of sickness and all bad thoughts, to set the world back on its axis. Each stamp is followed by the swift lifting heavenward of a smallish, cylindrical basket that we call a *vikapuhich*. The body of the basket is decorated with bold, shiny black designs on a creamy ground. It has been split lengthwise and attached to a hazel stick handle that is wrapped in finely tanned buckskin. A small bunch of yellowhammer feathers is attached at one end.

A popular symbolic interpretation of this basket is that of family, home and village. The *vikapuhich* contains a prayer for the world to be in balance. The basket is lifted to heaven and then retracted, bringing with it the spirit world's acknowledgement and luck. In unison the line of dancers then stamp out all that is bad. Over and over the basket is raised, then retracted, followed by the stamping out of sickness. Accompanied by songs originally inspired by the wind, the dance soon brings on a collective illumination: the elders cry, the young yearn.

Last fall I attended the Yurok Jump Dance at Pekwon, an ancient village about fifteen miles from the mouth of the Klamath River. After ten days, the time of the culmination dance had arrived. I had the distinct honor of choreographing the Pekwon camp's display of wealth, when all the regalia that has been contributed is brought out "to dance," in accordance with Indian law. So, the dance skirts of deerhide were laid out on the earthen floor. Then I brought armload after armload of Jump Dance baskets into the open air ceremonial house. They were stacked into a pile to hip level and four feet long. I carried into the house the fifty necklaces of shell and glass beads which were then laid across the baskets. I brought in the four remaining broad buckskin head-bands, each decorated with the brilliant crimson-scarlet of at least forty pileated woodpeckers. Finally, the fifty eagle feather plumes were sent in, making a magnificent sight.

I ran back to the regalia-camp to make sure that nothing had been left behind. As I was returning to the dance, I heard someone running up behind me. I turned and saw a Yurok man named Pordie Blake. He said, "Here. Put this in. I just finished it up this morning," and handed me a small, twelve-inch-long Jump Dance basket. It was pure white except for the dark orange-shafted yellowhammer feathers bunched at its end, and the shiny black design that ran along its side. I immediately perceived it as a newborn. It was light, perfect in proportion, and wonderful to behold. The spectators were already visibly transfixed by the sheer volume of regalia and the frenzy for which the culmination dance is noted. Nevertheless, as I carried the new little basket into the dance house, there was an audible sigh, a look-at-the-beautiful-baby sigh. The world renewal was now complete with the entrance of the basket.

Ada Charles, the white-haired Yurok woman who had woven the little basket cylinder, sat with Pordie, the regalia maker in his mid-forties who had assembled its parts (the hazel stick, yellowhammer feathers, and buckskin) into its finished state. Earlier in the week the Pekwon dancemakers had choreographed a tribute dance to Ada. Each of nine dancers had held a basket she had made. The central dancer had lifted to heaven the first Jump Dance basket she had ever made, back when she was sixteen years old. Included in the line had been a brand new basket, the companion to the little basket I was about to carry into the dance house. The world was being made with the old and the new.

Twenty-two men and four women dance in the culmination dance. Each man raises a basket into the air, and then stamps out all sickness and bad thoughts. In the end the dancers separate into two lines, one side going west and one side going east. They dance and sing pointing the baskets north and south, and then into the sunrise and sunset. They spread their prayers all around this world and the sky-world and bring back the luck. They fix the world for us all.

I am a singer and dancer, and oddly, this was the first dance at which I participated as a spectator. For the first time I saw the weavers and regalia makers "look on" at the dance. Guests to the ceremony are invariably moved by the experience. It is truly a wonderful spectacle, and it is repeated every two years. The basket-makers and owners bring out the baskets, and prepare them, telling their families and friends where each basket came from, who wove it, and how their family came to own it. All along the Klamath River the baskets come out. We believe the baskets are alive and want to dance. That is why they were created, to help us fix the world.[144]

Every significant act in the daily life of the Kwakiutl, native to British Columbia, had a ritual and a prayer connected with it. Erna Gunther, in *Further Analysis of the First Salmon Ceremony*, gives an example: "The fisherman catches four silver salmon and the canoe-builder throws four chips behind the tree because the Kwakiutl, like the Tsimshian, have four as their ritual number. There is a very definite formula to these prayers. The animal or plant prayed to is called 'Friend, Supernatural One.' It is thanked for giving of its substance. It is asked to keep illness and death from the devotee."[145] The following passage, a translation by Franz Boas of material dating around 1900, suggests the pervasiveness of this ritualism. A Kwakiutl woman cuts the roots of a young cedar tree, while speaking to it respectfully, prayerfully and in a spirit of thanksgiving.

"Look at me, friend! I come to ask for your dress, for you have come to take pity on us; for there is nothing for which we cannot use you, for you are really willing to give us your dress. I come to beg you for this, long life-maker, for I am going to make a basket for lily roots out of you. I pray, friend, not to feel angry with me on account of what I am going to do to you, and I beg you, friend, to tell your friends about what I ask of you. Take care, friend! Keep sickness away from me, so that I may not be killed by sickness or in war, O friend!"[146]

Grandfather Great Spirit
All over the world the faces of living ones are alike.
With tenderness they have come up out of the
*   ground.*
Look upon your children that they may
face the winds and walk the good road to the
*   Day of Quiet.*
Grandfather Great Spirit
Fill us with the Light.
Give us the strength to understand, and the eyes to
*   see.*
Teach us to walk the soft Earth as relatives to all
*   that live.*

Lakota prayer[147]

NOTES

INTRODUCTION

Note: Quoted matter in the introduction for which citations are not given will be cited later in the text.

1. Quoted in Stephen Little, *Visions of the Dharma: Japanese Buddhist Paintings and Prints in the Honolulu Academy of Arts* (Honolulu: The Honolulu Academy of Arts, 1991), p. 165.

2. Quoted in Matthew Fox, *Original Blessing* (Santa Fe: Bear & Company, 1983), p. 65.

3. Amadou Hampâté Bâ, "Earth, Moon, and Sun," trans. Ellen Draper, *Parabola*, vol. XIV, no. 3 (1989), p. 52.

4. Mircea Eliade, *The Sacred and the Profane: The Nature of Religion,* trans. Willard R. Trask (San Diego: Harcourt Brace Jovanovich, 1959), p. 13.

5. Quoted in *The Sun: A Magazine of Ideas,* Issue 189 (August 1991), p. 40.

6. Quoted in J. Baird Callicott and Roger T. Ames, eds., *Nature in Asian Traditions of Thought: Essays in Environmental Philosophy* (Albany: State University of New York Press, 1989), pp. 73–74.

7. See Graham Parkes, "Human/Nature in Nietzsche and Taoism," in *Nature,* p. 81; and Wing-Tsit Chan, trans. and comp., *A Source Book in Chinese Philosophy* (Princeton, NJ: Princeton University Press, 1969), p. 153. Philosopher Huston Smith offers a luminous translation of the significance of *Tao,* the Way:

> There is a being, wonderful, perfect;
> It existed before heaven and earth.
> How quiet it is!
> How spiritual it is!
> It stands alone and it does not change.
> It moves around and around, but does not on this account suffer.
> All life comes from it.
> It wraps everything with its love as in a garment, and yet it claims no honor,
>   it does not demand to be Lord.
> I do not know its name, and so I call it Tao, the Way, and I rejoice in its
>   power.

See Huston Smith, "Tao Now," in Ian G. Barbour, ed., *Earth Might Be Fair: Reflections on Ethics, Religion and Ecology* (Englewood Cliffs, NJ: Prentice-Hall, 1972), p. 81.

8. I use the words *Earth* and *world* to mean our planetary domicile, the third satellite out from the Sun. *Earth* with a lower case *e* refers to soil, and by extension to land, country and nation.

9. Gregory Bateson, *Mind and Nature: A Necessary Unity* (New York: Dutton, 1979), p. 8.

10. Ibid., p. 11.

11. Ibid., p. 86.

12. Sōetsu Yanagi, *The Unknown Craftsman: A Japanese Insight into Beauty* (Tokyo and New York: Kodansha International/USA, 1984), pp. 115, 117.

13. Rainer Maria Rilke, "Ninth Elegy," in *Duino Elegies,* trans. David Young (New York: W. W. Norton, 1978), p. 83.

14. See Kenneth Brower, ed., text by Stephen C. Jett, photographs by Philip Hyde, *Navajo Wildlands* (San Francisco: A Sierra Club/Ballantine Book, 1967), p. 124.

15. Quoted in John Michell, *The Earth Spirit: Its Ways, Shrines and Mysteries* (New York: Crossroad, 1975), p. 4.

16. C. G. Jung, *Alchemical Studies,* trans. R. F. C. Hull, Bollingen Series XX, vol. 13 (Princeton, NJ: Princeton University Press, 1976), p. 92.

17. E. E. Evans-Pritchard, *The Nuer* (Oxford: Clarendon Press, 1940), p. 120.

18. Ilias Venezis, *Aiolian Land* (Montreal: McGill University Companions to Modern Greek Studies, p. 316.

19. Quoted in Barbara Bode, *No Bells to Toll: Destruction and Creation in the Andes* (New York: Paragon, 1990), p. 149.

20. Quoted in Karan Singh, *Essays on Hinduism,* rev. ed. (Delhi: Ratna Sagar, 1990), pp. 117–18.

21. Alan Ereira, *The Elder Brothers: A Lost South American People and Their Message About the Fate of the Earth* (New York: Knopf, 1992), p. 215.

22. Quoted in Paul Devereux, *Earth Memory: Sacred Sites—Doorways into Earth's Mysteries* (St. Paul, MN: Llewellyn Publications, 1992), p. 31.

23. *Akwesasne Notes,* vol. 7, no. 5 (Early Winter 1975), p. 35.

24. Quoted in Richard Broome, *Aboriginal Australians: Black Response to White Dominance 1788–1980* (North Sydney, NSW: Allen & Unwin Australia, 1982), p. 196.

25. Quoted in Jill Purce, *The Mystic Spiral: Journey of the Soul* (London: Thames and Hudson, 1975), p. 17.

26. *Cultural Survival Quarterly,* vol. 7, no. 3 (1983), p. 57.

27. *Akwesasne Notes,* vol. 14, no. 3 (Early Summer 1982), p. 21.

28. Noni Jabavu, *The Ochre People* (London: John Murray, 1963), p. 93.

29. Ogotemmêli in Marcel Griaule, *Conversations with Ogotemmêli: An Introduction to Dogon Religious Ideas* (Oxford: Oxford University Press, 1970), p. 157.

30. Ibid., pp. 156, 158.

31. *The Song of Songs.* Interpretation by Matthew Fox. See interview with Fox in *The Sun,* Issue 189, August 1991.

32. Quoted in Bode, *No Bells to Toll,* p. 140.

33. N. Scott Momaday, foreword to *Native American Stories,* ed. Joseph Bruchac (Golden, CO: Fulcrum Publishing, 1991).

34. Yanagi, *The Unknown Craftsman,* pp. 214–15.

35. Quoted in Jennifer Isaacs, comp. and ed., *Australia Dreaming: 40,000 Years of Aboriginal History* (Sydney, NSW: Lansdowne Press, 1980), p. 186.

36. Maurice Kenny, "Spawning," in *Songs from This Earth on Turtle's Back,* ed. Joseph Bruchac (Greenfield Center, NY: Greenfield Review Press, 1983), pp. 129–30.

37. Mircea Eliade, *Ordeal by Labyrinth: Conversations with Claude-Henri Rocquet,* trans. Derek Coltman (Chicago: University of Chicago Press, 1982), pp. 6–7, 10–11.

38. Yanagi, *The Unknown Craftsman,* pp. 115, 118.

39. *And Woman Wove It in a Basket . . . ,* a 60-minute documentary film (1989) about Netti Jackson Kuneki, master basket-weaver of the Klickitat tribe of the Yakima Indian Nation in Washington State. A film by Bushra Azzouz, Marlene Farnum and Netti Kuneki. Distributed by Women Who Make Movies, New York City.

40. Pitseolak, *Pitseolak: Pictures Out of My Life,* from recorded interviews by Dorothy Eber (Seattle: University of Washington Press, 1972), n.p.

41. Friedrich Wilhelm Nietzsche in Graham Parkes, "Human/Nature in Nietzsche and Taoism," in *Nature,* p. 89. See also Nietzsche, *Thus Spake Zarathustra,* trans. Thomas Common, Prologue, sec. 4 (New York: Modern Library, 1950) p. 11.

42. Joseph Campbell, *The Masks of God: Primitive Mythology,* vol. 1 (New York: Viking, 1959), p. 65.

43. Octavio Paz, *The Labyrinth of Solitude: Life and Thought in Mexico,* trans. Lysander Kemp (New York: Grove Press, 1961), p. 173.

44. See Charles Ross, *Sunlight Convergence Solar Burn: The Equinoctial Year, September 23, 1971 through September 22, 1972* (Salt Lake City: University of Utah Press, 1976).

45. Robert Lawlor, *Sacred Geometry: Philosophy and Practice* (New York: Thames and Hudson, 1989), p. 70.

46. Ibid., p. 73.

I. ABORIGINAL AUSTRALIA

1. This constitutes a part of a much longer "Statement of Protest" by Aborigines and their supporters—during the 1982 Commonwealth Games—against the racism in Queensland. See Roger Moody, ed., *The Indigenous Voice: Visions and Realities,* vol. 1 (London: Zed Books, 1988), pp. 360–61.

2. Quoted in Henry Reynolds, *Dispossession: Black Australia and White Invaders* (Sydney: Allen & Unwin Australia, 1989), p. 89. This extract appeared in a pamphlet on land rights and the need for a national policy (in a chapter entitled "Aboriginal Ideology and Philosophy of the Land") prepared by the National Aboriginal Conference in Canberra, n.d.

3. Quoted in T. G. H. Strehlow, *Aranda Traditions* (Carlton, Victoria: Melbourne University Press, 1947), p. 142.

4. Edwin Bernbaum, *Sacred Mountains of the World* (San Francisco: Sierra Club Books, 1990), p. 190. Bernbaum's book is an exquisite meditation on the many great peaks of the world. The author has experienced the mountains himself as living entities, embodiments of humanity's deepest spiritual yearnings and reservoirs of the eternal verities.

5. See W. E. H. Stanner, *White Man Got No Dreaming* (Canberra: Australian National University Press, 1979), p. 135.

6. "The Dreaming organizes experience," writes Fred Myers, "so that it *appears* to be continuous and permanent." See Fred R. Myers, *Pintupi Country, Pintupi Self* (Washington, DC: Smithsonian Institution, 1986; Berkeley: University of California Press, 1991), pp. 48, 53.

7. For a fuller explanation of this concept see W. E. H. Stanner, *On Aboriginal Religion,* Oceania Monograph no. 11 (Sydney: University of Sydney, 1959–63), p. 10.

8. Nancy D. Munn, "Transformation of Subjects into Objects in Walbiri and Pitjantjatjara Myth," in Max Charlesworth, Howard Morphy et al., eds., *Religion in Aboriginal Australia* (St. Lucia, Queensland: University of Queensland Press, 1986), p. 68.

9. Strehlow, *Aranda Traditions,* p. 17.

10. Quoted in Myers, *Pintupi Country, Pintupi Self,* p. 47.

11. See Stanner, *White Man Got No Dreaming,* p. 230.

12. Aboriginal National Land Rights Poster in International Work Group for Indigenous Affairs (IWGIA) Document no. 54, *Land Rights Now* (Copenhagen: IWGIA Publications, October 1985), p. 95.

IWGIA publicizes and campaigns against the oppression of indigenous peoples and actively supports their right to determine their own future in concurrence with their own efforts and desires: (1) by organizing research, examining their situation and publishing the information to a worldwide readership; (2) thereby furthering international understanding, knowledge and involvement in the cause of indigenous peoples; (3) by fighting racism and securing political, economical and social rights, as well as establishing the indigenous peoples' right to self-determination; (4) by arranging humanitarian projects and other forms of support to indigenous peoples and ethnic groups with a view to strengthening their social, cultural and political position. This includes practical and economic support for seminars and conferences. (IWGIA statement about its goals).

IWGIA receives its information from reports by scholars working directly in the relevant areas as well as from the indigenous peoples themselves.

13. Quoted in IWGIA Document no. 54, p. 4.

14. Quoted in Catherine H. and Ronald M. Berndt, *The Aboriginal Australians: The First Pioneers* (Carlton, Victoria: Pitman, 1983), p. 16.

15. Quoted in Jennifer Isaacs, comp. and ed., *Australia Dreaming: 40,000 Years of Aboriginal History* (Sydney: Lansdowne Press, 1980), p. 99.

16. Charlie Jampijinpa Gallagher in Penny Taylor, ed., *After 200 Years* (Canberra: Aboriginal Studies Press, 1988), p. 299.

17. Dick Roughsey, *Moon and Rainbow: The Autobiography of an Aboriginal* (Sydney: A. H. and A. W. Reed, 1971), p. 27.

18. L. Fison and A. W. Howitt, *Kamilaroi and Kurnai* (1880; reprint, Oosterhout, The Netherlands: Anthropological Publications, 1967), p. 25.

19. *Desert Stories,* a half-hour documentary film about the Pintupi people of central Australia, 1984. A 29-minute documentary film about some engaging Pintupi storytellers and their stories in and around the Papunya Aboriginal Settlement near Alice Springs in central Australia. Directed and edited by Lindsay Frazer; written and narrated by Billy Marshall-Stoneking; produced by Nick Frazer. Network 0/28. Special Broadcasting Service, 1984.

20. Quoted in Margie K. C. West, *The Inspired Dream: Life as Art in Aboriginal Australia* (South Brisbane: Queensland Art Gallery, 1988), p. 41.

21. Quoted in Paul Memmot, "Social Structure and Use of Space Amongst the Lardil," in Nicolas Peterson and Marcia Langston, eds., *Aborigines, Land and Land Rights* (Canberra: Australian Institute of Aboriginal Studies, 1983), pp. 61–62.

22. As told by Australian cartographer of Aboriginal sacred sites, Arkady Volchok. Quoted in Bruce Chatwin, *The Songlines* (New York: Viking Penguin, 1987), p. 11.

23. Arkady Volchok explains the ground of this statement: "Sometimes," said Arkady, "I'll be driving my 'old men' through the desert, and we'll come to a ridge of sandhills, and suddenly they'll all start singing. 'What are you mob singing?' I'll ask, and they'll say [this]." Ibid., p. 14.

24. Roland Robinson, *The Man Who Sold His Dreaming* (Sydney: Currawong, 1965), pp. 6–7.

25. Ibid., p. 7.

26. James Cowan, *Mysteries of the Dream-Time: The Spiritual Life of Australian Aborigines* (Bridport, Dorset: Prism Press, 1989), p. 99.

27. Jack McPhee in Sally Morgan, *Wanamurraganya: The Story of Jack McPhee* (Fremantle, Western Australia: Fremantle Arts Centre Press, 1989), pp. 25, 75–77, 196.

28. Quoted in Broome, *Aboriginal Australians,* p. 14.

29. Quoted in James G. Cowan, *Letters from a Wild State* (New York: Bell Tower, 1991), p. xiv.

30. Ibid., pp. 58–59.

31. Quoted in Judith Ryan, *Mythscapes: Aboriginal Art of the Desert* (Melbourne: The National Gallery of Victoria, 1989), p. 30.

32. Kevin Gilbert in Moody, *The Indigenous Voice,* vol. 1, p. 21. Roger Moody's *The Indigenous Voice* (2 vols.) juxtaposes indigenous perspectives and worldviews on the fundamental questions of life from every corner of the globe in a truly irreplaceable document, an essential resource for indigenous and nonindigenous alike.

33. Robert Bropho, *Fringedweller* (Sydney: Alternative Publishing Co-operative, 1983), p. 34.

34. See Stanner, *White Man Got No Dreaming*, p. 143.

35. Ibid., p. 140.

36. Chatwin, *The Songlines*, p. 13.

37. Ibid., pp. 13–14.

"White men," writes Chatwin (recalling his conversation with Aboriginal Dan Flynn—an ex-Benedictine monk), "made the common mistake of assuming that, because the Aboriginals were wanderers, they could have no system of land tenure. This was nonsense. Aboriginals, it was true, could not imagine territory as a block of land hemmed in by frontiers: but rather as an interlocking network of 'lines' of 'ways through.' "

"All our words for 'country,' " said Flynn, "are the same as the words for 'line.' " Ibid., 56.

38. Quoted in Robinson, *The Man Who Sold His Dreaming*, pp. 59–60.

39. Ibid., p. 133.

40. Robinson, *The Man Who Sold His Dreaming*, p. 7.

41. Quoted in Robinson, pp. 7–8.

42. Big Bill Neidjie, Stephen Davis, and Allan Fox, *Australia's Kakadu Man* (Darwin: Resource Managers, 1986), p. 81.

43. See W. E. H. Stanner, *On Aboriginal Religion* (Sydney: University of Sydney Press, 1989), pp. 15, 21.

44. Quoted in Peter Sutton, ed., *Dreamings: The Art of Aboriginal Australia* (New York: George Braziller and The Asia Society Galleries, 1988), p. 19.

45. Ibid., pp. 13–14.

46. Quoted in Diane Bell, "Topsy Napurrula Nelson: Teacher and Philosopher and Friend," in Isobel White, Diane Barwick, and Betty Meehan, eds., *Fighters and Singers: The Lives of Some Australian Aboriginal Women* (Sydney: Allen & Unwin Australia, 1985), p. 2.

47. Ibid.

48. IWGIA Newsletter no. 37 (May 1984), p. 11.

49. Pat Dodson, National Co-ordinator of the National Federation of Land Councils, in an address to the National Press Club, quoted in IWGIA Document no. 54, p. 78.

50. Bell's discussion is focused upon the Arandic of central Australia, but many of her comments apply generally to Aboriginal societies. See Diane Bell, "Sacred Sites: The Politics of Protection," in Nicolas Peterson and Marcia Langton, eds., *Aborigines, Land and Land Rights* (Canberra: Australian Institute of Aboriginal Studies, 1983), pp. 281–82.

51. Jack McPhee in Morgan, *Wanamurraganya*, pp. 58–59.

52. Quoted in Moody, *The Indigenous Voice*, vol. 1, pp. 388–89.

53. Quoted in Isaacs, *Australia Dreaming*, p. 40.

We owe much of what we know today about Ayers Rock to the pioneering work of Charles P. Mountford. The mythological origin of the topographical features of Ayers Rock, the paintings and engravings in the many caves at the base of the monolith and the worldview of the Pitjantjatjara people (whose tribal country includes Ayers Rock) are the focus of his extraordinary work. See Charles P. Mountford, *Ayers Rock: Its People, Their Beliefs and Their Art* (Sydney: Angus & Robertson, 1965).

54. Quoted in Strehlow, *Aranda Traditions*, p. 51.

55. Ibid., p. 31.

56. Ibid.

57. Quoted in Francis Huxley, *The Way of the Sacred* (London: Bloomsbury Books, 1989), p. 130.

58. Quoted in IWGIA Newsletter no. 47 (October 1986), pp. 5–6. Tens of thousands of Aborigines live on the fringes of Australian towns, many of them in dire poverty and unimaginable humiliation. These "Fringedwellers" have lost touch with

much of their heritage but retain a strong sense of racial identity and connection to the land. For a deeply moving and unsentimental account of a Fringedweller's "existence," see Robert Bropho's remarkable portrayal of an impossible life ("I've been a fringedweller all my life in and around the metropolitan Perth area, living near the local junk tip at Eden Hill, under sheets of tin . . .") in Robert Bropho, *Fringedweller*, p. 1.

59. Robinson, *The Man Who Sold His Dreaming*, pp. 98–100.

60. Myers, *Pintupi Country, Pintupi Self*, p. 67.

61. Neidjie et al., *Australia's Kakadu Man*, pp. 14, 79.

62. Quoted in Memmott, "Social Structure and Use of Space Amongst the Lardil," pp. 61–62.

63. Quoted in Daniel Vachon and Philip Toyne, "Mining and the Challenge of Land Rights," in Peterson and Langton, *Aborigines, Land and Land Rights*, p. 307.

64. Quoted in Sutton, *Dreamings: The Art of Aboriginal Australia*, p. 19.

65. As Fred R. Myers so perceptively illustrates in the title of his innovative study of the Pintupi people of Australia's Western Desert, *Pintupi Country, Pintupi Self.*

66. See Kevin J. Gilbert, *Because a White Man'll Never Do It* (Sydney: Angus & Robertson, 1973), p. 3.

67. Quoted in Bill Edwards, "Pitjantjatjara Land Rights," in Peterson and Langton, *Aborigines, Land and Land Rights*, pp. 303–4.

68. Diane Bell, "Sacred Sites: The Politics of Protection," in Peterson and Langton, *Aborigines, Land and Land Rights*, p. 283.

69. Ibid.

70. Ibid.

The concept of "lifting up country" is symbolically expressed in ritual performances when the women hold up the sacred boards, which are spiritual metaphors for the land and its Law.

71. Quoted in Diane Bell, "Women and Aboriginal Religion," in Charlesworth et al., *Religion in Aboriginal Australia*, p. 301.

72. Kevin Gilbert, *People Are Legends: Aboriginal Poems by Kevin Gilbert* (St. Lucia, Queensland: University of Queensland Press, 1978), pp. 34–35.

73. Quoted in H. C. Coombs et al., eds., *Land of Promises: Aborigines and Development in the East Kimberley* (Canberra: Centre for Resource and Environmental Studies, Australian National University, 1989), n.p.

74. Quoted in Janine Roberts, *From Massacres to Mining: The Colonization of Aboriginal Australia* (London: CIMRA and War on Want, 1978), p. 133.

75. See Gilbert, *Because a White Man'll Never Do It*, p. 3.

76. Quoted in IWGIA Document no. 54, p. 4.

77. See Derick Ray, comp., *Australian Aboriginal Town Name Meanings* (Cambridge: British Society of Australian Philately, 1987), pp. 12–13.

78. Quoted in Moody, *The Indigenous Voice*, vol. 1, pp. 19–21.

79. Quoted in Jennifer Isaacs, *Aboriginality* (St. Lucia, Queensland: University of Queensland Press, 1989), p. 22.

80. Quoted in Taylor, *After 200 Years*, p. 172.

81. Pat Dodson in IWGIA Document no. 54, pp. 90, 92, 93. This is part of an address delivered by Pat Dodson to the National Press Club in Canberra. The National Federation of Land Councils comprises fifteen organizations throughout Australia working for Aboriginal land rights.

82. Pat Dodson, "Restore Dignity, Restore Land, Restore Life," in Jack Davis et al., eds., *Paperbark: A Collection of Black Australian Writings* (St. Lucia, Queensland: University of Queensland Press, 1990), pp. 326–29.

83. Robinson, *The Man Who Sold His Dreaming*, p. 6.

84. Ibid., pp. 106–7.

85. Quoted in Moody, *The Indigenous Voice*, vol. 1, p. 388.

86. Quoted in Raymond Evans, Kay Saunders, and Kathryn Cronin, *Race Relations in Colonial Queensland: A History of Exclusion, Exploitation and Extermination* (St. Lucia, Queensland: University of Queensland Press, 1988), pp. 380–81.

Killed by settlers in 1833, according to Aboriginal poet and playwright Jack Davis, Yagan was a leader and spokesperson for his people, the Nyoongarah, and was called the "Chief of Swan River." (Evans et al., above, however, suggest that Yagan was very much alive ten years later, in 1843.) Today, says Davis, he is an important symbolic figure to the Nyoongarah of the southwest of Western Australia. His death led to the Battle of Pinjarra (October 28, 1834), when a party of the 21st Regiment, six police and a group of settlers engaged the Murray River tribe, killing between fifteen and twenty and capturing more. One policeman died of wounds. See Jack Davis, *Kullark—The Dreamers* (Sydney: Currency Press, 1982), p. 6.

87. *Identity*, vol. 1, no. 8 (August 1973), p. 17.

88. Quoted in Coombs et al., *Land of Promises*, p. 93.

89. Quoted in Reynolds, *Dispossession*, p. 91.

90. W. E. Harney, *Life Among the Aborigines* (London: Robert Hale, 1957), p. 213.

91. Quoted in Reynolds, *Dispossession*, p. 89.

92. Kevin J. Gilbert, *Living Black: Blacks Talk to Kevin Gilbert* (Ringwood, Victoria: Penguin Books Australia, 1978), pp. 304–5.

"The use of 'aboriginality' grew out of the pre- and post-1967 Referendum periods and has been variously used in both political, social and artistic contexts," writes Australian art critic Michael O'Ferrall. Another art critic, Peter Sutton, describes its use in "the construction of a new tradition out of a variety of materials, underpinned both by official funding and by a relatively new conception: Aboriginality." See Michael A. O'Ferrall, *On the Edge: Five Contemporary Aboriginal Artists* (Perth: Art Gallery of Western Australia, 1989), p. 10.

93. Quoted in Isaacs, *Australia Dreaming*, p. 202.

94. Kath Walker, *Stradbroke Dreamtime* (Sydney: Angus & Robertson, 1972), p. 74.

95. Quoted in Isaacs, *Australia Dreaming*, p. 176.

96. Quoted in Isaacs, *Australia Dreaming*, p. 176.

97. Quoted in Janice Reid, ed., *Body, Land and Spirit: Health and Healing in Aboriginal Society* (St. Lucia, Queensland: University of Queensland Press, 1982), p. 154.

98. Quoted in Reynolds, *Dispossession*, p. 90.

99. Sally Morgan, *My Place* (1987; reprint, New York: Arcade Publishing, 1990), pp. 247–49.

Sally Morgan was born in Perth, Western Australia. Many of her extended family refer to themselves as Mulbas, the Aboriginal people of the Port Headland/Marble Bay area of Western Australia. "The term," explains Morgan, "is derived from the word for man or person in that people's language." (Ibid. p. 359).

100. Ibid., pp. 38–39, 306.

101. Quoted in Neidjie et al., *Australia's Kakadu Man*, p. 12.

102. Quoted in Taylor, *After 200 Years*, p. 29.

103. Quoted in Colin Tatz, ed., *Black Viewpoints: The Aboriginal Experience* (Sydney: Australia and New Zealand Book Company, 1975), p. 29.

104. Quoted in Reynolds, *Dispossession*, pp. 91–92.

105. Jack Davis, "The Day After Moree Murder," in *Us Fellas: An Anthology of Aboriginal Writing*, collected by Colleen Class and Archie Weller (Perth: Artlook Books, 1987), pp. 173–74.

106. Quoted in Moody, *The Indigenous Voice*, vol. 1, pp. 21–24.

107. Quoted in Davis et al., *Paperbark*, p. 338.

108. Paddy Japaljarri Stewart in *Yuendumu Doors—Kuruwarri* (Canberra: Australian Institute of Aboriginal Studies, 1987), p. 3. (All the Warlukurlangu artists are considered the authors of this book.)

109. Tess Napaljarri Ross explains that Warlpiri people bear one of the following names:

Napaljarri	Japaljarri	Napurrurla	Jupurrurla
Napangardi	Japangardi	Nangala	Jangala
Nakamarra	Jakamarra	Napanangka	Japanangka
Nungarrayi	Jungarrayi	Nampijinpa	Jampijinpa

She points out that "the names that begin with 'J' are used for men and the names that begin with 'N' are what the women call themselves. If you say 'Napaljarri,' then it is a woman; if you say 'Japaljarri,' then it is a man. . . . Everyone has one of these names. The people who have these names are related to each other." Ibid., p. 7.

Senior Aboriginal painter Paddy Japaljarri Stewart speaks about the significance of the Honey Ant Dreaming:

We who are living at Yuendumu, near the Yakurrukaji water, we are living at the Honey Ant Dreaming Site. Their underground chambers have created the natural soakages found all over this part of our country. That is what we have painted here.

Ibid., p. 107

110. The Warlukurlangu artists are careful to point out that a complex relationship exists between paintings, stories and Dreamings. "Dreaming tracks are long," they say, "and meet and cross other Dreaming tracks frequently. Each Dreaming then has many interactions with other Dreamings and with the land. Both stories and paintings concern only a few such interactions for each Dreaming, sometimes there are several paintings and stories about the same Dreaming, sometimes a single story and painting may concern more than one Dreaming." Each painting is loaded with meaning, full understanding of which is available only to full members (initiated) of Warlpiri society. Ibid., p. 2.

111. Tess Napaljarri Ross. Ibid., pp. 3, 7, 9.

112. Hyllus Maris in John Pilger, *A Secret Country* (London: Jonathan Cape, 1989), pp. 25–26.

113. A common sentence for criminal offenses in Britain during the eighteenth and early nineteenth centuries was "transportation." It meant being transported to the colonies—originally those in America, and then, after the Revolutionary War, to Australia. In an eighty-year period, beginning in 1788, more than 160,000 convicts arrived in Australia—many of them Irishmen who had taken part in rebellions against the British.

114. Quoted in IWGIA Newsletter no. 57 (May 1989), pp. 33–34, 36–40, 42–43.

115. A scene from *Babakiueria,* a 30-minute 16mm film directed by Don Featherstone, Australian Broadcasting Corporation, 1987.

116. Quoted in *IWGIA Yearbook* (1987), 41.

II. JAPAN

1. Quoted in David Edward Shaner, "The Japanese Experience of Nature," in J. Baird Callicott and Roger T. Ames, eds., *Nature in Asian Traditions of Thought,* p. 173.

2. *Haikai and Haiku,* trans. Sanki Ichikawa et al. (Tokyo: The Nippon Gakujutsu Shinkokai, 1958), p. xvii.

3. Quoted in *Japan: Voices from the Land,* a one-hour documentary written and produced by Peter Argentine; a WQED production from QED Communications, Inc., Pittsburgh, 1991.

4. Daisetz T. Suzuki, *Zen and Japanese Culture,* Bollingen Series LXIV (Princeton, NJ: Princeton University Press, 1989), pp. 261–62.

5. See Bernbaum, *Sacred Mountains of the World,* p. 56.

6. Interview with Sincho Tanaka in *Japan: Voices from the Land,* the documentary.

7. Donald Keene, *Living Japan* (Garden City, NY: Doubleday, 1959), p. 11.

8. Yanagi, *The Unknown Craftsman,* p. 113.

9. Ibid., pp. 114–15.

10. Ibid., pp 115–18.

11. Quoted in Keene, *Living Japan,* p. 12.

12. See Royall Tyler, "A Glimpse of Mt. Fuji in Legend and Cult" in *Journal of the Association of Teachers of Japanese,* vol. 16, no. 2 (Ann Arbor, MI, 1980), p. 154.

13. The *Manyōshū,* III, 319, The Nippon Gakujutsu Shinkokai Translation of One Thousand Poems (New York: Columbia University Press, 1965), p. 215.

14. Masanobu Fukuoka, *The Natural Way of Farming: The Theory and Practice of Green Philosophy,* trans. Frederic P. Metreaud (Tokyo and New York: Japan Publications, 1985), pp. 106–7.

15. Shaner, "The Japanese Experience of Nature," pp. 165–66.

16. Kakuzo Okakura, *The Book of Tea* (Tokyo and New York: Kodansha International/USA, 1989), p. 29.

17. Suzuki, *Zen and Japanese Culture,* p. 271.

18. See Suzuki, "Zen and the Art of Tea," in *Zen and Japanese Culture,* pp. 271–314.

19. Ibid., p. 278.

20. "The Cosmos in the Hand," from *Japan: Spirit and Form,* Shuichi Kato, host, a ten-part television program series, produced by NHK International, Inc. The series was broadcast over City University Television, New York (CUNY), 1992.

21. Ibid.

22. Suzuki, *Zen and Japanese Culture,* p. 314.

23. Interview with Claude Champi, "The Cosmos in the Hand."

24. Interview with Kichizaemon Raku XV, "The Cosmos in the Hand."

25. Quoted in Andrew Wilson, ed., *World Scripture* (New York: Paragon, 1991), p. 204.

26. Quoted in *Japan: Voices from the Land,* the documentary.

27. The other indigenous minority in Japan are the Okinawans, with a population of approximately one million. The Okinawans live on the Ryukyu islands, southwest of Kyushu. In addition, two other minorities are represented by the Burakumin and Korean populations. The four minorities comprise between 2 and 4 percent of the total Japanese population. The IWGIA reported that Japanese Prime Minister Nakasone denied the existence of *any* minority groups in Japan in a statement made in October 1986. See *IWGIA Yearbook 1986*—Indigenous Peoples and Human Rights—p. 45.

28. Donald L. Philippi, *Songs of Gods, Songs of Humans* (Princeton, NJ, and Tokyo: Princeton University Press and the University of Tokyo Press, 1979), p. 4.

29. Professor Douglas Sanders, "The Ainu as an Indigenous People," in *IWGIA Newsletter,* nos. 45–46 (1986), p. 123.

30. M. Inez Hilger, with the assistance of Chiye Sano and Midori Yamaha, *Together with the Ainu—A Vanishing People* (Norman, OK: University of Oklahoma Press, 1971), p. 41.

31. Ibid.

32. Philippi, *Songs of Gods,* p. 21.

33. Ibid.

34. For a broad overview of Ainu culture, see the *Kodansha Encyclopedia of Japan,* vol. 1 (Tokyo: Kodansha; New York: Kodansha International/USA, 1983), pp. 34–37.

35. Philippi, *Songs of Gods,* pp. 2–3.

36. Hilger, *Together with the Ainu,* p. 188.

37. Quoted in Sir James George Frazer, ed., *The New Golden Bough,* notes and forward by Dr. Theodor H. Gaster (New York: Criterion Books, 1959), p. 457.

38. Hilger, *Together with the Ainu,* pp. 97–98.

39. Yanagi, *The Unknown Craftsman,* p. 215.

40. *Kodansha Encyclopedia of Japan,* vol. 6, p. 367.

41. Saigyō in William R. LaFleur, "Saigyō and the Buddhist Value of Nature, Part II," in *History of Religions,* vol. 13, 1973–74, p. 237.

42. See LaFleur, "Saigyō," pp. 236–37.

43. Quoted in Masaharu Anesaki, *Art, Life, and Nature in Japan* (Rutland, VT: Charles E. Tuttle, 1984), p. 93.

44. Matsuo Bashō, *The Narrow Road to the Deep North and Other Travel Sketches,* trans. Nobuyuki Yuasa (Harmondsworth: Penguin, 1966), p. 71.

45. Suzuki, *Zen and Japanese Culture,* p. 254.

46. See ibid., pp. 255–56.

47. Ibid., pp. 258–59.

48. Bashō, *The Narrow Road to the Deep North,* p. 54.

49. Ibid., p. 33.

50. Quoted in Mary Evelyn Tucker, *Moral and Spiritual Cultivation in Japanese Neo-Confucianism: The Life and Thought of Kaibara Ekken (1630–1714)* (Albany: State University of New York Press, 1989), pp. 139–40.

51. Kaibara Ekken, *The Way of Contentment,* trans. Ken Hoshino (London: John Murray, 1913; Washington, DC: University Publications of America, 1979), pp. 54–55.

52. Mary Evelyn Tucker writes that when "the German physician and naturalist Philip Franz von Siebold (1796–1866) . . . visited Japan in the nineteenth century . . . [and] recognized the remarkable scope of Ekken's studies, [he] call[ed] him 'the Aristotle of Japan.' " (Tucker, p. 41.) Ekken's scope of interest and knowledge covered an amazing array of topics, including medicine, music, military tactics, zoology, taxonomy, law, mathematics, linguistics and the practice of ethics to mention just a few.

53. Ronald E. Kotzsch, *Macrobiotics: Yesterday and Today* (Tokyo and New York: Japan Publications, 1985), pp. 12, 19.

At the age of eighty-three, Kaibara Ekken wrote the *Yojokun (Japanese Secrets of Good Health),* a very modern and practical guide to health and longevity. "For Kaibara human life is meant not only to be long and healthy," writes Kotzsch, but also "it is meant to be enjoyable." The following excerpts from *Japanese Secrets* reveal Ekken's playful and profound spirit:

> Saints always expound on the delights of living. A poor fool like me can hardly understand the mind of saints, but at least I know that delight is something that Heaven and Earth meant living things to have, and something that man is born possessed of.
>
> Ibid., p. 16.

"Kaibara discourses at length on the subject of food—its choice, preparation, and manner of eating," continues Kotzsch. Precepts for daily living include:

> Eat rice as a daily, staple food.
> Eat fresh vegetables when they are in season . . .
> Above all do not overeat. Eat only to 80 to 90 percent of capacity, until just before one feels full.
> Before eating remember with gratitude the farmers and others who have produced the food, the parents and benefactors who have supplied it, and those who have cooked and served it.
> Remember too those who are without food, and one's unworthiness before such blessings.
> Never eat while angry or worried . . .
>
> Ibid., 16–17.

54. Tucker, *Moral and Spiritual Cultivation,* p. 3.

55. Ekken, *The Way of Contentment,* p. 17.

56. Quoted in Tucker, *Moral and Spiritual Cultivation,* p. 186.

57. Ibid., pp. 186–87.

58. Ibid., p. 4.

59. Ibid., p. 125.

60. Suzuki, *Zen and Japanese Culture*, p. 368.

61. Ibid., p. 365.

62. Ibid., p. 370.

63. Quoted in Misao Kodama and Hikosaku Yanagishima, eds. and trans., *Ryōkan the Great Fool* (Kyoto: The Kyoto Seika Jr. College Press, 1969), pp. 53–54.

64. Tetsuro Watsuji, *A Climate: A Philosophical Study,* trans. Geoffrey Bownas (Japanese Government Printing Bureau, Ministry of Education, 1961), pp. 204, 197.

65. Ibid., p. 192.

66. Ibid., p. 197.

67. Ibid., p. 196.

68. Quoted in Tetsushi Furukawa, "Watsuji Tetsuro, the Man and His Work," in Watsuji, *A Climate,* p. 213.

69. Ibid., p. 214.

70. Watsuji, *A Climate,* pp. 206–7. Watsuji drafted these thoughts in 1929.

71. See Furukawa, "Watsuji Tetsuro," pp. 226, 228–29.

72. Quoted in Furukawa, "Watsuji Tetsuro," p. 227.

73. Ibid., pp. 212–13.

74. Yanagi, *The Unknown Craftsman,* p. 214.

75. Shimpei Kusano, *frogs & others,* trans. Cid Corman and Ohno Hidetaka (New York: Grossman Publishers, 1969), p. 98.

76. Quoted in *A Zen Forest,* comp. and trans. Soiku Shigematsu (New York: Weatherhill, 1981), p. 64.

77. "Sermon of Muso Kokushi at the Opening of Tenryū Monastery," in William Theodore De Bary, ed., *The Buddhist Tradition in India, China and Japan* (New York: Random House, a Vintage Books Edition, 1972), pp. 374–75.

78. D. T. Suzuki, introduction, in Eugen Herrigel, *Zen in the Art of Archery* (New York: Pantheon, 1953; New York: Vintage, 1971), p. vii.

79. Fukuoka, *The Natural Way of Farming,* p. 126.

80. Masanobu Fukuoka, *The Road Back to Nature,* trans. Frederic P. Metreaud (Tokyo and New York: Japan Publications, 1987), p. 226.

81. Quoted in Susan Peterson, *Shōji Hamada: A Potter's Way and Work* (New York: Kodansha International/USA, 1974), p. 92.

82. Bernard Leach, *Hamada: Potter* (New York: Kodansha International/USA, 1975), p. 136.

83. Ibid., pp. 135–36.

84. Satomi Myōdō, *Passionate Journey: The Spiritual Autobiography of Satomi Myodo,* trans. Sallie B. King (Boston and London: Shambhala Publications, 1987), pp. 7–9.

85. Daisetz Suzuki, *Japanese Spirituality,* trans. Norman Waddell, (Tokyo: Japan Society for the Promotion of Science, 1972; New York: Greenwood Press, 1988), pp. 111, 81.

86. Ibid., pp. 41, 45.

87. Shuichi Kato, *A History of Japanese Literature: The Modern Years,* vol. 3, trans. Don Sanderson (Tokyo: Kodansha International, 1983), p. 113.

88. Kunio Yanagita, *About Our Ancestors: The Japanese Family System,* trans. Fanny Hagin Mayer and Ishiwara Yasuyo (Tokyo: Japan Society for the Promotion of Science, 1970), pp. 73–75, 168–69.

Yanagita also wrote on the social and historical role of women. His "work might be called Japan's *Golden Bough,*" states cultural historian Shuichi Kato, adding, "its value as ethnographical material is incomparable." See Kato, *A History of Japanese Literature,* vol. 3, p. 130.

89. Fukuoka, *The Road Back to Nature,* p. 264.

90. Masanobu Fukuoka, *One-Straw Revolution: An Introduction to Natural Farming,* trans. Chris Pearce, Tsune Kurosawa and Larry Korn (Emmaus, PA: Rodale Press, 1978), p. 119.

91. Ibid., p. 117.

92. Fukuoka, *The Road Back to Nature,* p. 366.

93. Fukuoka, *The Natural Way of Farming,* p. 257.

94. Ibid., p. 133.

95. Ibid., p. 134.

96. Ibid., p. 268.

97. Ibid., p. 157.

98. Ibid., p. 5.

99. Ibid., p. 258.

100. Fukuoka, *The One-Straw Revolution,* pp. 19–21, 48, 76, 94.

101. Takashi Nagatsuka, *Earth,* trans. Yasuhiro Kawamura (Tokyo: Liber Press, 1986), pp. 41–43.

102. Dr. Junichi Saga, *Memories of Silk and Straw: A Self-Portrait of Small-Town Japan,* trans. Garry O. Evans (Tokyo and New York: Kodansha International/ USA, 1987), p. 13.

103. Ibid., p. 19.

104. Ibid., pp. 71–72.

105. Quoted in Graeme Wilson and Atsumi Ikuko, "The Poetry of Yamamura Bochō," *Japan Quarterly,* vol. 19, no. 4 (1972), p. 466.

106. Muso Soseki, "Temple of Eternal Light," in *Sun at Midnight: Poems and Sermons by Muso Soseki,* trans. W. S. Merwin and Soiku Shigematsu (San Francisco: North Point Press, 1989), p. 122.

107. Kazuaki Tanahashi, *Brush Mind* (Berkeley: Parallax Press, 1990), p. 131.

108. Quoted in *Dream Window: Reflections on the Japanese Garden,* a 57-minute documentary film produced by the Office of Communications, the Smithsonian Institution in association with KajimaVision, Tokyo, 1992. Directed by John Junkerman and written by Peter Grilli. Senior producer, Laura T. Schneider.

109. Interview with Toru Takemitsu, *Dream Window.*

110. Quoted in *Dream Window.*

111. Interview with Makoto Ooka, *Dream Window.*

112. Soseki, "Dialogues in the Dream," in *Sun at Midnight,* pp. 162–64.

113. Interview with Toru Takemitsu, *Dream Window.*

114. Interview with Sobin Yamada, *Dream Window.*

115. Quoted in Shigematsu, *A Zen Forest,* p. 120.

116. Patia R. Isaku, *Mountain Storm, Pine Breeze: Folk Song in Japan* (Tucson: University of Arizona Press, 1981), p. 23.

117. Quoted in "Things as They Are," in *Japanese Tales,* ed. and trans. Royall Tyler (New York: Pantheon, 1987), p. 57. The bodhisattvas were beings who had attained enlightenment but had vowed to defer their own entry into Nirvana in order to help all other beings to enlightenment. See Little, *Visions of the Dharma,* p. 14.

118. Michiko Ishimure, "Pure Land, Poisoned Sea" (from *Kugai Jodo,* chapter 3, "What Yuki Said"), *Japan Quarterly,* vol. 18, no. 3 (1971), pp. 300–301, 305–6.

119. Poet and writer Kazuko Shiraishi (in "Orient in Me," *Japan Quarterly,* vol. 19, no. 2 [1972], p. 221) hints at one facet of *mono no aware:*

> When I begin on the writing of a poem I do not consciously think that I am Japanese or even that I am an Oriental; but when I finish the poem and examine what I have written, I am persistently surprised to discover in my own work those characteristics of feeling, of "heart," which are distinctively Oriental. Though neither literature in general nor poetry in particular is the product of a specific climate, it is interesting to recognize, especially in one's own work, that the weather of one's inmost soul does, as the years move on, permeate with its singular scent everything that one does.

120. Yoshiro Kunimoto, "The Fisherfolk of the North," *Japan Quarterly,* vol. 19, no. 1 (1972), p. 74.

121. Interview with Setsuko Yamazato, *Japan: Voices from the Land.*

122. Quoted in *The Sacred Landscape,* written and compiled by Frederic Lehrman (Berkeley: Celestial Arts Publishing, 1988), p. 29.

123. Quoted in Anesaki, *Art, Life, and Nature in Japan,* p. 126.

124. Soseki, "Reply to Gen'no Osho's Poem," in *Sun at Midnight,* p. 35.

125. Quoted in Shaner, "The Japanese Experience of Nature," p. 165.

126. Hokusai, *Hokusai: One Hundred Views of Mt. Fuji,* introduction and commentaries on the plates by Henry D. Smith II (New York: George Braziller, 1988), p. 8.

127. Tyler, "A Glimpse of Mt. Fuji," p. 144.

128. Quoted in Tyler, "A Glimpse of Mt. Fuji," p. 144.

129. Ibid.

130. From *The Manyōshū,* III, 319, The Nippon Gakujutsu Shinkokai Translation, p. 215.

131. Tyler, "A Glimpse of Mt. Fuji," p. 153.

132. Akahito Yamabé, "On a Distant View of Mount Fuji," in *The Manyōshū,* III, 317–18, The Nippon Gakujutsu Shinkokai Translation, pp. 187–88.

133. Dōgen, *Shōbōgenzō: Zen Essays of Dōgen,* trans. Thomas Cleary (Honolulu: University of Hawaii Press, 1986), p. 6.

134. Ibid., p. 2.

135. Ibid., p. 9.

136. Ibid., pp. 96–98.

137. Quoted in De Bary, *The Buddhist Tradition,* p. 277.

138. Hitoshi Takeuchi, "Mt. Fuji," in *Mt. Fuji,* photographs by Yukio Ohyama (New York: Dutton, 1987), p. 71.

139. Ibid., p. 72.

140. C. W. Nicol, "A Gift from the Mountain," in *Mt. Fuji,* p. 43.

141. Fukuoka, *The Natural Way of Farming,* pp. 119–20.

142. Nanao Sakaki, *Break the Mirror* (San Francisco: North Point Press, 1987), p. 46. For an appreciation of this unique poet, world traveler, committed trekker and "unofficial examiner of the mountains and rivers of all Japan," see Gary Snyder's foreword to *Break the Mirror.*

143. Suzuki, *Zen and Japanese Culture,* pp. 331, 333–35.

144. Minako Ohba, "Candle Fish," in *Unmapped Territories,* trans. and ed. Yukiko Tanaka (Seattle: Women in Translation, 1991), pp. 23–25.

145. Yasushi Inoue, "Under the Shadow of Mt. Bandai," trans. Stephen W. Kohl, in Van C. Gessel and Tomone Matsumoto, eds., *The Shōwa Anthology: Modern Japanese Short Stories, 1929–1984* (Tokyo and New York: Kodansha International, 1989), pp. 253–54, 266–68.

146. Quoted in J. Thomas Rimer, *A Reader's Guide to Japanese Literature* (Tokyo and New York: Kodansha International, 1988), p. 123.

147. Kazuaki Tanahashi, *Enku: Sculptor of a Hundred Thousand Buddhas* (Boulder, CO: Shambhala Publications, 1982), p. 8.

148. Quoted in Kato, *A History of Japanese Literature,* vol. 3, p. 132.

149. Zekkai, "Mountain Temple," in Donald Keene, comp. and ed., *Anthology of Japanese Literature: From the Earliest Era to the Mid-Nineteenth Century* (New York: Grove Press, 1955), p. 313.

150. Quoted in Daisetz Suzuki, *Sengai: The Zen Master* (London: Faber and Faber, 1971), p. 120.

151. Quoted in Little, *Visions of the Dharma,* p. 15.

152. Enku in Tanahashi, *Enku,* p. 12.

153. Attributed to Tea Master Rikyu's descendants, *Dream Window.*

154. Quoted in a video installation on the Japanese tea ceremony in the Japanese Gallery at the Metropolitan Museum of Art, February 1993.

155. Okakura, *The Book of Tea,* p. 21.

156. Ibid.

157. Ibid., p. 29.

158. Ibid.

159. Ibid., p. 111.

160. Ibid., pp. 109–10, 118–19.

161. Quoted in Suzuki, *Zen and Japanese Culture,* p. 244.

162. Quoted in Rimer, *A Reader's Guide to Japanese Literature,* p. 30.

163. For further details about Shōji Hamada's remarkable life, see the *Kodansha Encyclopedia of Japan,* vol. 3, p. 89.

164. Quoted in Leach, *Hamada,* pp. 14, 93, 103–4, 136–37, 295–96, 299.

165. Suzuki, *Sengai: The Zen Master,* p. 158.

166. Quoted in Conrad Hyers, *The Laughing Buddha: Zen and the Comic Spirit* (Wolfeboro, NH: Longwood Academic, 1989), p. 83.

167. Quoted in Leach, *Hamada,* p. 97.
Shōji Hamada was a close friend of Bernard Leach, Europe's most renowned potter. In 1920, he accompanied Leach to England and helped establish the Leach Pottery in St. Ives, Cornwall. *(Kodansha Encyclopedia of Japan,* vol. 3, p. 89.) The clear gentle call of the *hototogisu* (little cuckoo, which is by far the best-known cuckoo in Japan) is one of the most appreciated of all Japan's bird songs. Along with the *kakko,* another Japanese cuckoo, the *hototogisu* is the main character in many folktales. *Kodansha Encyclopedia,* vol. 2, p. 52.

168. Ekken, *Way of Contentment,* pp. 50–51.

169. Anonymous (twelfth century), from Tsutsumi Chunagon Monogatari, trans. Arthur Waley, in Keene, *Anthology of Japanese Literature,* pp. 170–72.

170. Quoted in Cynthea J. Bogel, Israel Goldman and Alfred H. Marks, *Hiroshige: Birds and Flowers* (New York: George Braziller, in association with the Rhode Island School of Design, 1988), p. 29. The Peony is a Person of Wealth and Station. The Japanese love all flowers; the peony is a favorite.

171. Sanki Ichikawa, "On the Japanese Cicada," *Japan Quarterly,* vol. 3, no. 4 (1956).

172. The world of the mythical *kappa* is the world of the legendary water goblin that has become almost emblematic of Japanese folklore.

173. Motojirō Kajii, "Mating," trans. Robert Ulmer, in *The Shōwa Anthology,* pp. 25, 27.

174. Suzuki, *Sengai: The Zen Master,* p. 84.

175. Ibid.

176. Corman and Hidetaka, translator's preface, in Shimpei Kusano, *frogs & others,* n.p.

177. Shimpei Kusano, *frogs & others,* p. 119.

178. Ibid., p. 39.

179. Ibid., p. 48.

180. Sugaware no Michizane, "The Spider," in Keene, *Anthology of Japanese Literature,* pp. 165–66.

181. Daigaku Horiguchi, "The Cicada," in Keene, *Landscapes and Portraits: Appreciations of Japanese Culture* (Tokyo and Palo Alto: Kodansha International, 1971), p. 143.

III: GREECE

1. Quoted in C. Th. Dimaras, *A History of Modern Greek Literature,* trans. Mary P. Gianos (Albany, NY: State University of New York Press, 1972), pp. 410–11.

2. Quoted in Sir James George Frazer, *The Worship of Nature* (New York: Macmillan, 1926; New York: AMS Press, 1976), p. 320.

3. Nikos Kazantzakis, *Report to Greco,* trans. P. A. Bien (New York: Simon and Schuster, 1965), p. 175.

4. Edith Hamilton, *The Greek Way* (New York: W. W. Norton, 1942), p. 338.

5. Mary Lefkowitz, "The Origins of Greece and the Illusions of Afrocentrists," *The New Republic,* February 10, 1992, pp. 29–36.

6. George Seferis, "Letter on 'The Thrush,' " in *On the Greek Style: Selected Essays in Poetry and Hellenism,* trans. Rex Warner and Th. D. Frangopoulos (Boston: Little, Brown, an Atlantic Monthly Press Book, 1966), pp. 103–4.

7. See H. D. F. Kitto, "The Greeks at War," in *The Greeks* (New York: Viking-Penguin, 1988), pp. 136–52.

8. Quoted in Hamilton, *The Greek Way,* p. 330. Plotinus was born in Egypt and studied at Alexandria under Ammonius Saccas, the great exponent of Neoplatonism. His birth date of A.D. 205 is questionable.

9. Henry Miller, *The Colossus of Maroussi* (London: Faber and Faber, 1945), pp. 74 ff.

10. Kitto, *The Greeks,* p. 252.

11. Lefkowitz, "The Origins of Greece" p. 32. Lefkowitz does emphasize the point that "[c]lassicists . . . know, at least as well as our critics, that much of our so-called knowledge of the past is based on educated guesswork and sensible conjectures." Ibid., p. 30.

Lefkowitz cites the reflections of the great Italian-Jewish historian, Arnaldo Momigliano, on what he considers to be a valued inheritance that is typically Greek:

. . . what I think is typically Greek is the critical attitude toward the recording of events, that is, the development of critical methods enabling us to distinguish between facts and fancies. To the best of my knowledge no historiography earlier than the Greek or independent of it developed these critical methods; and we have inherited the Greek methods.

12. Stewart Flory, *The Archaic Smile of Herodotus* (Detroit: Wayne State University Press, 1987), p. 82. Flory points out in his introduction that the Greek word *historia,* in Herodotus' time, meant "inquiry," and that a concept of history as we understand it did not exist.

13. Quoted in Robert Drews, *The Greek Accounts of Eastern History* (Washington, DC: The Center for Hellenic Studies, 1973), p. 147 n.

14. Bernhard Abraham Van Groningen, *In the Grip of the Past: Essay on an Aspect of Greek Thought* (Leiden: E. J. Brill, 1953), p. 50.

15. George Seferis, *Poems,* trans. Rex Warner (Boston: Nonpareil Books, 1978), p. 29.

16. Aristophanes, *Clouds,* in G. Lowes Dickinson, *The Greek View of Life* (New York: Collier Books, 1961), p. 45.

17. Quoted in Frazer, *The Worship of Nature,* p. 321.

18. Quoted in *The Pursuit of Greece: An Anthology,* selected by Philip Sherrard (Athens: Denise Harvey, 1987), p. 19.

19. Differing views exist concerning not only the authorship of the *Hymns* but also the period of time in which they were composed. We call the Homeric hymns "Homeric," states Greek translator Apostolos Athanassakis, "not because we believe that Homer composed them but merely because for a long time the ancients thought that Homer did compose them and, therefore, they referred to them as Homeric." When the Alexandrians dismissed the Homeric attribution, "the integrity and the worth of the hymns came under suspicion," says Athanassakis, and for this reason, he suggests, the hymns were neglected and fell into an unwarranted obscurity not only in antiquity but also in modern times. *The Homeric Hymns,* trans. Apostolos N. Athanassakis (Baltimore: Johns Hopkins University Press, 1976), p. viii.

Author Charles Boer puts it another way when he asks in his translation of *The Homeric Hymns,* "Who composed the *Homeric Hymns?*" He replies that "[t]he name 'Homer' has been assigned to a body of epic poetry that centered on the Trojan War (1220 B.C.) and continued to be narrated, revised and resung for the next several hundred years. Homer was the author (*aoidos* or 'singer') of the *Iliad* and the *Odyssey,* but these works show many layers of composition and a personal identity is only assigned to 'Homer' on the basis of argument for one of these 'layers' (probably an eighth century one) being more important than others." Charles Boer, trans., *The Homeric Hymns* (Irving, TX: Spring Publications, 1979), p. iii.

20. Athanassakis, *The Homeric Hymns,* pp. 67–68.

21. Charlene Spretnak, *The Lost Goddesses of Early Greece: A Collection of Pre-Hellenic Myths* (Boston: Beacon Press, 1984), p. 84.

22. Ibid., p. 24.

23. Quoted in Spretnak, *Lost Goddesses,* p. 37.

24. Spretnak points out that the Homeric Hymn is "clearly rooted in the Olym-

pian tradition because it addresses Gaia as 'Mother of the gods' and 'wife of starry Heaven.' Long before she was regarded as mother of the powerful deities, she herself was the powerful deity." Spretnak, p. 45.

25. Ibid., p. 46.

26. Ibid., pp. 47–49.

27. Plato, *Phaedo*, in *The Last Days of Socrates*, trans. Hugh Tredennick (London: Penguin, 1954), pp. 145–47.

28. Ibid., pp. 146–48.

29. Plato, *Critias*, trans. Rev. R. G. Bury, The Loeb Classical Library, vol. IX (1929; reprint, Cambridge: Harvard University Press, 1981), pp. 273–75.

30. *The Dialogues of Plato* (selections), trans. Benjamin Jowett (New York: Liveright Publishing, 1927), p. 441.

31. Ibid., p. 457.

32. Ibid., p. 446.

33. Quoted in *Sappho and the Greek Lyric Poets*, trans. Willis Barnstone (New York: Schocken, 1988), p. 254.

34. Quoted in James Adam, *The Religious Teachers of Greece* (Edinburgh: T. & T. Clark, 1909), p. 21.

35. Quoted in Albin Lesky, *A History of Greek Literature*, trans. James Willis and Cornelius de Heer (London: Methuen, 1966), p. 201.

36. Plato, *Phaedrus*, in *The Collected Dialogues of Plato*, trans. R. Hackforth, eds. Edith Hamilton and Huntington Cairns, Bollingen Series LXXI (Princeton, NJ: Princeton University Press, 1989), p. 525.

Pan is the goat-footed god of shepherds and flocks. This most delightful description of Pan (a small fragment of the work) is to be found in the *Homeric Hymns*, exquisitely translated by Charles Boer:

> *Pan,*
> *the pastoral god*
> *with magnificent hair . . .*
> *very noisy*
> *but laughing*
> *sweetly . . .*
> *And they decided to call him*
> > *Pan*
> *because he had delighted the minds of*
> > *all*

(See pp. 64–65.)

37. Athanassakis, *The Homeric Hymns*, p. xii.

38. Boer, *The Homeric Hymns*, p. iv.

39. Ibid., p. iii.

40. William Arrowsmith, in a review of Boer's *The Homeric Hymns* (jacket), n.d.

41. The Muses were the nine goddesses who presided over the arts and sciences, including poetry, music, dance and astronomy. They were the daughters of Zeus, ruler and father of the gods, and Mnemosyne, goddess of memory. Apollo and his twin sister, Artemis, were offspring of Zeus and Leto. Apollo was god of medicine, archery, music, the sun, and prophecy, and the ideal of youthful male beauty.

42. Boer, *The Homeric Hymns*, p. 88.

43. Ibid., p. 8

44. Ibid., p. 182.

45. Quoted in W. K. C. Guthrie, *The Greeks and Their Gods* (Boston: Beacon Press, 1955), pp. 53–54.

46. Spretnak, *Lost Goddesses*, pp. 99–101.

47. Quoted in Barnstone, *Sappho and the Greek Lyric Poets*, p. 186.

48. Spretnak, *Lost Goddesses*, p. 69.

49. Ibid., pp. 71–72.

50. Lilika Nakos in Deborah Tannen, *Lilika Nakos* (Boston: Twayne Publishers, 1983). Tannen describes the *kallikantzaroi* as "mischievous demons which are believed to cause annoying but not dangerous mishaps between Christmas Day and Epiphany (January 6th)." (*Lilika Nakos*, p. 178).

51. Ibid., pp. 152–53.

52. Quoted in Arthur Fairbanks, *The First Philosophy of Greece* (New York: Charles Scribner's Sons, 1898), p. 69.

53. Angelos Sikelianos in *Angelos Sikelianos: Selected Poems*, trans. Edmund Keeley and Philip Sherrard (Princeton, NJ: Princeton University Press, 1979), p. xiv.

54. Quoted in Humbert Wolfe, *Others Abide* (London: Ernest Benn, 1927), p. 85.

55. Quoted in K. D. White, *Country Life in Classical Times* (Ithaca, NY: Cornell University Press, 1977), p. 27.

56. See Aristophanes, *Birds*, ed. and trans. Alan 'H. Sommerstein (Teddington House, Warminster, Wilts.: Aris & Phillips, 1987), p. 2.

57. Ibid., 95, 97, 99.

58. Quoted in *Classical Studies in Honor of John C. Rolfe: Essays on Sophocles; Ancient Wit and Humor*, ed. George Depue Hadzsits (Freeport, NY: Books for Libraries Press, 1967), p. 141.

59. Quoted in Adam, *The Religious Teachers of Greece*, pp. 163–64.

60. Ibid., p. 164.

61. Sophocles, *The Theban Plays*, trans. E. F. Watling (Baltimore: Penguin, 1953), p. 92.

62. Theocritus, Idyll 7, "The Harvest Festival," in *Theocritus: The Idylls*, trans. Robert Wells (London: Penguin, 1989), p. 86.

63. Quoted in Rae Dalven, trans. and ed., *Modern Greek Poetry* (New York: Russell & Russell, 1971), p. 48.

64. Konstantinos Dapontes, "The Garden of Graces," in Sherrard, *The Pursuit of Greece*, 204–5.

65. Helen Dendrinou Kolias, trans., in Elisavet Moutzan-Martinengou, *My Story* (Athens, GA: The University of Georgia Press, 1989), p. ix.

66. Quoted in Moutzan-Martinengou, *My Story*, p. xx.

67. Ibid., p. xxi. Kolias quoting writer Maurice Rowdon on the environment of convents and the happiness they provided for many young girls.

68. Moutzan-Martinengou, *My Story*, pp. 5, 9, 10.

69. Kazantzakis, *Report to Greco*, p. 435.

70. Ibid., pp. 17–18.

71. Ibid., pp. 34, 435–36, 485–86.

72. Kazantzakis, *Zorba the Greek* (New York: Simon and Schuster, 1952), p. 32.

73. Kazantzakis, *Report to Greco*, p. 484.

74. Venezis, *Aiolian Land*, p. 153.

75. Ibid., pp. 41–42.

76. Yannopoulos, "The Greek Line," in Sherrard, *The Pursuit of Greece*, pp. 223–25.

77. George Seferis, "The Cistern," in Dalven, *Modern Greek Poetry*, p. 256.

78. George Seferis, *A Poet's Journal: Days of 1945–1951*, trans. Athan Anagnostopoulos (Cambridge: The Belknap Press of Harvard University, 1974), pp. 64–65.

79. Seferis, *Poems*, p. 49.

80. Seferis, *A Poet's Journal*, p. 59.

81. Marco Pallis, *The Way and the Mountain* (London: Peter Owen, 1961), pp. 30–31.

82. Quoted in Dalven, *Modern Greek Poetry*, p. 338.

83. Quoted in Barnstone, *Sappho and the Greek Lyric Poets*, p. 146.

84. Kazantzakis, *Report to Greco*, p. 175.

85. Thucydides, *The History of the Peloponnesian War*, trans. Richard Crawley (New York: Dutton, 1950), p. 122.

86. Isocrates, *Panegyricus*, trans. George Norlin, The Loeb Classical Library, vol. 1 (23–27) (New York: Putnam, 1928), p. 133.

87. Lilika Nakos in Tannen, *Lilika Nakos*, p. 142.

88. Ibid., pp. 153–54.

89. Quoted in Barnstone, *Sappho and the Greek Lyric Poets*, p. 161.

90. Quoted in Richard Stoneman, ed., *A Literary Companion to Travel in Greece* (Harmondsworth: Penguin, 1984), pp. 123–24.

91. Quoted in Vincent Scully, *The Earth, the Temple and the Gods: Greek Sacred Architecture* (New York: Praeger, 1969), p. 9.

92. Dionysios Solomos, "The Cretan," in Dalven, *Modern Greek Poetry*, p. 88.

93. Kostas Pasagianis, "Greek Travels," in Sherrard, *The Pursuit of Greece*, pp. 168–69.

94. Pallis, *The Way and the Mountain*, p. 13.

Marco Pallis was born in 1895 of Greek parentage, in Liverpool. He made his first mountain-climbing trek to Tibet in 1933, where he also became a student of Buddhism. He has written a second book, entitled *Peaks and Lamas* (London: Knopf, 1949).

95. Ibid., p. 17.

96. Ibid., pp. 18, 20–3.

97. Ibid., p. 32.

98. Seferis, "A Letter to a Foreign Friend," in *On the Greek Style*, p. 171.

99. Seferis, *A Poet's Journal*, p. 28.

100. Frederick J. E. Woodbridge, *Aristotle's Vision of Nature*, ed. John Herman Randall, Jr., with the assistance of Charles H. Kahn and Harold A. Larrabee (New York: Columbia University Press, 1966), p. 163. This is an interpretation by Woodbridge.

101. Kazantzakis, *Report to Greco*, p. 164.

102. Seferis, "A Letter to a Foreign Friend," p. 171.

103. Konstantine Mavroyannis, a passage from *Observations on the Climate of Athens* in Sherrard, *The Pursuit of Greece*, p. 26.

104. Seferis, *A Poet's Journal*, pp. 15, 64.

105. Quoted in Gregory Jusdanis, *The Poetics of Cavafy: Textuality, Eroticism, History* (Princeton, NJ: Princeton University Press, 1987), p. 23.

106. Quoted in Edith Hamilton, *The Greek Way*, p. 291. The full citation of Plato's admiration for Homer reads:

I have always from my earliest years had an awe of Homer and a love for him which even now [when he is about to criticize him] make the words falter on my lips. He is the great leader and teacher.

107. Seferis, *A Poet's Journal*, p. 49.

108. Homer, *Odyssey*, XI, 222–24, in Ennis Rees, trans., *The Odyssey of Homer* (New York: Macmillan, 1991), p. 180.

In an entry in his diary on Wednesday, October 23, 1946, George Seferis comments on the threatening beauty of the light in Greece extending its potential danger to Homer's "infirmity":

This light, this landscape, these days start to threaten me seriously. I close the shutters so I can work. I must protect myself from beauty . . . You feel your brain emptying and lightening . . . Today I understood why Homer was blind; if he had had eyes he wouldn't have written anything. He saw once, for a *limited* period of time, then saw no more. In Greece, alas, if you want to see all the time you must keep narrowing the diaphragm, as one does in photography . . .

Seferis, *A Poet's Journal*, p. 53.

109. Konstantinos Lardas, trans. *Mourning Songs of Greek Women* (New York: Garland Publishing, 1992), p. xi.

110. Katerina Anghelaki-Rook, "My Heart at Night," in Dinos Siotis and John Chioles, eds., *Twenty Contemporary Greek Poets* (San Francisco: Wire Press, 1979), p. 17.

111. Quoted in Fairbanks, *The First Philosophers of Greece*, p. 67.

112. Kazantzakis in an "Open Letter" to a periodical in Athens, quoted in Pandelis Prevelakis, *Nikos Kazantzakis and His Odyssey: A Study of the Poet and the Poem*, trans. Philip Sherrard (New York: Simon and Schuster, 1961), p. 34.

113. See Seferis, *On the Greek Style*, p. 18.

114. Quoted in Dimaras, *A History of Modern Greek Literature*, p. 411.

115. Yannopoulos, "The Greek Line," in Sherrard, *The Pursuit of Greece*, pp. 34–36.

116. Quoted in Dimaras, *A History of Modern Greek Literature*, p. 410.

117. Quoted in Stoneman, *A Literary Companion to Travel in Greece*, p. 14.

118. Seferis, *A Poet's Journal*, p. 146.

119. Seferis, "Astyanax," in *Poems*, p. 27.

120. Sikelianos in Keeley and Sherrard, *Angelos Sikelianos*, p. xv.

121. Ibid., pp. xiii–xiv.

122. Kazantzakis, *Report to Greco*, p. 159.

123. Quoted in James Olney, *Tell Me Africa: An Approach to African Literature* (Princeton, NJ: Princeton University Press, 1973), p. 149. Olney suggests that Socrates was "referring to the knowledge that the individual carries over from one incarnation to another; he was not speaking of rediscovery or recollection, nor of literal return, within the span of a single life." Ibid.

124. Sherrard, *The Pursuit of Greece*, p. 4.

125. Keeley and Sherrard, *Angelos Sikelianos*, p. xv.

126. Professor Willis Barnstone *(Sappho and the Greek Lyric Poets)* writes that Sappho was preceded by Archilochos "by some fifty years as the man to whom we can attribute a significant body of extant lyric poetry and is the very first individual voice in the Western lyric tradition. The earliest poet whose texts we know, and even possess in cuneiforms from the third millennium, is the Sumerian woman poet Enheduanna, from about 2300 B.C." (p. 269 n.).

A. R. Burn, in *The Lyric Age of Greece*, states that poetry was a common pursuit of women not only on Lesbos but also in other parts of Greece. He suggests that Sappho accepted her position as a woman poet as a natural course of events. References to other woman poets include the names Gongyla, Corinna, Myrtis and Praxilla. A. R. Burn, *The Lyric Age of Greece* (London: Edward Arnold, 1978), p. 229.

127. Barnstone, *Sappho and the Greek Lyric Poets*, p. 274. Professor Barnstone states that Sappho's work enjoyed a wide popularity in antiquity and that it was well preserved. The Church, however, condemned it as amoral and licentious, and ca. A.D. 380, the Bishop of Constantinople, Saint Gregory of Nazianzos ordered the burning of her writings wherever they existed. Again, in A.D. 1073, another burning of her works was mandated by Pope Gregory VII. For a broad discussion of these events and subsequent historical pillages and recoveries, see Barnstone, pp. 274–76.

128. Quoted in *Sappho, Poems and Fragments*, trans. Josephine Balmer (Secaucus, NJ: Meadowland Books, 1984), p. 27, no. 99.

The choice and juxtaposition of Sappho's words were also praised:

> *Like a mountain whirlwind*
> *punishing the oak trees,*
> *love shattered my heart.*

Barnstone, *Sappho and the Greek Lyric Poets*, p. 67.

129. The full quotation, attributed to Plato, is: "Some say nine Muses—but count again. / Behold the tenth: Sappho of Lesbos." Barnstone, p. 180.

130. Plato, *Phaedrus*, in *The Collected Dialogues of Plato*, p. 483.

131. Strabo, *Geography*. Strabo was a first century A.D. geographer. The full quotation appears as follows:

A contemporary of Pittakos and Alkaios was Sappho,—a marvel. In all the centuries since history began we know of no woman who in any true sense can be said to rival her as a poet.

Barnstone, *Sappho and the Greek Lyric Poets*, p. 65.

From the Scholiast on Lucian's *Portraits*, reports Barnstone, we have a picture of contrasts: Sappho is described as dark, unattractive and short, "like a nightingale with misshapen wings enfolding a tiny body"; then she is called "the delicious glory of the Lesbians." Barnstone, p. 271.

132. Barnstone, ibid., p. 269.

133. Balmer, *Sappho: Poems and Fragments*, no. 33.

134. Barnstone, *Sappho and the Greek Lyric Poets*, p. 69.

135. Balmer, *Sappho: Poems and Fragments*, n.p., no. 114—"nightingale" fragment; no. 110—"Hesperus" fragment. Hesperus is depicted in Greek art as a young boy carrying a torch. Ibid., p. 107.

136. Barnstone, *Sappho and the Greek Lyric Poets*, pp. 68, 73–74. Aphrodite is goddess of love and beauty; she sprang from the foam of the sea near Paphos in Cyprus.

137. Balmer, *Sappho*, no. 6.

138. Adam, *The Religious Teachers of Greece*, p. 19.

139. Quoted in Frazer, *The Worship of Nature*, pp. 49–50.

140. G. S. Kirk and J. E. Raven, *The Presocratic Philosophers* (1957; reprint Cambridge: Cambridge University Press, 1967), p. 184.

141. Ibid., p. 184 n.

142. Ibid., p. 185.

143. The author of more than forty books and pamphlets and several collections of poetry, Thomas Merton is perhaps best known for his inspirational and witty biographical account of seeking monkhood amidst the pratfalls of day-to-day life so humanly described in his *The Seven Storey Mountain*. His translations of selected teachings of Heraclitus' philosophy, "The Legacy of Herakleitos," appeared in *The Collected Poems of Thomas Merton* (New York: New Directions, 1977), pp. 767–74.

144. Robert S. Brumbaugh, *The Philosophers of Greece* (New York: Thomas Y. Crowell, 1964), p. 47.

145. This particular fragment of Heraclitus' teaching was translated by Philip Sherrard and appeared in his *The Pursuit of Greece*, p. 156.

146. Adam, *The Religious Teachers of Greece*, p. 356.

147. Quoted in Brumbaugh, *The Philosophers of Greece*, p. 133.

148. Ibid.

149. Ibid., p. 134.

150. Jowett, *The Dialogues of Plato*, pp. 532–33.

151. *Hippocrates*, trans. W. H. S. Jones, The Loeb Classical Library, vol. 1 (Cambridge: Harvard University Press, 1962), pp. 137, 331, 333, 345, 347, 351.

IV. AFRICA

1. Chinua Achebe, *Hopes and Impediments* (New York: Doubleday, 1989), p. 92.

2. Cosmas Okechukwu Obiego, *African Image of the Ultimate Reality: An Analysis of Igbo Ideas of Life and Death in Relation to Chunkwu-God* (Frankfurt am Main: Peter Lang, 1984), p. 144.

3. Prince Modupe, *I Was a Savage* (London: Museum Press, 1958), p. 26.

4. Quoted in John S. Mbiti, *Introduction to African Religion*, 2d ed. (London: Heinemann Educational Books, 1991), p. 212.

5. Kwame Anthony Appiah, *In My Father's House* (New York: Oxford University Press, 1992) pp. 26–27.

6. John S. Mbiti, *African Religions and Philosophy*, 2d ed., rev. and enl. (Oxford: Heinemann Educational Books, 1990) pp. 26–27.

7. Quoted in Benjamin C. Ray, *African Religions* (Englewood Cliffs, NJ: Prentice-Hall, 1976), pp. 165–66.

8. *Nightline* with Ted Koppel, "Report on Famine in Ethiopia," July 8, 1991.

9. Bâ, "Earth, Moon, and Sun," *Parabola*, vol. XIV, no. 3 (1989), p. 50.

10. Modupe, *I Was a Savage*, p. 7.

11. Quoted in James Olney, *Tell Me Africa: An Approach to African Literature*, p. 112.

12. Quoted in Bernbaum, *Sacred Mountains of the World*, p. 141.

13. See ibid.

14. Kenneth David Kaunda, *Letter to My Children* (London: Longman, 1973), p. 17.

15. Mbiti, *Introduction to African Religion*, p. 212.

16. Ibid.

17. Kofi Awoonor, *The Breast of the Earth* (New York: NOK Publishers, 1975), p. 174.

18. Ogotemmêli in Griaule, *Conversations with Ogotemmêli*, p. 112.

19. K. A. Busia, *The Position of the Chief in the Modern Political System of Ashanti* (London: Frank Cass, 1968), p. 40.

20. Ibid.

21. Ibid., p. 27.

22. Ibid., p. 41.

23. Mbiti, *African Religions and Philosophy*, p. 31.

24. Quoted in John S. Mbiti, *The Prayers of African Religion* (Maryknoll, NY: Orbis Books, 1975), pp. 148–49.

25. J. H. Driberg, *People of the Small Arrow* (New York: Payson & Clarke, 1930), pp. 142–43.

26. Clement Agunwa, *More Than Once* (London: Longmans, Green, 1967), pp. 100–101.

27. Bâ, "Earth, Moon, and Sun," pp. 49–50.

28. Obiego, *African Image of the Ultimate Reality*, pp. 116–17.

29. Chinua Achebe, *Things Fall Apart* (New York: Astor-Honor, 1959, p. 26.

30. Kofi Anyidoho, *Earthchild* (Accra: Woeli Publication Services, 1985), pp. 43–44.

31. Quoted in Colin M. Turnbull, *The Forest People* (New York: Simon and Schuster, A Touchstone Book, 1962), p. 74.

32. Ibid., p. 83.

33. Ibid., p. 125.

34. Ibid., p. 30.

35. Ibid., pp. 92–93.

36. R. Mugo Gatheru, *Child of Two Worlds* (London: Heinemann Educational Books, 1964), pp. 6, 7.

37. Michelle Gilbert, "The Sources of Power in Akuropon-Akuapem: Ambiguity in Classification," in *Creativity of Power: Cosmology and Action in African Societies*, W. Arens and Ivan Karp, eds. (Washington, DC: Smithsonian Institution Press, 1989), p. 75.

38. Quoted in Gilbert, "Sources of Power," p. 59.

39. Modupe, *I Was a Savage*, 25–26.

40. Quoted in Susan Vogel, ed., *Africa Explores: 20th Century African Art* (New York: The Center for African Art, 1991), p. 276.

41. Quoted in Laurens Van Der Post, *The Lost World of the Kalahari* (New York: William Morrow, 1958), p. 246.

42. Naomi Kipury, *Oral Literature of the Maasai* (Nairobi: Heinemann Educational Books, 1983), p. 3.

43. Anthony K. Andoh, *The Science and Romance of Selected Herbs Used in Medicine and Religious Ceremony* (San Francisco: The North Scale Institute, 1987), pp. 40, 24.

44. Quoted in Andoh, *The Science and Romance of Selected Herbs,* p. 40.

Professor Emeritus Richard Evans Schultes is Director and Curator of Economic Botany at the Botanical Museum of Harvard University.

45. Andoh, *The Science and Romance of Selected Herbs,* p. 18. Andoh cites an example of this "re-discovery" in his discussion of the ancient Egyptians' use of cabbage seeds "to prevent intoxication." He tells us that "today, cabbage juice is being used to treat alcoholism" (quoting Adele G. Dawson's work, in *Health, Happiness, and the Pursuit of Herbs* [Brattleboro, VT: Stephen Green Press, 1980]). Garlic, he says, was so highly valued as a natural cure-all that (quoting Dawson again) "fifteen pounds of it was the going rate for an able-bodied slave."

46. Ecclesiastes 3:1.

47. Andoh, *The Science and Romance of Selected Herbs,* pp. 17–18, 40–41.

48. Quoted in Maureen Slattery, catalog ed., *Modern Days, Ancient Nights: Thirty Years of African Filmmaking* (New York: The Film Society of Lincoln Center, 1993), p. 24.

49. Quoted in Melville J. Herskovits and Francis S. Herskovits, *Dahomean Narrative* (Evanston, IL: Northwestern University Press, 1970), p. 63. The Herskovitses suggest that "hope for the future prominence of the clan" is an apt interpretation.

50. Quoted in Ulli Beier, ed., *An Introduction to African Literature: An Anthology of Critical Writing* (London: Longman Group, 1979), p. 239.

51. Bessie Head, *Serowe: Village of the Rain Wind* (London: Heinemann Educational Books, 1981), pp. ix–xiii.

52. Bessie Head, *A Question of Power* (New York: Pantheon, 1973), p. 11.

53. Ibid.

54. Review by Ronald Blythe, *The Sunday Times,* London, n.d.

55. For further details about the history, characteristics and influence of the Green Tree in the village life of Serowe, see Head, *Serowe,* pp. xvii–xviii.

56. Bessie Head, "The Green Tree," *Transition,* vol. 4, no. 16 (1964), p. 33. This phrase refers to a passage in "The Green Tree" that speaks of strangers traversing the land, "fugitives from the south fleeing political oppression." Head writes: "It is good that they do not know the passion we feel for this parched earth. We tolerate strangers because the things we love cannot be touched by them."

57. Head, "The Green Tree," p. 33.

58. Olney, *Tell Me Africa,* p. 207.

59. Cheikh Hamidou Kane, *Ambiguous Adventure,* trans. Katherine Woods (London: Heinemann Educational Books, 1963. Originally published in France as *L'aventure ambiguë* in 1962), p. 112.

60 Ibid., pp. 139–40, 148–50.

61. Tepilit Ole Saitoti, *The Worlds of a Maasai Warrior* (New York: Random House, 1986), pp. 136–37.

62. See Kaunda, *Letter to My Children.*

63. Kenneth Kaunda and Colin Morris, *A Humanist in Africa* (Nashville, TN: Abingdon Press, 1966), pp. 22–24.

64. Quoted in *African Heritage: Intimate Views of the Black Africans from Life, Lore, and Literature,* ed. Jacob Drachler (New York: Crowell-Collier Press, 1963), pp. 94–95.

65. Peter Abrahams, *Tell Freedom: Memories of Africa* (New York: Knopf, 1966), pp. 43–47.

66. Kofi Nyidevu Awoonor, *Comes the Voyager At Last* (Trenton, NJ: Africa World Press, 1992), p. 43.

67. Ibid., pp. 43–44.

68. Quoted in Oladele Taiwo, *Social Experience in African Literature* (Enugu, Nigeria: Fourth Dimension, 1986), p. 165.

69. Jomo Kenyatta, *Facing Mount Kenya: The Tribal Life of the Kikuyu* (1938; reprint, London: Martin Secker & Warburg, 1959), p. xxi.

70. Jomo Kenyatta, *My People of Kikuyu* (London: Oxford University Press, 1966), pp. 23–24.

71. Kenyatta, *Facing Mount Kenya,* p. 311.

72. Ibid., p. 317.

Land ownership in Kikuyu society is not recognized. It can, however, be *held* in a number of different ways: privately, collectively, and in trust; always in partnership, never in proprietorship. Ibid., pp. 310–12; also look at Chapter 2.

73. In the Preface to his book *Facing Mount Kenya,* Jomo Kenyatta points out that "Gikuyu" is the correct spelling of his tribal society (the strict phonetic spelling is "Gekoyo") and that "Kikuyu" is the preferred European usage, but incorrect.

74. Ibid., pp. xxi, 21, 316–18.

75. Ngugi wa Thiong'o (James Ngugi), *Weep Not, Child* (1964; reprint, New York: Collier-Macmillan, 1969), pp. 33, 35.

76. Ibid., p. 31.

77. Kofi Nyidevu Awoonor, *Contemporary Authors Autobiography Series,* vol. 13 (Detroit: Gale Research Inc., 1991), p. 41.

78. Ibid., p. 41.

79. Awoonor, *The Breast of the Earth,* pp. 282–83.

80. Jack Mapanje and Landeg White, comps., *Oral Poetry of Africa: An Anthology* (New York: Longman, 1983), p. 52.

81. Camara Laye, *The Dark Child: The Autobiography of an African Boy,* trans. James Kirkup and Ernest Jones (New York: Farrar, Straus & Giroux, 1954; New York: Hill and Wang, 1992), pp. 55–58, 60–62.

82. K. Kia Bunseki Fu-Kiau, *The African Book Without Title* (Privately published, 1980), pp. 18, 20.

83. Ibid., p. 22.

84. Ibid., p. 29.

85. Ibid., pp. 27, 29, 60.

86. See Bernbaum, *Sacred Mountains of the World,* p. 135.

87. Mircea Eliade, *Patterns in Comparative Religion,* trans. Rosemary Sheed (New York: New American Library, 1974), p. 99.

88. See Bernbaum's treasure-trove, *Sacred Mountains of the World,* a thought-provoking and important contribution to an understanding of mountains as living entities, cosmic centers, profound spiritual loci of truth, and in the author's own case, as physical and mental worlds to scale and to learn from.

89. Kenyatta, *Facing Mount Kenya,* pp. 234, 236–37. See pp. 3–6 for Kenyatta's recapitulation of his tribal origin legend, with *Kere-Nyaga* assuming center stage.

90. Ibid., pp. 236–37.

91. Ibid., p. 253.

92. Awoonor, *The Breast of the Earth,* p. 226.

93. Ibid., p. 255. Awoonor argues that Tutuola's works, "because of their clear antecedents, cannot be discussed as novels, but rather as romances which base themselves on the Yoruba folk tale." Awoonor suggests that Tutuola's highly significant storytelling is "[c]ast in the mold of what Northrop Frye calls the 'naive quest romance,' " demonstrating how his stories "follow the pattern of the folk story in which the man or animal hero or heroine departs in order to acquire knowledge, wealth, food, and the wherewithal for survival in an uncertain world. The features of the quest are the trials, labors, revelations which the hero experiences on his journey." Tutuola's marvelous creative impulse lies in his ability to link the multiple "aspects of the quest through more than one story," says Awoonor, thereby establishing a unified universe of wisdom. Ibid., pp. 226–50.

94. Quoted in Michael Charles Tobias and Harold Drasdo, eds., *The Mountain Spirit* (Woodstock, NY: Overlook Press, 1979), pp. 125–26.

95. Gatheru, *Child of Two Worlds,* p. 1.

96. Ibid., pp. 2–3.

97. Quoted in Elizabeth Roberts and Elias Amadon, eds., *Earth Prayers* (San Francisco: HarperCollins, 1991), p. 219.

98. Mustapha Tlili, *Lion Mountain,* trans. Linda Coverdale (New York: Arcade, 1990), pp. 3, 8–9, 13, 17.

99. Bâ, "Intermediaries for the Sacred Force," *Parabola,* vol. XIV, no. 2 (1989), p. 11.

100. For these and additional biographical and anecdotal details about Bâ's extraordinary life and work, see Daniel Whitman's foreword to and translation of Amadou Hampâté Bâ's *Kaidara* (Washington, DC: Three Continents Press, 1988).

101. Bâ, "Earth, Moon, and Sun," p. 49.

102. Bâ, "Intermediaries for the Sacred Force," pp. 11–12.

In the African classic *Conversations with Ogotemmêli,* a series of thirty-three consecutive conversations about Dogon cosmology and sacred traditions—between French ethnologist Marcel Griaule and blind elder Ogotemmêli, a Dogon of Africa's Western Sudan—the mythical and divine aspects of the craft of pottery making are explained:

> The mat on which the woman works, is a symbol of that of the first human couple. The craft of pottery is like a person on a mat. In molding the clay the woman is imitating the work of God when he modeled the earth and the first couple. She is creating a being, and the round pot is like a head resting on the mat, a head or a womb. . . .
>
> The mat on which the potter works has eighty threads one way and eighty threads the other. It is woven like one square of the pall that covers the dead, but with fibers of baobab instead of cotton. . . .
>
> Patterns made on pots in this way [as in the mat] make one think one has one's mat with one for repose wherever one goes. . . .
>
> "And what," Ogotemmêli was asked, "of the pebble with which the clay is struck?"
>
> "The stone," was the reply, "which the woman rolls in the clay is the symbol of the food which will be cooked in the pot."
>
> "So a humble pot," adds Griaule, "is an epitome of the universe, with its own mat on its surface."
>
> Griaule, *Conversations with Ogotemmêli,* pp. 89–90.

103. Bâ, "Intermediaries for the Sacred Force," p. 9.

104. Ibid., pp. 10–11.

105. Awoonor, *The Breast of the Earth,* p. 60. Mahogany and wawa are the woods that are commonly used for traditional and religious art. Effigies in ancestral shrines are generally made of clay.

106. Ibid., p. 60.

107. A. A. Y. Kyerematen, *Panoply of Ghana* (New York: Praeger, 1964), p. 118.

108. Quoted in Awoonor, *The Breast of the Earth,* p. 89. Awoonor's discussion of the language of drumming, its revelatory poetic nature and its vital role in Ewe poetry in addition to the intuitive characteristics embedded in the calling of the musician and the poet, is fascinating.

109. Quoted in Kyerematen, *Panoply of Ghana,* p. 60.

110. Quoted in Awoonor, *The Breast of the Earth,* p. 162.

111. Camara Laye, *The Dark Child,* p. 75.

In addition to *The Dark Child,* Camara Laye's works include *A Dream of Africa* and *The Radiance of the King.* All three books are about return, re-discovery, reunion and re-collection, ideally, literally and symbolically.

112. Olney, *Tell Me Africa,* p. 136.

113. Laye, *The Dark Child,* p. 35.

114. Ibid., pp. 31–33.

115. Modupe, *I Was a Savage,* p. 27.

116. Quoted in Mbiti, *The Prayers of African Religion,* p. 69.

117. Odette St. Lys, *From a Vanished German Colony; A Collection of Folklore,*

Folk Tales and Proverbs from South-West Africa (London: Gypsy Press, 1916), pp. 149–50.

In a letter dated *Umtata*, Dec. 1st, 1879, the Bishop of St. John's wrote the following comments on this luminous passage:

> I have just translated what I regard as a literary gem. It contains two songs [I've included only one]. I have had it by me for sometime, but could not translate it without a Kxosa Kafir, as there were some archaisms in it, and allusions which . . . one . . . acquainted with the songs could explain . . .

> (See p. 149 n.)

118. Herskovits, *Dahomean Narrative*, Introductory Page.

119. Quoted in Wilson, *World Scripture*, p. 567.

120. Harold Courlander, *A Treasury of African Folklore* (New York: Crown, 1975), p. 117.

121. Henry John Drewal and John Pemberton III, *Yoruba: Nine Centuries of African Art and Thought* (New York: Harry N. Abrams and the Center for African Art, 1989), p. 15.

122. Mbiti, *Introduction to African Religion*.

123. Kwame Gyekye, *The Unexamined Life* (Accra: Ghana Universities Press, 1988), pp. 31–32.

124. Bâ, "Earth, Moon, and Sun," p. 52.

125. Courlander, *A Treasury of African Folklore*, p. 66.

126. Mbiti, *Introduction to African Religion*, p. 208.

127. Quoted in *Millennium: Wisdom and the Modern Modern World*, host: David Maybury-Lewis, a 10-part PBS/BBC television series, broadcast May 1992.

128. Mbiti, *Introduction to African Religion*, p. 210.

129. Herskovits, *Dahomean Narrative*, introductory page.

130. Wilson, *World Scripture*, p. 567.

131. Mbiti, *Introduction to African Religion*, p. 210.

132. Ibid., p. 208.

133. Ibid., p. 209.

134. K. Kia Bunseki Fu-Kiau, *The African Book Without Title*, pp. 3–4, 22.

135. Ibid., p. 51. Fu-Kiau describes *Muntu* (person) as a "set of concrete social relationships; he is a system of systems; the pattern of patterns being." Ibid., p. 13.

136. Ibid.

137. Ibid., p. 49. Fu-Kiau firmly believes that proverbs "tell us how lawful, philosophical, systematic and practical African people were in their own world." He points out that "one must understand that a proverb, for African people and those with a basically oral literature, is not seen and understood in the way [the] western world sees and understands it. For us, because of lack of material to write on in the past, proverbs are principles, theories, warehouses of knowledge, booklets, taped information, and, above all, they have *'force de loi,'* force of law, in judiciary circumstances." Ibid., p. 63.

138. Fu-Kiau describes *Kânda* as "the structural base of the African community life as well as its organizational patterns." Ibid., p. 23.

In traditional African law, *Kânda* is everything. Fu-Kiau's own description of his early community life is illuminating:

> I grew up in a village community of at least 1,000 inhabitants (before it knew the rural exodus). There was no single policeman; the jail was unknown, no secret agent i.e. a people's watchdog; it did not have a bureau of investigation, no sentry to watch on people's goods. In day time the village was practically . . . empty without a single person to take care . . . [of] unlocked doors. Strangers were always welcomed. Everyone felt responsible to everybody else in the community and its neighborhood. When a community member suffered, it was the community as a

whole that suffered. Until my age of 25 it was very nice to live in that community, literally a community without problem. Such communities still exist in many parts of the world known as "developing regions" where the imperialistic arms race did not yet trouble the peace.

Ibid., p. 18.

139. Ibid., pp. 50–53, 56–58, 62.
140. Courlander, *A Treasury of African Folklore,* p. 182.
141. Ibid., pp. 472–73
142. Teplit Ole Saitoti is a Maasai writer, lecturer and tribal elder who divides his time between his city home and a remote village in Tanzania. He was a focus of a *National Geographic Special,* entitled "Serengeti Diary," aired over PBS, August 12, 1990. Mr. Saitoti was speaking about Maasai poetry.
143. Mapanje and White, *Oral Poetry of Africa,* p. 64.
144. Personal interview with the poet and novelist, July 5, 1993. Mr. Awoonor gave the author this folktale.
145. Noni Jabavu, *The Ochre People: Scenes from a South African Life* (London: John Murray, 1963), pp. 24–25.

Jomo Kenyatta, father of the modern state of Kenya, echoes very similar feelings about the social, ritual and economic currency of cattle in his own people's culture. The Kikuyus' "[c]attle are their wealth and pride; they play a part in every business transaction and at every ceremonial gathering, and a man's standing in the tribe is reckoned largely by his cattle." Kenyatta, *Kenya: The Land of Conflict,* (Manchester, England: Panaf, 1945), p. 17.

Solomon Ole Saibull describes a comparable relationship within the Maasai culture of East Africa: "An intimate bond exists between the Maasai and their cattle. They know their cattle by voice, by color, and by eye, and will call them by name. These self-sufficient herders have a spartan life style, and know nothing of luxury. Their herds provide them with all they need: milk, blood, a simple cheese and meat; dung for fuel, plaster for their huts which are made from dung mixed with earth, hides for bed covering and garments, urine for cleansing hands, tanning leather and cleaning gourds, butterfat for their rituals and baby food." (Solomon Ole Saibull, and Rachel Carr, *Herd and Spear: The Maasai of East Africa* (London: Collins and Harvill, 1981), p. 37.

146. *Herdsmen of the Sun,* a 52-minute documentary directed by Werner Herzog, 1988.
147. Olney, *Tell Me Africa,* pp. 65–66.
148. Jabavu, *The Ochre People,* p. 177. Her first autobiographical work was *Drawn in Color* (London: John Murray, 1960).
149. The Mpondo had "at least fifty-seven different terms describing cattle of different markings, as well as five terms describing the horns. A man had a name for every beast he owned and composed praise songs for his favorites. Among the Basotho, there is a saying: *'Dikgomo ke banka ya Mosotho'* (Cattle are the bank of a Mosotho)." Leonard Thompson, *A History of South Africa* (New Haven: Yale University Press, 1990), p. 18.
150. Jabavu, *The Ochre People,* pp. 159–61.

V. SOUTH AMERICA: THE KOGI

1. *From the Heart of the World: The Elder Brothers' Warning,* a documentary film by Alan Ereira: a 90-minute production of BBCTV in association with the Goldsmith Foundation, 1990.

British historian Alan Ereira went to Columbia in 1988 to film a story about the Spanish Armada and the gold that was the Holy Grail for sixteenth-century Spain. After filming in the Museo del Oro in Bogota, a museum renowed for its collection of more than fifteen thousand pieces of pre-Columbian gold (some of the finest pieces being of Tairona origin—the Kogi ancestors), the BBC asked Ereira to investigate the Kogi connection while he was there. Thus began an extraordinary odyssey that is best encapsulated in the author's own words: "I am not an experienced explorer," began Ereira,

I am an historian of sorts, who makes television programmes. I do not relish danger and detest discomfort. I have never thought of myself as physically tough and prefer a comfortable chair to even a short walk. I have no particular knowledge of anthropology or archaeology, and have never been to South America before. But the Kogi have decided that they have to break their long silence. And I was the person they decided could best help them. . . . Faced by the threat of complete destruction [by the Spanish in the sixteenth century], they were forced to decide what was really central to them, what it would mean to survive. . . . [T]he emphasis of Kogi society became, and remains, an emphasis on the life of the mind—a life which is almost incomprehensible to us.

Fundamental to that survival is the maintenance of a physical separation between their world and our own. Every intrusion made into their territory—by tourists, by anthropologists, by robbers, by peasants, by seekers after wisdom or profit—is a threat. They are hidden, and have developed a culture of silence and secrecy. Communication with the outside world is taboo: children are taught to hide from strangers, and adults regard all outsiders as dangerous. Everything about the Kogi is concealed. . . .

They have learned that hospitality is the most dangerous virtue on earth. . . .

They see us as moral idiots, greedy beyond all understanding. Over and over again they speak of us sacking, looting the planet, tearing at its flesh without respect. The highest morality is understanding that for everything that is taken, something must be given back. . . . The Kogi demand that we behave responsibly, that we begin to take care of the world. They are demanding an ethical revolution on our part, in which greed and selfishness are tempered by awe, and by a sensitivity to the earth as a living—and now perhaps dying—totality.

If we fail to respond, they say, all life will be destroyed very soon. They have seen the signs, and they are profoundly fearful. Since I have lived with them, I have learned to trust their judgement.

Alan Ereira, *The Elder Brothers: A Lost South American People and Their Message About the Fate of the Earth* (New York: Knopf, 1992), pp. 7–9, 12.

2. Quoted in Warwick Bray, *Gold of El Dorado: The Heritage of Colombia* (New York: Harry N. Abrams, 1979), n.p.

3. *From the Heart of the World,* the documentary.

4. As to "planet in miniature," historian Alan Ereira makes the following comments:

The Sierra, taken as a whole, is a completely self-sufficient system, and if it was designed as a home for humanity the architect could hardly have done a better job. . . . But the Sierra is a strange world. Its form, this natural pyramid, reaching from the sea to the sky, an island outcrop, does make it unique. Its range of habitats and environments, the incredible diversity of plant and animal life, does truly make it a model of the larger world. Its placing, between northern and southern continents, with day and night twelve hours each all year round, without seasonal changes of temperature, seems almost unnatural to a northerner like myself. The expression "The Heart of the World" is not simply a conceit. . . . The Kogi see the whole of the Sierra as a single entity, a sacred world in the heart of the larger world. . . . They have to maintain the harmony of the Heart of the World by making offerings, which they call "payments," at a multitude of sites. If this is not done, then the harmony of the Heart of the World is upset and the larger world too becomes chaotic.

Ereira, *The Elder Brothers,* pp. 83, 119.

Likewise, the Diné (Navajo people) of the American Southwest say "we who are the People are the heart of the world." (Navajo origin legend.)

5. Gerardo Reichel-Dolmatoff, in "Funerary Customs and Religious Symbol-

ism Among the Kogi," in Patricia J. Lyon, ed., *Native South Americans: Ethnology of the Least Known Continent* (Boston: Little, Brown, 1974; Prospect Heights, IL: Waveland Press, 1985), p. 290.

Most of what we know about the mysterious world of the Kogi comes from the dedicated efforts and trail-blazing studies of Gerardo Reichel-Dolmatoff and his wife, Alicia. Born in Austria, educated in Vienna, Munich and Paris, Reichel-Dolmatoff became a resident of Colombia in 1939. As government anthropologists, he and his wife conducted excavations and organized archaeological and ethnological research all over the country for more than four decades. Reichel-Dolmatoff has written several books and numerous articles on Colombian aboriginal cultures, many of which have yet to be translated into English.

Alan Ereira's journey to film and record the Kogi is a valuable contribution to this knowledge.

6. Quoted in Gerardo Reichel-Dolmatoff, "Training for the Priesthood Among the Kogi of Colombia," in *Enculturation in Latin America: An Anthology,* ed. Johannes Wilbert, vol. 37 (Los Angeles: Latin American Center Publications, University of California, 1976), p. 287.

7. Reichel-Dolmatoff, "Training for the Priesthood," p. 269.

8. Ereira, *The Elder Brothers,* p. 50.

9. *From the Heart of the World,* the documentary.

10. Ereira, *The Elder Brothers,* p. 163.

11. Gregory Mason, *South of Yesterday* (New York: Henry Holt, 1940), p. 321.

12. Quoted in Reichel-Dolmatoff, "The Great Mother and the Kogi Universe: A Concise Overview," *Journal of Latin American Lore,* vol. 13, no. 1 (1987), p. 108.

13. "It is said that, originally, the Mother was pure thought *(aluna),*" writes Reichel-Dolmatoff. "The term *aluna,*" he continues, "has the multiple meanings of thought, memory, spirit, soul, mind, imagination and frequently the Great Mother is described as an invisible force floating upon the dark primeval waters." Reichel-Dolmatoff, "The Great Mother and the Kogi Universe," p. 84.

Mama Valencia explains the meaning of *aluna* in this way:

Everything we do is an event not only in the physical world but also in the spirit world. We live in a world shaped in spirit. Every tree, every stone, every river, has a spirit form, invisible to the Younger Brother. This is the world of *aluna,* the world of thought and spirit. *Aluna* embraces intelligence, soul and fertility: it is the stuff of life, the essence of reality. The material world is underpinned, shaped, given life and generative power in *aluna,* and the *Mama's* work is carried out in *aluna.*

Quoted in Ereira, *The Elder Brothers,* p. 63.

14. *From the Heart of the World,* the documentary.

15. Quoted in Ereira, *The Elder Brothers,* p. 156.

The *Mamas* told Ereira:

In Colombia all the land was sacred; you could not dig out oil, you could not build a highway, cut open a hillside, you could not do that. Serankua [the Creator] said, in Colombia, take care of the Sierra Nevada. So we remained like this; and that is why today when the *Mama* begins to have a pot made [and digs clay from the earth], he gives tribute in *aluna* so that no illness will appear.

Ibid., p. 158.

16. Tomb robbing is a large-scale activity in Colombia, particularly among the Colombian peasantry. In the last fifty years, spectacular gold pieces made by pre-Colombian civilizations have found their way to the Museo del Oro in Bogota. The Kogi, however, have laid claim to their Tairona ancestors' graves, believing that the fecundity of the Earth is determined by the presence of gold. They are deeply aggrieved by the pillaging of these graves, which they consider to be exceptionally sacred sites, and they fear for the very life of Earth itself. The looting is not something new to them. The *Mamas* remind us that it began with the Spanish soldiers:

> When Columbus came
> they took away the things that were ours.
> They took away our gold.
> They took away all our sacred gold.
> They set dogs on us and we had to flee,
> we ran in fear,
> and as we ran we left everything behind us.
> We had sacred gold pieces when they set dogs on us.
> We lost them.
> They took our soul.
> They took everything.
>> Quoted in Ereira, *The Elder Brothers*, pp. 140–41.

17. Ibid., pp. 142, 160, 163, 217, 224–25.

18. Reichel-Dolmatoff, "The Loom of Life: A Kogi Principle of Integration," *Journal of Latin American Lore*, vol. 4, no. 1 (1978), p. 15.

19. The act of weaving from a mythological perspective opens up this concept considerably. Reichel-Dolmatoff learned from the Kogi that it was the Great Mother herself who taught at the time of Creation. "In the beginning of time," he writes, "the Mother Goddess took a spindle and pushed it upright into the newly created and still soft earth, right in the center of the snow peaks of the Sierra Nevada, saying: 'This is the central post *(kalvasankaw)!*' And then, picking from the top of the spindle a length of yarn, she drew with it a circle around the spindle-whorl and said: 'This shall be the land of my children!'

"The spindle itself was a male/female symbol, the male hardwood shaft piercing the female softwood disk. A Kogi spindle, then, is a model of the cosmos (as is the case with the Dogon of the Sudan); the flat disk of the spindle-whorl is our earth and on top of it rests the high, cone-shaped body of cotton yard wound tightly around the world axis. . . . The sun, by spiraling around the world, spins the Thread of Life and twists it around the cosmic axis." Ibid., pp. 13–14.

Similarly, in Navajo mythology, the loom and the art of weaving were the original acts of Creation. In fact, to weave is to create the fabric of the universe itself:

Spider woman instructed the Navajo women how to weave on a loom which Spider Man told them how to make. The crosspoles were made of sky and earth cords, the warp sticks of sun rays, the healds of rock crystal and sheet lightning. The batten was a sun halo, white shell made the comb. There were four spindles: one a stick of zigzag lightning with a whorl of cannel coal; one stick of flash lightning with a whorl of turquoise; a third had a stick of sheet lightning with a whorl of abalone; a rain streamer formed the stick of the fourth, and its whorl was white shell.
>> Gladys A. Reichard, *Spider Woman: A Story of Navajo Weavers and Chanters* (Glorieta, NM: The Rio Grande Press, 1968), frontispiece.

20. Ereira, *The Elder Brothers*, p. 96.

21. Ibid., p. 94.

22. Ibid.

23. Ibid.

24. Ibid., p. 96.

25. Reichel-Dolmatoff, "The Loom of Life," pp. 12–13.

26. Ibid., p. 15.

27. Quoted in Reichel-Dolmatoff, "The Loom of Life," p. 12.

28. Ibid., p. 13.

29. Ibid.

30. Ibid., p. 23.

31. Quoted in Ereira, *The Elder Brothers*, pp. 176–77.

32. Quoted in Reichel-Dolmatoff, "The Loom of Life," p. 24.

33. Reichel-Dolmatoff, "The Loom of Life," p. 23.

34. Reichel-Dolmatoff, "Training for the Priesthood," p. 268.
35. Quoted in Ereira, *The Elder Brothers*, p. 10.
36. Reichel-Dolmatoff, "The Loom of Life," pp. 21–23.
37. Ibid., p. 22.
38. Ibid., p. 23.
39. Quoted in *National Geographic*, May 1991, p. 82.
40. Quoted in Ereira, *The Elder Brothers*, p. 7.
41. Ibid., p. 212.
42. Quoted in Reichel-Dolmatoff, "The Great Mother and the Kogi Universe," p. 111.

VI. NATIVE NORTH AMERICA

1. Quoted in Moody, *The Indigenous Voice*, vol. 2, pp. 69–70.
2. Quoted in Alfonso Ortiz, *The Tewa World: Space, Time, Being and Becoming in a Pueblo Society* (Chicago: University of Chicago Press, 1969), p. 13.
3. Luther Standing Bear, *Land of the Spotted Eagle* (Lincoln: University of Nebraska Press, 1978), p. 45.
4. Quoted in *Parabola*, vol. XII, no. 4 (1987), p. 44.
5. Black Elk, *The Sacred Pipe: Black Elk's Account of the Seven Rites of the Oglala Sioux*, rec. and ed. Joseph Epes Brown (Norman, OK: University of Oklahoma Press, 1953; Baltimore: Penguin, 1971), p. 72.
6. Alphonso Ortiz in *Indian Affairs* (Newsletter of the Association on American Indian Affairs), no. 116 (Summer 1988), p. iv.
7. Ibid. (For a lively and detailed account of the Taos Pueblo's struggle to regain its sacred Blue Lake, see R. C. Gordon-McCutchan, *The Taos Indians and the Battle for Blue Lake* (Santa Fe, NM: Red Crane Books, 1991).
8. Luther Standing Bear, *Land of the Spotted Eagle*, 43–45.
9. Quoted in Anita Parlow, *Cry, Sacred Ground: Big Mountain U.S.A.* (Washington, DC: The Christic Institute, 1988), p. 162.
10. N. Scott Momaday, *The Way to Rainy Mountain* (1969; reprint, Albuquerque: University of New Mexico Press, 1991), p. 5.
11. Quoted in *A Song from Sacred Mountain*, ed., interviews and writing by Anita Parlow (Pine Ridge, SD: Oglala Lakota Legal Rights Fund, 1983), p. 76.
12. Alphonso Ortiz, "Look to the Mountaintop," in E. Graham Ward, ed., *Essays in Reflection II* (Boston: Houghton Mifflin, 1973), p. 90.
13. Quoted in Parlow, *Cry, Sacred Ground*, p. 48.
14. Quoted in John (Fire) Lame Deer and Richard Erdoes, *Lame Deer: Seeker of Visions* (New York: Simon and Schuster, 1972), p. 138.
15. *Native Corn Report*, Cornell American Indian Agriculture Program, no. 1 (Summer 1991), pp. 1, 6.
16. Nigel Pride, *Crow Man's People: Three Seasons with the Navajo* (London: Constable, 1982), p. 218.
17. Quoted in International Work Group for Indigenous Affairs (IWGIA) Document no. 68 (1991), p. 122.
18. Ronald Wright, *Stolen Continents: The "New World" Through Indian Eyes* (Boston: Houghton Mifflin, 1992), pp. 126–27.
19. Quoted in *Stolen Continents*, p. 128.
20. Quoted in *On Our Ground: The Complete Writings of William Apess, A Pequot*, ed. Barry O'Connell (Amherst: University of Massachusetts Press, 1992), p. 295. For a discussion of the role of Philip as a "father" of Pequot country and leader of an alliance of New England Indians against the English colonists in a bitter war in the seventeenth century, see O'Connell's introduction, pp. xviii–xxiv.
21. Black Hawk in *Black Hawk: An Autobiography*, ed. Donald Jackson (Historical Society of Iowa, 1833; Chicago: Prairie State Books, 1990), p. 101
22. Quoted in Ernest Wallace and E. Adamson Hoebel, *The Comanches: Lords of the South Plains* (Norman, OK: University of Oklahoma Press, 1952), p. 283.

23. Quoted in Melvin R. Gilmore, *Prairie Smoke* (New York: Columbia University Press, 1929; St. Paul: Minnesota Historical Society, 1987), p. 36.

24. Quoted in Stephen Hirst, *Havsuw'Baaja: People of the Blue Green Water* (Supai, AZ: The Havasupai Tribe, 1985), p. 204.

25. Quoted in Ernest Thompson Seton, *The Gospel of the Red Man* (New York: Doubleday Doran, 1936), pp. 58–59. The occasion that prompted this explanation of the meaning of homeland was a 1912 proposed government offer to the Crows for another land cession. It was turned down.

26. Quoted in D'Arcy McNickle, *The Surrounded* (New York: Dodd, Mead, 1936; Albuquerque: University of New Mexico Press, 1980), p. 70.

27. See Matthew Fox, ed., *Western Spirituality: Historical Roots, Ecumenical Routes* (Santa Fe: Bear & Company, 1981), pp. 322–24. With the permission of Sr. José Hobday, who writes for *Creation Spirituality* magazine.

28. Forrest Carter, *The Education of Little Tree* (Albuquerque: University of New Mexico Press, 1986), pp. 9–10, 7.

29. Joseph Bruchac, review of *The Education of Little Tree, Parabola*, vol. XIV, no. 2 (1989), p. 112.

30. See Lawrence Clayton, "Forrest Carter/Asa Carter and Politics," *Western American Literature*, May 1986, pp. 19–26.

31. Review by Joseph Bruchac, p. 112.

32. Carter, *The Education of Little Tree*, pp. 102–3.

33. N. Scott Momaday, "Native American Attitudes to the Environment," in *Seeing with a Native Eye*, ed. Walter Holden Capps (New York: Harper & Row, 1976), p. 80. Expanding on this theme of "reciprocal appropriation," Momaday moves to the concept of "appropriateness" and its vital significance to Native American thinking and self-knowledge. He states:

The idea of "appropriateness" is central to the Indian experience of the natural world. It is a fundamental idea within his philosophy. I recall the story told to me some years ago by a friend, who is not himself a Navajo, but was married for a time to a Navajo girl and lived with her family in Southern Utah. And he said that he had been told this story and was passing it on to me. There was a man living in a remote place on the Navajo reservation who had lost his job and was having a difficult time making ends meet. He had a wife and several children. As a matter of fact, his wife was expecting another child. One day a friend came to visit him and perceived that this situation was bad. The friend said to him "Look, I see that you're in tight straits, I see you have many mouths to feed, that you have no wood and that there is very little food in your larder. But one thing puzzles me. I know you're a hunter, and I know, too, there are deer in the mountains very close at hand. Tell me, why don't you kill a deer so that you and your family might have fresh meat to eat?" And after a time the man replied, "No, it is inappropriate that I should take life just now when I am expecting the gift of life."

The implications of that idea, and the way in which the concept of appropriateness lies at the center of that little parable is a central consideration within the Indian world. You cannot understand how the Indian thinks of himself in relation to the world around him unless you understand his conception of what is appropriate; particularly what is morally appropriate within the context of that relationship.

Ibid., pp. 81–82.

34. N. Scott Momaday, "The Man Made of Words," in *Indian Voices*, 1st Convocation of American Indian Scholars at Princeton University (San Francisco: Indian Historical Press, 1970), pp. 164–66.

35. Joseph Bruchac, *Near the Mountains* (Fredonia, NY: White Pine Press, 1987), pp. 63, 37, 34, 19.

36. Quoted in Moody, *The Indigenous Voice*, vol. 1, p. 374.

37. *Canadian Association in Support of the Native Peoples* (CASNP—Toronto) Bulletin, vol. 18, no. 2 (October 1977), pp. 9–11.

38. Mary TallMountain, "You *Can* Go Home Again," in *I Tell You Now:*

Autobiographical Essays by Native American Writers, ed. Brian Swann and Arnold Krupat (Lincoln: University of Nebraska Press, 1987), p. 13.

39. Quoted in Harvey Arden and Steve Wall, *Wisdomkeepers: Meetings with Native American Elders* (Hillsboro, OR: Beyond Words Publishing, 1991), p. 26.

40. Interview with Bill Moyers in *Spirit and Nature*, a 90-minute PBS documentary aired June 5, 1991. Produced and directed by Gail Pellett; Executive Producer, Judith Davidson Moyers.

41. Quoted in Moody, *The Indigenous Voice*, vol. 2, p. 224.

42. George Tinker, "For All My Relations," *Sojourners*, January 1991, n.p.

43. Ibid.

44. Quoted in *Akwesasne Notes* (Early Summer 1976), p. 16.

45. Quoted in Parlow, *Cry, Sacred Ground*, p. 57.

46. Hirst, *Havsuw'Baaja*, p. 7.

47. Sister M. Inez Hilger, *Chippewa Child Life and Its Cultural Background*, Bureau of American Ethnology Bulletin no. 146 (Washington, DC: Smithsonian Institution, 1951), pp. 16–17.

Harry Holbert Turney-High describes similar cultural observances amongst the Flathead of Montana:

> Part of the mother's prenatal sewing consisted in making a lozenge shaped bag of buckskin about three and a half inches long, beaded and decorated as handsomely as possible. The umbilicus was then placed in this bag together with the pulverized needles of a very pungent fir. This was then attached to the head of the child's cradle-board. The cord was saved to prevent the baby from prying, lest it "keep digging around all the time." Such a child is thought to be searching for its umbilicus. One frequently hears an Old Indian cry out to a youngster who is digging in the bushes or forever looking under things, "What are you looking for, your umbilicus?"
>
> Children wore the umbilical sack on a necklace after they learned to walk. This they did until they were grown. It was never thrown away or discarded . . . even after the death of its owner.
>
> American Anthropological Association, *Memoirs*, no. 48, 1937, pp. 67–68.

48. Quoted in Parlow, *Cry, Sacred Ground*, p. 57.

49. Ibid.

50. Ibid., pp. 161–62.

51. Ibid., p. 162.

52. Billy Frank, Jr., in "Indians and Salmon: Making Nature Whole," *The New York Times*, November 26, 1992, p. C10.

53. Alice C. Fletcher recorded these extraordinary thoughts ca. 1884. Fletcher relates another experience, similar in thinking and conveyed to her by "a devout old Indian": "The tree is like a human being for it has life and grows, so we pray to it and put our offerings on it that the god may help us." Fletcher believed that "these manifestations of life" were more like "media of communication" rather than symbols or objects of worship. "As a consequence," she wrote, "the Indian stands abreast with nature." Alice C. Fletcher, "The Elk Mystery or Festival," Peabody Museum of Archaeology and Ethnology, *Reports*, no. 16 (1884), p. 276.

In contrast, Claude Lévi-Strauss views the Dakota passage as exemplary of "a metaphysical philosophy common to all the Sioux . . . according to which things and beings are nothing but materialized forms of creative continuity." Claude Lévi-Strauss, *Totemism* (Boston: Beacon Press, 1963), pp. 97–98.

54. Quoted in Frances Densmore, "Teton Sioux Music," Bureau of American Ethnology Bulletin no. 61 (1918), p. 214.

55. Arthur Amiotte, "The Road to the Center," *Parabola*, vol. IX, no. 3 (1984), pp. 46, 51.

56. Black Elk in *A Treasury of Traditional Wisdom*, pres. Whitall N. Perry (New York: Simon and Schuster, 1971), pp. 819–20.

57. With the permission of N. Scott Momaday.

58. Quoted in Parlow, *Cry, Sacred Ground,* p. 2.

59. Ibid., p. 46.

60. Ibid., p. 208.

61. For a historical, political, economic, cultural and up-to-date analysis of land rights and Native Nations in North America, see two excellent papers in IWGIA Document no. 68 (1992): Ward Churchill, "Genocide in Arizona?: The 'Navajo-Hopi Land Dispute' in Perspective"; Ward Churchill and Winona LaDuke, "Native America: The Political Economy of Radioactive Colonialism."

62. From "Dark Sky Over Black Mesa," in Senate Committee on Interior and Insular Affairs, *Problems of Electrical Power Production in the Southwest: Hearings Before the Committee on Interior and Insular Affairs,* Pt. 5, 28 May 1971.

63. Interview with Bill Moyers in *Spirit and Nature.*

64. Henrietta Mann, "Indian Religious Freedom Under Attack," *Indian Affairs,* no. 124 (Summer/Fall 1991), p. 1.

65. Henrietta Mann, "The Beautiful Earth Woman: American Myth and Reality," a paper given to the author by Dr. Mann.

66. Vine Deloria, Jr., *Sacred Lands and Religious Freedom* (New York: Association on American Indian Affairs, 1991), p. 7.

67. Bill Tallbull, "On the Tongue River Valley," in *Proceedings of the National Sacred Sites Caucus* (New York: Association on American Indian Affairs, August, 1991), p. 9.

68. Ibid., pp. 8–9.

69. Quoted in Moody, *The Indigenous Voice,* vol. 2, pp. 300–306.

70. *Out of the Silence,* photographs by Adelaide DeMenil, text by William Reid (New York: Harper & Row, 1971), pp. 54–56, 59–60, 62–63.

71. Popovi Da, "Indian Pottery and Indian Values," in *Explorations 1970* (Santa Fe: School of American Research, 1970).

72. Interview with Manfred Susunkewa in *Native Peoples,* Spring 1992, pp. 48–49.

73. Linda Hogan, *Mean Spirit* (New York: Atheneum; Toronto: Collier Macmillan Canada, 1990), pp. 339–40.

74. Ibid., pp. 357–58.

75. Black Elk, *The Sacred Pipe,* p. 75.

76. Quoted in Parlow, *Cry, Sacred Ground,* p. 52.

77. Quoted on an "Announcement" for *Visions from Akwesasne: Contemporary Iroquois Art,* curator Alex Jacobs, The American Indian Community, Gallery/Museum, New York, October 1990.

78. Quoted in T. C. McLuhan, *Dream Tracks* (New York: Harry N. Abrams, 1985), p. 86.
Dr. Edmund Carpenter's inquiry into the meaning of "life-lines" in Hopi designs led to this epigraph's illuminating explanation by an elderly Hopi artist from the Hopi village of Oraibi. "Life-line is the term used to describe a picture of an animal with a line drawn from its mouth to its lungs or heart," writes Carpenter. It is also a motif found woven into Pueblo basketry and painted on pots. The Cree Indians also use this design a great deal in their paintings. (Ibid., p. 199.) See also Edmund Carpenter, *Oh, What a Blow That Phantom Gave Me* (New York: Holt, Rinehart and Winston, 1972), p. 88.

79. Joseph Bruchac, ed., *Songs from This Earth on Turtle's Back* (Greenfield Center, NY: The Greenfield Review Press, 1983), p. xv.

80. Ibid.

81. Mann, "The Beautiful Earth Woman."

82. Ibid.

83. Quoted in *Navajo Wildlands,* text by Stephen C. Jett, photographs by Philip Hyde, ed. Kenneth Brower (San Francisco: The Sierra Club and Ballantine Books, 1969), p. 51.

84. Black Elk, *Black Elk Speaks,* as told through John G. Neihardt (Flaming Rainbow) (New York: William Morrow, 1932; Lincoln: University of Nebraska Press, a Bison Book, 1970), pp. 43, 85, 173.

85. Quoted in Ella E. Clark, *Indian Legends of the Pacific Northwest* (Berkeley: University of California Press, 1960), pp. 83–84.

86. Arthur C. Parker, *The Code of Handsome Lake: The Seneca Prophet,* New York State Museum, Museum Bulletin no. 163 (Albany: University of the State of New York, 1912), p. 47.

87. Tinker, "For All My Relations."

88. Ibid.

89. Chief John Snow, *These Mountains Are Our Sacred Places* (Toronto: Samuel Stevens, 1977), p. 149.

90. Quoted in Edward Goldsmith, *The Way* (London: Rider Books, 1992), p. xxi.

91. Quoted in *Navajo Wildlands*, p. 50.

92. Joseph Bruchac, *Indian Mountain* (Ithaca, NY: Ithaca House, 1971), p. 6.

93. Ortiz, "Look to the Mountaintop," p. 91.

94. Alphonso Ortiz, ed., *New Perspectives on the Pueblos* (Albuquerque: University of New Mexico Press, 1984), p. 143.

95. Ortiz, "Look to the Mountaintop," pp. 91–95.

96. Quoted in Aileen O'Bryan, *The Diné: Origin Myths of the Navajo Indians,* Bureau of American Ethnology. Bulletin 163 (Washington, DC: Smithsonian Institution, 1956), p. 29.

97. Quoted in Wilson, *World Scripture*, pp. 233–34.

98. Ortiz, *New Perspectives on the Pueblos*, p. 145. See Alphonso Ortiz's essay "Ritual Drama and the Pueblo World View" for a stimulating presentation of the conception of a Pueblo worldview as a means of "provid[ing] a people with a structure of reality." Ibid., pp. 135–161.

99. Ortiz, "Look to the Mountaintop," pp. 95–98, 103–4.

100. Snow, *These Mountains Are Our Sacred Places*, pp. 147–48.

101. Quoted in *And Woman Wove It in a Basket.* . . .

102. Snow, *These Mountains Are Our Sacred Places*, p. 6.

103. Ibid., p. 147.

104. Ibid., pp. 2, 4–5, 7, 11–13.

105. Quoted in Elizabeth Roberts and Elias Amidon, eds., *Earth Prayers* (San Francisco: HarperCollins, 1991), p. 146.

106. Quoted in T. C. McLuhan, *Touch the Earth* (1972; reprint, New York: Simon & Schuster, 1992), p. 176 n.

107. Quoted in Wilson, *World Scripture,* p. 31.

108. David Riesman, "The Oral and Written Traditions," in *Explorations in Communications,* Edmund Carpenter and Marshall McLuhan, eds. (Boston: Beacon Press, 1966), pp. 110–11.

109. Ruth Underhill, *The Autobiography of a Papago Woman,* American Anthropological Association, *Memoirs*, no. 46 (1936), p. 4.

110. Ibid., pp. 22–24.

111. Ibid., pp. 5, 10–13, 22.

The impact of the spoken or sung word on the young and the importance it has held and holds in Native American life is of particular interest to Native American leaders right now. Peterson Zah, former elected chairman of the Navajo Nation (1982–1986) and now a promotor of teaching the Navajo language, culture, history and tribal government, has said that "Indians have a belief that if you write it down, you're tying it down." He believes that "if you look at the Indian philosophy you see the whole universe revolves in a circular motion," and that this "constant motion" is an integral part of the dynamic process of the oral tradition "handed down from generation to generation and from people to people. When you hear it," he says, "you actually see the person saying those kinds of things [the teachings, the stories] and if you know and respect the person, it has a greater effect on you as an individual." Zah's grandparents were very important teachers in his life: "I had a great respect for both my grandmother and my grandfather, on both my father's and my mother's side. And so when they were telling me these things, an added dimension was the great respect that I have for those folks. And because of that the legends really stuck with me." Peterson Zah in *Parabola,* vol. XIV, no. 2 (1989), p. 57.

In "The Storytelling Seasons," Joseph Bruchac, Abenaki author and storyteller, offers some sensitive insights into the humanity, humaneness and awareness of all forms of life to be found in and learned from his own story-telling tradition. He writes:

> Whenever I think of the transmission of stories, my mind goes back to a certain time and place. I am standing behind the house of Mdawelasis, an Abenaki elder who spent most of life in the Adirondack town of Old Forge. It is early autumn. A basswood log has been stripped of its bark and laid across two sawhorses and the old man is working on it with his carving tools while I help him. The carving of poles is an old Abenaki tradition and I know that I have been allowed to help because he wants me to see how he does things, to learn in the old way by watching and doing. His name means "Little Loon" in Abenaki and as we work, we hear a sound from overhead, a whistling of wings. We look up and see a loon pass above us.
>
> "Heading for Moose River," he says as we watch until it is out of sight behind the trees. Then he nods and rubs his hand over the shape of the Turtle on the carved log. "There's thirteen squares on Turtle's shell," he says. "Always thirteen. One for each of the Abenaki nations. Sokoki, Cowasuck, Penacook, Pigwacket . . ." As he speaks those names, I know that I will remember. Everything in that moment, the smell of wood smoke in the air, the feel of the cool earth beneath our feet, the sound of his dog Awasos stretching on the old back porch, will be as clear in my memory as the whistling of that loon's wings—telling the old man that the time was right to share a story. So, too, my own mind was open to hear. And that was as important, for a story is truly told only when someone listens."

A little further on in his eloquent essay, Bruchac points out how the stories have sustained a special spirit and kept Native Peoples alive and strong: "More now than ever before," he continues,

> we need the gift of stories whch instruct and delight, explain and sustain. Such stories lead us—as that simple story told me by Mdawelasis on a clear autumn day —to an understanding of who we are and what our place is in the natural world. They help us find respect for ourselves and respect for the earth. They lead us towards understanding the sacred nature of the greatest story of all, that story which is told by the rising sun each dawn, the story of the gift of life.
>
> Joseph Bruchac in *Parabola,* vol. IV, no. 2 (1989), pp. 87, 92.

112. Parker, *The Code of Handsome Lake,* pp. 60–61.

113. Reported by Knud Rasmussen, *The Netsilik Eskimos: Social Life and Spiritual Culture,* Report of the Fifth Thule Expedition 1921–24, vol. III, nos. 1–2 (Copenhagen: Gyldendalske Boghandel, Nordisk Forlag, 1931), p. 16.

On another occasion, while reciting some of his songs for Rasmussen, Orpingalik again pointed out the significance of song in his life: "*My Breath:* This is what I call this song, for it is just as necessary to me to sing it as it is to breathe." He called his songs "comrades in solitude," wrote Rasmussen, and "he was always singing." Ibid., pp. 15, 321.

114. Ibid., p. 321.

115. See *The North American Indian,* 20 vols., written, illustrated and published by Edward S. Curtis, ed. Frederick Webb Hodge, introduction by Theodore Roosevelt, vol. 10 (The Kwakiutl), 1915, pp. 171–72.

116. Quoted in *Technicians of the Sacred,* 2d ed., rev. and enl., ed. Jerome Rothenberg (Berkeley: University of California Press, 1985), p. 15.

117. Ibid., p. 45.

118. See T. C. McLuhan, *Touch the Earth,* p. 25. Also see Edmund Carpenter, "The Eskimo and His Art," in *A Guide to the Peaceable Kingdom,* ed. William Kilbourn (Toronto: Macmillan of Canada, 1970), pp. 137–38.

119. Quoted in Melvin R. Gilmore, *Uses of Plants by the Indians of the Missouri River Region*, Thirty-third Annual Report of the Bureau of American Ethnology (1919; reprint, Lincoln: University of Nebraska Press, 1977), pp. 27, 29.

120. Linda Hogan, "Walking," *Parabola*, vol. XV, no. 2 (1990), pp. 15–16.

121. See *Navajo Wildlands*, p. 124.

122. Quoted in Wilson, *World Scripture*, p. 205.

123. Louis Littlecoon Oliver, *Chasers of the Sun: Creek Indian Thoughts* (Greenfield Center, NY: The Greenfield Review Press, 1990), p. 5.

124. *The Potlatch: A Strict Law Bids Us Dance*, a 60-minute documentary by Canadian filmmaker Dennis Wheeler, 1975. Produced by Tom Shandel; directed by Dennis Wheeler; written by Brian Shein and Dennis Wheeler.

125. Quoted in Joseph Epes Brown, *The Spiritual Legacy of the American Indian* (New York: Crossroad, 1982), p. 123.

126. *Li Chi: Book of Rites*. An Encyclopedia of Ancient Ceremonial Usages, Religious Creeds, and Social Institutions, trans. James Legge, vol. 1 (New Hyde Park, NY: University Books, 1967), p. 367.

127. Ibid., pp. 370–71.

128. Linda Hogan, "All My Relations," *Parabola*, vol. XVII, no. 1 (1992), p. 33.

129. Ibid., p. 35.

130. Ibid.

131. Ibid., pp. 33–35.

132. Parker, *The Code of Handsome Lake*, p. 55.

133. Quoted in Thomas Berry, *The Dream of the Earth* (San Francisco: Sierra Club Books, 1988), p. 16.

134. Alice C. Fletcher and Francis La Flesche, *The Omaha Tribe* (Washington, DC: Bureau of American Ethnology, *Annual Report*, no. 27 (1905–1906), p. 115.

135. Ibid., p. 116.

136. Ibid., pp. 116–17.

137. Quoted in John Bierhorst, ed., *The Sacred Path* (New York: William Morrow, 1983), p. 129.

138. Black Elk, *Black Elk Speaks*, pp. 192–93.

139. Parker, *The Code of Handsome Lake*, pp. 102–3.

140. Quoted in Frazer, *The Golden Bough*, p. 487.

141. Ibid.

142. Julian Lang, "The Basket and World Renewal," *Parabola*, vol. XVI, no. 3 (1991), p. 85.

143. Thomas Buckley, "The One Who Flies All Around the World," *Parabola*, vol. XVI, no. 1 (1991), p. 8.

144. Lang, "The Basket and World Renewal," pp. 83–85.

145. Erna Gunther, *Further Analysis of the First Salmon Ceremony* (Seattle: University of Washington Press, 1928), p. 142.

146. Franz Boas, *Ethnology of the Kwakiutl*, based on data collected by George Hunt (Washington, DC: 35th Annual Report of the Bureau of American Ethnology [1913–1914], 1921), pp. 617–19.

147. Quoted in Roberts and Amidon, *Earth Prayers*, p. 184.

SELECT BIBLIOGRAPHY

INTRODUCTION

And Woman Wove It in a Basket.... A 60-minute documentary film by Bushra Azzouz, Marlene Farnum and Nettie Kuneki, 1989. Distributed by Women Who Make Movies, New York City.

Barbour, Ian G., ed. *Earth Might Be Fair: Reflections on Ethics, Religion, and Ecology.* Englewood Cliffs, NJ: Prentice-Hall, 1972.

Bateson, Gregory. *Angels Fear: Towards an Epistemology of the Sacred.* New York: Macmillan, 1987.

———. *Mind and Nature: A Necessary Unity.* New York: E. P. Dutton, 1979.

Berry, Thomas. *The Dream of the Earth.* San Francisco: Sierra Club Books, 1988.

Bhagavad Gita: The Song of God. Trans. Swami Prabhavananda and Christopher Isherwood. 1944. 4th ed. Hollywood, CA: Vedanta Press, 1987.

Blossfeldt, Karl. *Art Forms in Nature: Examples from the Plant World Photographed Direct from Nature.* New York: E. Weyhe, 1929.

Bode, Barbara. *No Bells to Toll: Destruction and Creation in the Andes.* New York: Paragon House, 1990.

Bord, Janet. *Mazes and Labyrinths of the World.* London: Latimer New Dimensions, 1976.

Broome, Richard. *Aboriginal Australians: Black Response to White Dominance 1788–1980.* North Sydney, NSW: George Allen & Unwin Australia, 1982.

Callicott, Baird, and Roger T. Ames, eds. *Nature in Asian Traditions of Thought: Essays in Environmental Philosophy.* Albany: State University of New York Press, 1989.

Campbell, Joseph. *The Masks of God: Primitive Mythology.* 4 vols. New York: Viking Press, 1959–68.

Cook, Theodore Andrea. *The Curves of Life.* London: Constable and Co., 1914; Reprint. New York: Dover Publications, 1979.

Coomaraswamy, Ananda K. *The Transformation of Nature in Art.* Cambridge: Harvard University Press, 1934.

Corbin, Henry. *Spiritual Body and Celestial Earth.* Trans. Nancy Pearson. Bollingen Series XCI, vol. 2. Princeton, NJ: Princeton University Press, 1977.

Crosby, Alfred W. *Ecological Imperialism.* Cambridge: Cambridge University Press, 1986.

Devereux, Paul. *Earth Memory: Sacred Sites—Doorways into Earth's Mysteries.* St. Paul, MN: Llewellyn Publications, 1992.

Dubos, René. *The Wooing of Earth.* New York: Charles Scribner's Sons, 1980.

Eliade, Mircea. *Ordeal by Labyrinth: Conversations with Claude-Henri Rocquet.* Trans. Derek Coltman. Chicago: University of Chicago Press, 1982.

————. *Patterns in Comparative Religion*. Trans. Rosemary Sheed. New York: New American Library, 1974.

————. *The Sacred and the Profane: The Nature of Religion*. Trans. Willard R. Trask. San Diego: Harcourt Brace Jovanovich, 1959.

Eriera, Alan. *The Elder Brothers: A Lost South American People and Their Message About the Fate of the Earth*. New York: Alfred A. Knopf, 1992.

Evans-Pritchard, E. E. *The Nuer*. Oxford: Clarendon Press, 1940.

Fox, Matthew. *The Coming of the Cosmic Christ*. San Francisco: Harper & Row, 1988.

————. *Original Blessing*. Santa Fe: Bear & Company, 1983.

————, ed. *Western Spirituality: Historical Roots, Ecumenical Routes*. Santa Fe: Bear & Company, 1981.

Frick, Thomas. *The Sacred Theory of the Earth*. Berkeley: North Atlantic Books, 1986.

Griaule, Marcel. *Conversations with Ogotemmêli: An Introduction to Dogon Religious Ideas*. Oxford: Oxford University Press, 1970.

Hughes, Donald J. *Ecology in Ancient Civilizations*. Albuquerque: University of New Mexico Press, 1975.

Huxley, Aldous. *The Perennial Philosophy*. 1944. New York: Harper & Row, Harper Colophon edition, 1970.

Huxley, Francis. *The Way of the Sacred*. London: Bloomsbury Books, 1989.

Hyams, Edward. *Soil and Civilization*. New York: Harper & Row, 1976.

Hyers, M. Conrad, ed. *Essays on Religion in the Comic Perspective*. New York: Seabury Press, 1969.

Jung, C. G. *Alchemical Studies*. Trans. R. F. C. Hull. Bollingen Series XX, vol. 13. Princeton: Princeton University Press, 1976.

Kenny, Maurice. "Spawning." In Joseph Bruchac, ed., *Songs from This Earth on Turtle's Back*. Greenfield Center, NY: Greenfield Review Press, 1983.

Lawlor, Robert. *Sacred Geometry: Philosophy and Practice*. New York: Thames and Hudson, 1989.

Levine, Louis D., ed. *Man in Nature*. Toronto: Royal Ontario Museum, 1975.

Lippard, Lucy R. *Overlay: Contemporary Art and the Art of Prehistory*. New York: Pantheon Books, 1983.

Little, Stephen. *Visions of the Dharma: Japanese Buddhist Paintings and Prints in the Honolulu Academy of Arts*. Honolulu: The Honolulu Academy of Arts, 1991.

Lonegren, Sig. *Labyrinths: Ancient Myths and Modern Uses*. Glastonbury, Somerset: Gothic Image, 1991.

Lonergan, Anne, and Caroline Richards. *Thomas Berry and the New Cosmology*. Mystic, CT: Twenty-Third Publications, 1987.

Lowenthal, David, and Marilyn J. Bowden, eds. *Geographies of the Mind: Essays in Historical Geosophy*. New York: Oxford University Press, 1976.

Matthews, William Henry. *Mazes and Labyrinths: A General Account of their History and Developments*. London: Longmans, Green, 1922.

Michell, John. *The Earth Spirit: Its Ways, Shrines and Mysteries*. London: Thames and Hudson, 1975.

Momaday, N. Scott. Foreword. *Native American Stories*. Ed. Joseph Bruchac. Golden, CO: Fulcrum Publishing, 1991.

Morgan, William N. *Prehistoric Architecture in the Eastern United States*. Cambridge: The MIT Press, 1980.

Nasr, Seyyed Hossein. *Man and Nature: The Spiritual Crisis of Modern Man*. London: George Allen & Unwin, a Mandala Book, 1976.

Nietzsche, Friedrich Wilhelm. *Thus Spake Zarathustra*. Baltimore: Penguin Books, 1961.

O'Bryan, Aileen. *The Diné: Origin Myths of the Navajo Indians*. Bureau of American Ethnology Bulletin 163. Washington, DC: Smithsonian Institution, 1956.

Paz, Octavio. *The Labyrinth of Solitude: Life and Thought in Mexico*. Trans. Lysander Kemp. New York: Grove Press, 1961.

Pitseolak. *Pitseolak: Pictures Out of My Life.* From recorded interviews by Dorothy Eber. Seattle: University of Washington Press, 1972.

Purce, Jill. *The Mystic Spiral: Journey of the Soul.* London: Thames and Hudson, 1975.

Read, Herbert. *The Meaning of Art.* rev. ed. London: Faber and Faber, 1984.

Rilke, Rainer Maria. *Duino Elegies.* Trans. David Young. New York: W. W. Norton, 1978.

Ross, Charles. *The Substance of Light: Sunlight Dispersion, the Solar Burns, Point Source/Star Space.* La Jolla, CA: La Jolla Museum of Contemporary Art, 1976.

———. *Sunlight Convergence Solar Burn.* Salt Lake City: University of Utah Press, 1976.

Singh, Karan. *Essays on Hinduism.* rev. ed. Delhi: Ratna Sagar, 1990.

Sopher, David E. *Geography of Religions.* Englewood Cliffs, NJ: Prentice-Hall, 1967.

Sorrell, Roger D. *St. Francis of Assisi and Nature.* New York: Oxford University Press, 1988.

Thompson, D'Arcy Wentworth. *On Growth and Form.* 2 vols. Cambridge: Cambridge University Press, 1968.

Tuan, Yi-Fu. *Topophilia: A Study of Environmental Perception, Attitudes, and Values.* Englewood Cliffs, NJ: Prentice-Hall, 1974.

Tzu, Lao. *Tao Te Ching.* Trans. D. C. Lau. Harmondsworth: Penguin Books, 1963.

Venezis, Ilias. *Aiolian Land.* Montreal: McGill University, 1987.

Washburn, Dorothy, and Donald W. Crowe. *Symmetries of Culture: Theory and Practice of Plane Pattern Analysis.* Seattle: University of Washington Press, 1988.

Yanagi, Sōetsu. *The Unknown Craftsman: A Japanese Insight into Beauty.* Tokyo and New York: Kodansha International/USA, 1984.

Young, Louise B. *The Unfinished Universe.* New York: Simon and Schuster, 1986.

ABORIGINAL AUSTRALIA

Anderson, Michael. "A Call for Justice." *Identity.* vol. 1, no. 8, August 1973.

Babakiueria. A 30-minute 16-mm film directed by Don Featherstone, and produced by Julian Pringle. An Australian Broadcasting Corporation Film, 1987.

Beckett, Jeremy R. *Past and Present: The Construction of Aboriginality.* Canberra: Aboriginal Studies Press, 1988.

Bell, Diane. *Daughters of the Dreaming.* Melbourne and North Sydney, NSW: McPhee Gribble Publishers in association with George Allen & Unwin Australia, 1983.

Bell, Diane, and Pam Ditton. *Law, the Old and the New: Aboriginal Women in Central Australia Speak Out.* Canberra: Published for Central Australian Aboriginal Legal Aid Services by *Aboriginal History,* 1980.

Bernbaum, Edwin. *Sacred Mountains of the World.* San Francisco: Sierra Club Books, 1990.

Berndt, Catherine H., and Ronald M. Berndt. *The Aboriginal Australians: The First Pioneers.* Carlton, Victoria: Pitman Publishing, 1983.

Berndt, Ronald M., and Catherine H. Berndt, eds. *Aboriginal Sites, Rights, and Resource Development.* Perth: Published for the Academy of the Social Sciences in Australia by University of Western Australia Press, 1982.

———. *Aborigines of the West: Their Past and Present.* Nedlands, W. Australia: University of Western Australia Press, 1979.

———. *Love Songs of Arnhem Land: Three Faces of Love: Traditional Aboriginal Song-Poetry.* Chicago: University of Chicago Press, 1978.

———. *Man, Land and Myth in Northern Australia: The Gunwinggu People.* East Lansing: Michigan State University Press, 1970.

———. *The Speaking Land: Myth and Story in Aboriginal Australia.* Ringwood, Victoria: Penguin Books Australia, 1989.

Broome, Richard. *Aboriginal Australians: Black Response to White Dominance 1788–1980.* North Sydney, NSW: George Allen & Unwin Australia, 1982.

Bropho, Robert. *Fringedweller*. Sydney: Alternative Publishing Co-operative, 1983.
Caruana, Wally. *Aboriginal Art*. New York: Thames and Hudson, 1993.
Charlesworth, Max, and Howard Morphy et al. *Religion in Aboriginal Australia*. St. Lucia, Queensland: University of Queensland Press, 1986.
Chatwin, Bruce. *The Songlines*. New York: Viking Penguin, 1987.
Coombs, H. C. *Kulinma: Listening to Aboriginal Australians*. Canberra: Australian National University Press, 1978.
Coombs, H. C., et al., eds. *Land of Promises: Aborigines and Development in the East Kimberley*. Canberra: Centre for Resource and Environmental Studies, Australian National University, 1989.
Cowan, James G. *Letters from a Wild State: Rediscovering Our True Relationship to Nature*. New York: Bell Tower, 1991.
————. *The Mysteries of the Dream-Time: The Spiritual Life of Australian Aborigines*. Bridport, Dorset: Prism Press; Lindfield, NSW: Unity Press, 1989.
Crumlin, Rosemary, ed. *Aboriginal Art and Spirituality*. North Blackburn, Victoria: Collins Dove, 1991.
Davis, Jack, et al., eds. *Paperbark: A Collection of Black Australian Writings*. St. Lucia, Queensland: University of Queensland Press, 1990.
Desert Stories. A 29-minute documentary film about the Pintupi people of central Australia. Directed by Lindsay Frazer; written by Billy Marshall-Stoneking; produced by Nick Frazer. Network 0/28. Special Broadcasting Service. 1984.
Dodson, Pat. "Address to the National Press Club." In *Land Rights Now*. International Work Group for Indigenous Affairs (IWGIA) document no. 54. Copenhagen: IWGIA Publications, October 1985.
————. "Restore Dignity, Restore Land, Restore Life." In Jack Davis et al., eds. *Paperbark: A Collection of Black Australian Writings*. St. Lucia, Queensland: University of Queensland Press, 1990.
Edwards, W. H., ed. *Traditional Aboriginal Society: A Reader*. South Melbourne: Macmillan Co. of Australia, 1987.
Elkin, A. P. *Aboriginal Men of High Degree*. 2d ed. St. Lucia, Queensland: University of Queensland Press, 1977.
Evans, Raymond, Kay Saunders, and Kathryn Cronin. *Race Relations in Colonial Queensland: A History of Exclusion, Exploitation and Extermination*. 1975. Reprint. St. Lucia, Queensland: University of Queensland Press, 1988.
Fison, L., and A. W. Howitt. *Kamilaroi and Kurnai*. 1880. Reprint. The Netherlands: Anthropological Publications, 1967.
Gale, Fay, ed. *We Are Bosses Ourselves: The Status and Role of Aboriginal Women Today*. Canberra: Australian Institute of Aboriginal Studies, 1983.
Gilbert, Kevin J. *Because a White Man'll Never Do It*. Sydney: Angus & Robertson, 1973.
————. *The Blackside: People Are Legends, and Other Poems*. South Yarra, Melbourne, Victoria: Hyland House, 1990.
————. *The End of Dream-Time*. Sydney: Island Press, 1971.
————. *Living Black: Blacks Talk to Kevin Gilbert*. Ringwood, Victoria: Penguin Books Australia, 1978.
————, ed. *Inside Black Australia: An Anthology of Aboriginal Poetry*. Ringwood, Victoria: Penguin Books Australia, 1988.
————. *People Are Legends: Aboriginal Poems by Kevin Gilbert*. St. Lucia, Queensland: University of Queensland Press, 1978.
Glass, Colleen, and Archie Weller. comps. *Us Fellas: An Anthology of Aboriginal Writing*. Perth, W. Australia: Artlook Books, 1987.
Harney, W. E. *Life Among the Aborigines*. London: Robert Hale, 1957.
————. *The Significance of Ayers Rock for Aborigines*. Darwin: Northern Territories Reserves Board, 1968.
Harris, Stewart. *This Is Our Land*. Canberra: Australian National University Press, 1972.
Huxley, Francis. *The Way of the Sacred*. London: Bloomsbury Books, 1989.

International Work Group for Indigenous Affairs (IWGIA) document no. 54 "Land Rights Now." Copenhagen: IWGIA Publications, October 1985.
International Work Group for Indigenous Affairs (IWGIA) newsletter no. 57. Copenhagen: IWGIA Publications, May 1989: pp. 33–43.
Isaacs, Jennifer. *Aboriginality: Contemporary Aboriginal Paintings and Prints*. St. Lucia, Queensland: University of Queensland Press, 1989.
———. *Australia Dreaming: 40,000 Years of Aboriginal History*. Sydney: Lansdowne Press, 1980.
———. *Australia's Living Heritage: Arts of the Dreaming*. Sydney: Lansdowne Press, 1984.
Lawlor, Robert. *Voices of the First Day: Awakening in the Aboriginal Dreamtime*. Rochester, VT: Inner Traditions International, 1991.
Montagu, Ashley. *Coming into Being Among the Australian Aborigines*. 1937. 2d ed. London: Routledge and Kegan Paul, 1974.
Moody, Roger, ed. *The Indigenous Voice: Visions and Realites*. 2 vols. London and Atlantic Highlands, NJ: Zed Books, 1988.
Morgan, Sally. *My Place*. New York: Arcade Publishing, 1990.
———. *Wanamurraganya: The Story of Jack McPhee*. Fremantle, W. Australia: Fremantle Arts Centre Press, 1989.
Mountford, Charles P. *Ayers Rock: Its People, Their Beliefs and Their Art*. Sydney: Angus & Robertson, 1965.
Myers, Fred R. *Pintupi Country, Pintupi Self*. Washington, DC: Smithsonian Institution, 1986; Berkeley and Los Angeles: University of California Press, 1991.
———. "Representing Culture: The Production of Discourse(s) for Aboriginal Acrylic Paintings." *Cultural Anthropology*, vol. 6, no. 1, 1991: pp. 26–62.
Neidjie, Big Bill, Stephen Davis, and Allan Fox. *Australia's Kakadu Man*. Darwin: Resource Managers, 1986.
O'Ferrall, Michael A. *On the Edge: Five Contemporary Aboriginal Artists*. Perth: Art Gallery of Western Australia, 1989.
Peterson, Nicolas, and Marcia Langston, eds. *Aborigines, Land and Land Rights*. Canberra: Australian Institute of Aboriginal Studies, 1983.
Pilger, John. *A Secret Country*. London: Jonathan Cape, 1989.
Ray, Derick, comp. *Australian Aboriginal Town Name Meanings*. Cambridge: British Society of Australian Philately, 1987.
Reid, Janice, ed. *Body, Land and Spirit: Health and Healing in Aboriginal Society*. St. Lucia, Queensland: University of Queensland Press, 1982.
Reynolds, Henry, comp. *Dispossession: Black Australia and White Invaders*. Sydney: George Allen & Unwin Australia, 1989.
———. *Frontier: Aborigines, Settlers, and Land*. Sydney and Boston: George Allen & Unwin, 1987.
———. *The Other Side of the Frontier: Aboriginal Resistance to the European Invasion of Australia*. Ringwood, Victoria: Penguin Books, 1982.
Roberts, Janine. *From Massacres to Mining: The Colonization of Aboriginal Australia*. London: CIMRA and War on Want, 1978.
Robinson, Roland. *The Man Who Sold His Dreaming*. Sydney: Currawong Publishing Co., 1965.
Ross, Tess Napaljarri. *Yuendumu Doors—Kuruwarri/The Warlukurlangu Artists*. Canberra: Australian Institute of Aboriginal Studies, 1987.
Roughsey, Dick. *Moon and Rainbow: The Autobiography of an Aboriginal*. Sydney: A. H. and A. W. Reed, 1971.
Ryan, Judith. *Mythscapes: Aboriginal Art of the Desert*. Melbourne: The National Gallery of Victoria, 1989.
Shaw, Bruce. *Banggaiyerri: The Story of Jack Sullivan*. Canberra: Australian Institute of Aboriginal Studies, 1983.
Shaw, Bruce, and Grant Ngadbidj. *My Country of the Pelican Dreaming: The Life of an Australian Aborigine of the Gadjerong, 1904–1977*, as told to Bruce Shaw. Canberra: Australian Institute of Aboriginal Studies, 1981.

Shoemaker, Adam. *Black Words, White Page: Aboriginal Literature 1929–1988.* St. Lucia, Queensland: University of Queensland Press, 1989.
Spencer, Sir Baldwin. *The Arunta: A Study of a Stone Age People.* 2 vols. London: Macmillan & Co., 1927.
Stanner, W. E. H. *On Aboriginal Religion.* Sydney: University of Sydney Press, 1989.
——. *White Man Got No Dreaming.* Canberra: Australian National University Press, 1979.
Strehlow, T. G. H. *Aranda Traditions.* Carlton, Victoria: Melbourne University Press, 1947.
——. *Songs of Central Australia.* Sydney: Angus & Robertson, 1971.
——. *The Sustaining Ideals of Australian Aboriginal Societies.* Adelaide: Printed for Aborigines Advancement League of South Australia, 1962.
Sutton, Peter, ed. *Dreamings: The Art of Aboriginal Australia.* New York: George Braziller and The Asia Society Galleries, 1988.
Tatz, Colin, ed. *Black Viewpoints: The Aboriginal Experience.* Sydney: Australia and New Zealand Book Co., 1975.
Taylor, Penny, ed. *After 200 Years.* Canberra: Aboriginal Studies Press, 1988.
Thompson, Liz, comp. *Aboriginal Voices: Contemporary Aboriginal Artists, Writers and Performers.* Brookvale, NSW: Simon & Schuster Australia, 1990.
Visions of Mowanjum: Aboriginal Writings from the Kimberley. Adelaide: Rigby Publishers, 1980.
Walker, Kath. *My People: Oodgeroo.* Milton, Queensland: Jacaranda Press, 1990.
——. *Stradbroke Dreamtime.* Sydney: Angus & Robertson, 1972.
——. *We Are Going Home: Poems.* New York: Citadel Press, 1965.
Weeks, Stephen Cone, et al., eds. *Aratjara: Art of the First Australians.* Düsseldorf and London: Conceived and published by Bernhard Luthi and Gary Lee, 1993.
West, Margie K. C. *The Inspired Dream: Life as Art in Aboriginal Australia.* South Brisbane: Queensland Art Gallery, 1988.
White, Isobel, Diane Barwick, and Betty Meehan, eds. *Fighters and Singers: The Lives of Some Australian Aboriginal Women.* North Sydney, NSW: George Allen & Unwin Australia, 1985.
Yu, Peter. Interview. In *International Work Group for Indigenous Affairs* (IWGIA) newsletter no. 57. Copenhagen: IWGIA Publications, May 1989: pp. 33–43.
Yuendumu Doors—Kuruwarri/Warlukurlangu Artists. Canberra: Australian Institute of Aboriginal Studies, 1987.

JAPAN

Anesaki, Masaharu. *Art, Life, and Nature in Japan.* Rutland, VT and Tokyo, Japan: Charles E. Tuttle Co., 1984.
Bashō, Matsuo. *The Narrow Road to the Deep North and Other Travel Sketches.* Trans. Nobuyuki Yuasa. Harmondsworth: Penguin Books, 1966.
Bernbaum, Edwin. *Sacred Mountains of the World.* San Francisco: Sierra Club Books, 1990.
Blyth, R. H. *Japanese Humour.* Tokyo: Japan Travel Bureau, 1957.
Bogel, Cynthea J., Israel Goldman, and Alfred H. Marks. *Hiroshige: Birds and Flowers.* New York: George Braziller in association with the Rhode Island School of Design, 1988.
Callicott, J. Baird, and Roger T. Ames. *Nature in Asian Traditions of Thought: Essays in Environmental Philosophy.* Albany: SUNY Press, 1989.
Cunningham, Michael R. *The Triumph of Japanese Style: 16th–Century Art in Japan.* Cleveland: The Cleveland Museum of Art, 1991.
De Bary, William Theodore, ed. *The Buddhist Tradition in India, China and Japan.* New York: Random House, a Vintage Books Edition, 1972.
Dōgen. *Shōbōgenzō: Zen Essays by Dōgen.* Trans. Thomas Cleary. Honolulu: University of Hawaii Press, 1986.
Dream Window: Reflections on the Japanese Garden. A 57-minute documentary film

produced by the Office of Telecommunications, the Smithsonian Institution in association with KajimaVision, Tokyo, 1992. Written by Peter Grilli and directed by John Junkerman. Senior producer, Laura T. Schneider.

Earhart, H. Byron. *Japanese Religion: Unity and Diversity*. Encino, CA: Dickenson Publishing Co., 1974.

———. *Religions of Japan: Many Traditions Within One Sacred Way*. New York: Harper & Row, 1984.

Ekken, Kaibara. *The Way of Contentment*. Trans. Ken Hoshino. Washington, DC: University Publications of America, 1979.

Frazer, Sir James George, ed. *The New Golden Bough*. New York: Criterion Books, 1959.

Fukuoka, Masanobu. *The Natural Way of Farming: The Theory and Practice of Green Philosophy*. Trans. Frederic P. Metreaud. Tokyo: Japan Publications, 1985.

———. *One-Straw Revolution: An Introduction to Natural Farming*. Trans. Chris Pearce, Tsune Kurosawa and Larry Korn. Emmaus, PA: Rodale Press, 1978.

———. *The Road Back to Nature*. Trans. Frederic P. Metreaud. Tokyo: Japan Publications, 1987.

Gessel, Van C., and Tomone Matsumoto, eds. *The Shōwa Anthology: Modern Japanese Short Stories: 1929–1984*. Tokyo and New York: Kodansha International, 1989.

Hayakawa, Masao. *The Garden Art of Japan*. Trans. Richard L. Gage. New York and Tokyo: Weatherhill/Heibonsha, 1977.

Herrigal, Eugen. *Zen in the Art of Archery*. New York: Vintage Books, 1971.

Hilger, M. Inez, with the assistance of Chiye Sano and Midori Yamaha. *Together with the Ainu—A Vanishing People*. Norman, OK: University of Oklahoma Press, 1971.

Hokusai. *Hokusai: One Hundred Views of Mt. Fuji*. Intro. and commentaries on the plates by Henry D. Smith II. New York: George Braziller, 1988.

Hyers, Conrad. *The Laughing Buddha: Zen and the Comic Spirit*. Wolfeboro, NH: Longwood Academic, 1989.

Ichikawa, Sanki. "On the Japanese Cicada." *Japan Quarterly*, vol. 3, no. 4 (1956): pp. 487–90.

Ichikawa, Sanki, et al. *Haikai and Haiku*. Tokyo: The Nippon Gakujutsu Shinkokai, 1958.

Ienaga, Saburo. *Painting in the Yamato Style*. Trans. John M. Shields. New York and Tokyo: Weatherhill/Heibonsha, 1973.

Isaku, Patia R. *Mountain Storm, Pine Breeze: Folk Song in Japan*. Tucson: University of Arizona Press, 1981.

Ishida, Eiichiro. *Japanese Culture: A Study of Origins and Characteristics*. Tokyo: University of Tokyo Press, 1974.

Ishimure, Michiko. "Pure Land, Poisoned Sea." Chapter 3, "What Yuki Said," in *Kugai Jodo. Japan Quarterly*, vol. 18, no. 3 (1971): pp. 299–306.

Japan: Spirit and Form. Shuichi Kato, host. A ten-part television series produced by NHK International, Inc. The series was broadcast over City University Television, New York (CUNY), 1993.

Japan: Voices from the Land. A 60-minute documentary written and produced by Peter Argentine; a WQED production from QED Communications, Inc., Pittsburgh, 1991.

Kato, Shuichi. *A History of Japanese Literature*. 3 vols. Tokyo and New York: Kodansha International, 1983.

Keene, Donald, comp. and ed. *Anthology of Japanese Literature: From the Earliest Era to the Mid-Nineteenth Century*. New York: Grove Press, 1955.

———. *Landscapes and Portraits: Appreciations of Japanese Culture*. Tokyo and Palo Alto: Kodansha International, 1971.

———. *Living Japan*. Garden City, NY: Doubleday & Co., 1959.

Kodama, Misao, and Hikosaku Yanagishima, eds. and trans. *Ryōkan The Great Fool*. Kyoto: The Kyoto Seika Jr. College Press, 1969.

Kotzsch, Ronald E. *Macrobiotics: Yesterday and Today.* Tokyo and New York: Japan Publications, 1985.

Kunimoto, Yoshiro. "The Fisherfolk of the North." *Japan Quarterly,* vol. 19, no. 1 (1972): pp. 73–82.

Kusano, Shimpei. *Asking Myself/Answering Myself.* New York: New Directions Books, 1984.

———. *frogs & others.* Trans. Cid Corman and Ohno Hidetaka. New York: Grossman Publishers, 1969.

LaFleur, William R. "Saigyō and the Buddhist Value of Nature, Part II." In *History of Religions,* vol. 13 (1973–74): pp. 227–46.

Lawton, Thomas, and Linda Merrill. *Freer: A Legacy of Art.* Washington, DC, and New York: Freer Gallery of Art, Smithsonian Institution, in association with Harry N. Abrams, 1993.

Leach, Bernard. *Hamada: Potter.* New York: Kodansha International/USA, 1975.

Lehrman, Frederic. *The Sacred Landscape.* Berkeley: Celestial Arts Publishing, 1988.

The Manyōshū: The Nippon Gakujutsu Shinkokai Translation of One Thousand Poems. New York: Columbia University Press, 1965.

Myōdō, Satomi. *Passionate Journey: The Spiritual Autobiography of Satomi Myōdō.* Trans. Sallie B. King. Boston: Shambhala Publications, 1987.

Nagatsuka, Takashi. *Earth.* Trans. Yasuhiro Kawamura. Tokyo: Liber Press, 1986.

Ohba, Minako. "Candle Fish." In Yukiko Tanaka, trans. and ed. *Unmapped Territories.* Seattle: Women in Translation, 1991.

Okakura, Kakuzo. *The Book of Tea.* 1906. Reprint. Tokyo and New York: Kodansha International/USA, 1989.

Okazaki, Jōji. *Pure Land Buddhist Painting.* Trans. Elizabeth ten Grotenhuis. New York and Tokyo: Kodansha International and Shibundo, 1977.

Ooka, Makoto, et al. *Mt. Fuji.* Photographs by Yukio Ohyama. New York: E. P. Dutton, 1987.

Pearson, Richard, et al. *Ancient Japan.* Washington, DC: the Arthur M. Sackler Gallery and the Smithsonian Institution, 1992.

Peterson, Susan. *Shōji Hamada: A Potter's Way and Work.* New York: Kodansha International/USA, 1974.

Philippi, Donald L. *Songs of Gods, Songs of Humans: The Epic Tradition of the Ainu.* Princeton and Tokyo: Princeton University Press and the University of Tokyo Press, 1979.

Rimer, J. Thomas. *A Reader's Guide to Japanese Literature: From the Eighth Century to the Present.* Tokyo: Kodansha International, 1988.

Saga, Dr. Junichi. *Memories of Silk and Straw: A Self-Portrait of Small-Town Japan.* Trans. Garry O. Evans. Tokyo and New York: Kodansha International/USA, 1987.

Sakaki, Nanao. *Break the Mirror.* San Francisco: North Point Press, 1987.

Sanders, Douglas. "The Ainu as an Indigenous People." *IWGIA Newsletter,* nos. 45–46 (1986): pp. 119–25.

Shigematsu, Soiku, comp. and trans. *A Zen Forest.* New York and Tokyo: Weatherhill, 1981.

Slawson, David A. *Secret Teachings in the Art of Japanese Gardens: Design Principles /Aesthetic Values.* Tokyo: Kodansha International, 1991.

Soseki, Muso. *Sun at Midnight: Poems and Sermons by Muso Soseki.* Trans. W. S. Merwin and Soiku Shigematsu. San Francisco: North Point Press, 1989.

Suzuki, Daisetz. *Japanese Spirituality.* Trans. Norman Waddell. New York: Greenwood Press, 1988.

———. *Sengai: The Zen Master.* London: Faber and Faber, 1971.

———. *Zen and Japanese Culture.* Bollingen Series LXIV. Princeton, NJ: Princeton University Press, 1989.

Tanahashi, Kazuaki. *Brush Mind.* Berkeley: Parallax Press, 1990.

———. *Enku: Sculptor of a Hundred Thousand Buddhas.* Boulder, CO: Shambhala Publications, 1982.

Tanaka, Yukiko, trans. and ed. *Unmapped Territories*. Seattle: Women in Translation, 1991.

Tucker, Mary Evelyn. *Moral and Spiritual Cultivation in Japanese Neo-Confucianism: The Life and Thought of Kaibara Ekken (1630–1714)*. Albany: State University of New York Press, 1989.

Tyler, Royall. "A Glimpse of Mt. Fuji in Legend and Cult." *Journal of the Association of Teachers of Japanese*, vol. 16, no. 2 (1980): pp. 140–65.

——, ed. and trans. *Japanese Tales*. New York: Pantheon Books, 1987.

Ueda, Makoto. *Matsuo Bashō*. New York: Twayne Publishers, 1970.

Watsuji, Tetsuro. *A Climate: A Philosophical Study*. Trans. Geoffrey Bownas. Tokyo: Japanese Government Printing Bureau, Ministry of Education, 1961.

Wilson, Andrew, ed. *World Scripture*. New York: Paragon House, 1991.

Wilson, Graeme, and Atsumi Ikuko. "The Poetry of Yamamura Bocho." *Japan Quarterly*, vol. 19, no. 4 (1972): pp. 458–66.

Yanagi, Sōetsu. *The Unknown Craftsman: A Japanese Insight into Beauty*. New York: Kodansha International/U.S.A, 1984.

Yanagita, Kunio. *About Our Ancestors: The Japanese Family System*. Trans. Fanny Hagin Mayer and Ishiwara Yasuyo. Tokyo: Japan Society for the Promotion of Science, 1970.

GREECE

Adam, James. *The Religious Teachers of Greece*. Edinburgh: T. & T. Clark, 1909.

Alexiou, Stylianos, Maria Theocharis et al. *Historia Tou Ellenikou Ethnous*. Athens: Ekdotike Athenon, 1971.

Aristophanes. *Birds*. Ed. and trans. Alan H. Sommerstein. Teddington House, Warminster, Wiltshire: Aris & Phillips, 1987.

Athanassakis, Apostolos N., trans. *The Homeric Hymns*. Baltimore: Johns Hopkins University Press, 1976.

Balmer, Josephine, trans. *Sappho, Poems and Fragments*. Secaucus, NJ: Meadowland Books, 1984.

Barnstone, Willis, trans. *Sappho and the Greek Lyric Poets*. New York: Schocken Books, 1988.

Boer, Charles, trans. *The Homeric Hymns*. Irving, TX: Spring Publications, 1979.

Brumbaugh, Robert S. *The Philosophers of Greece*. New York: Thomas Y. Crowell, 1964.

Burn, A. R. *The Lyric Age of Greece*. London: Edward Arnold, 1978.

Clogg, Richard. *A Concise History of Greece*. New York: Cambridge University Press, 1992.

Dalven, Rae, trans. and ed. *Modern Greek Poetry*. New York: Russell & Russell, 1971.

Dickinson, G. Lowes. *The Greek View of Life*. New York: Collier Books, 1961.

Dimaras, C. Th. *A History of Modern Greek Literature*. Trans. Mary P. Gianos. Albany: State University of New York Press, 1972.

Drews, Robert. *The Greek Accounts of Eastern History*. Washington, DC: The Center for Hellenic Studies, 1973.

Fairbanks, Arthur. *The First Philosophers of Greece*. New York: Charles Scribner's Sons, 1898.

Flory, Stewart. *The Archaic Smile of Herodotus*. Detroit: Wayne State University Press, 1987.

Frazer, Sir James George. *The Worship of Nature*. New York: The Macmillan Co., 1926; New York: AMS Press, 1976.

Guthrie, W. K. C. *The Greek Philosophers: From Thales to Aristotle*. New York: Harper & Row, Harper Torchbooks/The Academy Library, 1960.

——. *The Greeks and Their Gods*. Boston: Beacon Press, 1955.

Hadzsits, George Depue, ed. *Classical Studies in Honor of John C. Rolfe*. 1931. Reprint. Freeport, NY: Books for Libraries Press, 1967.

Hamilton, Edith. *The Greek Way.* 1930. Reprint. New York: W. W. Norton, 1942.
Hampe, Roland, and Erika Simon. *The Birth of Greek Art, from the Mycenaean to the Archaic period.* New York: Oxford University Press, 1981.
Hesiod. Trans. Richmond Lattimore. Ann Arbor: University of Michigan Press, 1959.
Hippocrates. Trans. W. H. S. Jones. 1923. Reprint. The Loeb Classical Library, vol. 1. Cambridge: Harvard University Press, 1962.
Homer. *Odyssey.* Trans. Robert Fitzgerald. New York: Vintage Books, 1974.
Huxley, G. L. *The Early Ionians.* New York: Humanities Press, 1966.
Isocrates. *Panegyricus.* Trans. George Norlin. The Loeb Classical Library, vol. 1. New York: G. P. Putnam's Sons, 1928.
Jay, Peter, ed. *Anthologia Graeca: The Greek Anthology and Other Ancient Greek Epigrams.* New York: Oxford University Press, 1973.
Jusdanis, Gregory. *The Poetics of Cavafy: Textuality, Eroticism, History.* Princeton, NJ: Princeton University Press, 1987.
Kazantzakis, Nikos. *Report to Greco.* Trans. P. A. Bien. New York: Simon and Schuster, 1965.
———. *Zorba the Greek.* Trans. Carl Wildman. New York: Simon and Schuster, 1952.
Kirk, G. S., and J. E. Raven. *The Presocratic Philosophers.* 1957. Reprint. Cambridge: Cambridge University Press, 1967.
Kitto, H. D. F. *The Greeks.* New York: Viking Penguin, 1988.
Lardas, Konstantinos, trans. *Mourning Songs of Greek Women.* New York: Garland Publishing, 1992.
Lefkowitz, Mary. "The Origins of Greece and the Illusions of Afrocentrists." *The New Republic,* February 10, 1992, pp. 29–36.
Lesky, Albin. *A History of Greek Literature.* Trans. James Willis and Cornelis de Heer. London: Methuen & Co., 1966.
Merton, Thomas. *The Collected Poems of Thomas Merton.* New York: New Directions, 1977.
Miller, Henry. *The Colossus Of Maroussi.* London: Faber and Faber, 1945.
Moutzan-Martinengou, Elisavet. *My Story.* Trans. Helen Dendrinou Kolias. Athens, GA: The University of Georgia Press, 1989.
Pallis, Marco. *The Way and the Mountain.* London: Peter Owen, 1961.
Plato. *Critias.* Trans. Rev. R. G. Bury. 1929. Reprint. The Loeb Classical Library, vol. IX. Cambridge: Harvard University Press, 1981.
———. *The Dialogues of Plato.* Selections from the translation of Benjamin Jowett. New York: Liveright Publishing Corp., 1927.
———. *Phaedo.* Trans. Hugh Tredennick. In *The Last Days of Socrates.* London: Penguin Books, 1954.
———. *Phaedrus.* Ed. Edith Hamilton and Huntington Cairns. *The Collected Dialogues of Plato.* Bollingen Series LXXI. Princeton, NJ: Princeton University Press, 1989.
Prevelakis, Pandelis. *Nikos Kazantzakis and His Odyssey: A Study of the Poet and the Poem.* Trans. Philip Sherrard. New York: Simon and Schuster, 1961.
Ricks, David. *The Shade of Homer: A Study in Modern Greek Poetry.* Cambridge: Cambridge University Press, 1989.
Scully, Vincent. *The Earth, the Temple and the Gods: Greek Sacred Architecture.* New York: Frederick A. Praeger, 1969.
Seferis, George. *On the Greek Style: Selected Essays in Poetry and Hellenism.* Trans. Rex Warner and Th. D. Frangopoulos. Boston: Little, Brown and Co., an Atlantic Monthly Press Book, 1966.
———. *Poems.* Trans. Rex Warner. Boston: Nonpareil Books, 1978.
———. *A Poet's Journal: Days of 1945–1951.* Trans. Athan Anagnostopoulos. Cambridge: The Belknap Press of Harvard University, 1974.
Sherrard, Philip, ed. *The Pursuit of Greece: An Anthology.* Athens: Denise Harvey & Co., 1987.

Sikelianos, Angelos. *Angelos Sikelianos: Selected Poems*. Trans. Edmund Keeley and Philip Sherrard. Princeton, NJ: Princeton University Press, 1979.

Siotis, Dinos, and John Chioles, eds. *Twenty Contemporary Greek Poets*. San Francisco: Wire Press, 1979.

Sophocles. *The Theban Plays*. Trans. E. F. Watling. Baltimore: Penguin Books, 1953.

Spretnak, Charlene. *Lost Goddesses of Early Greece: A Collection of Pre-Hellenic Myths*. Boston: Beacon Press, 1984.

Stoneman, Richard, ed. *A Literary Companion to Travel in Greece*. Harmondsworth: Penguin Books, 1984.

Tannen, Deborah. *Lilika Nakos*. Boston: Twayne Publishers, 1983.

Theocritus. *Theocritus: The Idylls*. Trans. Robert Wells. London: Penguin Books, 1989.

Thucydides. *The History of the Peloponnesian War*. Trans. Richard Crawley. New York: E. P. Dutton, 1950.

Trypanis, C. A. *Greek Poetry: From Homer to Seferis*. Chicago: University of Chicago Press, 1981.

Tsatsos, K., I. Kakrides, and Karl Schefold et al. *Hellenike Mythologia*. 5 vols. Athens: Ekdotike Athenon, 1986.

Van Groningen, Bernhard Abraham. *In the Grip of the Past: Essay on an Aspect of Greek Thought*. Leiden, The Netherlands: E. J. Brill, 1953.

Venezis, Ilias. *Aiolian Land*. Ed. Anne Farmakides. Montreal: McGill University, 1987.

Vlastos, Gregory. *Socrates: Ironist and Moral Philosopher*. Ithaca, NY: Cornell University Press, 1991.

White, K. D. *Country Life in Classical Times*. Ithaca, NY: Cornell University Press, 1977.

Wolfe, Humbert. *Others Abide*. London: Ernest Benn, 1927.

Woodbridge, Frederick J. E. *Aristotle's Vision of Nature*. Ed. John Herman Randall, Jr., with the assistance of Charles H. Kahn and Harold A. Larrabee. New York: Columbia University Press, 1966.

AFRICA

Abraham, W. E. *The Mind of Africa*. Chicago: University of Chicago Press, 1962.

Abrahams, Peter. *Tell Freedom: Memories of Africa*. New York: Alfred A. Knopf, 1966.

Achebe, Chinua. *Hopes and Impediments*. New York: Doubleday & Co., 1989.

———. "If One Thing Stands, Another Will Stand Beside It": An Interview with Chinua Achebe. *Parabola*, vol. XVII, no. 3 (1992), pp. 19–27.

———. *Things Fall Apart*. New York: Astor-Honor, 1959.

Agunwa, Clement. *More than Once*. London: Longmans, Green & Co., 1967.

Akiga, Benjamin. *Akiga's Story: The Tiv Tribe as Seen by One of Its Members*. 1939. Trans. Rupert East. Reprint. London: Oxford University Press, 1965.

Andoh, Anthony K. *The Science & Romance of Selected Herbs Used in Medicine & Religious Ceremony*. San Francisco: The North Scale Institute, 1987.

Anyidoho, Kofi. *Earthchild*. Accra: Woeli Publication Services, 1985.

Appiah, Anthony Kwame. *In My Father's House*. New York: Oxford University Press, 1992.

Arens, W., and Ivan Karp, eds. *Creativity of Power: Cosmology and Action in African Societies*. Washington and London: Smithsonian Institution Press, 1989.

Awoonor, Kofi. *The Breast of the Earth*. New York: NOK Publishers International, 1975.

———. *Comes a Voyager at Last: A Tale of Return to Africa*. Trenton, NJ: Africa World Press, 1992.

———. *Contemporary Authors Autobiography Series*. vol. 13. Detroit: Gale Research, 1991.

————. *The Latin American and Caribbean Notebook*. vol. 1. Trenton, NJ: Africa World Press, 1992.

————. *This Earth, My Brother....* London: Heinemann Educational Books, 1972.

Bâ, Amadou Hampâté. *Kaidara*. Trans. Daniel Whitman. Washington, DC: Three Continents Press, 1988.

————. "Earth, Moon, and Sun." *Parabola,* vol. XIV, no. 3 (1989): pp. 48–52.

————. "Intermediaries for the Sacred Force." *Parabola,* vol. XIV, no. 2 (1989): pp. 9–12.

Beier, Ulli, ed. *An Introduction to African Literature: An Anthology of Critical Writing*. London: Longman Group, 1979.

Bernbaum, Edwin. *Sacred Mountains of the World*. San Francisco: Sierra Club Books, 1990.

Brincard, Marie-Thérèse. *The Art of Metal in Africa*. New York: The African-American Institute, 1982.

Busia, K. A. *The Position of the Chief in the Modern Political System of Ashanti*. London: Frank Cass & Co., 1968.

Césaire, Aimé. *Return to My Native Land*. Trans. John Berger and Anna Bostock. Harmondsworth: Penguin Books, 1969.

Courlander, Harold. *A Treasury of African Folklore*. New York: Crown Publishers, 1975.

Davidson, Basil. *The African Genius: An Introduction to African Cultural and Social History*. Boston and Toronto: Atlantic-Little, Brown Books, 1969.

————. *The Lost Cities of Africa*. Boston: Little, Brown & Co., 1987.

Drachler, Jacob, ed. *African Heritage: Intimate Views of the Black Africans from Life, Lore, and Literature*. New York: Crowell-Collier Publishing, 1963.

Drewal, Henry John, and John Pemberton III. *Yoruba: Nine Centuries of African Art and Thought*. New York: Harry N. Abrams and The Center for African Art, 1989.

Driberg, J. H. *People of the Small Arrow*. New York: Payson & Clarke, 1930.

Edwards, Paul, comp. *Modern African Narrative: An Anthology*. London: Thomas Nelson and Sons, 1966.

Eliade, Mircea. *Patterns in Comparative Religion*. Trans. Rosemary Sheed. New York: New American Library, 1974.

Fisher, Angela. *Africa Adorned*. New York: Harry N. Abrams, 1984.

Fu-Kiau, K. Kia Bunseki. *The African Book Without Title*. Privately published, 1980.

Gatheru, R. Mugo. *Child of Two Worlds*. London: Heinemann Educational Books, 1964.

Gillon, Werner. *A Short History of African Art*. 1984. Reprint. New York: Penguin Books, 1991.

Griaule, Marcel. *Conversations with Ogotemmêli: An Introduction to Dogon Religious Ideas*. London: Oxford University Press, 1970.

Gyekye, Kwame. *The Unexamined Life*. Accra: Ghana Universities Press, 1988.

Head, Bessie. "The Green Tree." *Transition,* vol. 4, no. 16 (1964), p. 33.

————. *A Question of Power*. New York: Pantheon Books, 1973.

————. *Serowe: Village of the Rain Wind*. London: Heinemann Educational Books, 1981.

Herskovits, Melville J., and Francis S. Herskovits. *Dahomean Narrative*. Evanston, IL: Northwestern University Press, 1970.

Jabavu, Noni. *The Ochre People: Scenes from a South African Life*. London: John Murray, 1963.

Janheinz, Jahn. *Muntu: An Outline of the New African Culture*. Trans. Marjorie Grene. New York: Grove Press, 1961.

Kane, Cheikh Hamidou. *Ambiguous Adventure*. Trans. Katherine Woods. London: Heinemann Educational Books, 1963.

Kaunda, Kenneth. *A Humanist in Africa: Letters to Colin M. Morris from Kenneth D. Kaunda*. Nashville, TN: Abingdon Press, 1966.

————. *A Letter to My Children*. London: Longman, 1973.

Kenyatta, Jomo. *Facing Mount Kenya: The Tribal Life of the Kikuyu*. 1938. Reprint. London: Martin Secker & Warburg, 1959.

——. *My People of Kikuyu*. 1942. Reprint. London: Oxford University Press, 1966.

Kipury, Naomi. *Oral Literature of the Maasai*. Nairobi: Heinemann Educational Books, 1983.

Kyerematen, A. A. Y. *Panoply of Ghana: Ornamental Art in Ghanaian Tradition and Culture*. New York: Frederick A. Praeger, 1964.

Laye, Camara. *The Dark Child: The Autobiography of an African Boy*. Trans. James Kirkup and Ernest Jones. New York: Farrar, Straus and Giroux, 1954; New York: Hill and Wang, 1992.

——. *The Radiance of the King*. Trans. James Kirkup. New York: Collier-Macmillan, 1971. Originally published as *Le Regard du Roi* (Paris: Plon, 1954).

Mapanje, Jack, and Landeg White, comps. *Oral Poetry of Africa: An Anthology*. New York: Longman , 1983.

Mbiti, John S. *African Religions and Philosophy*. 2d ed., rev. and enl. Oxford: Heinemann Educational Books, 1990.

——. *Introduction to African Religion*. 2d ed. London: Heinemann Educational Books, 1991.

——. *The Prayers of African Religion*. Maryknoll, NY: Orbis Books, 1975.

Modupe, Prince. *I Was a Savage*. London: Museum Press, 1958.

Morell, Karen L. *In Person: Achebe, Awoonor, and Soyinka at the University of Washington*. Seattle: African Studies Program, Institute for Comparative and Foreign Area Studies, University of Washington, 1975.

Nicol, Davidson. *Africa: A Subjective View*. 1964. Reprint. Accra: Longmans, Green & Co. in association with Ghana Universities Press, 1967.

Obiego, Cosmas Okechukwu. *African Image of the Ultimate Reality: An Analysis of Igbo Ideas of Life and Death in Relation to Chunkwu-God*. Frankfurt am Main: Peter Lang, 1984.

Okri, Ben. *The Famished Road*. New York: Anchor Books, 1993.

Ole Saibull, Solomon. *Herd and Spear: The Maasai of East Africa*. London: Collins and Harvill Press, 1981.

Olney, James. *Tell Me Africa: An Approach to African Literature*. Princeton, NJ: Princeton University Press, 1973.

Ray, Benjamin C. *African Religions*. Englewood Cliffs, NJ: Prentice-Hall, 1976.

Roberts, Elizabeth, and Elias Amadon, eds. *Earth Prayers*. San Francisco: HarperCollins, 1991.

St. Lys, Odette. *From a Vanished German Colony: A Collection of Folklore, Folk Tales and Proverbs from South-West Africa*. London and Dublin: Gypsy Press, 1916.

Saitoti, Tepilit Ole. *The Worlds of a Maasai Warrior*. Berkeley: University of California Press, 1986.

Serequeberhan, Tsenay. *African Philosophy: The Essential Readings*. New York: Paragon House, 1991.

Sieber, Roy. *African Textiles and Decorative Arts*. New York: Museum of Modern Art, 1972.

Siroto, Leon. *African Spirit Images and Identities*. New York: Pace Editions, 1976.

Soyinka, Wole. *Myth, Literature and the African World*. 1976. Reprint. Cambridge: Cambridge University Press, 1990.

Taiwo, Oladele. *Social Experience in African Literature*. Enugu, Nigeria: Fourth Dimension Publishing Co., 1986.

Thompson, Leonard. *A History of South Africa*. New Haven: Yale University Press, 1990.

Tlili, Mustapha. *Lion Mountain*. Trans. Linda Coverdale. New York: Arcade Publishing, 1990.

Tobias, Michael Charles, and Harold Drasdo, eds. *The Mountain Spirit*. Woodstock, NY: Overlook Press, 1979.

Turnbull, Colin M. *The Forest People*. New York: Simon and Schuster, a Touchstone Book, 1962.

Tutuola, Amos. *My Life in the Bush of Ghosts*. New York: Grove Press, 1954.

————. *The Palm-Wine Drinkard*. New York: Grove Press, 1953.

————. "The Yoruba and the Hill Spirits." In Michael Charles Tobias and Harold Drasdo, eds. *The Mountain Spirit*. Woodstock, NY: Overlook Press, 1979.

Van der Post, Laurens. *The Lost World of the Kalahari*. New York: William Morrow and Co,, 1958.

Vogel, Susan. *Africa Explores: 20th Century African Art*. New York: The Center for African Art, 1991.

————, ed. *For Spirits and Kings: African Art from the Paul and Ruth Tishman Collection*. New York: The Metropolitan Museum of Art, 1981.

wa Thiong'o, Ngugi [James Ngugi]. *Weep Not, Child*. New York: Collier-Macmillan, 1969.

Waciuma, Charity. *Daughter of Mumbi*. Nairobi: East African Publishing House, 1969.

Wauthier, Claude. *The Literature and Thought of Modern Africa*. Washington, DC: Three Continents Press, 1979.

Wilson, Andrew, ed. *World Scripture*. New York: Paragon House, 1991.

SOUTH AMERICA: THE KOGI

The Art of Precolumbian Gold: The Jan Mitchell Collection. Curator of the exhibition, Julie Jones. New York: The Metropolitan Museum of Art, 1985.

Bray, Warwick. "Across the Darien Gap: A Colombian View of Isthmian Archaeology." In *The Archaeology of Lower Central America*. Ed. Frederick W. Lange and Doris Z. Stone. Albuquerque: University of New Mexico, 1984.

————. *The Gold of Eldorado: The Heritage of Colombia*. New York: Harry N. Abrams, 1979.

Ereira, Alan. *The Elder Brothers: A Lost South American People and Their Message About the Fate of the Earth*. New York: Alfred A. Knopf, 1992.

From the Heart of the World: The Elder Brothers' Warning. An 88-minute documentary film by Alan Ereira. Written and produced by Alan Ereira. A BBC TV production in association with the Goldsmith Foundation, 1990. Distributed by Mystic Fire Video, New York City.

Knowlton, Elizabeth. *The Naked Mountain*. 1933. Reprint. New York and London: G. P. Putnam's Sons, 1953.

Mason, Gregory. *South of Yesterday*. New York: Henry Holt & Co., 1940.

Mason, John Alden. "Archaeology of Santa Marta, Colombia: The Tairona Culture." Anthropological Series, vol. 20, no. 1. Chicago: Field Museum of Natural History Publications, 1931–36.

Mayr, J. D., ed. *The Sierra Nevada of Santa Marta*. Bogota: Mayr & Cabal, 1985.

Meggers, Betty Jane. *Prehistoric America: An Ecological Perspective*. New York: Aldine Publishing Co., 1979.

Moser, Brian and Donald Taylor. *The Cocaine Eaters*. New York: Taplinger Publishing Co., 1967.

Reichel-Dolmatoff, Gerardo. *Colombia*. New York: Frederick A. Praeger, 1965.

————. "Cultural Change and Environmental Awareness: A Case Study of the Sierra Nevada de Santa Marta, Colombia." *Mountain Research and Development*, vol. 2, no. 3, 1982: pp. 289–98.

————. "Funerary Customs and Religious Symbolism Among the Kogi." In *Native South Americans: Ethnology of the Least Known Continent*, ed. Patricia J. Lyon. Boston and London: Little, Brown & Co., 1974; Prospect Heights, IL: Waveland Press, 1985: pp. 289–301.

————. *Goldwork and Shamanism: An Iconographic Study of the Gold Museum, Bogota*. Medellín: Compania Litografica Nacional, 1988.

————. "The Great Mother and the Kogi Universe: A Concise Overview." *Journal of Latin-American Lore*, vol. 13, no. 1, 1987: pp. 73–113.

————. *Los Kogi: Una Tribu de la Sierra Nevada de Santa Marta*. 2 vols. Bogota: Nueva Biblioteca Colombiana, 1985.

————. "The Loom of Life: A Kogi Principle of Integration." *Journal of Latin-American Lore,* vol. 4, no. 1, 1978: pp. 5–27.

————. "A Preliminary Study of Space and Time Perspective in Northern Colombia." *American Antiquity,* vol. 19, no. 4 (April 1954): pp. 352–65.

————. *The Sacred Mountain of Colombia's Kogi Indians*. Leiden, The Netherlands: E. J. Brill, 1990.

————. *San Augustin: A Culture of Colombia*. New York: Frederick A. Praeger, 1972.

————. "Some Kogi Models of the Beyond." *Journal of Latin-American Lore,* vol. 10, no. 1, 1984: pp. 63–85.

————. "Training for the Priesthood Among the Kogi of Colombia." *Enculturation in Latin America: An Anthology,* vol. 37. Series ed., Johannes Wilbert. Los Angeles: Latin-American Center Publications, University of California, 1976: pp. 265–88.

NATIVE NORTH AMERICA

Allen, Paula Gunn. *Grandmothers of the Light: A Medicine Woman's Source Book*. Boston: Beacon Press, 1991.

Amiotte, Arthur. "The Road to the Center." *Parabola,* vol. IX, no. 3 (1984): pp. 46–51.

Arden, Harvey, and Steve Wall. *Wisdomkeepers: Meetings with Native American Elders*. Hillsboro, OR: Beyond Words Publishing, 1991.

Bierhorst, John, ed. *The Sacred Path*. New York: William Morrow and Co., 1983.

Black Elk. *The Sacred Pipe: Black Elk's Account of the Seven Rites of the Oglala Sioux*. Rec. and ed. Joseph Epes Brown. Norman, OK: University of Oklahoma Press, 1953; Baltimore: Penguin Books, 1971.

Black Hawk. *Black Hawk: An Autobiography*. Ed. Donald Jackson. 1833; Reprint, Chicago: Prairie State Books, 1990.

Boas, Franz. *Ethnology of the Kwakiutl* (based on data collected by George Hunt). Washington, DC: Bureau of American Ethnology, 35th Annual Report, 1913–14.

Brown, Joseph Epes. *The Spiritual Legacy of the American Indian*. New York: Crossroad Publishing Co., 1982.

Bruchac, Joseph. *Near the Mountains*. Fredonia, NY: White Pine Press, 1987.

————. *Songs from This Earth on Turtle's Back*. Greenfield Center, NY: Greenfield Review Press, 1983.

Buckley, Thomas. "The One Who Flies All Around the World." *Parabola,* vol. XVI, no. 1 (1991): pp. 4–9.

Bunzel, L. Ruth. *The Pueblo Potter: A Study of Creative Imagination in Primitive Art*. New York: Columbia University Press, 1929. Reprint. New York: Dover Publications, 1972.

Canadian Association in Support of the Native Peoples (CASNP). Bulletin. vol. 18, no. 2 (1977): pp. 3–58.

Capps, Walter Holden, ed. *Seeing with a Native Eye: Essays on Native American Religion*. New York: Harper & Row, 1976.

Carpenter, Edmund. "The Eskimo and His Art." In *A Guide to the Peaceable Kingdom*. Ed. William Kilbourn. Toronto: Macmillan of Canada, 1970.

————. *Oh, What a Blow That Phantom Gave Me*. New York: Holt, Rinehart & Winston, 1972.

Carter, Forrest. *The Education of Little Tree*. Albuquerque: University of New Mexico Press, 1986.

Clark, Ella E. *Indian Legends of the Pacific Northwest*. Berkeley: University of California Press, 1960.

Curtis, Edward S. *The North American Indian*. 20 vols. Ed. Frederick Webb Hodge. Seattle, WA: E. S. Curtis; Cambridge, MA.: The University Press, 1907–30.

Da, Popovi. "Indian Pottery and Indian Values." In Richard L. Spivey, *Maria*. Flagstaff, AZ: Northland Press, 1979.

Deloria, Jr., Vine. *Sacred Lands and Religious Freedom*. New York: Association on American Indian Affairs, 1991.

De Menil, Adelaide and William Reid. *Out of the Silence*. New York: Harper & Row, 1971.

Densmore, Frances. *Teton Sioux Music*. Bureau of American Ethnology Bulletin no. 61, 1918.

Fletcher, Alice C. "The Elk Mystery or Festival." Peabody Museum of Archaeology and Ethnology, *Reports*, no. 16, 1884.

Frank, Jr., Billy. "Indians and Salmon: Making Nature Whole," *The New York Times*, November 26, 1992.

Frazer, Sir James George. *The Golden Bough: A Study in Magic and Religion*. New York: Macmillan, 1940.

Gilmore, Melvin R. *Prairie Smoke*. 1929. Reprint. St. Paul: Minnesota Historical Society, 1987.

———. *Uses of Plants by the Indians of the Missouri River Region*. Thirty-third Annual Report of the Bureau of American Ethnology, 1919. Reprint. Lincoln: University of Nebraska Press, 1977.

Glenbow-Alberta Institute. *The Spirit Sings: Artistic Traditions of Canada's First Peoples*. Toronto: McClelland and Stewart and the Glenbow Museum, 1987.

Goldsmith, Edward. *The Way*. London: Rider Books, 1992.

Gunther, Erna. *Further Analysis of the First Salmon Ceremony*. Seattle: University of Washington Press, 1928.

Hilger, Sister M. Inez. *Chippewa Child Life and Its Cultural Background*. Bureau of American Ethnology Bulletin no. 146. Washington, DC: Smithsonian Institution, 1951.

Hirst, Stephen. *Havsuw'Baaja: People of the Blue Green Water*. Supai, AZ: The Havasupai Tribe, 1985.

Hogan, Linda. *Mean Spirit*. New York: Atheneum; Toronto: Collier-Macmillan Canada, 1990.

———. "Walking." *Parabola*, vol. XV, no. 2 (1990): pp. 14–16.

Hyde, Philip (photographs), and Stephen C. Jett (text). *Navajo Wildlands*. Ed. Kenneth Brower. San Francisco: Sierra Club/Ballantine Books, 1967.

International Work Group for Indigenous Affairs (IWGIA). Document no. 68. "Critical Issues in Native North America. Copenhagen: IWGIA Publications, 1992.

Lame Deer, John, and Richard Erdoes. *Lame Deer: Seeker of Visions*. New York: Simon and Schuster, 1972.

Lang, Julian. "The Basket and World Renewal." *Parabola*, vol. XVI, no. 3 (1991): pp. 83–85.

Lévi-Strauss, Claude. *Totemism*. Boston: Beacon Press, 1963.

Mann, Henrietta. "The Beautiful Earth Woman: American Myth and Reality." A paper given to the author by Dr. Mann.

McLuhan, T. C. *Dream Tracks: The Railroad and the American Indian, 1890–1930*. New York: Harry N. Abrams, 1985.

———. *Touch the Earth*. New York: Outerbridge and Dienstfrey, 1971. Reprint. New York: Simon & Schuster, a Touchstone Book, 1992.

McNickle, D'Arcy. *The Surrounded*. 1936. Reprint. Albuquerque: University of New Mexico Press, 1980.

Momaday, N. Scott. *House Made of Dawn*. New York: Harper & Row, 1969.

———. "The Man Made of Words." In *Indian Voices*, 1st Convocation of American Indian Scholars at Princeton University. San Francisco: Indian Historical Press, 1970.

———. *The Names*. New York: Harper & Row, 1977.

———. *The Way to Rainy Mountain*. 1969. Reprint. Albuquerque: University of New Mexico Press, 1991.

Moody, Roger, ed. *The Indigenous Voice: Visions and Realities*. 2 vols. London and Atlantic Highlands, NJ: Zed Books, 1988.

Nabokov, Peter, ed. *Native American Testimony: A Chronicle of Indian-White Relations from Prophecy to the Present, 1492–1992.* New York: Viking Penguin, 1991.

Oliver, Louis Littlecoon. *Chasers of the Sun: Creek Indian Thoughts.* Greenfield Center, NY: Greenfield Review Press, 1990.

O'Bryan, Aileen. *The Diné: Origin Myths of the Navajo Indians.* Bureau of American Ethnology Bulletin no. 163. Washington, DC: Smithsonian Institution, 1956.

O'Connell, Barry, ed. *On Our Ground: The Complete Writings of William Apess, A Pequot.* Amherst: University of Massachusetts Press, 1992.

Ortiz, Alfonso. "Look to the Mountaintop." *Essays in Reflection II:* Ed. E. Graham Ward. Boston: Houghton Mifflin, 1973.

———. *New Perspectives on the Pueblos.* Albuquerque: University of New Mexico Press, 1984.

———. *The Tewa World: Space, Time, Being and Becoming in a Pueblo Society.* Chicago: University of Chicago Press, 1969.

Ortiz, Simon J. *Earth Power Coming: Short Fiction in Native American Literature.* Tsaile, AZ: Navajo Community College, 1983.

Parker, Arthur C. *The Code of Handsome Lake: The Seneca Prophet.* New York State Museum, Museum Bulletin no. 163. Albany: University of the State of New York, 1912.

Parlow, Anita. *Cry, Sacred Ground: Big Mountain U.S.A.* Washington, DC: The Christic Institute, 1988.

———. *A Song from Sacred Mountain.* Pine Ridge, SD: Oglala Lakota Legal Rights Fund, 1983.

Perry, Whitall N. *A Treasury of Traditional Wisdom.* New York: Simon and Schuster, 1971.

Petrone, Penny, ed. *First People, First Voices.* Toronto: University of Toronto Press, 1983.

Peyer, Bernd C., ed. *The Singing Spirit: Early Short Stories by North American Indians.* Tucson: University of Arizona Press, 1989.

The Potlatch: A Strict Law Bids Us Dance. A 53-minute documentary film narrated by Gloria Cranmer Webster, directed by Dennis Wheeler, written by Brian Shein and Dennis Wheeler, and produced by Tom Shandel. 1975. Distributed by Canadian Filmmakers Distribution West, Vancouver.

Pride, Nigel. *Crow Man's People: Three Seasons with the Navajo.* London: Constable and Co., 1982.

Rasmussen, Knud. *The Netsilik Eskimos: Social Life and Spiritual Culture.* Report of the Fifth Thule Expedition 1921–24, vol. III, nos. 1–2. Copenhagen: Gyldendalske Boghandel, Nordisk Forlag, 1931.

Riesman, David. "The Oral and Written Traditions." In Edmund Carpenter and Marshall McLuhan, eds. *Explorations in Communications.* Boston: Beacon Press, 1966.

Riley, Patricia, ed. *Growing Up Native American.* New York: William Morrow and Co., 1993.

Robert, Elizabeth, and Elias Amidon, eds. *Earth Prayers.* San Francisco: HarperCollins, 1991.

Rothenberg, Jerome, ed. *Technicians of the Sacred.* 2d ed., rev. and enl. Berkeley: University of California Press, 1985.

Sarris, Greg. *Keeping Slug Woman Alive: A Holistic Approach to American Indian Texts.* Berkeley: University of California Press, 1993.

Seton, Ernest Thompson. *The Gospel of the Red Man.* New York: Doubleday Doran, 1936.

Snow, Chief John. *These Mountains Are Our Sacred Places.* Toronto: Samuel Stevens Publishers, 1977.

Southcott, Mary E. (Beth). *The Sound of the Sacred Drum: The Sacred Art of the Anishnabec.* Erin, Ont.: Boston Mills Press, 1984.

Standing Bear, Luther. *Land of the Spotted Eagle.* 1933. Reprint. Lincoln: University of Nebraska Press, 1978.

Susunkewa, Manfred. Interview by Tom Wallis. *Native Peoples,* Spring 1992: pp. 46–49.

Swann, Brian, and Arnold Krupat, eds. *I Tell You Now: Autobiographical Essays by Native American Writers.* Lincoln: University of Nebraska Press, 1987.

Tallbull, Bill. "On the Tongue River Valley." *Proceedings of the National Sacred Sites Caucus.* New York: Association on American Indian Affairs, August 1991.

Tinker, George. "For All My Relations." *Sojourners,* January 1991.

Truettner, William H., ed. *The West as America: Reinterpreting Images of the Frontier 1820–1920.* Washington, DC: Smithsonian Institution Press, 1991.

Underhill, Ruth. *The Autobiography of a Papago Woman.* American Anthropological Association, *Memoirs,* no. 46, 1936.

Walker Art Center and the Minneapolis Institute of Arts. *American Indian Art: Form and Tradition.* New York: E. P. Dutton, 1972.

Waters, Frank. *Book of the Hopi.* New York: Viking Press, 1963. Reprint. New York: Penguin Books, 1982.

Wilson, Andrew. *World Scripture: A Comparative Anthology of Sacred Texts.* New York: Paragon House, 1991.

Wright, Ronald. *Stolen Continents: The "New World" Through Indian Eyes.* Boston: Houghton Mifflin, 1992.

PERMISSIONS

Oxford University Press for an excerpt from *My People of Kikuyu* by Jomo Kenyatta, copyright © 1966, 1967, 1968 by Oxford University Press. Foreword copyright © 1966 Mzee Jomo Kenyatta.

Penguin Books Ltd., UK, for an excerpt from *The Idylls by Theocritus,* translated by Robert Wells, translation, Introduction and Notes copyright © 1988 by Robert Wells; an excerpt from *The Last Days of Socrates,* translated by Hugh Tredennick, copyright © 1954 by Hugh Tredennick; an excerpt from *The Theban Plays* by Sophocles, translated by E. F. Watling, copyright © 1953 by E. F. Watling.

Peter Owen Publishers, London, for excerpts from *The Way and the Mountain* by Marco Pallis, copyright © 1961 by Marco Pallis.

Princeton University Press for excerpts from *Zen and Japanese Culture,* Bollingen Series LXIV, by Daisetz T. Suzuki, copyright © 1959 by Princeton University Press, renewed 1987.

Random House, Inc., for an excerpt from *The Buddhist Tradition in India, China and Japan* by William Theodore de Bary, copyright © 1969 by William Theodore de Bary.

Bill Reid for an excerpt from *Out of the Silence,* text by Bill Reid, photographs by Adelaide DeMenil (New York: Harper & Row Publishers, 1971). Copyright © 1971 by the Amon Carter Museum of Western Art. All rights reserved.

Rider Books, an imprint of Random House UK Ltd., for an excerpt from *The Way* by Edward Goldsmith, copyright © 1992 by Edward Goldsmith.

Samuel Stevens for excerpts from *These Mountains Are Our Sacred Places* by Chief John Snow, copyright © 1977 by Chief John Snow.

Schocken Books for quotations from *Sappho and the Greek Lyric Poets,* translated and annotated by Willis Barnstone, copyright © 1962, 1967, 1988 by Willis Barnstone, published by Pantheon Books, a division of Random House, Inc.

School of American Research Press for excerpts from "Indian Pottery and Indian Values" by Popovi Da, in *Exploration 1970,* © 1970 by the School of American Research, Santa Fe, NM.

Simon & Schuster, Inc., for excerpts from *Report to Greco* by Nikos Kazantzakis, copyright © 1961 by Helen N. Kazantzakis, copyright renewed © 1993 by Helen N. Kazantzakis. English translation copyright © 1965 by Simon & Schuster, Inc.

Smithsonian Institution, Office of Telecommunications, for excerpts from two interviews—with Toru Takemitsu and Sobin Yamada—in *Dream Window: Reflections on the Japanese Garden,* a 57-minute documentary film produced by the Office of Telecommunications, Smithsonian Institution, in association with KajimaVision, Tokyo, 1992. Senior Producer: Laura T. Schneider. Directed by John Junkerman. Written by Peter Grilli.

Sojourners, 2401 15th St., N.W., Washington, DC 20009, for excerpts from "With Drum and Cup" (aka "All My Relations"), an interview with George Tinker, January 1991.

Spring Publications, Inc., Dallas, for excerpts from *The Homeric Hymns,* translated by Charles Boer, copyright © 1970 by Charles Boer. All rights reserved.

State University of New York Press for an excerpt from *Journey in Search of the Way* (aka *Passionate Journey: The Spiritual Autobiography of Satomi Myōdō*), translated and annotated by Sallie B. King, copyright © 1993 by the State University of New York Press.

Shincho Tanaka for permission to quote from his interview in *Japan: Voices from the Land,* a WQED production, Pittsburgh, 1991.

Transition for an excerpt from "The Green Tree" by Bessie Head, in *Transition,* vol. 4, no. 16, 1964.

PICTURE CREDITS

page 20

    Geographical Line Drawing. Drawn by Yuri Numata.

page 33

    The Cell and Its Genetic Components, the coiled structure of double-stranded DNA. Photograph © Hughes Medical Institute, Peter Arnold, Inc.

    Cucurbita, pumpkin tendrils. From *Art Forms in Nature,* published by Universe Books, New York, 1967. Photographs by Karl Blossfeldt. Reproduced with permission of the publisher.

    The Cochlea of the Human Ear. Artwork. Photograph © Alex Grey, Peter Arnold, Inc.

page 34

    An Ammonite. Computer illustration by Susan Now.

    Silphium laciniatum, compass plant, rosinweed. From *Art Forms In Nature,* published by Universe Books, New York, 1967. Photographs by Karl Blossfeldt. Reproduced with permission of the publisher.

    Helix of hemoglobin. Photograph © Leonard Lessin, Peter Arnold, Inc.

    Adiantum pedatum, American maidenhair fern. From *Art Forms In Nature,* published by Universe Books, New York, 1967. Photographs by Karl Blossfeldt. Reproduced with permission of the publisher.

    Fingerprint. Photograph © Leonard Lessin.

    Aspidium filix mas, shield fern. From *Art Forms In Nature,* published by Universe Books, New York, 1967. Photographs by Karl Blossfeldt. Reproduced with permission of the publisher.

page 35

    Charles Ross, *Solar Burn Spiral,* 1971–72. Photo construction. 36" x 96". Reproduced with the permission of the artist.

page 38

Darby Jampijinpa Ross (b. ca. 1910, Warlpiri), *Emu Dreaming,* 1987. Synthetic polymer on canvas, 12.1 x 91.5 cm. (47⅝ x 36"). Collection: National Gallery of Victoria, Melbourne.

page 45

Gagudju White Spirit Figure, rock painting. Photograph by Reg Morrison.

page 58

Mick Namarari Tjapaltjarri (b. 1926, Pintupi), *Bandicoot Dreaming,* 1991. Synthetic polymer on canvas, 182 x 150 cm. (71⅝ x 59"). Collection: Museums and Art Galleries of the Northern Territory, Darwin. Copyright: Aboriginal Arts Agency, Cammeray, NSW.

page 79

Pearl-shell pendant. Artist unknown. Kimberley, Western Australia. Charcoal; H: 17 cm. (6¾"). Elkin Collection, National Museum of Australia, Canberra.

page 90

Bronwyn Bancroft (b. 1958, Koori), *Corroboree Created,* 1992. Gouache on paper, approx. 36" x 25". Courtesy The Jan Weiss Gallery, New York City.

page 109

Ellen José, *Sea Scape,* 1987. Linocut on rice paper, 15 x 15 cm. Reproduced with the permission of the artist.

page 116

Kano Hogai (1828–1888), Kannon, *The Bodhisattva Avalokitesvara,* Japan, Meiji period, 19th century. Hanging scroll, 165.7 x 84.8 cm. Courtesy of the Freer Gallery of Art, Smithsonian Institution, Washington, DC. Accession number 02.225.

page 123

Painting by Icho, *Water.* From Frederic Spiegelberg, *Zen, Rocks, and Waters* (New York: Pantheon Books, 1961), Reproduced with the permission of Frederic Spiegelberg.

page 158

Tawaraya Sotatsu, *Waves at Matsushima,* Momoyama-Edo period, 17th century. Detail from folding screen, 166.0 x 369.9 cm. Courtesy of the Freer Gallery of Art, Smithsonian Institution, Washington, DC. Accession number 06.231 detail.

page 164

Katsushika Hokusai (1760–1849), *The Great Wave off Kanagawa* from *The Thirty-six Views of Fuji,* 1823–29, woodcut. The Metropolitan Museum of Art, Henry L. Phillips Collection, bequest of Henry L. Phillips, 1939. Accession number JP2972.

page 184

Enku, *Koma-Inu,* ca. 1675–1695. From Kazuaki Tanahashi, *Enku: Sculptor of a Hundred Thousand Buddhas* (Boulder: Shambhala Publications, 1982), Plate 61. Reproduced with the permission of Kazuaki Tanahashi. Photograph by Tetsuo Kuruhara.

page 189

Jōmon Earthenware Jar, Japan, ca. 3000–2500 B.C. Glazed clay; H: 50.2 cm. (19¾"). Courtesy of the Freer Gallery of Art, Smithsonian Institution, Washington, DC. Accession number 74.5.

page 192

Temple Ornament. Asuka, early Nara period, 7th century. Gilt bronze. From the catalogue of the exhibition of the Japan House Gallery: *Hōryū-Ji: Temple of the Exalted Law* (New York: Japan Society, 1981). Courtesy of the Japan Society, Inc.

page 204

Sirenes, emerging from flowers; silver, 5th century B.C. Part of the handle of an urn. Archaeological Museum, Thessaloniki.

page 226

Late Minoan Period Vase, ca. 1500–1400 B.C. The Metropolitan Museum of Art, Rogers Fund, 1922. Accession number 22.139.76.

page 242

Gold Pendant, Crete, ca. 1600 B.C. National Archaeological Museum, Athens.

A Coin from Knossos, Crete, 2nd century B.C. The American Numismatic Society, New York; the Adra M. Newell Collection ex Berlin duplicates.

Bronze Wire Fibula, Greece, 10th century B.C. L: 15 cm. (5¹⁵⁄₁₆"). The Metropolitan Museum of Art, Fletcher Fund, 1937. Accession number 37.11.18.

page 276

Janus Headdress, Nigeria or Cameroon, 19th–20th century. Courtesy of The Pace Gallery, New York City.

page 281

Akwanshi stone carvings, southeastern Nigeria. From Philip Allison, *African Stone Sculpture* (New York: Frederick A. Praeger, 1968), Plate 47. An imprint of Greenwood Publishing Group, Inc., Westport, CT. Reprinted with the permission of Greenwood Publishing and Lund Humphries Publishers Ltd., London.

page 282

Ancient Bushman Rock Painting, Ceremonial Dance, Zimbabwe. From Leo Frobenius and Douglas C. Fox, *African Genesis* (Berkeley: Turtle Island Foundation, 1983), plate 263.

page 302

   Yoruba Mask (Gelede), Republic of Benin, West Africa, 20th century. Wood; H: 61 cm. (24"). Photograph by Jerry L. Thompson. The Metropolitan Museum of Art. Gift of Paul and Ruth Tishman, 1990. Accession number 1990.336.

page 316

   Turkana Earrings, Kenya. Brass; L: 2 in. Collected by S. A. Barrett in 1929. Milwaukee Public Museum. Accession number 36985/9486.

   Coiled Wire Bangle, Kenya or Tanzania. Collected in 1947/48. H: 8 in. Phoebe A. Hearst Museum of Anthropology, The University of California at Berkeley. Accession number 5-799c.

page 327

   Tiv Brass Ring, Nigeria. Collected in 1950. H: 5½ in. The H. D. Gunn Collection, Lincoln University, Pennsylvania.

   Tiv-carved wooden spoon, Nigeria, 19th–20th century. L: 48.3 cm. (19"). The Paul and Ruth Tishman Collection of African Art. Loaned by the Walt Disney Company. Photograph by Jerry L. Thompson.

page 335

   Mongo Necklace (iron), Zaire. W: 12.5 cm. Collection of Jean Pierre and Anne Jernander-De Vriese. Brussels.

page 360

   Tairona pendant. Cast and gilt tumbaga. H: 6.1 cm. (2⅜"). Collection of the Boltin Picture Library, Croton-on-Hudson, New York.

page 374

   David B. Williams (Ojibwa), *Untitled,* 1980. Watercolor on paper, 77.0 x 57.5 cm. Donated by S. Roger Yake and Lyla J. Yake in honor of the Walpole Island Indian Band. McMichael Canadian Art Collection, Kleinburg, Ontario. Accession number 1987.37.26.

page 381

   Petroglyph exhibiting labyrinthine spiral. Dinnebito Wash, Arizona. Photograph © Dan Budnik, 1977.

page 401

   Lolita Concho, *Canteen,* ca. 1983, Acoma Pueblo, New Mexico. Collection of the Newark Museum. Purchase 1983, The Members' Fund. Photograph © the Newark Museum. Accession number 83.423.

page 404

   Pima Basketry Tray, Sacatón, Arizona, 1900–1915. 9¾" in diameter. Courtesy of the National Museum of the American Indian, Smithsonian Institution. Negative number 11/415.

Diegueño Basket, Southern California. 14½" in diameter. Courtesy of the National Museum of the American Indian, Smithsonian Institution. Negative number 15/4625.

page 405

Gelineau Fisher (Ojibwa), *Untitled*, 1984. Acrylic on paper, 56.7 x 76.2 cm. Donated by S. Roger Yake and Lyla J. Yake in honor of the Walpole Island Indian Band. McMichael Canadian Art Collection, Kleinburg, Ontario. Accession number 1987.37.23.

page 434

Redware Bowl, Mogollón; Gila County, Arizona, 900–1000. Polychrome redware, 11½" in diameter. Courtesy of the National Museum of the American Indian, Smithsonian Institution. Negative number 23/1909.

Black-on-White Ware Bowl, Anasazi; Coconino County, Arizona, 1250–1300. 4¼ x 8¼". Courtesy of the National Museum of the American Indian, Smithsonian Institution. Negative number 18/9175.

page 445

Eunice Carney, *Dance Boots*, ca. 1986. Kutchin Athapascan; Alaska. Collection of the Newark Museum. Purchase 1986, The Members' Fund. Accession number 86.32.

page 457

Roy Thomas (Ojibwa), *Serpent Man*, 1975. Acrylic on canvas, 119.3 x 113.0 cm. McMichael Canadian Art Collection, Kleinburg, Ontario. Accession number 1975.49.1.

page 466

Hopi symbols from Frank Waters, *Book of the Hopi* (New York: The Viking Press, 1963). Redrawn by Susan Now.

COLOR INSERT
PICTURE CREDITS

C–1

Simon Ngumbe (b. 1911, Murrinh-Patha), *RainbowSnake and Children,* ca. 1972. Natural pigments on bark, 62 x 24.6 cm. (24³/₈ x 9⁵/₈″). Collection: Art Gallery of Western Australia, Perth.

C–2

Whirling Snakes or Whirling Mountain. A sandpainting of the Navajo Shooting Chant, 1930s. From Franc J. Newcomb and Gladys A. Reichard, *Sandpaintings of the Navajo Shooting Chant* (New York: Dover Publications, 1975), Plate X. Courtesy Dover Publications.

C–3

Great Serpent Mound, near Peebles, Ohio. Photograph by Richard Cooke III.

C–4

Mineo (Katô) Okabe, *Oribe Ware Round Dish,* ca. 1960. Property of the Art Institute of Chicago, gift of Margaret Gentles. Accession number 1961.967. Photograph by Dr. Frederick Baekeland.

C–5

Athena. Marble, ca. 525 B.C. Acropolis Museum, Athens.

C–6

Pansy Napangati (b. ca. 1945, Luritja/Warlpiri), *Rainbow Serpent at Pikilli,* 1989. Acrylic on canvas, 288 x 159 cm. Courtesy Gabrielle Pizzi Collection, Melbourne. Copyright: Aboriginal Artists Agency, Cammeray, NSW.

C–7

Tairona Figure Pendant, Colombia. Metalwork, gold. 14th–16th century. H: 13.4 cm. (5¹/₄″), W: 16.5 cm. (6¹/₂″). Metropolitan Museum of Art, gift of the H. L. Bache Foundation, 1969. Accession number 69.7.10. (View #2.)

C–8

Gold Breastplate, Mycenae period, ca. 1300 B.C. Museum of Heracleion, Crete.

C–9

Hiroshige (1797–1858), *Crane and Wave,* mid-1830s. Woodblock print, *koban* (quarter-block), 12.7 x 18.4 cm. (5⅛ x 7⅜″). From the Abby Aldrich Rockefeller Collection of Japanese Prints, Museum of Art, Rhode Island School of Design. Accession number 34.040.

C–10

Bamileke people, *Cameroon Palm Wine Container,* 20th century. H: 23½″. Collection of the Newark Museum. Purchase 1982, Wallace M. Scudder Bequest Fund. Accession number 82.115. Photograph © the Newark Museum.

C–11

Charlie Egalie Tjapaltjarri (Warlpiri/Papunya), *Corroboree Dancing,* ca. 1972. Synthetic polymer on board, 775 mm x 430 mm. Courtesy Lauraine Diggins Fine Art Pty Ltd., Melbourne. Copyright: Aboriginal Artists Agency, Cammeray, NSW.

C–12

Tairona Nose Ornament. Cast gold; W: 6.6 cm. (2⅝″), Colombia. Collection of the Boltin Picture Library, Croton-on-Hudson, New York.

C–13

Leopard (slate), Scepter of the King, Minoan Civilization, 1700–1500 B.C. Museum of Heracleion, Crete.

C–14

Kosode with Snow-Laden Orchids, Mid-Edo period, mid-eighteenth century. From the catalogue of the exhibition of Japan House Gallery, *Kosode: 16th–19th Century Textiles from the Nomura Collection* (New York: Japan Society, 1984). Courtesy of the Japan Society, Inc.

C–15

Fante tribe, Ghana, *Cloth of the Great,* 20th century. Collection of the Newark Museum. Purchase 1986, The Members' Fund. Accession number 86.238.

C–16

Goyce Kakegamic (Cree), *A Nest of Birds,* ca. early 1970s. Acrylic on paper, approx. 25″ x 33″. Courtesy T. C. McLuhan.

INDEX

Alexios Comnenos, Emperor, 231
Alkinoos, King, 227
"All My Relations" (Hogan), 468–70
All Powerful One, African names for, 285
aluna (world of spirit), 365, 368
Amazon rain forest, 24, 299
American Academy of Arts and Sciences, 391
American Indian Movement, 423
Amiotte, Arthur, 407–8
ammonite fossil, 34
Ana (Earth-Spirit), 288–90
Anakreon, 218
Anasazi people, 401, 414, 434
Ancient Japanese Culture (Watsuji), 136
Anderson, Michael, 86–87
Andes, 23, 29
Andoh, Anthony K., 297–300
Andoh, Joseph, 298
Anghelaki-Rook, Katerina, 258
animals
   in Africa, 354–58
   in Japan, 194–201
animism, 103
Anishnawbe tribe, 457
Antheia (flower goddess), 224
antiquities, Japanese, 136
Anyaneanyane (Awakening) (Akan drum prelude), 340–341
Anyidoho, Kofi, 291
Anyte, 223
Apache tribe, 375, 446, 460
Aphrodite, 222, 224, 262, 263, 268
Apollo, 218, 220, 229, 231
   hymn to, 221
Apollodorus, 269˙
Appiah, Kwame Anthony, 278
Aranda, 39

Arapaho tribe, 415
archetypes, Greek, 212, 222
Arctic Watershed, 395
Ariston, 271
Aristophanes, 207, 208, 210, 227–29
Aristotle, 206, 254, 273
Arkadia, 223
Arnold, Matthew, 15
Arrow Covenant, 379
Arrow Renewal Ceremony, 416–417, 436
art
   African, 339
   Byzantine, 231
   Japanese, 186–91, 251
   Native North American, 425–430
Arukun tribe, 74
Asae Yaa (Earth), 284
Asclepiadae, 273
Ashanti people, 284, 340, 347
Asia Minor disaster, 245
Aspects de la civilisation africaine (Bâ), 338
Assiniboine tribe, 387
Association of American Indian Affairs, Religious Freedom Coalition Project, 415
Asuka era, 136
Athapascan tribe, 445
Atharva-Veda, 23
Athena, 222–23
Athens, 208, 244, 246, 260, 271
Athos, Mount, 231
Attica, 216, 223, 260–62
Australia, 18, 19
   track line to North America from, 20
   See also Aboriginal Australians
Autobiography of a Papago Woman, The (Underhill), 458–60

Hokusai, Katusushika, 164, 172, 175
Holding, Clyde, 59
Holy Elements, 412, 413
"Homage to Mount Fuji" (anonymous), 182
Homecoming, The (Thiong'o), 24
homeland, Greece as, 243–46
Homer, 26, 218, 227, 240, 256–257, 265, 270
Homeric Hymns, 211–12, 219–221
"Homing Call of Earth, The" (Anyidoho), 291
Honshu, 124
Hopi tribe, 373, 412, 429–30, 433, 467
Horiguchi, Daigaku, 201
Horyu-ji Buddhist temple, 192
Hosono (Japan), 181
House Made of Dawn (Momaday), 391
Huaraz (Peru), 23, 29
humanism
    African, 278
    Greek, 203, 272
Humanist in Africa, A (Kaunda), 309–10
humor
    African, 340, 346–52
    Native North American, 375
hunting in Africa, 337–38, 357–358
Hupa tribe, 474, 475
Hydro-Quebec, 394
"Hymn to the Earth" (Atharva-Veda), 23–24
hymns
    Greek, 211–12, 219–21
    see also songs

Ibadan (Nigeria), 331
Ichikawa, Sanki, 197

Icho, 123
Idylls (Theocritus), 230
Igbo people, 287–90
Iglulik tribe, 463
Ikarian Dreamers (Nakos), 225, 245
Ikxzréeyav (Spirit-beings), 476
Ilbalintja tribe, 64–65
Iliad (Homer), 256
Iliff School of Theology, 398
illo tempore (primordial time), 248
In the Grip of the Past (Groningen), 208
India, 23, 134, 299
indifference, mountains of, 172–182
Industrial Revolution, 310
infinity, mathematical symbol for, 21
Ingassana people, 279–80
Inoue, Yasushi, 178–81
Inouye, Daniel, 378
Institute of Culture and Creation Spirituality, 387
interdependence, principles of, 99
interspecies awareness, 168
Inuit people, 32, 394
Io, 249
Ionia, light in, 254
Ionian Sea, 232
Iroquois Confederacy, 373, 382, 383, 400, 415, 433
Ishigaki Island, 169
Ishimure, Michiko, 166
Islam, 251, 279
Isocrates, 244
Italy, 232
    light in, 254
Ivory Coast, 336, 347
Iwamuro (Japan), 134

Jabavu, Noni, 27, 357–58
Jacobs, Alex, 433

Miller, Henry, 207–8
Miller, Roy Andrew, 172
Millingimbi (Australia), 47
Minamata disease, 166
Mingei (Folk Crafts), 188
Minoans, 222–23, 226
Miskito tribe, 27
missionaries, 344–45
Missouri River, 385, 387
Mistra, 243
Modeste, 387
Modupe, Prince, 27, 277, 280,
    295–96, 343
Mogollón people, 434
Mohave electrical plant, 412
Mohawk Nation, 30, 398
Mojave tribe, 447
Moke, 293
Momaday, N. Scott, 26, 30, 378,
    391–93, 409–11
Mongo tribe, 335
Monogue, David, 412
Montana, University of, 415
Monument Valley, 410
Morgan, Sally, 24, 48, 95–97
Moritake, Takeichi, 125
Moss Temple (Saiho-ji), 158
mountains, 28–32
    African, 280–81, 326, 328–33
    Australian, 40
    Greek, 231, 247–54
    Japanese, 118–20, 171–82
    North American, 403, 412,
        437, 445–56
    South American, 362–63, 370
Moutzan-Martinengou, Elisavet,
    232–33
Mumbulla, Jack, 62
Mumbulla, Percy, 54
Mumbulla Mountain (Australia),
    61–63
mundumugo (medicine man),
    331
Munggurrawuy, 56

Muses, 218
    hymn to, 220
music
    African, 340–41
    Japanese, 162
    see also songs
Mwene-Nyaga (High God), 317–
    318, 328, 329
Myers, Fred, 68
My Life in the Bush of Ghosts
    (Tutuola), 329
My People of Kikuyu (Kenyatta),
    317–18
My Place (Morgan), 95–97
Mykonos, 238
Myōdō, Satomi, 142–43
myrrh, 299
mythology
    African, 329
    Greek, 212

Nagatsuka, Takashi, 152–54
Nakogee, Chief Emile, 396
Nakos, Lilika, 225, 245
Nambe (New Mexico), 448
Nangala, 72
Nanyarwanda people, 285
Nara period, 136, 172, 192
Native North American
    Freedom-Exercise of
    Religion Act (1993), 378
Native North Americans, 19, 24,
    26, 373–479
    art of, 425–30
    ceremonies of, 467–80
    Creation myths of, 433–44
    mountains and, 445–56
    nature of land in thought of,
        383–402
    sacred sites of, 29, 406–25,
        431–32
    songs of, 457–65
    see also specific tribes

origin legends
  Australian Aboriginal, 61; *see also Dreaming, The*
  Navajo, 19, 437, 445, 464
Orpingalik, 460–61
Ortiz, Alphonso, 29, 375, 379, 446–48, 449–51
Ortiz, Simon, 394
Osage tribe, 398–400, 431, 440
Ōsawa (Japan), 181

Pagosa Springs (Colorado), 379
Paha Sapa (Black Hills), 423
Paiakan, 24
Pallis, Marco, 27, 241, 250–52
Palm-Wine Drinkard, The (Tutuola), 329
Pan, 219, 250
Pan-Africanist Congress, 303
Panegyricus (Isocrates), 244
Papago tribe, 387, 405, 458–460
Papunya Tula, 43
paradox of truth, 270
Parthenon, 246, 262
Pasagianis, Kostas, 248–50
Passamaquoddy tribe, 462
Passionate Journey (Myōdō), 142–43
patriarchal mythology, 212
patriotism, 244
patterns, 19, 119, 370
Pawurrinji (Australia), 56–57
Paz, Octavio, 33
Peabody Coal Company, 412–15
pearl shells, 79
Peloponnesian War, 207, 271
Peloponnesos, 223, 248
Pequot tribe, 384
Pericles, 209, 244
Perictione, 271
Peru, 23, 29
Peule tribe, 338

Phaeacia, 227
Phaedrus (Plato), 213–17, 273, 274
Phaistos, 203
Pharos, 239
Philip, King, 384
Philippi, Donald, 125
Philippines, 27
philosophy
  African, 307, 309, 336, 347
  Greek, 207, 266–74; *see also specific philosophers*
Phoebus Apollo, 228
Physics (Aristotle), 254
pilgrimage, 251–52
Pima tribe, 405, 447
Pindar, 218, 246
Pintupi people, 42, 43, 48, 51, 68
Pitjantjatjara tribe, 29, 41, 63, 71
Pitseolak, 32
placenta ceremonies, 279–80
plants, 293–300
  reciprocity with, 194–201
Plato, 19, 206, 208, 213–17, 219, 256, 266, 271–74
Plotinus, 207
Plutarch, 205, 272
Po Lo-t'ien, 161
poetry
  African, 310–11, 340, 354–55
  Ainu, 125
  Greek, 211–12, 218–21, 223, 225, 226, 230, 239–41, 243, 246, 247, 256–58, 266–74
  Japanese, 121, 129–31, 133, 134, 138–39, 142, 156, 171–73, 175, 176, 181, 182, 185, 187, 188, 193, 199–201
  Native American, 393
  see also songs
Pokanoket tribe, 384
Polynesia, 27
Poseyemu (Creator), 451

Shukagku-In imperial garden, 160

Shumunkot (Japan), 125

Shungopavi (Hopi village), 429

Sierra Club, 441

Sierra Nevada de Santa Marta, 28

Sierra Nevada de Santa Marta (Colombia), 362–63, 370

Sikelianos, Angelos, 225, 264

silences, 277, 296

Simbi and the Satyr of the Dark Jungle (Tutuola), 329

Sinai, Mount, 231

Sioux Nation, 373, 380, 387, 406–7, 419, 452

sirens, 205

Six Nations, 397

Sky Woman, 435–36

Sleeping Ute, 410

Smith, Katherine, 382

Smohalla, 418

Smyrna, 245

Snake Dance, 449

Snow, Chief John, 451–55

Snowy Mountains (Australia), 40

Snpoilshi River, 387

Socrates, 206, 208, 213–15, 217, 219, 265, 267, 271–72

Solar Burn Spiral (Ross), 35

Solomos, Dionysios, 247

solstice marker, 381

Somalia, 296

Son'en, 16

Song of Songs, The, 28

Song of the Earth Spirit (Navajo origin legend), 21

songs
of Aboriginal Australians, 47–51
of Africans, 284–87, 296
of Ainu, 125
of Greeks, 219, 257, 267–68
of Native Americans, 457–65

Sophocles, 207, 229

Soseki, Muso, 123, 140–41, 157, 159–62, 171

Sotatsu, Tawaraya, 158

Sōtō Zen school, 173

soul, identification of soil and, 22–23

Sousou people, 277, 280, 295

South Africa, 27, 303, 305, 311, 347–49, 352

South America, 18, 19, 359–71
See also specific countries and regions

"Spider, The" (Michizane), 201

spiral, 32–36
African, 277
Greek origin of, 222
in nature, 31, 32, 77

Spretnak, Charlene, 212

Squaw Dance, 449

Standing Bear, Luther, 375, 377–378

Standing Rock Sioux, 419

Stanner, W. E. H., 42

staple food plants, 300

Stewart, Paddy Japalijarri, 106, 108

Stonehenge, 30

Stoney tribe, 442, 451–55

Strabo, 267

Strehlow, T. G. H., 41, 64

Sudan, the, 22, 27, 286

Sun Dance, 376, 377, 407–8, 436

supplication, ceremony of, 340

Supreme Court, U.S., 378

Survival Gathering, 423–25

Susunkewa, Manfred, 429–30

Suzuki, Daisetz, 22, 117, 121, 122, 130, 141, 144–46, 176–77, 192, 199

Swan Valley (Australia), 65–67

Sweet Medicine, 416–17

Swimme, Brian, 470